UK SOCIETY
WORK, URBANISM
AND INEQUALITY

UK SOCIETY WORK, URBANISM AND INEQUALITY

Edited by Philip Abrams and Richard Brown

Contributors:
Philip Abrams
Richard Brown
Robert Burgess
Paul Corrigan
Brian Elliott
Philip Stanworth
Steve Redhead
Hilary Wainwright

Weidenfeld and Nicolson
London

First published 1984

George Weidenfeld & Nicolson Limited
91 Clapham High Street, London SW4

British Cataloguing in Publication Data

UK society: work, urbanism and inequality.
   1. Great Britain — Social conditions —
   1945–
   I. Abrams, Philip II. Brown, Richard
   941.085'8 HN385.5

ISBN 0 297 78486 2
ISBN 0 297 78529 X

Typeset by Composer Typesetting, Bath
Printed and bound in Great Britain by The Pitman Press, Bath

Contents

Contributors

Introduction to the 1978 Edition
Philip Abrams
Late Professor of Sociology, University of Durham

Chapter 1 Brian Elliott
Senior Lecturer in Sociology, University of Edinburgh

Chapter 2 Robert Burgess
Lecturer in Sociology, University of Warwick

Chapter 3 Richard Brown
Professor of Sociology, University of Durham

Chapter 4 Hilary Wainwright
Popular Planning Unit, Greater London Council

Chapter 5 Philip Stanworth
Lecturer in Sociology, University of York

Chapter 6 Steve Redhead
Senior Lecturer in Law, Manchester Polytechnic

Chapter 7 Paul Corrigan
Head of the Department of Applied Social Studies, Polytechnic of North London

Tables

Figures

Acknowledgements

The publishers wish to thank the following who have kindly given permission for the use of copyright materials:

The Appletree Press Ltd for tables from *Religion, Education and Employment: Aspects of Equal Opportunity in Northern Ireland*, edited by R. J. Cormack and R. D. Osborne.

Basil Blackwell and the author for a table from Ivan Reid, *Social Class Differences in Britain* (second edition).

Cambridge University Press and A.B. Atkinson and A.J. Harrison for a table from *The Distribution of Personal Wealth in Britain*; and the Press and R. Whitley for a figure from 'The City and Industry', in *Elites and Power in British Society*, edited by P. Stanworth and A. Giddens.

Carfax Publishing Company and B. Main and D. Raffe for data from 'The "transition from school to work" in 1980/1' in the *British Educational Research Journal*, Vol. 9.

Counter Information Services for data from *Women under Attack*, Anti-report No. 15.

Gower Publishing Company Ltd and H. Richardson, J. Vipond and R. Furbey for a map from their book, *Housing and Urban Spatial Structure*.

Granada Publishing Ltd and J.W.B. Douglas for a table from *The Home and the School*.

Heinemann Educational Books and the Chartered Institute of Public Finance and Accountancy for two tables from J. Mortimore and T. Blackstone: Economic and Social Research Council, *Disadvantage and Education*, originally published in CIPFA, *Statistical Information Service*.

Peter Davies Ltd and J.W.B. Douglas, J.M. Ross and H.R. Simpson, for a table from *All Our Future*.

The Controller of Her Majesty's Stationery Office for tables and text reproduced or adapted from the following publications: Central Statistical Office, *Social Trends*, Nos 6, 12 and 13; Department of Education and Science, *Aspects of Secondary Education in England, Education Statistics for the United Kingdom*, 1982, *The Organisation of Secondary Education*, 1965, *Statistics of Education*, Vol. 2, *School Leavers*, 1979, and *Statistics of Teachers in Service in England and Wales*, 1980; Department of Employment, *British Labour Statistics: Historical Abstract 1886–1968, New Earnings Survey*, 1982 and 1983, and *Employment Gazette*; Department of the Environment, *Housing and Construction Statistics*, 1972–82, *Inner Cities Information Note*, No. 1, 1982, and *National Dwelling and Housing Survey*, 1977–8; Department of Health and Social Security, *Health and Personal Social Service Statistics for England*, 1975; Office of Population Censuses and Surveys, *Census 1971:*

Economic Activity, General Household Survey, 1976, 1979, 1980 and 1981; *West Indian Children in our Schools* (Rampton Report); *Higher Education* (Robbins Report); and Welsh Office, *Statistics of Education*.

Kogan Page Ltd for data from a paper by A. Little in *The World Yearbook of Education*, 1981, edited by J. Megarry, S. Nisbet and E. Hoyle.

Longman Group Ltd and G. Cameron for tables from *The Future of the British Conurbations*, edited by G. Cameron.

The Low Pay Unit for a table from C. Pond and S. Winyard, *The Case for a National Minimum Wage*.

Macmillan Ltd for a table from G.G.C. Routh, *Occupation and Pay in Great Britain 1906-1979*.

Methuen and Company and L. Hannah for data from Professor Hannah's *The Rise of the Corporate Economy*.

The New Statesman for data from *Hear this, Brother* by A. Coote and P. Kellner.

Oxford University Press for data from S. Nyman and A. Silberston, 'The Ownership and Control of Industry', in *Oxford Economic Papers*, Vol. 30: and the Press and the respective authors for tables from J.H. Goldthorpe, *Social Mobility and Class Structure in Modern Britain*, and from A.H. Halsey, A. Heath and J.M. Ridge, *Origins and Destinations: Family, Class and Education in Modern Britain*.

Routledge and Kegan Paul Ltd and L. Cantor and I.F. Roberts for a figure from *Further Education Today: a critical review*.

The Society for Research into Higher Education for a table from *Access to Higher Education*, edited by O. Fulton.

Tieto Ltd, the British Journal of Industrial Relations, and G.S. Bain and R. Price for data from their articles in that journal on 'Union growth revisited' and 'Union growth in Britain'.

The Universities' Statistical Record for tables from *University Statistics 1980*, Vol. 1, 'Students and Staff'.

The publishers would like to point out that every effort has been made to obtain all relevant permissions, but that if anyone has been overlooked they apologize and will make amends in future editions.

Introduction to the 1984 Edition

Richard K. Brown

At the time of his death in October 1981, Philip Abrams had initiated the preparation of a second edition of *Work, Urbanism and Inequality*, first published in 1978. His aim then was, and remains for us, to produce a discussion and analysis of central features of our society which includes a considerable body of substantive material, of 'information' about social conditions and social processes within that society, but does so in a way which is critical and sceptical, theoretically informed and interpretative, explicitly not letting 'facts' speak for themselves. As his introduction to the 1978 edition (which is reproduced with only minor omissions in this volume) makes clear, Philip Abrams saw such an enterprise as a central part of the task of sociology as an intellectual discipline; it was necessary both to question commonsense and taken-for-granted understandings of our social world and to offer a more satisfactory account, an account which is 'better' in that it places 'factual' and descriptive material in the context of an analysis of social relations and structure. Such an account—or possibly accounts—will suggest that some of the 'facts' about our society have meanings other than those conventionally given to them; and will show how social situations are socially constructed through the actions of members of the society and then further interpreted and reinterpreted in the course of social life. They will indicate, too, how such situations might be explained even if they do not in themselves constitute full explanations.

Although the sub-title to the first edition—*UK Society*—has been made the main title of this one, our intention also remains to offer an explicitly selective treatment of our society, to consider certain fundamental themes and key institutions in depth rather than providing a comprehensive 'sociology' of contemporary Britain and Northern Ireland. Four of the contributors to the first edition have substantially updated and revised, and in some areas completely rewritten, their chapters. These are all centrally concerned with the themes and topics listed in our sub-title, 'work, urbanism and inequality'. Brian Elliott shows how recent developments and changes in the city reflect and themselves create systematic inequalities of conditions and opportunity. Richard Brown discusses the nature of and changes in the division of labour and the continuing inequalities in the distribution of the costs and rewards deriving from work. Hilary Wainwright considers the position of women and shows how the domestic division of labour, still seen as 'natural and inevitable', constrains the sexual division of wage labour to women's continuing disadvantage, despite the legislation and other measures designed to end such inequalities. Philip Stanworth considers those in positions of power and privilege, the 'elites', discusses their social origins and modes of access to such positions, and by considering the inter-connections between various elites is able to outline something of the nature of power and its exercise.

The other three contributors all represent changes from the earlier edition and increase the scope and coverage of our discussion. Paul Corrigan concentrates on only one element in the material considered in his earlier chapter on 'deviance and deprivation' and focuses on the development of the Welfare State in Britain, some of the contradictions within it and how they have been interpreted within different theoretical frameworks. Deviance is one element in an entirely new contribution by Steve Redhead who shows how both what is considered 'deviant' and what represents 'law and order' are closely related, far from unproblematic and reflect some of the most basic inequalities in our society. The final new contribution by Robert Burgess reviews the educational systems of the United Kingdom and discusses how they too, despite explicit commitments to equality of opportunity, reflect and reinforce underlying social inequalities. Although the range of our discussions has been extended in this way, we are well aware that (as is acknowledged in Philip Abrams' introduction to the first edition) a number of important elements of social structure and areas of social experience receive little or no direct consideration. Thus there is little in detail on many aspects of the family, on religion, leisure, race relations, many areas of political activity, and so on, though there are references to each of them. We make no apology for such selective treatment; it is essential for practical reasons if nothing else. Nor do we claim that our selection of topics is the only possible one. It is, however, one which covers undeniably central problems and issues, and provides a solid basis for an understanding of UK society as a whole.

Each contributor has approached his or her task in the way they considered the most appropriate in the light of the material to be covered, the state of our existing knowledge, and what they define as the central questions. There has deliberately been no overall constraining framework, no imposed consensus as to theoretical perspective or mode of presentation. Quite apart from such a pluralism being a more appropriate reflection of the current state of sociological research and opinion, it has the added advantage of greater interest and possibly of fresh insights for the reader. What is clear, however, is that despite such differences of approach certain common themes emerge from many or all of the chapters. Without attempting to provide a comprehensive list some of the more important of them can usefully be discussed, very briefly, under two headings.

In the first place each contributor has had to cope with certain methodological problems. Our title is 'UK Society', but in what sense is there such a (single) society? Considering the question relatively superficially, much of the statistical material on which we have drawn refers to Britain (excluding Northern Ireland) or only to England and Wales, and perhaps the most important single source, the Census, is published separately for England and Wales, Scotland, and Northern Ireland. More fundamentally, the legal systems, the educational systems, and some parts of the administration of social welfare are similarly separate, although the existence of one central government and one legislature results in there being more than just a family resemblance between them. The question of the 'unity' of the United Kingdom is clearly a very live political issue and it can neither be ignored nor altogether satisfactorily resolved within a sociological account such as this one.

Whatever the societal unit is taken to be, each contributor has also had to decide how to use the 'factual' and especially the quantitative material available. Some of these difficulties have been technical, and in some cases only temporary, like the unavailability at the time of writing of the full results of the 1981 Census or the changing categorizations of occupations within social classes or socio-economic groups which make comparisons over time hazardous. Others are more fundamental. Even the most basic descriptive material has to be considered in the light of the ways in which it has been collected and presented. Because of the difficulties of interpretation which arise from such considerations, Steve Redhead has chosen to conduct his discussion without reference to the undoubtedly highly contentious statistical data on crime and deviance. The remaining contributors have all, to a greater or lesser extent, included such data, at the same time trying to indicate their limitations; they have felt that although, for example, statistics relating to wealth and income, or to unemployment, are highly mediated reflections of social conditions, used with care and with reservations they can still tell us something about the nature of the society in which we live and the changes which are occurring within it.

Secondly, it is clear that there are significant points of contact and common ground between the separate contributions, ones which could in time provide a basis for a more extensive and comprehensive analysis of our society. Two of them can be outlined. Perhaps the most common sociological frame of reference for understanding British society has been that centred around one or other notion of social class. Analysis in terms of class differences and class relations has certainly helped to explain many aspects of social life. What emerges from the discussions in this volume, however, is that it is inadequate to limit one's explanation of social differentiation to class alone, even if that term is used in a much more sophisticated and theoretically satisfactory way than, for example, merely referring to occupation. Differentiation in terms of sex or gender, race or ethnic origin, and age have all been shown to be important for understanding educational and occupational opportunities, inequalities in the law, access to positions of wealth and privilege, and differing life chances within the city. Such dimensions of differentiation cannot be reduced to or subsumed within class differences. Indeed with respect to some areas of social experience religion and region may be further important independent lines of social differentiation. As a result social analysis becomes very much more complex, but hopefully also more adequate.

A second shared theme discernible in these chapters is the need to pay attention to the political and economic forces which influence and constrain social processes and social institutions. The problems of the inner city, unemployment or 'law and order', for example, cannot be understood without taking account of Britain's declining economic position in the world (seen most starkly in the collapse of, especially traditional, manufacturing industry) and of the way in which the resulting problems have been 'managed' politically. Of course, the influences and constraints are not all in one direction; as Philip Stanworth shows, the nature of Britain's economic development and decline reflects the dominance of commercial and financial elites; and the aims and ethos of finance capital have been sustained and perpetuated through a class-divided educational system, especially in England, as the socially and politically dominant region in UK society.

Thus the need to take explicit account of the political economy of UK society is very clear. Indeed one of the consequences of preparing a revised version of contributions some six years after the first has been to reveal the important influences of government policies and actions on all the subjects discussed in this volume, and, more generally, to accentuate the central part played by the state in determining the nature of social conditions and social processes in UK society. In a number of areas the policies pursued by recent governments through the apparatus of the British state are clearly the subject of critical comment: for example, the consequences of economic policies for the city or for levels of unemployment, the policies for social welfare or the handling of law and order issues. Yet at a more fundamental level we should welcome this evidence that political initiatives make a difference. The persistence of problems of urban deprivation, educational inequality, alienation from work, sexual inequalities, and so on over many decades, or even centuries, can all too easily lead to an overdetermined view of society, to a judgement that, by and large, things are as they have to be. Whilst acknowledging that there are constraints, both from within the society and from outside, the emphasis on political initiatives and actions, and more generally on the relative autonomy of politics and the state, implies that it is also possible to act so as to bring about desired changes. Our discussions show that UK society has changed and is changing; many past changes may be the unintended consequences of actions taken with other aims in view, but some represent the result of deliberate choices. This volume should serve not only to help provide an informed understanding of the nature of our society today, but also to provide a basis for action to change society for the better in the future.

Introduction to the 1978 Edition
social facts and sociological analysis

Philip Abrams

It seems sensible to begin by saying what this book is not. It is not an expanded version of *Britain in Figures*.[1] Although it contains a good deal of statistical evidence, quantitative information and tabulated data it is not meant to be any sort of definitive presentation of that type of evidence. It is not, for example, an attempt to emulate the invaluable series published annually by the Central Statistical Office, *Social Trends*.[2] There would really be no point in trying to improve on the way in which the CSO gathers official statistical data and, letting the data speak for themselves, offers a year by year commentary on the directions of social change. One of the things this book seeks to do is to talk about official statistics while deliberately *not* letting those sorts of 'facts' speak for themselves. Again, the book does not offer an alternative to A. H. Halsey's *Trends in British Society since 1900*.[3] Halsey and his colleagues have done one of the jobs that *Social Trends* has never yet quite achieved in assembling a genuinely long range and comprehensive digest of quantitative information about British society, together with a series of critical and politically alert commentaries on the social problems indicated by that evidence. But here, too, the evidence is for the most part not itself questioned; the assumption again is that 'the data' do provide a more or less reliable picture of British social relations and social structure. This book is more sceptical than that. Where Halsey is comprehensive we have been selective; he has something to say about virtually every aspect of British society while we have concentrated on exploring a selection of the key aspects of that society in rather greater depth. On the other hand, while we are concerned to apply sociology as a system of theory and interpretation to the available 'facts' about UK society, the book is not a guide to applying social research methods to the study of practical social problems; it is not a companion volume to Albert Cherns' *Sociotechnics*;[4] nor do we discuss in detail the methodological issues involved in the sociological interpretation of 'given' empirical data in the way that Barry Hindess has done in *The Use of Official Statistics in Sociology*.[5] Nor, finally, is this another attempt at 'the sociology of modern Britain'.

A vital function of sociology as an intellectual discipline is to open the fortified windows of commonsense knowledge and let the gales of uncertainty blow through. Determining what sociologists can claim to know about UK society is in large part a matter of freeing ourselves from the uncritical trust in 'facts' to which we are all too readily disposed, and trying to rediscover the social reality of the relationships and conditions to which the 'facts' refer. We start therefore by putting 'facts' in question — especially statistical 'facts'. A principal object of this book is to suggest the sociological meaning of the sort of information about UK society which we normally take on trust.

As Paul Corrigan pointed out in his discussion of juvenile law-breaking, our problem is
not that the information presented to us in statistical tables and official reports is totally
misleading; it is simply that, for the sociologist, it is not totally correct either. It is, as he
put it, a peculiar type of 'refracted', or partly distorted, knowledge.[6] The task of
sociology is to seek a more reliable image. The problem is two-sided. On the one hand
there is a meaningless fascination about a great deal of 'factual' information which grips
the imagination and tempts us to believe we have learned something significant: in 1975
beer production in Britain totalled 40 million barrels; there were 52,000 confectioners'
shops and 47,000 hairdressers; 75,000 children were taken into care by local authorities;
and 5.11 million metric tons of sulphur dioxide were emitted into the air. Plainly, the
accumulation of statistical scraps and tit-bits of this sort is almost wholly without value
until the bits and pieces are given some sort of meaningful context; for the sociologist
this means a context of structured social relationships. On the other hand, the same types
of 'facts' can acquire a dangerous meaningfulness of their own, precluding awareness of
unstated realities which the information masks. Thus, it is well known that the population
of the UK is ageing dramatically; successive censuses reveal a steady and rapid increase
in both the number and proportion of the elderly in the population. We had 5.7 million
people over the age of 65 in 1941 (in a total population of 48 million) and an estimated
9.6 million in 1975 (in a total population of 56 million). Figures such as these point
powerfully to the growing importance (and cost) of the social problem of dependency in
old age. The trouble is that they tend to point too powerfully, suggesting that the social
problem springs simply from biological characteristics (the infirmity of the old) and
demographic changes (increases in life-expectancy and decreases in the birth rate). What is
obscured is that the problem of dependency in old age is also *socially* created—by the
family as a domestic institution, retirement as an economic institution and pensions as a
political institution; in each case the particular sorts of institutions we have constructed
help in turn to construct the problem of the elderly.

The problem of applying sociology to information of this sort about UK society therefore becomes primarily a problem of placing such information in its proper context of
social relations and social structure. That is what this book tries to do. We have taken
three of the most fundamental concerns of sociology—the division of labour, urbanism
and inequality—and, from the available evidence, tried to develop an analysis of contemporary UK society. The result is something less than a portrait of a whole society;
although it does perhaps confirm that in making these three themes central to their
analysis of industrial societies, classical sociologists were forging an intellectual perspective
of considerable and continuing explanatory power. Work, community and inequality
provide a framework within which effective sense can still be made of the structures
and experiences of an industrial society, and it is hoped that the studies in this book will
do just that. Perforce, many matters of 'obvious' importance are wholly or largely ignored
as a result of this treatment. To some extent this is because our approach necessarily cuts
across some of the more conventional categories of social description. . . . More generally,
although there are indeed some topics—religion, leisure, the monarchy—which are totally
overlooked, we have, through this narrowing of focus, sought to give a sociological
account of the UK *as a society*, a social system, even if we have not given an account of
everybody in it or of the whole range of activities and experiences it contains.

The position we have taken is then that the application of sociology to the understanding of UK society—or any other society—is essentially a critical exercise involving the re-working of commonsense knowledge, facts and evidence from the viewpoint of a distinct intellectual perspective. It is a position well summarized by Tom Burns in his now famous lecture on 'Sociological Explanation'. Having examined a series of major examples of sociological work and shown how their success in every case lay in their ability to unmask everyday stereotypes about the social world, he concludes:

> In this last instance, as in all the others, sociology defines itself as a critical activity. The purpose of sociology is to achieve an understanding of social behaviour and social institutions which is different from that current among the people through whose conduct and the institutions exist; an understanding that is not merely different but new and better. The practice of sociology is criticism. It exists to criticise claims about the value of achievement and to question assumptions about the meaning of conduct. It is the business of sociologists to conduct a critical debate with the public about its equipment of social institutions.[7]

Straightforward, thorough, descriptive reporting is an important element in this debate; it establishes the appropriate basis for discussion. Burns cites the impact of the *Our Towns* study of the condition of children evacuated from city slums in 1940 as an example: 'The astonishing feature of the *Our Towns* report . . . was not the squalor and unseemliness of the children but the blank ignorance of all other sections of society about them and the circumstances of urban life which had produced them'. After its publication the formation of social policy in health, housing and education simply had to proceed on a new basis. Some of the more recent findings about work, wealth and poverty discussed later in this book have had a very similar influence. But good descriptive reporting is only one of the essential ingredients of the debate between sociology and society. The other is a strategic understanding of what the descriptions could mean, a larger conception of how the institutions and behaviour being described relate to behaviour, institutions and experience in the rest of society. Such a perspective is implicit in our decision to concentrate the analysis of UK society in this book within the framework of inequality, urbanism and the division of labour.

The intellectual history of sociology is indissolubly tied to the material history of industrialization. And the immediate experience of the transition to industrialism has almost invariably been one in which life seems to be dominated by a dramatic explosion of the division of labour, a transformation of old patterns of inequality and rapid and extensive if not ubiquitous urbanization. It would have been odd indeed if these phenomena and the peculiar problems of social integration, progress and values which they posed had not become the substantive core of a social science concerned above all to understand the nature of industrial society. What we find in the best sociology, whether in the writings of Marx, Durkheim and Weber or in the more modern writings of Bell, Sennett or Castells, is a sustained attempt to relate these phenomena of industrialization to one another and to grasp the underlying realities of structure and process from which they spring. Such works are only secondarily a matter of record or description; the distribution of persons to occupations, the scale and pace of urbanization, hierarchies of stratification and rates of social mobility are the distinctive phenomena to which sociological analysis refers. But the analysis itself is primarily concerned with the inter-relationships of such phenomena, not with their incidence. It is in the ways they act on one another that the division of labour, inequality and urbanism reveals and constitutes the peculiar social structure and dynamics of industrial societies. And it is towards an understanding of that interaction that sociology, pure or applied, consistently moves.

Attempts to isolate any one of these dimensions of industrialization from the others have, almost without exception, proved disastrous — most conspicuously in the efforts of Louis Wirth and his successors to develop a sociology of the urban community without reference to the contexts of inequality and the social division of labour in which cities exist. Emile Durkheim, whom I would regard as having done more than any other single writer to give modern sociology its special intellectual character, came close to a similar sterility in his own pioneering analysis of the division of labour. Only at the very end of *The Division of Labour in Society* does Durkheim actually place the division of labour *in* society, recognizing that the specialization of functions, the logical implications of which he had so brilliantly unravelled in the body of his book, also occurred in settings constructed historically in terms of the power of some social groups and the powerlessness of others.[8] Nevertheless, he does recognize this 'forcing' of the division of labour; and so concludes in the end that the actual working out of the ambiguous tendencies of the division of labour in any industrial society — tendencies towards both individual rationality and social meaninglessness, towards both cohesion and division in society — will have to be left as an open empirical question for the sociologist to resolve. And its resolution will be in part a matter of understanding the ways in which the history of the division of labour is contained within the history of social inequality and in turn acts on it. . . .

Marx and Weber were more sensitive than Durkheim to the interdependence of inequality and the division of labour; and also more aware of the ways in which the typical social forms of industrial society such as the city were expressions of that interdependence. Yet there is a surprising consensus among all three of the most eminent founding fathers of sociology on the nature of the sociological task. From the point of view of the individual the rise of industrial capitalism created a world which is simultaneously a world of emancipated self-interest, rational personal action, and collective irrationality, chaos and constraint. The moral absurdity of the situation of the individual is to be understood, perhaps even transcended, through social analysis of the bonds between the division of labour and the structure of inequality. Experiences of personal life — suicide, poverty, religion, the city or whatever form of experience might be in question — are to be explained by their location within that relationship.

This is a strong doctrine and it immediately indicates the second great danger that faces any attempt to unite sociology and social description in an effective, applied social analysis. The first danger is that of taking the findings of descriptive enquiries too much on trust, of allowing the data to speak for themselves. The second is that of allowing the wisdom or at least the logic of sociological theory to speak for *itself*, brutally imposing what inferentially must be on whatever commonsense appears to have observed. Applied sociology has to negotiate a passage between these two hazards and it can do so only by taking both social facts and sociological analysis quite seriously. It is in other words a matter of balance: of constantly looking at 'the evidence' from the point of view of theory, and of constantly looking at 'theory' from the point of view of the evidence. On each side of the balance perhaps the most important and valuable question the sociologist can ask is simply 'so what?' It is this sort of balance that the various chapters of this book seek to maintain, a balance that is at once fragile, sceptical and constructive.

FROM FACTS TO ANALYSIS: THE PROBLEM OF AGE

Two examples will perhaps help to make clear just how difficult this type of balance is to achieve. Let us take first a field of social enquiry in which evidence has tended to dominate theory—the study of age; and then a field in which theory has tended to dominate evidence—the study of urban communities. In both cases the challenge to the applied sociologist is to use the apparently weaker element to subvert the apparent authority of the stronger.

Demographic data, basic information about rates of birth, marriage, death and migration, are commonly treated as one of the 'hardest' types of evidence available to the social scientist. At the same time it is well known that predictions and projections based on demographic data are, of all types of social prediction, the ones most likely to go wrong. The fact that in the late 1970s Britain is experiencing a so-called 'crisis of teacher-training'—that is to say we are training far more teachers than government is willing to pay to teach—is a direct result of the official belief that the high marriage and birth rates of the early 1960s were themselves social facts which could be treated as a given and continuing basis for social policy. The belief that information about fertility in 1960 could provide a basis for knowing what sort of families people would have in the 1970s is the immediate cause of the prospect of unemployment that faces so many student teachers in 1978. Yet there is a sense in which demographers never learn. In the early 1960s we were told with complete confidence that the population of the United Kingdom would increase towards a figure of 66 millions by the end of the century. Today, in the 1976 edition of *Social Trends*, we are told no less confidently that the probable population of the United Kingdom in the year 2001 is a mere 59 million. Seven million people more or less have been demographically written off. Yet the basic datum on which both projections are based is the same; it is the number of women of child-bearing age already or prospectively in the population at the moment when the projection is made; coupled with the assumption that these women will behave in exactly the same way as their immediate predecessors. On the basis of this information and on this assumption the demographer concludes that the child-bearing behaviour of tomorrow's adults can be extrapolated in a law-like manner from his knowledge of the child-bearing behaviour of the adults of the immediate past.[9]

The belief that the incidence of a given type of behaviour at a given moment in time constitutes a social fact of general significance is here given a rigidity and force of a quite remarkable nature. As a result the history of demography is a history of endlessly revised projections. And yet, despite the fact that generation after generation of parents have spectacularly failed to behave in the way demographers expected them to behave, demography continues to flourish. Instead of abandoning the whole business of demographic projection and recognizing that family size, to say nothing of family relationships, are too susceptible to changing social pressures and personal choices to be treated as social facts in this simplistic way, the demographer tends simply to produce a new projection offered with all the authority of the one that has just been discredited.

Demography thus provides an exceptionally clear example of the way in which social description falls short of social analysis. Contemporary demographic facts about the UK would include the following. First, the births that have already occurred, together with our existing ability to prolong life, will mean that there will be very many fewer children of compulsory school age in the 1980s than there have been in the recent past, that there will be a short-term increase in the demand for higher education followed by a decline from the late 1980s to the end of the century, that there will be a quite rapid increase in the population of working age during the next decade and that there will be a considerable increase in the numbers of very old people between the ages of 75 and 85. Second, and only a little more speculatively, one could suggest that these changes will in turn entail a number of further changes; for example, a quite dramatic increase in the number of one-person households, since at present about three-quarters of such house-holds consist of single elderly people. The current projection is that the 3.5 million one-person households in the country in 1970 will have increased to 5.5 million by 1990. And thirdly it might not be unreasonable to argue that certain well-established trends in patterns of marriage and divorce will continue along broadly the same lines to the end of the century. Thus, both marriage and divorce have been becoming more popular and it is not implausible to suppose that both trends will persist. Between 1931 and 1973 the ratio of married people in Great Britain rose from 56 per cent to 67 per cent of the adult population. In 1931 only 25 per cent of women from 20 to 24 years old were married; but in 1973 the ratio was 58 per cent. At the same time there were 121,000 divorces in England and Wales in 1975, over three times as many as ten years earlier; and there were 116,000 re-marriages—marriages which were not the first marriage for one or both partners. Taken together such figures point to the strong probability of there being an increasing number of children living in families which do not consist of both their natural parents.

But what does all this tell us about the family as a social institution in UK society, or more specifically about the social significance of age and the social organization of the life-cycle? How can we make the leap from demographic data to sociological under-standing? A slightly closer look at the problem might be helpful. Demography was after all one of the earliest social sciences. It took shape against the background of an essentially pre-industrial social order—in England, for example, between 1660 and 1720. Its methods tended to reflect the social realities of such social orders; realities in which rates of marriage, fertility and mortality were all relatively fixed from generation to generation and in which trends in any of the three matured slowly over very long periods of time and in a more or less invariable manner. Plagues, wars and famines apart, demo-graphic data did look like social facts in pre-industrial societies. In the more 'ideal-typical' versions of such societies, biological age and inherited social identity were the cardinal sources of social organization, status and hierarchy. To know a person's kin and age was to know almost everything of social importance about him. The 'natural' phases of the life-cycle provided a stable basis for the social division of labour, power, privilege and identity. By contrast the extent to which age and kin control an individual's social destiny and status (or even reliably indicate them) in advanced industrial societies is remarkably slight. Of course people are still assigned to age-specific roles, such as child-hood, adolescence and old age, in relatively inflexible ways; and the social organization of the life-cycle is still an important dimension of social organization as a whole. But for all the excitement about 'youth culture' and the 'generation gap' in the last two decades the striking thing about industrial societies is how little, comparatively speaking, age determines.

The same is increasingly true of the other basic elements of demographic enquiry. The law-like constraints of the life-cycle and of biological inheritance that are experienced in pre-industrial societies are being progressively relaxed in other areas too. The technologies of birth control and the politics of divorce and women's liberation have freed people from subjection to the social 'facts' of marriage and fertility rates. Medicine, and institutional and social care, are progressively making even the facts of mortality variable. Death was of course the beginning of demography. It was the predictability of death by gender, age, occupation and medical history that permitted the formation and profitability of life-insurance organization. And it was from this basis that demography as a predictive, statistical social science sprang. By undermining the certainties on which demography was constructed, advanced industrialism makes the understanding of the life-cycle sociologically problematic in a way it has not been for a long time. As the predictions began to be falsified the need for an independent analysis of the social meaning of the data became steadily more evident. The demographic profile of contemporary UK society is easy to draw and not especially controversial. What is controversial is the meaning of that profile for social change and social policy.

One would begin by conceding that UK society is indeed becoming an older society. In 1900 the median age of our population was 24; today it is 34; by the end of the century we are told that it will be 38. Of all demographic projections those concerning mortality are the least unreliable since the normal tendency of medicine to extend life, and the normal propensity of human beings to avoid death, are about as reliable as any social data can be. To put it more directly; given a falling birth rate since the early 1960s and greater longevity among the old, the proportion of retired and dependent persons in the population as a whole has to increase. *Social Trends* expresses it rather opaquely as an increase in the 'upper quartile' of the age distribution of the population from 40 per cent in 1901 to 50 per cent in 1971. Another way of putting it is to note that there were 2.4 million people over the age of retirement in 1901, 5.7 million in 1941, 7.1 million in 1971 and the figure now projected for the year 2001 is 8.5 million. In other words Britain is an ageing society in quite a dramatic sense; with an overall population growth of 45 per cent since 1900 the number of people over the age of retirement has increased by 196 per cent. At the same time, although the number of people under the age of 16 has fractionally increased in absolute terms, it has declined as a proportion of the population as a whole. So that while the overall 'dependency' ratio—the proportion of the population that on grounds of age will have to be supported by others—may be said to have changed very little in the first three-quarters of this century (from 35 per cent to 38 per cent), its *constitution* has changed remarkably and in a way that gives us a new and acute social problem. At least it does for so long as we treat men over 65 and women over 60 as necessarily 'economically inactive'; but this again is a political not a demographic fact.

Unreliable as projections based on fertility rates and marriage rates are now recognized to be, the implications of our survival rate taken in conjunction with current levels of fertility are quite impressive. At present women are marrying younger (the average age of first marriage is now 23 as compared with 26 in 1900); as are men (25 now as compared with 27 in 1900) and, except in the professional middle classes, all married couples are having fewer children. Elizabeth Still has shown that graduates of higher education have now become the most prolific section of the population so far as child-bearing is concerned.[10] More generally the increasing popularity of marriage seems to be negatively related to family size. As marriage and parenthood both become increasingly matters of choice it seems that marriage is being chosen more frequently and parenthood less frequently. The current birth rate of 12.4 live births per 1,000 of the population is the lowest the country has had this century, compared with figures of 18 in 1961 and 29 in 1901. We do not know of course whether these trends will continue. It is difficult for example to know what allowance to make for the possible effects of future economic changes on people's attitudes to the 'value' of children. But for the moment we plainly have a population profile with a bulging forehead (of the elderly) and a receding chin (of the young)—a profile which, however sceptical one may be about the reliability of demographic projections, already has a serious message for policy-makers.

Yet here we hit upon a difficulty. Although demographic description indicates the existence of the social problem, it does not indicate its nature—if anything it misrepresents it. Demography encourages the interpretation of the problem of dependence in old age as a 'natural' hazard of the life-cycle and obscures the extent to which it is, rather, an effect of a particular social division of labour; and of particular relations of social inequality. The point is hardly new but it is one that almost always needs to be made when one attempts to move from this sort of descriptive evidence to an adequate understanding of the social relations of the family.

In Britain this point was made as long as eighty years ago by Seebohm Rowntree in his path-finding analyses of the social causes of poverty. In *Poverty: a Study of Town Life* Rowntree examined the relationship between poverty and the life-cycle and showed with devastating clarity that while the incidence of poverty was indeed strongly associated with particular phases of the life-cycle, its causes were to be found not in the life-cycle as such, but in the relationship between the social organization of age and an equally socially organized division of labour.[11] Anyone looking at Rowntree's chart (figure 0.1), where the life-cycle is expressed as a series of age-specific waves of poverty and affluence, can see that the periodic reductions of well-being which he identified are a consequence not of biological facts alone, but of the relationship between the life-cycle and the labour market. In that relationship it is the structure of the labour market which has to be regarded as the variable element and therefore as the proper target of social policy. What was needed was not just old age pensions but a change in the relationship between the family and the economy.

Demographic data, then, like other descriptive evidence, tell us something about the location and scale of our social problems. But they cannot on their own tell us why those problems exist or what should properly be done about them. To move from description to analysis some *theoretical* bridge has to be built between the evidence and its possible meaning. However reluctantly, Rowntree was forced to conclude that this bridge was constituted by the wage economy. Looking at similar data today we must be at least as determined to resist the suggestion that the dependency of the old is merely a function of age. Of course old people do become crippled by arthritis and other disabilities, the biological process of ageing does take its toll. But we also institutionalize age and this is a socially variable matter. In many primitive societies age is institutionalized on the basis of authority; in modern UK society it is institutionalized on the basis of dependency. The social description of age masks the extent to which we have *created* age as a certain sort of social relationship. Perhaps at the present time in the UK the real 'problem' of old age is not that of dependency and disability at all, but that of retirement. It is important to remember that only a minute proportion of the elderly are in residential care—for

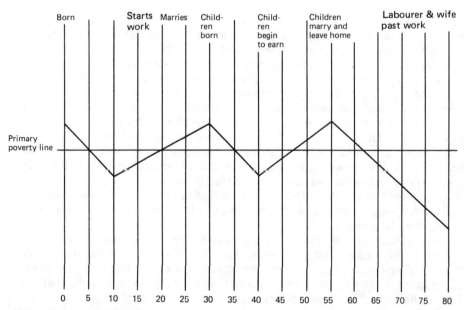

Figure 0.1   Poverty and the Life Cycle
Source: adapted from B. Seebohm Rowntree, *Poverty: a Study of Town Life* (London 1910).

example 7 per cent of those over 75 in 1960—and there is some evidence that the figure is if anything falling. But they all face the issue of being old in a society where the social division of labour makes being old a form of redundancy. As Phillipson puts it in a recent analysis of the social creation of retirement:

> One of the major innovations to have occurred in the twentieth century has been the emergence of retirement as a major part of the life-cycle. In addition the character of the retirement period has changed, and continues to change at a dramatic pace. From a point where it seemed merely a short stage (particularly for men) before death, there is now evolving a multi-staged period at least part of which, for increasing numbers, may mark a real measure of choice and scope to pursue diverse social activities. The evolution of ideas about the retirement stage in the life-cycle has developed in a hesitant manner, reflecting both ambiguities in social attitudes toward old age and competing economic and social priorities—these producing tension in the relationship between the work and post-work spheres and in the latter's cultural and social legitimation.[12]

He goes on to trace the particularly close connection in that evolution between the social position and treatment of the elderly and fluctuations in the supply and demand for labour in the wage economy as a whole. Against this background the problem of the elderly disappears and is replaced by the problem of the relationship of all age-groups to one another within an encompassing division of labour. Social policy for its part, having just begun to shift its attention from the idea of institutional care to that of domiciliary care, is now called upon to make a further move away from the idea of concentrating 'care' on a particular age group; and towards that of protecting and enhancing the family as a setting for relationships of reciprocity across the life-cycle as a whole. For despite the many suggestions in the demographic data which might be thought to point towards a weakening of family life, one of the plainest and firmest findings of more intensive sociological research is that the family in fact remains the strongest and most highly valued basis for social attachment UK society possesses.[13] Sociologically, the tough resilience of family relationships is not surprising; it follows from the discipline's earliest and most fundamental insights into the nature of solidarity, reciprocity and attachment. Had our discussion of the problem of old age in the contemporary UK started from the works of Durkheim, or Simmel, LePlay or Malinowski rather than from the latest census data, the descriptive evidence would not have presented us with the relatively isolated problem of old age; but with the much more analytically fruitful question of the extent to which family relationships in the general setting of an advanced industrial society can survive as a basis for practical solidarity and attachment between individuals. That is in itself a controversial question, but at least it is a question which recognizes the social context of social problems.

Thus the first hazard of applied sociology is that of taking the fruits of social description too much on trust; and its first task is to reinterpret social description from the point of view of sociological theory. Nevertheless the second task is to pay proper respect to the findings of descriptive enquiries; and the second great hazard is that of allowing the logic of sociological theory to overwhelm the hard evidence of common-sense. This hazard has been particularly acute in sociological discussions of community.

FROM ANALYSIS TO FACTS: THE PROBLEM OF COMMUNITY

The apparent weakening of the family indicated in many descriptive studies is as nothing compared to the loss of community predicted by the whole tradition of sociological theory. Because sociology came into being as an attempt to apprehend the nature and dynamics of the transition to industrialism, it tended to identify the emergent industrial world in terms of a series of stark polarities, or contrasts-of-type, between pre-industrial and industrial societies. The most characteristic of these centred on the idea of community. Virtually without exception the pioneers of sociology understood industrialization to involve a disintegration of the bonds of community. Community became, as Robert Nisbet puts it, 'the most fundamental and far-reaching of sociology's unit ideas'.[14] The term referred not only to attachments grounded in locality but, much more generally, to an inclusive moral cohesion believed to have characterized pre-industrial society. As Nisbet remarks again: 'the word . . . encompassed all forms of relationship which are characterized by a high degree of personal intimacy, emotional depth, moral commitment, social cohesion and continuity in time. Community is founded on man conceived in his wholeness rather than in one or another of the roles, taken separately, that he may hold in a social order.' Since the essential nature of industrial society involved an explosion of the division of labour which splintered people's lives into separated roles, industrialization logically threatened community. The theme is endlessly reiterated, becoming one of the commonplaces of sociological wisdom. The loss of community was associated especially with the growth of industrial cities which were contrasted not just with the past, but with the countryside as well. It is in the early urban sociology of Simmel and Wirth that these ideas are most directly presented. But this theme was not the sole preserve of sociologists. It was Benjamin Disraeli who gave it one of its crispest statements:

> There is no community in England; there is aggregation, but aggregation under circumstances which make it rather a dissociating than a uniting principle . . . In great cities men are brought together by the desire of gain. They are not in a state of co-operation but of isolation, as to the making of fortunes; and for the rest they are careless of neighbours. Christianity teaches us to love our neighbour as ourself; modern society acknowledges no neighbour.[15]

Ruth Glass has suggested that this tendency to contrast urban present and rural past in terms of community, and to the disadvantage of urban present, is a peculiar tendency of British intellectuals. While there is some truth in this, it is also the case that this particular contrast pervades the whole of sociology, European and American as much as British. A representative passage from Louis Wirth may speak for the whole sociological tradition, both in its assertion of the loss of community and in its belief in the vital importance of the city as a distinctive social form of industrial society:

> The multiplication of persons in a state of interaction under conditions which make their contact as full personalities impossible produces that segmentalization of human relationships which has sometimes been seized upon by students of the mental life of the cities as an explanation of the 'schizoid' character of urban personality. . . . Characteristically, urbanites meet one another in highly segmental roles. They are, to be sure, dependent upon more people for the satisfactions of their life-needs than are rural people and thus are associated with a greater number of organised groups, but they are less dependent upon particular persons, and their dependence upon others is confined to a highly fractionalized aspect of the other's round of activity. This is essentially what is meant by saying that the city is characterized by secondary rather than primary contacts. The contacts of the city may indeed be face to face but they are nevertheless impersonal, superficial, transitory and segmental. The reserve, the indifference and the blasé outlook which urbanities manifest in their relationships may thus be regarded as devices for immunizing themselves against the personal claims and expectations of others.[16]

The most remarkable thing about the body of doctrine and inference which such a passage represents is that it is so deeply rooted in the logic of sociological analysis that it has successfully resisted modification, despite a glaring absence of confirmatory evidence and the uncomfortable presence of a good deal of evidence pointing in a contrary direction. To begin with the analysis as a whole can not be fully validated as we lack thorough empirical studies of the supposed pre-industrial 'base-line' from which the loss of community is believed to have developed. We simply don't know what community in eighteenth-century England was like and it is unlikely that we shall ever be able to gain such knowledge. For the most part early sociologists treated the presence of strong communities in pre-industrial societies as axiomatic; and subsequent advocates of the loss of community thesis have been increasingly constrained to do the same. More disturbingly, quite a large number of descriptive studies of contemporary industrial societies, including the UK, have suggested that the various elements of community are in fact quite strongly present in such societies, even in their most highly urbanized areas.[17] The paradox of the sociology of community is the coexistence of a body of theory which constantly predicts the collapse of community and of a body of empirical studies which finds community alive and well.

In practice the problem is not quite as clear-cut as that, nor is the difficulty all on one side. Nevertheless, if we take one theme from the field of community studies as an example, that of neighbouring, we can see that this is a field where applied sociology has been quite severely hampered by the general predominance of theory over description. In line with the tendency of community theory as a whole, the prediction emerging from sociological analysis about neighbouring has been that it, too, will be eroded with the development of industrialism. For Wirth again 'the bonds . . . of neighbourliness . . . are likely to be absent or, at best, relatively weak' in urban industrial milieux. And in a comprehensive and perceptive review of the whole literature on neighbouring, Suzanne Keller was able to condense conventional wisdom into a number of quite sharply focused propositions explaining why attachment and interaction among neighbours must be expected to be less important and less intense in the typical settings of industrial societies (cities) than in the typical settings of pre-industrial societies (villages). From this point of view the UK is one of the most 'industrial' of nations. Its population density, 601 people per square mile, is one of the highest in the world; and that population is predominantly urban. The ratio of those living in urban areas to those living in the countryside is about $3\frac{1}{2}$: 1, with approximately a third of the population living in seven great conurbations. Keller summarizes the analysis as follows:

1. As crises diminish in number and kind, where, that is, self-sufficiency increases, neighbour relations will diminish in strength and significance.
2. As new forms of social control arise, the significance of neighbouring as a means of social control will recede in importance.
3. Where neighbouring is a segmental activity in an open system rather than an integral part of a closed system, it will be a highly variable and unpredictable phenomenon.
4. Since all three conditions are more true of urban than of pre- or suburban areas, neighbouring should diminish in extent, significance and stability in cities.[18]

More recently and in very much the same spirit, Key has claimed to have shown that 'there is a negative relationship between the size of the community in which people reside and the frequency with which they participate in social relationships involving other people residing in portions of the community contiguous to their residence.'[19]

One difficulty with this sort of argument is that a large number of empirical studies have documented the existence of intensive and extensive neighbourliness in highly urbanized areas, the best known in this country being the work of Young and Wilmott in Bethnal Green.[20] A further difficulty is that even when the effects predicted for urban industrial societies *are* observed it is not at all clear that the effects that occur *in* cities or in industrial societies are in fact caused *by* cities or by industrialism. The implicit causal relation asserted in the theory of community has proved extraordinarily difficult to demonstrate explicitly. That is one reason why modern urban sociology, represented in this book by Brian Elliott's chapter, has increasingly moved away from the idea of the city as a distinct social entity, found in the work of Simmel and Wirth, towards a type of analysis in which cities are treated merely as settings in which the characteristic relationships of some larger social structure and some more inclusive division of labour work themselves out. It is a move away from urban sociology towards the political economy of towns. Alternatively, one could say that it is an attempt to place the analysis of urbanism within the broader sociological analysis of the division of labour and social inequality, instead of allowing it to remain a seemingly independent and isolated branch of the discipline.

But to return to community and to neighbouring. The concept of community for its part is slowly being evicted from British sociology; not because there is agreement on the empirical collapse of community; but rather because the term has come to be used so variously and different relationships, identified as those of community, have been discovered in so many different contexts that the word itself has become almost devoid of precise meaning. In particular there has been a determined effort to detach the study of social relationships from the study of spatial relationships—two themes which are hopelessly jumbled together in the traditional idea of community. The problem of solidarity is, recent authors have suggested, one that should be separated, as a matter of principle, from the problem of the effects of spatial arrangements on social relationships. As Pahl says in an important article developing this theme: 'any attempt to tie particular patterns of social relationships to specific geographical milieux is a singularly fruitless exercise'.[21] And Stacey, in a parallel argument about the 'myth of community studies', concludes that 'our concern as sociologists is with social relationships; a consideration of the social attributes of individuals living in a particular geographic area is therefore not sociology, although it may well be an essential preliminary to sociological analysis'.[22] In sum, there is now a prevailing scepticism about the possibility of studying spatial relationships sociologically; and a resulting insistence that in so far as the concept of community implicitly prejudges the nature of such relationships it should be expelled from the dictionary of sociology.

Where does that leave the study of neighbouring in contemporary industrial society? Obviously, unlike the concept of community, the concept of neighbouring *must* have spatial connotations: neighbours are defined as people who live close to each other. So the sociological problem about neighbours has to be one that includes a question about the effects on social relationships of different ways of living close to others. More generally, the issue is to determine what type of social and/or spatial circumstances are associated with what types of relationships between neighbours. And here again such evidence as there is tends to belie the predictions of sociological theory. Two findings emerge especially strongly from the whole body of research. One concerns prevailing social norms about neighbourliness; the other involves the conditions under which members of our society are likely to be 'good' neighbours. So far as the norms of neighbourliness are concerned it seems clear that neighbourliness is very widely understood, in both town and country, and for that matter in both present and past, as a three-dimensional relationship composed of friendliness, helpfulness and distance.[23] Ideally, normatively, a neighbour is someone who is agreeable when casually encountered, there when you want them in an emergency and yet who does not 'live in your pocket'; who, while being both friendly and helpful, also respects your privacy. Not only is this norm widely diffused in contemporary UK society, but the circumstances under which such a norm can actually be realized in relationships between neighbours are also widely understood.

Thus, although the urban–rural contrast does not stand up to scrutiny, it seems that the nature of the locale in which people live does affect patterns of neighbouring in some quite definite ways. For example, the social homogeneity of a neighbourhood and the average length of residence of its inhabitants are both factors which seem to vary positively with the intensity and extensiveness of neighbouring.[24] There are also well-established social class variations, characterized by Keller as 'working class solidarity, middle class selectivity and suburban sociability'.[25] But these are typically much finer, subtler and more complex than the familiar generalizations would suggest. For example, one of the most recent English studies reports 'no clear dichotomy' in either behaviour or attitudes to neighbouring between classes but, within this 'general similarity of response', notes that working-class people tend to 'see' their neighbours more often, and that the street is a more common meeting place for them than for middle-class people—a difference which would seem to spring from variations in built-form, mobility and occupation rather than from class as such.[26] More generally, class differences in neighbouring would appear to be rooted in the ways in which the meaning of class is bound up with and affected by (for example) mobility, income, kinship, age, residential arrangements, social service provision, occupational patterns; in other words more specific influences operating within the worlds of class. A typical instance is the finding of one study that while working class people express rather more positive attitudes about the desirability of contact with neighbours than middle-class people, this difference is not reflected in any degree of greater neighbouring activity. The authors explain this absence of variation by pointing out that the working-class people in their study *did* have a great deal more to do with their relations than the middle-class people.[27] For practical purposes kinship replaced neighbouring in the functions through which strong relationships with neighbours might have been constructed. Similar observations could be made about the relationship between neighbouring and built-form, mobility, stages in the life-cycle and numerous other factors. What emerges consistently throughout is that neighbourliness is a social relationship facilitated or impeded by a wide array of social-structural influences but determined by none of them. Disraeli was wrong: modern society *does* acknowledge neighbours. And the social analysis of neighbouring is slowly moving away from the sweeping application of deterministic social theory towards the detailed empirical rediscovery of the conditions under which it does so.

Applied sociology is, therefore, a dialogue between social theory and social description. In the chapters that follow we attempt to develop such a dialogue about UK society seen from the point of view of three of the most crucial and distinctive concerns of sociological analysis. We have not tried to take the further step, often also thought of as applied sociology, of deriving proposals for policy from our analysis, but will be satisfied if the sort of analysis we offer here enables the discussion of policy to proceed in a more perceptive context of interpretation. To adapt a famous observation: philosophers have sought to change the world; the task, however, is to interpret it.

Notes to Introduction to the 1978 Edition

1   A. Sillitoe, *Britain in Figures* (Penguin edn. 1971).
2   HMSO, *Social Trends* (1971-6).
3   A. H. Halsey (ed.), *Trends in British Society since 1900* (London 1972).
4   A. Cherns (ed.), *Sociotechnics* (London 1976).
5   B. Hindess, *The Use of Official Statistics in Sociology* (London 1973).
6   P. Corrigan, 'Deviance and Deprivation' in P. Abrams (ed.), *Work, Urbanism and Inequality: UK Society Today* (London 1978), pp. 249-96.
7   T. Burns, 'Sociological Explanation', *British Journal of Sociology*, Vol. 18 (1967).
8   E. Durkheim, *The Division of Labour in Society* (London 1933), esp. Bk. 3.
9   P. Abrams, 'Age and Generation' in P. Barker (ed.), *A Sociological Portrait* (Penguin edn. 1972).
10 E. Still, 'The Fashion for Families', *New Society* (8 June 1967.)
11 B. Seebohm Rowntree, *Poverty: a Study of Town Life* (London 1910).
12 C. Phillipson, *The Emergence of Retirement*, Working Papers in Sociology, No. 14, University of Durham (1977).
13 See, especially, E. Shanas and G. Streib, *Social Structure and the Family* (Wiley 1965).
14 R. Nisbet, *The Sociological Tradition* (London 1966), p. 47.
15 Cited in R. Nisbet, *op. cit.*
16 L. Wirth, 'Urbanism as a Way of Life', *American Journal of Sociology*, Vol. 44 (1938).
17 See, especially, C. Bell and H. Newby, *Community Studies* (London 1971).
18 S. Keller, *The Urban Neighbourhood* (New York 1968).
19 W. H. Key, 'Urbanism and Neighbouring', *Sociological Quarterly* (1965), p. 384.
20 M. Young and P. Wilmott, *Family and Kinship in East London* (London 1957).
21 R. E. Pahl, 'The Rural-Urban Continuum', *Sociologia Ruralis*, Vol. 6 (1966).
22 M. Stacey, 'The Myth of Community Studies', *British Journal of Sociology*, Vol. 20 (1969).
23 F. Robinson and P. Abrams, *What We Know About the Neighbours*, Rowntree Research Unit, University of Durham (1977).
24 See especially, H. Gans, *The Levittowners* (Penguin edn. 1967) and 'Urbanism and Suburbanism as Ways of Life' in R. Pahl (ed.), *Readings in Urban Sociology* (Oxford, 1968); also P. Wilmott, *The Evolution of a Community* (London 1963).
25 S. Keller, *op. cit.*
26 Kingston Polytechnic, *The Buxton Report* (1976).
27 *Ibid.*

1
Cities in the Eighties: the growth of inequality

Brian Elliott

INTRODUCTION

What is happening in our cities? The urban riots in 1981 in Brixton, Southall and Toxteth, along with smaller disturbances in other districts prior to and following these much publicized affairs suggest that all is not well. When people take their grievances onto the street and do battle with the police or with particular ethnic groups, we can be sure that important tensions, anxieties and senses of frustration or injustice exist. One hardly needs a degree in social science to be aware of some of the problems. Any interested observer surveying the character of many of our inner city streets or the dereliction of old industrial areas or the boarded-up windows of many public housing estates can identify the symptoms of change and decline. The evidence is there in the steel shuttered shop-fronts, in the desolate landscape of littered public spaces, in the graffiti on the walls and hoardings or the squalor of lifts and landings in the high-rise towers. Frequently though, one has only to travel a short distance to encounter very different scenes: the discreet opulence of Georgian squares; the tastefully restored Victorian villas behind substantial walls; the ordered domesticity of the owner-occupied suburban 'semis'. It is the contrasts that are so striking and convey the sense of a divided society. Those with jobs, those on above average earnings can continue to enjoy the fruits of the consumer society. They can buy their new cars, plan their continental holidays, work in congenial surroundings and choose to live convivially in the smartened-up areas of the central city, in the leafy suburbs or in the pleasant towns and villages some distance from the metropolitan areas.

Now, as always, our cities provide physical evidence of what is happening and what has happened in our social systems. The record is there in the bricks and mortar, in the general organization of space and in the social institutions of our urban places. Our purpose in this chapter is to look at the city as one way of documenting some of the major changes that have taken place in Britain in the recent past and as a way of capturing important ongoing processes. We need to be concerned not only with broad trends but also with those ideas, ideals and objectives that find expression in the programmes of government. That seems especially vital in the 1980s, for over the past few years we have had in power a government which proclaims the 'radicalism' of its particular conservative philosophy. While we should be careful not to attribute too much influence to governments, not to be taken in by their rhetoric, it is the thesis of this chapter that the Thatcher administrations have been trying to alter the conditions of our lives in some profound ways and that their specifically urban policies are a part of that endeavour. Simply put, the so-called 'New Right' seeks to promote long-term growth and prosperity through the encouragement of market forces and accepts that this will lead to greater inequality. In order to achieve its objectives it argues that we must break with and even reverse many of the policies of the post-war years. It is for this reason that the election of 1979 was a watershed in the pattern of our social and economic development. Looking at our cities we can already begin to see some of the effects of these changes of policy.

THE BACKGROUND

First, however, we need to sketch the general character of post-war urban development. The Labour government came to power committed to a radical restructuring of British society. As part of this commitment, and drawing upon ideas that had been debated over many years, it put in hand measures designed not simply to repair bomb damage but to reshape our urban environments in a fundamental way.[1] Most of the ideas found their expression in the Town and Country Planning Act of 1947. The effects of that Act and of subsequent pieces of legislation through the 1950s and 1960s were immensely important. As a nation we engaged in the creation of new towns, we expanded smaller urban centres, cleared slums and rebuilt central areas and spent millions of pounds on huge public housing schemes. We conducted what were really massive social experiments, but we did remarkably little to monitor them, to assess their impact on the people concerned. Planning took shape and largely remained an enterprise engaged, above all, with the physical environment. At the point of its real development in the immediate post-war years, planning looked not to the social sciences but to those disciplines which traditionally manipulated the built environment: architecture and engineering.[2] Of course, there were always some who saw their task in a broader framework and attempted to relate their spatial preoccupations to the likely social consequences. It should also be noted that from the mid-sixties onwards the patterns of recruitment into planning changed[3] with far more geographers, economists and sociologists joining the profession and the amount of specifically social research on urban problems and policies increased substantially. Nonetheless, when one looks back over those years, there is no escaping the primacy of the physical and spatial considerations in British planning nor the depressing frequency with which the failure to attend to *social* needs was reported by those who set out to study new areas of housing.[4]

The creation of the original post-war legislation was really the product of several distinct and sometimes conflicting interests. On the one hand, there was the deeply entrenched concern over the growth of cities. In the 1920s and 1930s there certainly had been very considerable growth, especially in the major towns and cities. London, for instance, grew from six million to eight million between 1919 and 1939, and much more importantly, it expanded its land area almost five times.[5] The extension of road and rail networks and the government subsidies to developers and builders[6] produced a rapid expansion of the major urban areas and these developments excited some ancient fears about the growth of the city. There can be no doubt that post-war legislation reflected this fear: the urban sprawl had to be contained; the countryside preserved. Thus a principal aim of planning was deeply conservative, seeking to prevent change, defending the interests of rural landowners and giving expression to the old mistrust of the city. But planning was not all negative. Alongside the conservatives, indeed allied with them at least for a while, we find advocates of more radical change. Men like Abercrombie and Osborn saw planning as an instrument for a more equitable distribution of resources, as a way of really ameliorating the lot of those condemned for years to live in squalor. Their claim to represent a more radical vision resides principally in their willingness to establish a high degree of public control of land and its development. The problems of cities could not be solved unless the free market in land was curtailed and public ownership established. Thus two very different views came together, each representing separate interests and seeking solutions to different problems but united, at least for a while, in their determination to see the machinery of rational planning set up. The alliance, however, was fragile and as the real import of the 1947 legislation was appreciated by those who owned land or who hoped to benefit from land development, it was shattered. By 1958, under a Tory government, the public control envisaged by the Act was largely removed.[7] By the mid-fifties planning in Britain was firmly established as a conservative force, its enthusiasm for containing urban growth an obvious representation of the interests of the counties and its engagement with social issues centred on the desire to produce harmonious, consensual 'communities'. Again the practical goals of establishing 'balanced' communities and carefully contrived 'neighbourhood units' drew support from diverse quarters. As the first study of the new town[8] revealed, the Right wing could construe 'balancing' the community, that is, providing a broad social mix, as a scheme which would ensure community leadership by the middle class; for naive socialists the idea had appeal as a move in the destruction of class barriers.

In the 1960s the coalition of interests which had shaped planning and housing began to break up. The effects of urban renewal programmes, the boom in office building and central city development schemes led to much social conflict and to a widespread recognition that planning was not the rational, non-partisan business which its practitioners pretended. There was a growing awareness that the planning apparatus as it stood was poorly equipped to deal with the complex economic and social problems in the cities. There was an increasing appreciation of the fact that, all too often, planning decisions helped to promote the material interests of the property developers, rather than the interests of poorly housed residents, and that the whole machinery of planning was inaccessible and insensitive to the needs of ordinary citizens. Governments might vie with each other in setting targets for housing completions – '400,000 homes a year' promised by the Tories in 1960 was capped by '500,000 homes a year' from Labour in 1964 – but more and more people understood that there were serious disadvantages in the kinds of urban development which this promoted. The period of Labour government from 1964 to 1970 saw some important changes. A new Town and Country Planning Act in 1968 called for structure plans to deal with broad economic and social considerations and action area plans to tackle the problems of particular small areas. The issue of public participation was taken up by the Skeffington Committee a year later and provisions were made for a greater involvement of the public in the planning process. Also in 1969 the Community Development projects began their work in a dozen areas of 'deprivation' up and down the country. There was in the period of that first Wilson government some optimism that programmes for the shaping of our cities could be freed from the elitism and paternalism of the earlier period and that broader and more radical approaches (especially if linked to developing policies for economic planning, education and welfare)

would lead to greater equality and opportunity. Sadly, the mood did not last. Just as one
can trace in, say, the sociology of education, a growing scepticism and disillusionment
with the effects of educational reform, so too, by the 1970s, one finds a growing
pessimism and despair in the discussions of urban planning and of housing policy.

For twenty-five years or so, there existed in Britain a broad area of agreement on those
policies which shaped the Welfare State and this included urban policies. This is not to
deny that there were important differences between the major parties. Labour was always
more concerned to promote public housing than was the Tory Party; the latter favoured
relatively weak controls over building, land development and rents whereas Labour
imposed a freeze on office construction, passed a Community Land Act and sought to
give tenants greater security. But for all that there were important points of agreement.
David Donnison and Paul Soto have expressed it well when they identify four fundamental beliefs which appear to have been very widely held:

> First, that the community should 'level up'the distributions of income and living con-
> ditions by bringing those at the bottom of these distributions closer to their averages;
> second, that rational inquiry and analysis, monitoring social conditions and reporting
> on the plight of those at the bottom of the heap would eventually gain the support of
> public opinion and move democratic governments to act; and third, that the state was
> the natural and principal instrument for achieving this social progress. Fourth, and most
> important of all, was the assumption that although governments would regulate the
> processes of economic development, succour the casualties of economic growth and
> stimulate the economy or steer it in particular directions, the economic motor itself
> would keep turning – and so, too, would the motor of demographic growth which
> assumed a constantly expanding demand for the economy's products.[9]

By the mid-seventies all of these beliefs were being called in question. They were challenged by events: by the oil crisis and by successive sterling crises; by the general decline
in the competitiveness of our economy and the reorganization on a global scale of
capitalist activity. Old industries continued to run down and new ones were slow to start.
Unemployment was rising at a time when the demands for labour were falling and to cap
it all, the actual size of the potential workforce was increasing. Government's capacity to
steer or manage this economy was made to look doubtful.

But those central beliefs were also challenged politically, from the Left as well as the
Right, each arguing that a more radical approach was necessary. It was, however, the
'Radical Right' which put together a programme that gave it electoral success. Since 1979
the Conservative Party in government has been pursuing policies, including urban policies,
which are indeed different from those of previous years. They are policies predicated on a
rejection of most of those beliefs that characterized the 'Butskellite' consensus.

However, before we embark on a discussion of the new policies we must survey what
seem to be some very important general changes.

COUNTER-URBANIZATION AND THE DECLINE OF MANUFACTURING EMPLOYMENT

Probably the most striking general change – let's call it a 'secular trend' – is the flow of population *out* of our major cities. This is a remarkable tendency because it reverses the drift from less urbanized to more urbanized areas which accelerated so dramatically with the industrial revolution. For the past eighty years or so this has been a thoroughly urbanized society, at least in the sense that the vast majority of the population has lived in urban centres. By 1901, 75 per cent of the people in England and Wales were city dwellers and that figure grew only marginally to the 80.8 per cent recorded in the 1951 Census. Since the sixties, however, the pattern has been changing. By 1971, 78.3 per cent lived in the cities, reflecting both the voluntary and the contrived dispersal of fractions of the urban population. Although we do not, as yet, have any very detailed analyses of the 1981 Census data, it is clear that the general trend is continuing.

Most of the discussion of 'counter-urbanization' is focused on the major urban areas: the seven large conurbations, London, Clydeside, Merseyside, South East Lancashire, Tyneside, West Midlands and West Yorkshire. In his paper on 'Statistical trends of the British conurbations'[10] Douglas McCallum presents a detailed picture of what has been happening.

Tables 1.1 and 1.2, and figure 1.1 (all from McCallum's paper) enable us to see that there has been a substantial change since the early sixties. Up to that point, while most conurbations experienced slower growth than was found in the population as a whole, they did not actually decline. London was an exception to this, losing 2 per cent of its population between 1951 and 1961. From 1961 the substantial losses of population are clearly seen in the graph. The West Midland conurbation continued its upward path for a further decade, but then it too began to conform to the general trend. Alone among the conurbations West Yorkshire continued to increase its numbers into the 1970s. There can be no doubt that the decade between 1960 and 1970 marks a very important break with historical patterns of city development. Quite suddenly the major urban centres began to experience population decline, losing almost one million inhabitants in a period when the population of the country as a whole grew by 3.5 million. Putting it into even broader perspective, as McCallum does, by 1974 the major conurbations held fewer people than they had in 1931. They had shrunk by 4.5 per cent while in the rest of the country the population grew by over 39 per cent in the period 1931 to 1974.

Conurbations are large areas and it is soon apparent when one looks at the demographic data that the loss of population does not occur evenly across these major urban districts. Rather it is accounted for in large part by the flight from inner city districts. Thus, you find that while some of the central areas may have lost more than one-third of their population between 1931 and the 1970s, the outer districts experienced growth of 22 per cent on average. We are observing then some very sizeable migrations, migrations in which the inflows are substantially smaller than the outflows. Some 800,000 individuals moved into the big cities during the period 1966 to 1971, most of them coming from outside the regions in which the metropolitan areas were set. At the same time 1.7 million people moved out, chiefly to other smaller urban centres within the same region.

The movements of population, together with other changes in the economic structures of the large urban centres, have meant that the overall occupational profiles of the conurbations look rather different from that of the country at large. Managerial, professional, technical, supervisory and skilled workers have been best placed to make the move to smaller, growing centres. Excluding Greater London, the conurbations have proportion-

Table 1.1 Population of the Conurbations, 1901–74 (thousands)

Conurbation	1901	1911	1921	1931	1951	1961	1971	1974
Central Clydeside	1,374	1,498	1,618	1,688	1,759	1,802	1,728	1,658
Greater London	6,586	7,256	7,488	8,216	8,348	8,183	7,452	7,174
Merseyside	1,030	1,157	1,263	1,347	1,382	1,384	1,267	1,207
South East Lancashire	2,117	2,328	2,361	2,427	2,423	2,428	2,393	2,376
Tyneside	678	762	816	827	836	855	805	781
West Midlands	1,483	1,635	1,773	1,933	2,237	2,347	2,372	2,353
West Yorkshire	1,524	1,590	1,614	1,655	1,693	1,704	1,728	1,737
Total: 7 conurbations	14,792	16,226	16,933	18,093	18,678	18,703	17,745	17,286
Rest of Great Britain	*22,208*	*24,605*	*25,836*	*26,702*	*30,176*	*32,581*	*36,234*	*37,132*
Total: Great Britain	*37,000*	*40,831*	*42,769*	*44,795*	*48,854*	*51,284*	*53,979*	*54,418*

Based on:
'English conurbations 1901–51' from *1951 Census England and Wales, General Tables*, Table 3.
'Scottish conurbations 1931–51' from *1951 Census of Scotland, General Tables*.
'English conurbations 1961' from *1961 Census England and Wales*.
'Scottish conurbations 1961' from *1961 Census Scotland*.
All conurbations 1901–21 estimated from constituent area data in the relevant Census volumes 1901, 1911 and 1921.
All conurbations 1974 data are from Registrar General Estimates, Office of Population Census and Surveys.

Note: In many cases there were small changes in conurbation boundaries between Censuses; this is not generally significant, except that for Greater London the fall in population for 1961–71 is somewhat exaggerated because of the change in definition consequent upon the creation of the GLC.

Source: McCallum (1980).

Table 1.2 Rates of Population Change in the Conurbations, 1901–74 (percentage change over period shown)

Conurbation	1901–11 (%)	1911–21 (%)	1921–31 (%)	1931–51 (%)	1951–61 (%)	1961–71 (%)	1971–4 (%)	1951–74 (%)
Central Clydeside	+ 9.0	+ 8.0	+ 4.3	+ 4.2	+ 2.4	– 4.1	– 4.1	– 5.7
Greater London	+10.2	+ 3.2	+ 9.7	+ 1.6	– 2.0	– 8.9	– 3.7	–14.1
Merseyside	+12.3	+ 9.2	+ 6.7	+ 2.6	+ 0.1	– 8.5	– 4.7	–12.7
South East Lancashire	+10.0	+ 1.4	+ 2.8	– 0.2	+ 0.2	– 1.4	– 0.7	– 1.9
Tyneside	+12.4	+ 7.1	+ 1.3	+ 1.1	+ 2.3	– 5.8	– 3.0	– 6.6
West Midlands	+10.2	+ 8.4	+ 9.0	+15.7	+ 4.9	+ 1.1	– 0.8	+ 5.2
West Yorkshire	+ 4.3	+ 1.5	+ 2.5	+ 2.3	+ 0.6	+ 1.4	+ 0.5	+ 2.6
Total: 7 conurbations	+ 9.7	+ 4.4	+ 6.9	+ 3.2	+ 0.1	– 5.1	– 2.6	– 7.5
Rest of Great Britain	+10.8	+ 5.0	+ 3.4	+13.0	+ 8.0	+11.2	+ 2.5	+23.1
Total: Great Britain	+10.4	+ 4.7	+ 4.7	+ 9.1	+ 5.0	+ 5.3	+ 0.8	+11.4

Note: All periods are ten years, except 1931–51 (twenty) and 1971–4 (three); hence, rates of change are not exactly comparable between the ten-year inter-censal periods and the other periods.

Source: McCallum (1980)

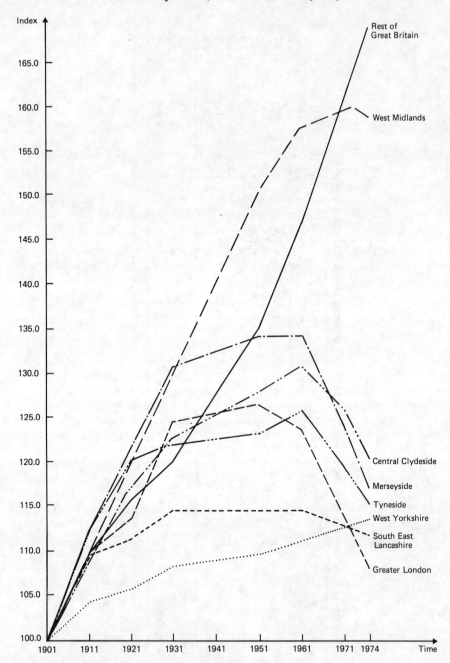

Figure 1.1   Index of Population Growth : Conurbations, 1901–79
Source: McCallum (1980).

ally fewer males in the professional and managerial groups of the Registrar General's classification and more semi-skilled and unskilled workers. Moreover, the trend seems to be for these disparities to become more marked. The growth of professional and managerial occupations in the major cities (again leaving London aside) has been noticeably lower than in the rest of the country, while at the other end of the distribution the proportion of semi and unskilled workers has remained substantially above that for non-conurbation Britain.

The importance of these general changes is hard to exaggerate. Britain is becoming a more divided, more unequal society and one of the principal lines of that division can be seen in the very different opportunities for work, career mobility, education, leisure, personal fulfillment and standards of comfort afforded in settlements of varying size. The general decline of the British economy has been, and continues to be, felt most acutely in our major cities, not only in the inner city areas but within whole regions which surround them. The results of one of the most recent studies of urban and regional growth patterns makes this very plain. Fothergill and Gudgin argue that:

> . . . urban structure has been the dominant influence on the pattern of employment change in recent years. Britain's cities are experiencing a rapid loss of manufacturing jobs while small towns and rural areas are quite successful in retaining and expanding their manufacturing base. As a general rule, the larger and more industrial a settlement the faster its decline . . . The most urbanized regions, such as the North West, are experiencing the worst falls in industrial employment, while in regions characterized by small towns and rural areas, such as East Anglia, industry is more buoyant.[11]

In a careful and detailed examination of changes in primary, secondary and tertiary sectors of the economy, the authors argue that the most important factor in the patterns of growth and decline across the country is found when we look at what has been happening to manufacturing industry. Changes in primary industries like agriculture and mining, which have obviously declined, and opportunities in service jobs, which have certainly increased, are of much lesser effect than the patterns of de-industrialization of the areas dominated by large urban centres or the expansion of manufacturing employment in small town or rural areas. Moreover, from their analysis it emerges that it is the specifically urban structure of a region which does most to account for these observed differences in manufacturing employment. In those areas with the highest proportions of the population living in cities and in those areas containing the biggest cities, the decline of industrial employment is most marked. Their conclusions suggest that neither the industrial structure, that is the precise mix of different types of manufacturing activity, nor the movement of industrial firms, enables us fully to grasp what has been going on. The overall picture of growth and decline is most substantially affected by what has been happening to manufacturing in the cities. Our principal urban centres have experienced loss of population, mass unemployment and the appearance of widespread poverty, largely as a result of the fact that manufacturing establishments have found their urban locations profoundly restricting. Fothergill and Gudgin, in trying to explain the urban-rural shift, seek to appraise the various competing accounts and are led to argue that:

> The explanation which is best able to fit the evidence turns out to be surprisingly simple: manufacturing is in decline in the cities because a higher proportion of firms

in cities are in 'constrained locations', restricted by old-fashioned premises, hemmed
in by existing urban development and with no room for expansion. This means that in
cities investment in machinery displaces labour on the shop floor and thus reduces
employment. The same displacement of labour from existing floor space occurs in
small towns and rural areas, of course, but the greater room for expansion also allows
investment in factory extensions and the construction of new factories on greenfield
sites, and this is more than sufficient to produce a net increase in employment in these
locations.[12]

In other words, it is not closures, not lock, stock and barrel relocations, not the
decisions of foreign-owned multinationals to move their operations around the country or
the globe, that account for the marked changes in the level and areal redistribution of
manufacturing jobs, but the balance between expansion and contractions. The pattern is
obviously a complicated one and there are clearly differences from one urban centre to
another, but the general argument that is advanced stresses the severe limitations experienced by manufacturing firms located in the old urban areas. And interestingly, the
broad picture of urban-rural redistribution and the processes which give rise to it seem to
be very similar in countries outside the UK, for instance in the United States.

At this very general level then, our cities are recording and reflecting fundamental
changes in the nature of our political economy. The decline of industrial manufacturing is
registered in shifts of population and jobs away from those northern and peripheral
centres which grew up in the nineteenth century. Economic activity and population have
been moving southward. And in north and south alike the tendency over the past twenty
years or so has been for an obvious 'decentralization', a movement out of the major cities
of people and jobs.

Starting with observations about demography and employment is necessary, but what
about the changes that have been taking place within the conurbations and the smaller
towns? One important aspect of this is, of course, housing.

CHANGING PATTERNS OF HOUSING PROVISION

One of the most fundamental changes in the structure of our cities since the war can be
found by looking at the housing market. In 1947 only 26 per cent of households in
Britain owned their own home. A few, 13 per cent, had council houses and flats but the
majority, 61 per cent, rented from private landlords. The pattern in which only a
minority owned housing was long established and although it is impossible to get accurate
statistics, it is likely that around the beginning of this century about 90 per cent of all
households lived in accommodation rented from private landlords. During the 1920s and
1930s, an extraordinary burst of building activity took place along the major transportation routes into all major cities. With government subsidies to railway companies and
builders, enormous areas of suburban housing were constructed, and many clerks and
artisans and others of comparatively modest means became house owners. At the same
time, local authorities began to attack the problem of the slums and the more general
problems of housing the poor, and embarked on ambitious programmes of public housing.
After 1945 these trends continued until, by 1972, half of all households in Great Britain
were living in owner-occupied houses; the local authorities and new town corporations

provided accommodation for nearly a third and the private landlords' share was reduced to a mere 18 per cent.

The reasons for the restructuring of the housing market are not hard to find. They relate principally to three things. First, the changing aspirations of a great many families and individuals. The pre-war, speculatively built estates had demonstrated that with a reasonable income and tolerable job security an artisan or a clerical worker really could own his or her own house. When the Tories came to power in 1951, they sought to extend private ownership and, in a generally favourable economic climate, were able to sustain and encourage the development of the private house market. The Labour Party, which has traditionally put great stress on the need for more public housing to provide for the poor, had become by 1964 sharply sensitive to the changing ambitions and interests of a large and growing group of house owners. By the 1970s the idea of a 'property owning democracy' was supported by all the major political parties. Thus, the number of private landlords declined because economic and social conditions enabled the widespread formation of many small households able to acquire a mortgage and the benefits of owner-occupation.

Secondly, the pressure on landlords came from the public sector. If Labour came to accept a part of a traditional Tory commitment to private ownership, the Tories for their part mostly accepted the view that support for local authority housing was a necessary and sizeable responsibility. Although encouragement was given by the Heath government for the sale of council houses, there was no serious challenge to the principle of public housing. Indeed, under Tory governments the renewal of slum clearance programmes in the fifties and the encouragement of ambitious programmes of urban redevelopment in the sixties ensured that local authorities would supplant many private landlords and even dispossess a good many owner-occupiers.

Thirdly, there are the economics of landlordism. Ever since 1915 there have been controls on rent levels and on the conditions of eviction, and over the years these have made most forms of private rental economically unattractive. Evidence presented in the First Report of the Environment Committee in the House of Commons in 1982[13] illustrated this. Data on registered rents (which make up less than one-quarter of all rents) suggested that the median figure for an unfurnished property was £540 per annum and that over the period 1970 to 1980 such rents failed to keep pace with inflation. A 1976 survey of unregistered rents presented an even bleaker picture. Median rents here were around £4 per week. There were, of course, considerable variations up and down the country with London figures for unregistered rents some 70 per cent above those charged elsewhere. But even in London the returns on private rental were deemed by most landlords to be grossly inadequate and in consequence many were anxious to sell. David Eversley's comment, made in 1975, provided an accurate assessment of some of the prime reasons for the enthusiasm of many landlords to unburden themselves of the housing they owned:

> The rising price of even old property, the improvement grant obtainable on a very large scale after 1969 with no ties as to the future tenure of the premises and the accelerated processes which created more small households with relatively high purchasing power, all played a role.[14]

One disturbing aspect of the changes in this sector of the market is the fact that the

decline in the number of privately rented dwellings is not matched by a comparable
decline in the number of households or persons living in them. Although overcrowding
in the privately rented sector declined during the 1970s, it is still noticeably higher here
than in other sectors, especially in the furnished properties. It is also true that in the
privately rented market there are far more houses and flats classified as 'unfit' and more
than one-third of all rental units required substantial repairs done to them.[15] Much of this
housing is found in the old declining districts near the city centres, transmitted by inheritance to owners who take no interest in it but leave all management to lawyers or agents
to whom it is frequently more troublesome than profitable.[16]

The pressure on the small, declining stock of privately rented housing is enormous, for
the demand for cheap accommodation close to the heart of the city is maintained by
young people moving in search of jobs or in pursuit of college education, by immigrants
seeking a niche in the housing system and by old folk who are reluctant to leave familiar
areas and wish to maintain households separate from their children.

The election of the Thatcher government in 1979 signalled some important changes in
the housing market as in many other areas. Figures on tenure patterns over the 1972-82
decade give us some preliminary indications of what has been going on.

Table 1.3   Dwellings: Tenure Types as a Percentage of Total Housing Stock, 1972-82

Area	Rented from local authority or new town corporation	Owner-occupied	Rented from private landlord
England			
1972	28.2	53.4	18.4
1977	29.6	55.5	14.9
1982	26.9	61.1	12.0
Wales			
1972	28.2	56.7	15.1
1977	29.0	58.8	12.2
1982	26.1	63.8	10.1
Scotland			
1972	52.8	31.7	15.5
1977	54.4	34.1	11.5
1982	53.4	37.2	9.4
Great Britain			
1972	30.5	51.5	18.0
1977	31.9	53.6	14.5
1982	29.3	59.0	11.7

Source: Department of the Environment, *Housing and Construction Statistics 1972-82* (HMSO
1983).

Between 1972 and 1977 the two major tenure forms continued to grow, with private
ownership increasing somewhat more rapidly than forms of publicly provided housing.
Private rental continued its decline. But the really interesting change is indicated by the
comparison of the 1977-82 figures. The growth of owner-occupation increases quite

sharply, especially in England and Wales. (Notice how different the housing profile is for Scotland.) Correspondingly, the figures for local authority or new town housing show a noticeable decline. Other data make it clear that the real change occurs after 1979, in other words, as a consequence of Conservative policy.

The government is committed to three main policies. First, to give private landlords a better deal. However, the provisions of the 1980 Housing Act will do very little to slow down, let alone reverse, the general decline in private landlordism. Its effect is essentially cosmetic. Secondly, the government wishes to expand owner-occupation and to this end it has increased the level of mortgage subsidy. Thirdly, and most importantly, it wishes to encourage the sale of publicly owned housing, which means property held by new towns and by some forms of housing association as well as local authority housing. The effect of this latter policy is beginning to be quite substantial, especially in England and Wales. Data presented in the Department of the Environment's *Housing and Construction Statistics 1972-1982*[17] volume allow us to see this. In 1978 sales of all kinds of local authority dwellings amounted to 30,620; in 1979 they rose to 42,460; in 1980 to 85,700; in 1981 to 106,485 and in 1982 to 205,825. The huge increase of nearly 100,000 sales between 1981 and 1982 is almost entirely accounted for by a dramatic rise in sales to sitting tenants. For the first time since the war we have a government which is concerned, not simply to slow down or even halt the growth of public sector housing, but positively to shrink the size of that sector as far as possible. It is a remarkable change and one that has profound implications for the lives of the less well off members of our society.

The effect of this attack on public housing, then, is already evident. The implementing of the second general policy, that of increasing owner-occupation, has been advanced chiefly through the means of encouraging council tenants to buy. It has not been greatly assisted by the general effects of monetarist policies, for as table 1.4 shows, the overall level of construction activity, including that in the private sector, has fallen sharply since 1979.

It is, of course, true that a decline in the rate of housing construction began in the years of the Callaghan government. The data show that public sector house-building fell quite sharply between 1977 and 1978, but after 1979 there is also contraction in the private sector. Whether we seek to assess it in terms of housing starts or housing completions,[18] it is quite clear that one of the effects of recent government policy has been a substantial reduction in house-building activity. The most recent indications are that there has been some modest recovery in private house construction in 1983, but against this there will be an even lower level of activity in the public sector.

The implications of the new policies need to be thought about with some care. It is the belief of the Thatcher government that giving council tenants the statutory right to buy their houses will help solve the country's housing problems. There are good reasons to doubt this. The housing pressure group Shelter has produced an interesting appraisal of the pros and cons of the policy, focusing attention on the assumptions that underlie it.[19] It is argued by those responsible for housing that 'the sale of council houses will save money'. Drawing on studies of council house sales in Birmingham, Leeds, Glasgow and Aberdeen, the authors of the Shelter document show that this assertion cannot be accepted at face value. It is true that many purchasers will gain from the resale of houses bought at very large discounts (up to 60 per cent of market values); local authorities will gain in the short term but lose in the long term;[20] and the government, because it

Table 1.4 Stock of Dwellings[1] by Tenure and Change, 1961–70 to 1981

	1961–70	1971–75	1976	1977	1978	1979	1980	1981
Stock of dwellings – at end of period (millions)								
Owner-occupied	9.57	10.76	10.96	11.16	11.39	11.62	11.91	12.21
Rented from local authorities or new town corporations	5.85	6.40	6.56	6.70	6.79	6.84	6.82	6.76
Other tenures	3.77	3.19	3.09	3.01	2.93	2.86	2.80	2.72
Total	19.19	20.35	20.61	20.87	21.11	21.32	21.53	21.69
Annual net gain (annual averages) (thousands)								
New construction								
Local authorities	152	118	136	127	102	79	80	58
New town corporations	9	12	16	16	10	9	8	11
Housing associations	4	10	16	25	23	18	21	19
Government departments	5	2	2	2	1	1	1	–
Total public sector	170	142	168	170	136	107	110	88
Private sector	198	178	155	143	152	142	130	117
Total new construction	368	320	323	313	288	249	240	205
Other changes[2]	–109	– 94	– 64	– 55	– 42	– 39	– 31	– 42
Total net gain	259	226[3]	259	258	246	210	209	163

Notes:
1 Figures for inter-censal years are based on estimated changes since the previous Census. Figures for 1981 are based on estimated changes since the 1971 Census. See Appendix, Part 8: Dwellings.
2 Comprises net gain from conversions, and losses from slum clearance and other reasons.
3 Including an increase of 32,000 dwellings in the privately rented and other tenure category arising from definitional changes in the 1971 Census.

Source: Department of the Environment, *Housing and Construction Statistics*.

provides what is virtually a perpetual subsidy in the form of mortgage interest relief, will lose. It is also asserted by the government that the policy of council house sales will help achieve a better social mix and balance of tenure, but again the evidence does not support the claim. In practice, it is a case of the better-off tenants buying the most desirable kinds of council houses in the 'best' areas, and the effects of this will be even sharper forms of social segregation. The suggestion that the present policy can be carried through without any adverse effects on the existing or prospective council tenants will not stand up to scrutiny either. Not only will the existing stock of public housing be reduced at a time when new construction has virtually ceased, but what remains will be a residue of poorer, less desirable houses. The waiting lists will lengthen, the general conditions of the public housing stock will deteriorate and overcrowding, already a problem in some areas of council housing, will increase. The problems for the poor will grow more acute.

The regressive character of current housing policies is revealed very starkly when one considers just how the great expansion of one tenure, owner-occupation, has been encouraged over the past twenty years. Since 1962 and the abolition of Schedule A tax levied on house owners, the level of public subsidy given to purchasers has increased a hundredfold. By 1982 more than £2,000 million per annum was being spent in this way. It is a vast subsidy distributed to the better off, for it is obvious from all official data that owner-occupiers are on average considerably wealthier than those who rent from the local authorities. The effect of mortgage tax relief, coupled with the fact that the capital gains made on family housing are immune from any tax liability, has meant that owner-occupation is not only the cheapest way for individuals to house themselves but also the most profitable investment they can make. Over the last decade or so several writers have analysed the potential for accumulation that house ownership confers.[21] *The Financial Times* all-shares index shows a fivefold increase over the years 1935 to 1980, but house prices increased more than forty-one times. The effects are registered not simply in the growth of individual 'nest-eggs', but in the entire pattern of investment in Britain as money that might otherwise have found its way, at least in part, into the recapitalising of our industry has been diverted into property.

The specifically sociological significance of the growth of owner-occupation has been much debated. The suggestion that we should look at diverse tenures as creating 'housing classes' with the outright owners and mortgage payers constituting specifically privileged classes has been explored,[22] as has the related issue of whether or not owner-occupation really leads to the ideological 'incorporation' of large sectors of the population.[23] There is a good deal to be said for extending our analyses of material interests to include those generated by our systems of consumption, as well as those of production, but attempts to link changes in consciousness, particularly as these are expressed in political orientations, need to be treated cautiously. Home owners do have distinctive economic interests (given the system of subsidy) and no doubt these do play some part in shaping political attitudes and behaviour, particularly in terms of local struggles, but we should be very careful about imputing any simple shifts in political orientations or conceptions of class interest merely on the basis of domestic property ownership. Owner-occupiers constitute a large fraction of the population and among them there are substantial differences in the kinds of 'stakes' that they have in our economic and political systems. The point that Ball makes in his recent book is right: rather than asking 'what does owner occupation do to the political consciousness of the owner occupier?' we would be better to examine 'the

conditions under which the structure of owner-occupied housing provision gained
political hegemony over state housing policy and sustained its dominant position'.[24]

Under the Thatcher government the dominance of owner-occupation is not simply
being 'maintained'. It is being actively developed, through the council house sales policy
and through the raising of the upper limits on mortgages qualifying for tax relief. The
housing system is becoming more and more inequitable. At the moment when greater
benefits are conferred upon those who can afford to buy, the provision for those who
cannot is being drastically reduced. Cuts in rate support grants, the imposition of strict
cash limits on local authorities prevent both new building and adequate programmes of
maintenance. And on top of this in 1984 it is proposed to cut the housing benefits pay-
able to the poor and to encourage further increases in council house rents.

POVERTY AND INEQUALITY IN THE CITY

The appearance of greater inequalities within our cities and the specific urban policies
which contribute to these really has to be seen as part of a general change in British
society. In the 1980s Britain is becoming a society with markedly greater economic disparities between sectors of its population. Moreover, the widening of the gaps between
rich and poor cannot be seen simply as the unanticipated consequences of particular
policies. Rather they are the product of two things: first a deliberate attempt to seek
economic growth through the provision of incentives for risk-taking and entrepreneur-
ship; and secondly, the effort to restore what are seen as traditional and necessary social
inequalities, eroded by the 'mania' for egalitarianism which allegedly characterized the
programmes of governments, Conservative as well as Labour, throughout the 1960s and
1970s.[25] So, those who benefited substantially from the fiscal and other policies in the
period 1979 to 1983 were the wealthiest groups. Those earning more than £40,000 per
year in 1983 experienced a growth of more than 25 per cent in their earnings over the
previous three years; those who were in the lowest decile of earners had experienced a
decline in their real earnings of almost the same proportion. In addition, according to the
Inland Revenue annual statistics in 1983[26] the distribution of wealth, for the first time
in a long while, showed some tendency for the very top wealth-holders to increase their
share of all wealth (though whether this is the start of a trend we shall have to wait a
while to see).

The incidence of poverty rose dramatically in the years 1979 to 1982. More and more
people became dependent on Supplementary Benefit—a 70 per cent increase from
December 1970 to December 1982 is recorded in the Scottish data, for instance.[27] Of
course, the main factor was the steep rise over these years in the numbers out of work,
but there were disturbing increases, too, in the number of single parents and their families
and among the sick and disabled. Low pay among male manual workers and women also
put many on or below the poverty line. The problem then was widespread, but the concentration of poor people in the major industrial cities and their regions was a particularly
noticeable feature.

It is important to stress the fact that inequalities and the specific features of contemporary poverty are widespread because in the urban literature there has been, over several
years now, a tendency to portray these matters as somehow peculiar to what is called the

'inner city'. Concern about these areas in Britain began in the early 1970s and by the middle of that decade was reflected in reports on the inner districts of several major cities and in 1977 in the *Policy for the Inner Cities*.[28] The urban riots in 1981 gave further reason for concentrating attention on inner city areas. Without wishing to deny that many of the central areas of the conurbations do indeed face severe economic problems, we need to recognize that the processes operating there are also at work in other districts.

Most discussions of changes in the inner city began by pointing to the evident decline in population in many districts. Thus, the Inner Areas Studies report[29] showed how in Liverpool the population of the inner area was approximately 300,000 in 1971, but forty years earlier the same area had housed 725,000, and that in the Small Heath district of Birmingham the population fell from 50,000 to 32,000 between 1951 and 1976. At the same time it was evident that in the inner areas of many major cities there were concentrations of deprivation, neighbourhoods where many were unemployed or impoverished, where overcrowding was rife, housing conditions deplorable and educational provision inadequate. With the example of American cities before them, this had led some commentators to argue that, just as the outward migration of the relatively wealthy left a poor (and mainly black) population to inhabit the inner areas there, so similar patterns of migration and changes in occupational structure were turning British inner cities into traps for the poor. Thus, Pahl in an essay 'Poverty and the Urban System'[30] has suggested that the general shift towards a service economy produced marked inequalities, evident in the spatial organization of the city. His argument was that as the professional and technical occupations grew, and with them the opportunities for highly paid work, so also there developed a series of menial, unskilled jobs supporting these new activities. Within the city there were areal concentrations of these professional and technical occupations and, whereas the professionals themselves were able to afford to live well away from their centrally situated offices, those on whom they depended were less well placed. For them, the limitations of money dictated that they live near their work and this meant struggling for a place in the areas of greatest housing stress. Following Harvey's suggestions[31] that there were unforeseen redistributions of real income taking place in the city, Pahl argued that we might be witnessing processes of pauperization as a result of the entrapment of these lowly paid service workers in areas where housing costs were extremely high and public resources frequently thinly distributed.

The suspicion that processes like these could be in train persuaded other researchers to look more precisely at the issues, and Lomas[32] examined the suggestion that there were real concentrations of the low paid, unskilled workers in the central areas. Although the available data were far from perfect, he was able to show that at least in London, the less skilled workers were not becoming increasingly segregated from the rest of society and concentrated in the inner city. Many semi- and unskilled workers were to be found in areas a long way from the city core, which is not surprising when one considers the policies of industrial and residential location which have been pursued since the 1930s.

It is true that within the inner districts the unskilled made up a higher proportion of the occupied population than in other districts, but the differences were not very large, nor was the proportion itself very substantial. In a later study Hamnett[33] compared the patterns for 1961, 1966 and 1971 and his analysis of Census material for those years corroborated Lomas' conclusion. It seemed then that one of the fears expressed in the Strategic Plan for the South East was not really justified: the expansion of service industry did not appear to trap large numbers of low-skilled workers in the inner city. The very high concentrations of unskilled employees remain in those districts associated with traditional manufacturing and warehousing, by no means all in the central areas of the city.

Thus Lomas' work specifically challenged the idea that the central area contained an inordinately high concentration of low paid workers. The data from the New Earnings Survey and the 1966 Census did not support the suspicion either; nor was it encouraged by Hamnett's findings. It is true that some of the occupations picked out by Pahl as representative of the changes taking place, such as messengers, clerks and catering and hotel workers, were associated with the central area but as a fraction of all low-paid workers they were not very significant. Overall, low pay was not markedly biased towards the inner city districts.

Most of those who commented on this 'pauperization' thesis linked their remarks about the concentration of poverty in the inner city to assessments of the economic position of coloured immigrants and Lomas' data did indeed show that there was a marked concentration of black immigrants in the less skilled jobs, and that they were mainly to be found in areas of housing stress near the city centre. However, to talk of black 'ghettos' at that point seemed hardly warranted since black households made up a majority of residents only in very small areas; the situation, it was argued, was not yet analogous to that in many major American cities, but there most certainly was a spatial representation of the life chances of black immigrants. It was also true that among the black population, and especially among the young men, unemployment was noticeably higher than for the population of London as a whole. Even in periods when the demand for labour was high, as in the mid-sixties, the central areas did contain enclaves of high unemployment and among the immigrant groups the geographical concentration of unemployment was easily seen. Lomas[34] showed that more than half the West Indian unemployed, for example, were found in just six Employment Exchange Areas.

Since those early studies there has been a good deal of research focused on the 'inner city'.[35] Governments of both major parties have developed policies specific to these areas and public and journalistic attention has been given to them as a consequence of the Scarman[36] Report which followed the outbursts of violence in Brixton.

The general depopulation of many of the inner city areas has continued, as early analyses of the 1981 Census statistics are beginning to reveal. The Inner Cities Directorate[37] has presented a report on the changes observable between 1971 and 1981 in Merseyside, which among the conurbations shows the greatest proportional and absolute loss of population. Some 150,000 people have left the Merseyside region, but the most substantial reductions have without doubt been in the inner city area. It has lost almost a quarter (23.8 per cent) of its 1971 population. Outflows from the district of Toxteth (scene of some of the 1981 rioting) have been even greater in proportional terms. It is worth noticing though that Kirkby, an area of modern public housing, has also seen considerable population decline.

The effects of the migration and the demographic structures of the most deprived areas have been predictable enough. Such districts are left with high dependency ratios; that is high proportions of the elderly and the young and relatively few between the ages of thirty-five and sixty-four. There are high proportions of unemployed youngsters and very few income earners in their mature years. The economic and social effects are profound.

Table 1.5   Population Change in Merseyside, 1971–81

Area	Population		Percentage change
	1971	1981	
Merseyside	1,656,575	1,511,915	− 8.7
Liverpool	610,116	509,981	−16.4
Inner city area	331,606	252,696	−23.8
Outer city area	278,510	275,285	− 7.6
Toxteth	97,263	71,869	−26.1
Knowsley	194,095	172,957	−10.9
Kirkby	60,070	50,901	−15.3
St Helens	189,001	189,759	+ 0.4
Sefton	307,549	299,724	− 2.5
Wirral	355,814	339,494	− 4.6

Source: Department of the Environment, Inner Cities Directorate, *Information Note No. 1* (1982).

The same report also gives some indication of what has been happening in terms of employment in Merseyside over the 1971–81 decade. Overall, the conurbation has seen a decline of more than 15 per cent in the numbers of residents in work and once again the decreases have been much larger in the inner city areas and in Toxteth in particular. Some 16.3 per cent of the economically active residents in the Merseyside area were out of work in 1981 and at the ward level we can find areas where double this proportion are out of a job. Most seriously of all, it is the young people who bear the brunt of worklessness and in some wards more than half of the sixteen to twenty-four year-old males have no employment.

Table 1.6   Employment Change in Merseyside, 1971–81

Area	Residents in work		Percentage change
	1971	1981	
Merseyside	692,464	587,059	−15.2
Liverpool	257,140	190,113	−26.1
Inner city area	137,328	90,200	−34.3
Outer City area	119,812	99,913	−16.6
Toxteth	38,443	23,623	−38.6
Knowsley	76,030	63,842	−16.0
Kirkby	22,503	17,375	−22.8
St Helens	82,873	78,914	− 7.2
Sefton	128,682	122,594	− 4.7
Wirral	147,739	133,596	− 9.6

Source: Department of the Environment, Inner Cities Directorate, *Information Note No. 1* (1982).

Behind these bleak statistics lie the day-to-day realities of life in inner city districts and it is much the same whether in Liverpool or Glasgow or parts of London. It consists of a constant struggle to make ends meet. It is rich only in fear: fear of the next unpayable fuel bill; fear of another humiliating and probably frustrating encounter with the officials in the DHSS offices; fear, especially for the isolated elderly, of robbery or physical violence; fear among the young and the black that once again they will be stopped and questioned by the police if they gather on the streets. There is little that offers hope. The prospects of better housing, of some substantial improvement in the decaying environment of the inner city, appear remote and over it all hangs the imminence of yet more closures of the factories or workshops. No one has captured better the everyday experiences of life in these areas than Paul Harrison.[38] Take his description of Andreas T., a fifty-six year-old Greek Cypriot who works in a small clothing factory in Hackney, basting collars and lapels by hand. He suffers from muscular dystrophy which has weakened his legs.

> Andreas has been laid off at Christmas time every year for three years, for six weeks in 1979, three months in 1980 and nine weeks in 1981. The first two occasions he did not claim supplementary benefit, though he would have been entitled to around £15 a week extra on top of his lay-off pay. 'To tell you the truth, I feel ashamed to go there (to the social security office). Each time I thought it would go on only for a few weeks and it would pass and everything would be all right. But this time I had to claim social security. All these years in England, we saved, not much, but something. Over the last three years we had to spend it, all of it, and we had to cash two life insurance policies. Now we got nothing.'[39]

As Harrison sees it, Andreas' situation can only get worse in 1983. He is dependent on his car to get to work, but the costs of repairs or of replacement seem beyond his means. Without a car he will lose his job. Given his high transport and housing costs, he would actually be ten to fourteen pounds better off on the dole; 'But I don't want to give my work up. I don't want to be a parasite. If I can't work, I'm going to be so depressed I would die.'[40]

Perhaps we should note that Andreas does not live in the inner city. His story reminds us that the economic problems of the inner city are not neatly contained there. They spread over a much wider area. And pursuing that thought we quickly recognize that both the statistical data and the more ethnographic accounts tell us that there are many districts outside the inner city, most obviously the larger suburban public housing estates, which display similar features. A study of one large council estate in Edinburgh, built only ten years ago, reveals that it has already become notorious for the inadequacy of much of its housing. The room sizes and internal amenities may meet Parker-Morris standards, but many flats are damp. It is feared that a few blocks may have serious structural faults, whilst many are plagued by a host of less fundamental problems resulting from poor construction. But it is the social and economic issues that do most to point out the similarities between an area like this and some of the districts close to the centre of the city. In the Wester Hailes estate it is difficult to let houses. Many people dislike the place and move out of the flats there. The area has a very unbalanced age structure; it has few recreational or shopping facilities and those are pretty basic. Above all, it houses many who are poor and many who are unemployed.

. . . overall male unemployment [is] around 26 per cent, with 38 per cent of 16–19 year-olds and 37 per cent of 20–24 year olds not being in work.[41]

Large scale unemployment, the feature of the early eighties in Britain, has been added to the familiar problems facing those living in the large public housing estates. Joblessness and attendant poverty become the common experience for many people in both the inner city and the less desirable areas of peripheral public housing. And the similarities do not stop there. In the 1950s and 1960s much was written about the destruction of 'community'. The focus, of course, was upon the ways in which urban renewal and later, comprehensive redevelopment programmes had swept away old working-class districts. The bulldozers, it was suggested, destroyed much more than bricks and mortar. Accounts like Harrison's suggest that even in inner city areas where a good deal of the old housing remained, the effects of some redevelopment together with insidious processes of migration have done much to erode the social ties and moral orders that once characterized working-class districts. We can accept that there was a tendency to romanticize working-class life, but there was surely some truth in the arguments about how, at least in the more stable areas, strong bonds between people and strong attachments to the local neighbourhood did develop. The 'mutuality of the oppressed', as Raymond Williams phrased it, referred to patterns of support and reciprocal aid, to local institutions like pubs, pawn shops[42] and parlour stores, geared to the economic circumstances of their clienteles and also to moral orders rooted in the experience of poverty. Life for generations had been hard and insecure, but it was made supportable by social and moral frameworks which were shared and by sanctions, codes and controls which were exercised by those who had to live by them.

The fragility of such social orders was easily demonstrated by those who studied urban renewal.[43] The breaking of familial bonds as young families were given priority over old people and childless couples and moved out to the new housing estates, the stranding of the aged in progressively deserted, decrepit areas where shops, cinemas and places of employment were shut down—all this was reported many times. So, too, were the problems of adjustment facing those who arrived in the new housing schemes, deprived of those social ties which had traditionally offered some protection against irregular employment. The studies of the 1980s suggest that such ties no longer exist or are much attenuated in old inner city districts as well as in the newer or most deprived housing estates. Perhaps Harrison's report is, as some critics have argued, too bleak, but it paints a convincing picture of isolation, suspicion and antagonism rather than community solidarity. And whereas it was the literature on housing estates which initially drew attention to the effects of bureaucratic rules upon the poor, we now find that the writing about the inner areas highlights these same features of repressive officialdom.

The fact that both inner city areas and peripheral public housing estates may share many of the same problems makes us realize that when it comes to framing social policy for our most urbanized regions, we need to address economic and political issues on a broad scale. And there is plainly a growing recognition of this. Nonetheless, from the mid-seventies on, it is the inner cities which have received most attention. Since the passing of the Labour government's Inner Urban Areas Act in 1978, we have had the establishment of central-local government 'partnerships' aimed at the economic regeneration of these areas in Liverpool, Birmingham, Manchester and Newcastle, and for

London: Lambeth, Hackney and the Docklands. In addition, some fifteen so-called 'programme areas' were identified for less comprehensive assistance. The partnerships allowed local authorities to give loans and grants for the acquisition and improvement of land and buildings and the provision of infrastructure. They also allowed assistance to small companies and the distribution of grants for the payment of industrial rents. The hope was that, coupled with existing planning powers vested in local authorities and with a greater degree of coordination of the efforts of several ministries, these new measures would lead to the economic revitalizing of these areas and thus the creation of new and permanent jobs.

It is hard to argue that these schemes have had major impact. From the beginning there have been problems of finance, problems of administrative coordination and a host of political difficulties. The Labour government found it hard enough to provide the public funds on which the partnerships would depend, and since 1979 the Conservative concern to restrict public expenditure and to rely more on private investment has seriously limited the implementation of these plans. The most serious factor has been the scarcity of public monies, but it also has to be said that private enterprise has so far produced a disappointing response. Few companies, commercial or industrial, have been eager to invest in the inner city. Nor have the hopes that small business would play an important role in the regenerative process been realized.

By 1983 it had become quite plain that any substantial relief of the problems of the inner city would hinge on two things. First, a considerable growth in the level of economic support by central government; secondly, a willingness on the part of that government to intervene much more extensively, both in the affairs of the private sector and in the affairs of local authorities. Many of the latter have found it politically difficult to arrange the sizeable redistribution of funds that would be called for. A government fervently committed to the 'free market' and, at least in theory, to the reduction in central intervention is unlikely to accept these responsibilities.[44]

SOCIAL SEGREGATION

So far we have been concerned largely with the so-called deprived areas in the city but we need to look, too, at the changing social and spatial arrangements in a wider perspective. For many years the patterns of land use and their development have attracted the attention of sociologists, geographers and economists. One of the early accounts of London's social ecology was provided by Westergaard in his contribution to *London: Aspects of Change*.[45] Using data from the 1951 and 1961 Censuses he showed how selective migration had produced a series of concentric rings in which the status of residents increased with distance from the centre. But, as ever, the pattern was by no means perfect. The rings which were clearly developed to the south of the Thames were broken in the east and west, with long arms of working-class housing extending from the East End out beyond the boundary of the conurbation, and from the West End high status accommodation stretching into the north-western suburbs.

Westergaard also provided data on journeys to work, housing patterns, the structure of employment and the demographic profiles of various areas. It requires little imagination to see that variations or changes in demographic structure must have quite profound effects upon the patterns of neighbourhood life, the development of institutions and the forms of social organization.[46] Westergaard's account did not link the demographic structure to specific social patterns, but it did offer a useful description of the broad alignments of age and sex groupings which were found in particular districts. In the Central and West End areas the age structure was markedly different from that in the city as a whole, with very high proportions of young adults and very small proportions of children. Such areas provided work, educational and recreational opportunities, but they did not offer suitable homes for people later in their lives. In the middle-ring suburbs the relatively low fertility and mortality of the middle-class inhabitants produced a demographic profile characterized by a small number of children and a large number of elderly people. By contrast, the outer suburbs and particularly the areas of large public housing schemes typically had very high proportions of children and young married adults and few in any other category. In the late sixties and early seventies, the effects of differences in age structures and in particular the effects of generational imbalances attracted attention as a consequence of work by Jane Jacobs and Oscar Newman.[47] Continuing concern with vandalism, neglect and petty crime, especially evident in public housing areas, gives some of their ideas relevance even now. Of course, some attempts have been made to produce more balanced population structures in housing estates, but through the 1970s it remained administratively convenient, publicly justifiable and economical to create estates which were almost exclusively for young families and to pay little attention to the social consequences.

The ecology of London continued to attract attention and in 1973 Young and Willmott[48] produced another description of the patterns of class segregation in the metropolis. Their conclusion was that between 1951 and 1966 the degree of segregation increased with the professional and managerial groups becoming more concentrated in the central residential district, the suburban quarters and the outer metropolitan area. Working-class people became more concentrated in a cross running east to west along the Thames valley, north along the Lea and south roughly along the valley of the Wandle. The trend then was towards more sharply delineated class areas.

A study of Edinburgh's urban structure, completed in 1975, produced some very interesting findings which in many respects ran parallel to those of Young and Willmott.[49] Using the 1966 Census data, Richardson and his colleagues assessed the degree of class segregation in the city by means of Duncan and Duncan's 'index of dissimilarity'. The index expressed the percentage of one social class which would have to change homes in order to be distributed among the enumeration districts in the city in exactly the same proportions as another class. The authors regrouped the Registrar General's seventeen socio-economic groups into six classes: (i) professional workers; (ii) employers and managers; (iii) non-manual workers; (iv) foreman; (v) skilled manual and own account workers; (vi) personal service workers, semi-skilled manual workers and agricultural workers (vii) unskilled manual workers; and they showed that Edinburgh was very highly segregated. Comparison with the figures for other cities which have been studied in this way made that plain. If we take the indices between the highest and the lowest class in Edinburgh the figure is 71 compared with 54 in Chicago, 46 in Oxford, 44 in Oslo and 53 in the outer metropolitan area of Kent.[50] Using another measure, the 'index of segregation', which measures the degree to which each social class is contained within relatively homogeneous areas, the researchers were able to demonstrate that the upper and lower ends of the social hierarchy were very highly segregated. Again, the statistics show this kind of separation to be more marked in Edinburgh than in other urban areas on which we had comparative data.

Richardson and his colleagues also provided a map outlining the class differences between enumeration districts. The technique employed was essentially similar to that used by Moser and Scott.[51] Districts were categorized according to the proportion of their populations in the top two socio-economic groups (as defined in the 1966 Census).

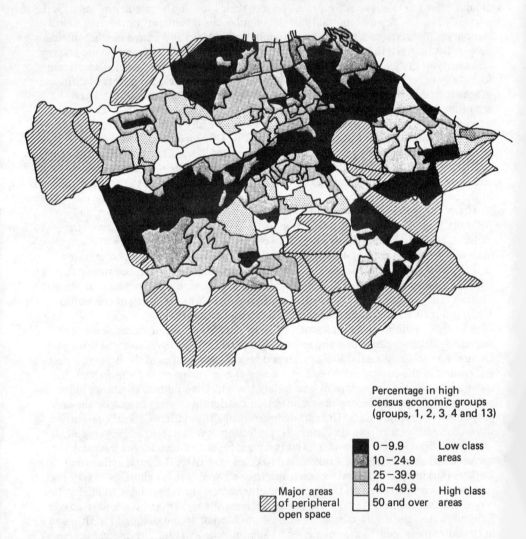

Percentage in high
census economic groups
(groups, 1, 2, 3, 4 and 13)

■	0 – 9.9	Low class areas
	10 – 24.9	
	25 – 39.9	
	40 – 49.9	High class areas
□	50 and over	

Major areas
of peripheral
open space

Figure 1.2   Social Segregation in Edinburgh
Source: H. Richardson, J. Vipond and R. Furbey, *Housing and Urban Spatial Structure*
(Farnborough 1975).

The pattern which emerged confirmed the high degree of spatial segregation, and the general shape was rather like that found by Willmott and Young in London. The most solidly working-class areas had developed around the port of Leith or on low ground which, in providing water or transportation routes, had attracted industry. The high class areas were concentrated in the west and north-west and were well insulated from the effects of industry. The map had a powerfully 'sectoral' as opposed to 'zonal' character and this in part reflected the interesting fact that many of the inner suburbs had not declined as the zonal theory implies, but had largely retained their social character and continued to attract families of relatively high socio-economic status. The analysis of house-purchase patterns over time, indeed, showed how many of the inner areas had proved more, not less, attractive to some of Edinburgh's wealthier citizens in recent years.[52] Like London, Edinburgh is marked by sharp differences in the class composition of its various districts and this research, using a wider array of techniques and sources of data, demonstrated even more clearly that the patterns of spatial segregation were becoming more, not less, marked.

In general, the literature on urban ecology has underlined the processes maintaining and indeed sharpening the segregation of different class and status groups in Britain. Few studies of city-wide patterns have been done of late (and in general sociological enthusiasm for such work has declined), but two particular aspects of spatial differentiation and the processes underlying it have continued to attract interest. The first of these focuses on the movement back into certain inner city areas by the relatively wealthy.

GENTRIFICATION

In sharp contrast to the idea that the general tendency is for inner city areas to become progressively more proletarian in character, an idea we considered earlier, we find in the literature a very different notion. It has been claimed that the most remarkable trend, at least in London, goes in the opposite direction. Ruth Glass[53] was the first to comment on the process whereby in some inner city areas those of lower economic status were displaced by others who were a good deal wealthier. She called the process 'gentrification'. There can be little doubt that her earlier observations exaggerated the scale of the changes, but over the past decade a number of studies have provided, in very different ways, corroboration of her general idea. Hamnett,[54] for instance, showed that between 1966 and 1971 the percentage of male managers and professionals in inner London increased by nearly 6 per cent and he argued that over the decade from 1961 to 1971 the figures indicate quite clearly an upward shift in the socio-economic composition of the inner districts. In part, this is explained by general changes in occupational structure, with the emergence of more and more professional, scientific and technical occupations and the reduction in less skilled jobs. This makes intelligible the fact that accompanying the increase in the proportion of these occupations near the city centre, there is also a sizeable 'export' of professional and managerial workers to the outer areas. In the more detailed reports of the process contained in Hamnett and Williams[55] we are able to see that the growth in the proportion of males in high socio-economic groups has not simply occurred in the districts where their kind were already numerous. That reinforcement of the patterns of segregation has occurred, but much more importantly, it can be demonstrated that there are some twenty-seven wards where we are really looking at a process of 'invasion'. What goes on has been well described, albeit satirically, by Jonathan Raban in *Soft City*.[56] He writes of the 'vaguely entrepreneurial cultural professions' from which these 'brahmins' come, and recounts how young, well-educated husbands and wives seek out desirable but run-down Victorian or Edwardian houses and set about refurbishing them. If the pioneer families have chosen wisely, which means selecting housing relatively close to existing high status areas, others soon follow in their footsteps. Property values rise, the landlords find it more and more attractive to sell out and one by one the existing, generally relatively poor, often elderly tenants are 'winkled' out and the house passes into the hands of another young writer, publisher or architect. It is easy to find much humour in the accounts.[57] However, the effect of the process on those displaced is not a matter for levity.

Explanations of the phenomenon really rest on three things. First, the changing conditions of the housing market and the prospects of profit for landlords, builders and estate agents. Secondly, the unintended consequences of government policies regarding rehabilitation and thirdly, the cultural choices and economic calculations of certain kinds of middle-class families.

The first point is perhaps the most important. We discussed earlier the fact that private landlords in Britain have, especially in the post-war period, found it generally much more profitable to sell their property than to continue to rent it. In some inner city areas landlords with those sizeable Georgian, Victorian or Edwardian houses which were originally built as family homes for the relatively wealthy have found that even multiple occupancy of these properties gave them poor returns. It made much better sense to sell and re-invest. Builders who could buy such property and refurbish it found that there was a ready market for it. Estate agents would, of course, derive money from such sale and resale processes.

Housing policies in the 1960s, when they involved the destruction of old, but once handsome, inner city areas came in for a good deal of criticism. There emerged a substantial lobby arguing for the preservation of styles and areas of domestic property. Some of the interest was essentially aesthetic or historical, but increasingly this was buttressed by economic arguments. It was, so it was claimed, cheaper to rehabilitate than rebuild. By the late 1960s, central government policy produced, through systems of municipal loans and grants, positive encouragement for the upgrading of the housing stock. The effects though were not quite what was expected. It was hoped that financial assistance provided by local authorities would benefit principally the owner-occupiers or the tenants in rented property. In fact, the benefits flowed mainly to landlords, property speculators and the relatively wealthy families who were able and prepared to undertake the improvement of previously rented housing. Although gentrification undoubtedly began before government introduced the home improvement loans and grants,[58] and the techniques for winkling out unwanted tenants had been in some landlords' repertoire for years, the 1969 legislation no doubt encouraged the displacement process. The unintended consequences were spelled out in the Counter Information Services Report.

In Hammersmith, for years a run-down working class area, the Council has paid out £950,000 in improvement grants, and property developers have received £700,000 of

Between 1971 and 1972 landlords and developers in Kensington and Chelsea received almost 70 per cent of the grants, in Hammersmith 67 per cent and in Westminster 64 per cent.[59]

Cheap flats became 'luxury apartments' or whole buildings were sold at a handsome profit.

But why was there increased demand for such inner city housing on the part of the young professionals and others? It is tempting perhaps to imagine that they were former suburban dwellers whose rational calculations about the costs and benefits of life in the city fringe had persuaded them to return to the centre. Certainly, city fathers lamenting the loss of rates revenue and the cultural disadvantages of the middle-class suburban exodus were hoping for such a return, but there seems to be little evidence that this is what happened. Rather, from Hamnett and Williams[60] we would conclude that most of those who were involved in the gentrification process were already, for the most part, inner city residents. Their choice of area seems really to have much to do with the cultivation of a particular kind of life style.

The consequences of gentrification can be simply stated. It has served chiefly to reduce the prospects of affordable rented housing close to the city centre for the relatively poor. It has increased the pressure on public housing, since a good many of the former residents were rehoused by the councils and it has driven labour out of the inner city. In some instances, too, it has led to sharp conflicts between incomers and groups of poor people attempting to retain the homes and the character of their neighbourhoods.[61] Against all this one has to weigh the improvement, structural and aesthetic, of those streets and squares in Barnsbury, Camden, Bayswater, Highgate and similar districts.

ETHNIC SEGREGATION

No account of social change in the British cities could ignore the issue of race. The appearance of black and Asian communities in London, Birmingham, Bradford and other urban areas has aroused passionate political debate and a good deal of academic interest. The urban riots of 1981 fuelled the former and gave greater relevance to the latter.

From the early sixties to the mid-seventies, the growth of the immigrant population was rapid. In 1961 there were fewer than 300,000 citizens from the New Commonwealth settled in Britain; by 1974 the figure was 1,744,000.[62] However, the rate of growth in recent years has been checked, partly by legislation restricting the flow of new immigrants and partly by a reduction in the rate of natural increase among those already settled here. Between 1966 and 1974 the black and Asian population grew from 2.1 per cent to 3.2 per cent of the total population, but the concern over the presence of those from the West Indies, Africa and the Indian subcontinent had less to do with this overall growth than with the emergence of areas with sizeable concentrations of migrants. By the mid-seventies certain districts of the cities were regarded not simply as immigrant districts but had already acquired specific ethnic identities. In London, for instance, Southall was 'Asian', Brixton 'West Indian'.

The concentrations of ethnic groups in the early years of the 1950s and 1960s arose primarily from the exclusion of immigrants from the two principal forms of housing. Rex and Moore's study of Sparkbrook[63] in Birmingham was the first serious attempt to describe and analyse the emergence of ethnic enclaves. Their account showed how the process worked. The immigrants were often excluded by the rules of eligibility from the public housing stock. As newcomers they could not meet the residency requirements and consequently could not even be put on the waiting list of some local authorities. At best they would rank low on the points system operated by those who would give them a place in the queue. And that place might easily be lost if, as often happened, the family moved and in the process crossed the administrative boundaries, say, from one London borough to another.

The owner-occupied sector of the housing system was generally not accessible either. Most immigrants were relatively poor and the greatest number were in unskilled or semi-skilled jobs. Most forms of private housing were beyond them. But even if they had the money for the down-payment, they found the gateway to home ownership guarded by the building society managers who were often unwilling to give loans to those they judged to be poor risks.

What was left then was the shrinking sector of privately rented flats and rooms, commonly expensive, mostly providing accommodation in run-down districts of the city, and to these areas many gravitated in the early years of their stay in Britain. Within such areas a few from the immigrant community would become landlords, typically purchasing a large property with a loan from a money-lender. If the rates of repayment were exceedingly high, at least the house would be large enough to split up and sub-let, generally to other immigrants, and in this way the debt could be managed.

In the late sixties the housing policies changed. The creation of General Improvement Areas and Housing Action Areas allowed city councils to address the problems of the twilight zones in which many immigrants lived, without programmes of demolition and the attendant rehousing of their populations. That would have meant letting sizeable numbers of council houses to immigrants, arousing expressions of resentment from the white population all too easy to imagine. Instead, the councils were able to enforce some upgrading of the very poor conditions of some of the worst housing in their cities. In a recent article describing the process, Rex[64] shows how the Housing Action Area powers enabled the local authorities to engineer improvements in districts in a highly selective way so that they could actually choose which houses *had* to be demolished and therefore which tenants they *had* to rehouse. The actions of councils then served to keep the black population in the old decrepit areas. Indeed, through the granting of council mortgages on properties in such places or through the policies of housing associations, they were able to direct other immigrant families into them.

If most immigrants began their stay in Britain in lodging houses, many contrived to move out of these places as soon as their wives and relatives joined them. After all, lodging houses might well contain individuals from several different ethnic groups. With the reunion of the family it was, for many Asians in particular, imperative that they move out and find a house or a flat where they could live more closely in accord with their cultural practices (which included, of course, the relative seclusion of their wives and daughters). Thus, many became the owners of small houses.[65] Despite the general tendency to purchase housing, others have become tenants in local authority housing especially where it has been possible to find council houses very near to the particular Indian or Pakistani community in which they have been living.[66] Some Asians are also beginning to move out of the inner areas to find housing in the suburbs, but the evidence is that the small businessmen and others who have acquired the means to buy such housing still retain strong ties and commitments to their ethnic community.[67] As far as the West Indian population is concerned, there appears to have been a very substantial change in housing tenure over recent years. According to the data presented by Cross[68], based on the 1977–8 *National Dwelling and Housing Survey*. West Indians are certainly no longer confined to lodging houses or other forms of privately rented housing. Instead they are the group, at least in Birmingham and London, most likely to occupy council housing.

Table 1.7   Proportion of Households in Local Authority Housing by Race, 1977–8 (per cent)

Racial Group	City			
	London		Birmingham	
	Inner	Outer	Inner	Outer
White	55.3	28.9	37.4	37.8
West Indian	60.9	42.3	37.9	47.5
Indian	32.6	11.6	3.3	13.1
Pakistani/Bangladeshi	33.8	22.1	7.6	(0)
Other	44.4	19.4	8.6	20.4
All	54.5	28.4	32.6	37.4
(N)	(14,297)	(143,848)	(1,351)	(4,413)

Source: Department of the Environment, *National Dwelling and Housing Survey, 1977–8* (1979).

However, this probably does not indicate any widespread movement of West Indians out of the inner city areas. In Birmingham at least, Ward is able to show that in these areas West Indians still made up 15 to 20 per cent of the council tenants whereas in the suburban council property they were very thinly represented.[69]

The fact that the largest number of Asian and West Indian immigrants and their families still live in the inner city is important for it means that they are still caught up in the areas with very high levels of unemployment, poor environmental conditions and levels of public provision. The survey referred to above gave evidence of the disadvantaged position of the black and Asian populations compared with white residents. From other sources we know that for black youths the rise in joblessness has been particularly marked and has risen dramatically in the last few years. As Cross puts it:

. . . in times of recession, age and race have a compound negative effect on our employment prospects.[70]

For black Britons the harshness of life in our cities is not captured adequately by commentary on housing conditions or employment prospects. Behind those evident inequalities, and indeed many other kinds, there is the pervasive influence of racism. This is not to say that we should account for such things by some general imputation that the housing officials, estate agents, employers or school-teachers have actively discriminated

Table 1.8   **Proportion of Household Heads Unemployed* (per cent)**

Racial Group	London		Birmingham	
	Inner	Outer	Inner	Outer
White	5.6	2.5	6.6	4.0
West Indian	9.5	7.1	14.3	15.4
Indan	7.0	3.0	11.9	5.4
Pakistani/Bangladeshi	12.9	5.6	6.6	(11.1)
Other	7.8	4.1	(10.5)	5.5
Total	6.3	2.8	8.2	4.2

* Those seeking work as proportions of those in labour market.

Source: Department of the Environment, *National Dwelling and Housing Survey 1977–8* (1979).

against the immigrants, or typically hold racist views, but the general importance of racism cannot be ignored. Hostility to West Indians and Asians is not confined to verbal abuse: it is manifest in many attacks on black people as the Home Office study which was set up two months before the riots in Brixton makes plain.[71] The authors estimated that, on the evidence of their survey, some 7,000 racially motivated incidents will be reported to the police in England and Wales in a year, and their respondents seemed quite convinced that the number of racial attacks had been increasing.

The data in table 1.9 indicate quite clearly that the victims of racially motivated incidents and crimes are much more likely to be blacks or Asians than white citizens. In the more detailed analysis of the particular types of incidents it is clear that Asians are the group subjected to some of the nastiest attacks. Arson, abusive telephone calls, window-smashing incidents are all largely directed against them. Many in the ethnic communities feel that the police, when such incidents are reported to them, fail to take the complaints seriously and rarely apprehend the attackers. Racial murders have gone unsolved; the actions of the Special Patrol Group in the 1976 Notting Hill Carnival are still remembered with bitterness; the use of the 'sus' law to stop and search black youths, together with periodic campaigns against crime (like the Swamp 81 campaign in Brixton), have meant that the police do not enjoy the trust of many in these communities.[72] The most recent inquiry into the attitudes of the Metropolitan force confirms the suspicions of blacks and Asians that racist views are widely held among the police, even if they do not generally manifest themselves in overtly discriminatory behaviour.[73]

Ethnic communities, then, are still to be found, mainly in the inner city districts of our major cities. They have emerged largely as a consequence of constraints in the housing and, to a lesser extent, the job markets in our urban centres. But they have arisen, too, out of the understandable desire to create conditions of mutual support: to live among co-religionists, to develop institutions that serve the distinctive cultural preferences of particular groups,[74] to contrive some insulation from the hostility of the white world. They should now be given support. There are some encouraging signs that housing officials, planners and politicians in some local areas are acknowledging this, but sadly there is little in the general policies regarding the inner cities which is specifically directed to the circumstances of ethnic minorities.

Table 1.9   Victims of Inter-racial Incidents and Criminal Offences with Strong Evidence of some Indications of a Racial Motive per 100,000 Population by Ethnic Origin of Victim

Ethnic origin of victim	Population size in survey areas (1)	Victims of racially motivated incidents, rate per 100,000 population	Victims of racially motivated criminal offences, rate per 100,000 population
White	16,047,100	1.4	0.9
Black	242,000	51.2	24.0
Asian	482,000	69.7	42.7
Other ethnic origin	239,800	11.3	8.8
Total	17,010,900	4.2	2.6

Note:
(1) Population figures for the English police force areas participating in the survey were obtained from the *National Dwelling and Housing Survey* 1977–8. Figures for the three divisions of Greater Manchester were taken from Manchester D Division Telford and Oldham only. Thames Valley police force was assumed to cover Berkshire, Buckinghamshire and Oxfordshire. Figures for the South Wales police force were taken from the 1971 Census population for Mid, South and West Glamorgan.

CONCLUSION

We have painted a rather bleak picture of what is going on in our cities, partly because most of the discussion relates to the large urban centres rather than to those smaller settlements or relatively rural areas into which many people and businesses are moving. In the future, it will be important to look more closely at these 'communities of hope'. But the central task of sociology is criticism. In the 1980s that means that our principal effort should be the monitoring and appraisal of those policies which, reversing many post-war trends, are leading now to greater inequalities. Alongside the exercises in sociography we require many more attempts to examine and understand the social and political philosophies of the 'New Right'.

Currently, there is an observable tension between two motifs in the ideology of neo-conservatism in Britain. The commitment to greater 'freedom' derives from several libertarian strands which stress the need for greater individual liberty and a freer rein for market forces. Such arguments owe most to the writings of Hayek on the one hand and Milton Friedman on the other.[75] But alongside the notions about freedom lie others about 'control'. The journalist, Peregrine Worsthorne, expressed a view which is undoubtedly held by members of many of those lobbies and pressure groups which grew up in the late seventies, a view which has found expression in some recent government policies including those concerned with central-local government relations. Writing in 1978 Worsthorne argued:

If one were to probe into the hearts of many potential and actual Tory supporters – and others besides – one might discover that what worried them most about contemporary Britain was not so much the lack of freedom as its excessive abundance. . . . The urgent need today is for the state to regain control over 'the people', to reassert its authority. . .[76]

Policies for our cities reflect both these ideological strands, the former—the libertarian tradition—informs the efforts to privatize the housing stock and to sell public resources in the forms of land and buildings to property entrepreneurs. The latter emerges in the demand for law and order and for closer surveillance and control over welfare claimants. Together, they lead to greater inequalities of both a material and a social kind.

The privatization measures in the cities are contributing handsomely to the profits of those engaged, for instance, in the rehabilitation of older housing areas or the development for commercial, industrial or residential purposes of city sites. Privatization of council houses will lead, as we suggested earlier, to a situation in which public housing will become more and more like 'welfare' housing in the USA. That is to say, housing for what the Victorians called a 'residuum'.

The 'freedom' that is enjoined will be freedom for those with means, with property. The 'control' which is called for, will be exercised most closely over those who are corralled in the worst housing areas, in districts with the most acute economic and social difficulties. Far from alleviating those structural conditions which underlay the urban violence in the early years of this decade, current policies seem likely to exacerbate them.

Notes to Chapter 1

1   Overviews of the development of planning in Britain are found in W. Ashworth, *The Genesis of Modern British Town Planning* (London 1954); M. Clawson and P. Hall, *Planning and Urban Growth, An Anglo-American Comparison*, (Baltimore 1973); D. Eversley, *The Planner in Society. The Changing Role of a Profession* (London 1973).

2   For comment on this see M. Broady, *Planning for People*, (London 1968).

3   For recent discussion of planners, their backgrounds and their commitments, see P. Knox and J. Cullen, 'Planners as urban managers: an exploration of the attitudes and self-image of senior British planners', *Environment and Planning*, 13 (1981).

4   See the studies by R. Durant, *Watling: A Survey of Social Life on a New Housing Estate*, (London 1959); L. Kuper, *Living in Towns*, (London 1953); J. M. Mogey, *Family and Neighbourhood: two studies in Oxford* (Oxford 1956).

5   P. Hall, H. Gracey, R. Drewitt, R. Thomas, *The Containment of Urban England*, (London 1973).

6   See A. Jackson, *Semi-Detached London* (London 1973).

7   R. Glass 'The Evaluation of Planning: Some Sociological Considerations', *International Social Science Journal*, Vol. XI (3), 1959, reprinted in A. Faludi (ed.), *A Reader in Planning Theory* (Oxford 1973).

8   H. Orlans, *Stevenage: A Sociological Portrait of a New Town* (London 1952).

9   D. Donnison and P. Soto, *The Good City. A Study of Urban Development and Policy* (London 1980), p. 29.

10   J. D. McCallum 'Statistical trends of the British Conurbations' in G. Cameron (ed.), *The Future of the British Conurbations* (London 1980).

11   S. Fothergill and G. Gudgin, *Unequal Growth, Urban and Regional Employment Change in the UK* (London 1982), p. 8.

12   *Ibid.*, pp. 68-9.

13   House of Commons, First Report of the Environment Committee, 1981-2, 'The Private Rented Sector', Vol. III, Appendices (1982).

14   D. Eversley, 'Landlords' Slow Goodbye', *New Society* (12 January 1975).

15   House of Commons, First Report of the Environment Committee 1981-2, *op. cit.*

16   B. Elliott and D. McCrone, 'Landlords in Edinburgh: Some Preliminary Findings', *Sociological Review*, 23 (3) (1975).

17   Department of the Environment, *Housing and Construction Statistics 1972-1982* (HMSO 1983).

18   *Ibid.*

19   Shelter (The Scottish Campaign for the Homeless), *Council House Sales: Who Pays* (Edinburgh 1979).

20   For details see B. Kilroy 'No Jackpot for Council House Sales', *Roof* (May 1977).

21   See for instance P. Saunders, *Urban Politics* (London 1979); R. Barrell and M. Farmer, 'Homes or Jobs: Maggie's Choice', *The Observer* (21 October 1979); M. Ball, *Housing Policy and Economic Power: The Political Economy of Owner Occupation* (London 1983).

22   It begins in J. Rex and R. Moore, *Race, Community and Conflict: A Study of Sparkbrook* (Oxford 1967); is developed in J. Rex, 'The Sociology of the Zone of Transition' in R. Pahl (ed.) *Readings in Urban Sociology* (Oxford 1968); and criticized by R. Haddon, 'The Location of West Indians in the London Housing Market', *New Atlantis* 2 (1) (1970). For more recent discussion see G. Pratt, 'Class Analysis and Urban Domestic Property: a critical examination', *International Journal of Urban and Regional Research*, 6 (4) (1982).

23   See J. A. Agnew, 'Home ownership and the capitalist social order' in M. Dear and A. Scott (eds), *Urbanization and Urban Planning in Capitalist Society* (London 1981); and J. Kemeny, 'Home Ownership and Privatization', *International Journal of Urban and Regional Studies*, 4 (1980).

24   M. Ball, *op. cit.*, p. 293.

25   This was very clearly expressed by Sir Keith Joseph in the interview he recorded for the Open University 'Down with Equality', *Open University Cassette* No. 302 01/04 (1976). The concern to re-establish old inequalities is explicitly stated by M. Cowling in his *Conservative Essays* (London 1978).

26   Inland Revenue, *Annual Statistics* (1983).

27   See G. M. Norris, 'Poverty in Scotland' in G. Brown and R. Cook (eds), *Scotland: The Real Divide. Poverty and Deprivation in Scotland* (Edinburgh 1983).

28   HMSO, *Policy for the Inner Cities*, Cmnd. 6845 (June 1977).

29   Department of the Environment, *Study of the Inner Areas of Conurbations* (June 1975).

30   R. Pahl 'Poverty and the Urban System' in M. Chisholm and A. Manners (eds), *Spatial Policy Problems of the British Economy* (Cambridge 1971).

31   D. Harvey, 'Social processes, spatial form and the redistribution of real income in an urban system' in M. Chisholm, A. Fray and P. Haggett (eds), *Regional Forecasting* (London 1971).

32   G. Lomas, 'Life and Labour in London' in D. Donnison and D. Eversley (eds), *London: Urban Patterns, Problems and Policies* (London 1973).

33   C. Hamnett, 'Social Change and Social Segregation in Inner London 1961-71', *Urban Studies*, 13 (3) (1976).

34   Lomas, *op. cit.*

35   See for instance C. Jones (ed), *Urban Deprivation and the Inner City* (London 1979); P. Lawless, *Urban Deprivation and Government Initiative* (London 1979); P. Lawless, *Britain's Inner Cities* (London 1981). A. Evans and D. Eversley (eds), *The Inner City*; P. Hall, *The Inner City in Context* (London 1981). For a journalist account see P. Harrison, *Inside the Inner City* (Harmondsworth 1983).

36   HMSO, *The Brixton Disorders 10-12 April 1981*, Report of An Inquiry by the Rt.

Hon. The Lord Scarman (1981).

37 Department of the Environment, Inner Cities Directorate, *Information Note No. 1* (1982).

38 P. Harrison, *op. cit.*

39 *Ibid*, pp. 57–8.

40 *Ibid.*, p. 58.

41 A Gilloran, *Wester Hailes Ten Years On*, Wester Hailes Representative Council (Edinburgh 1983), p. 20.

42 See M. Tebbutt, *Making Ends Meet: Pawnbroking and Working Class Credit* (Leicester 1983).

43 There grew up a very sizeable literature on programmes of redevelopment and renewal. In the United States one of the earliest and best assessments of these policies is H. Gans, *The Urban Villages* (New York 1962). See too the essays in his *People and Plans* (Harmondsworth 1972). Studies in Britain include N. Dennis, *People and Planning* (London 1970); and D. Muchnick, 'Urban Renewal in Liverpool: A Study of the Politics of Redevelopment', *Occasional Papers on Social Administration*, No. 33 (1970).

44 For discussion of the strategies and a good account of the views of both the Left and the Right in Britain on this issue see P. Lawless (1981), *op. cit.*

45 J. Westergaard, 'The Structure of Greater London' in Centre for Urban Studies, *London: Aspects of Change* (London 1964). For comment and description of other studies made in the sixties see R. J. Johnston, *Urban Residential Patterns* (London 1971).

46 The point was made very frequently by Durkheim and reinforced by Halbwachs. In the United States the work of the neo-ecologists like O. Duncan and L. Schnore proceeded from a similar conviction.

47 See their now 'classic' studies J. Jacobs, *The Death and Life of Great American Cities* (Harmondsworth 1964); and O. Newman, *Defensible Space* (New York 1973).

48 See P. Willmott and M. Young 'Social Class and Geography' in D. Donnison and D. Eversley (eds), *London: Urban Patterns, Problems and Policies* (London 1973); and P. Willmott and M. Young, *The Symmetrical Family* (London 1973).

49 H. Richardson, J. Vipond and R. Furbey, *Housing and Urban Spatial Structure: A Case Study* (Farnborough 1975).

50 *Ibid.*, p. 158.

51 C. Moser and W. Scott, *British Towns: A Statistical Study of their Economic and Social Differences* (Edinburgh 1961).

52 B. Elliott and D. McCrone, 'Urban Development in Edinburgh: A Contribution to the Political Economy of Place', *Scottish Journal of Sociology* 4 (1) (1980) gives further information on this for one of the inner suburbs.

53 R. Glass, 'Introduction' in Centre for Urban Studies (1964) *op. cit.*; and R. Glass, 'The Mood of London' in Donnison and Eversley (1973), *op. cit.*

54 Hamnett (1976), *op. cit.*

55 C. Hamnett and M. Williams, 'Social Change in London: A Study of Gentrification' *The London Journal*, 6 (1) (1980); and C. Hamnett and M. Williams, 'Gentrification in London 1961-1971. An Empirical and Theoretical Analysis of Social Change', CURS, University of Birmingham, RM71 (1979).

56   J. Raban, *Soft City* (London 1974).

57   See M. Williams, 'The New Raj: the gentrifiers and the natives', *New Society* (14 January 1982).

58   *Report of the Committee on Housing in Greater London* (Milner Holland Report) Cmnd. 2605 (HMSO 1965).

59   Counter Information Services, *The Recurrent Crisis of London: action report on the property developers* (London 1973).

60   C Hamnett and M. Williams, *op. cit.*

61   J. Ferris, *Participation in Urban Planning. The Barnsbury Case*, Occasional Papers in Social Administration No. 48 (London 1972).

62   'The Coloured Population of Great Britain', Runnymede Trust Occasional Reprint (1976).

63   J. Rex and R. Moore (1967), *op. cit.*

64   J. Rex, 'Urban Segregation and Inner City Policy in Great Britain' in C. Peach (ed.), *Ethnic Segregation in Cities* (London 1981).

65   See P. Jeffery, *Migrants and Refugees, Muslim and Christian Pakistani Families in Bristol* (Cambridge 1976).

66   For discussion of this see V. Robinson, 'Asians and Council Housing', *Urban Studies 17* (1980), and the same authors' discussion in 'The Development of South Asian Settlement in Britain and the Myth of Return' in C. Peach, (1981), *op. cit.*

67   S. Nowikowski and R. Ward, 'Middle Class and British? An Analysis of South Asians in Suburbia', *New Community* 7 (1978).

68   M. Cross, 'The Manufacture of Marginality' in E. Cashmore and B. Troyno (eds), *Black Youth in Crisis* (London 1982).

69   R. Ward and R. Sims, 'Social Status, The Market and Ethnic Segregation' in C. Peach, (1981), *op. cit.*

70   M. Cross, *op. cit.* See, too, J. Rex and M. Cross, 'Unemployment and Racial Conflict in the Inner City', *Working Papers on Ethnic Relations*, No. 16., SSRC Research Unit in Ethnic Relations (Birmingham 1982).

71   Home Office, *Racial Attacks* (London 1981).

72   The Journal *Race Today* provides much evidence of the suspicion and resentment of the police, particularly in London, and of efforts made by blacks and Asians to act collectively in defence of their interests. The theme is discussed in R. Moore, *Racism and Black Resistance in Britain* (London 1975) and in J. Rex, 'Black Militancy and Class Conflict' in R. Miles and A. Phizacklea, *Racism and Political Action in Britain* (London 1979). Specific comment on the 'SUS' laws can be found in B. Roberts, 'The Debate on "SUS"' in E. Cashmore and B. Troyna. (1982), *op. cit.*

73   See Policy Studies Institute, *Police and People in London* (London 1983).

74   For discussion of some of the ways in which Asians have developed self-contained social and economic structures, see the work of H. Aldrich and his associates. H. Aldrich, 'Asian Shopkeepers as a Middleman Minority: A Study of Small Business in Wandsworth' in D. Eversley and A. Evans (eds), *Inner City Employment* (London 1979); and H. Aldrich, J. Cater, T. Jones and D. McEvoy, 'Business Development and Self-Segregation: Asian Enterprise in Three British Cities' in C. Peach, *op. cit.*

75   See for instance F. A. Hayek, *The Road to Serfdom* (London 1944) and his *The Constitution of Liberty* (London 1960); M. Friedman, *Capitalism and Freedom* (Chicago 1982); and M. Friedman and R. Friedman, *Free to Choose* (London 1980). For discussion of both these authors and their importance in the 'New Right' see N. Bosanquet, *After the New Right* (London 1983).

76   P. Worsthorne, M. Cowling (eds), *Conservative Essays* (1978) *op. cit*. For some discussion of the movements which contributed to the emergence of the 'New Right', see B. Elliott, F. Bechhofer, D. McCrone and S. Black, 'Bourgeois Social Movements in Britain: repertoires and responses', *Sociological Review*, 30 (1) (1982).

2
Patterns and Processes of Education in the United Kingdom

Robert G. Burgess

INTRODUCTION

Education is big business in the United Kingdom.[1] Expenditure on education in the public sector in 1979–80 totalled £10,510 million and represented 5.2 per cent of the Gross National Product. In 1979–80 there were 38,000 maintained and non-maintained schools in which ten million pupils were taught by 588,000 teachers (see table 2.1).

Table 2.1　Numbers of Schools, Pupils and Teachers and Pupil/Teacher Ratios by School Type in the UK, 1979–80

	Schools	Pupils (000s)	Teachers (000s)	Pupil/teacher ratio
Public sector schools				
Nursery	1,236	54.9	2.5	21.6
Primary	26,764	5,317.1	237.0	22.4
Secondary	5,571	4,636.2	283.4	16.4
Non-maintained schools	2,655	597.6	46.1	13.0
Special schools	2,016	148.7	19.5	7.6
All schools 1979–80	38,242	10,754.6	588.5	18.3

Source: Department of Education and Science, *Education Statistics for the United Kingdom 1982 Edition* (HMSO 1982), p. iii.

In terms of post-compulsory education, half the sixteen to eighteen year-olds participated in an educational course: 16 per cent in schools and 38 per cent in non-advanced further education. There were also one in three nineteen and twenty year-olds continuing their education, with 14 per cent in part-time non-advanced further education and 14 per cent in full-time higher education. Overall five million people continued their education after their sixteenth birthday on a variety of courses, as shown in table 2.2.

Accordingly, 'education' is a familiar experience for many residents of the United Kingdom as they are actively involved in the educational system in some capacity. The result is that questions about education are commonplace. What school do you attend? Where do you teach? What did you do at school today? These are all part of day-to-day conversation. However, it is the sociologist's task to probe behind the answers to these

Table 2.2 Post-compulsory Students by Level and Mode of Course in the UK, 1979–80

	Number of persons (000s)
Schools	445
Non-advanced further education	
Full-time and sandwich	307
Part-time day	693
Evening	2,846
Total	**3,846**
Higher Education	
Full-time and sandwich	468
Part-time	268
Total	**736**
All post-compulsory, 1979–80	*5,027*

Source: Department of Education and Science, *Education Statistics for the United Kingdom 1982 Edition* (HMSO 1982), p. v.

questions to establish the patterns and processes that constitute the educational experiences of the inhabitants of the UK. Accordingly, sociologists have asked individuals about their educational careers and qualifications and studied their experiences of education in schools, colleges and classrooms.

However, such an assignment is no easy task as, not only are informants highly familiar with education and with educational settings, but so too are sociologists. Indeed the American sociologist, Howard Becker, comments in relation to the study of school classrooms:

> We may have understated a little the difficulty of observing contemporary classrooms. It is not just the survey method of educational testing or any of those things that keeps people from seeing what is going on. I think instead that it is first and foremost a matter of it all being so familiar that it becomes irresponsible to single out events that occur in the classroom as things that occurred even when they happen right in front of you. . . it takes a tremendous effort of will and imagination to stop seeing only the things that are conventionally there to be seen.[2]

As such, Becker argues that sociologists need to go into schools and classrooms with a view to going beyond the everyday educational experiences with which everyone is familiar.[3]

Sociologists have made some attempt at coming to terms with this issue by asking questions not only about the process of education, but also about the pattern and the practice; about structures and the ways in which those structures operate in a range of social and educational circumstances. The key questions that sociologists have posed about education have focused mainly on issues of equality of educational opportunity[4] with the result that the influence of social class on educational achievement and patterns of class mobility have had a prominent position in the literature. In turn, education has been linked with the economy and questions have been posed about the relationship between education and patterns of employment[5] and more recently unemployment.[6] However, such research questions have focused on educational input and output with the result that educational institutions were treated as 'black boxes' where central issues associated with teaching and learning were unquestioned. This deficiency has been rectified to some extent during the last fifteen years when an interactionist perspective has been used to study schools and classrooms, focusing on social and educational processes and the assumptions that have been made about teaching and learning. The result has been that the activities which take place within educational institutions are no longer seen as 'natural' or 'normal', but have been examined to see the way in which teachers and pupils mould the educational process.[7] Such an approach has meant that sociologists have focused not only on the processes involved in education, but also on the content of education, the curriculum and what it means to be educated.[8] However, as Banks[9] has noted, these approaches have been the subject of criticism from various writers; especially those working within a neo-Marxist perspective who have argued that it is important to pay some attention to the determining effects of social systems, especially the capitalist system, on schools and schooling. As a consequence, some attention has been given to examining interactions between teachers and pupils within a broad set of social structural forces.[10]

Alongside these changing theoretical, methodological and substantive interests, sociologists working within the field of education have, like other sociologists, taken account of the social, political and radical movements of the time, such as the 'New Left', the women's and students' movements, black power and counter-cultural movements. Of all such groups, it is the women's movement that has had the greatest impact upon recent British sociology, with the result that concepts and categories associated with gender have loomed large in much recent work. In particular, feminist accounts of education[11] have pointed to the dearth of systematic analyses of research in education that compare the experiences of boys and girls and men and women. Accordingly, questions on gender and social inequality have been placed on the research agenda alongside a consideration of the way in which sex and gender are routinely handled in the school and classroom.[12]

British sociologists have therefore adopted a number of different theoretical perspectives to ask critical questions about the patterns, practices and processes of education, especially in schools within the state educational system rather than within the independent sector. This chapter utilizes some of these sociological perspectives to examine major patterns of state education in the UK.[13] Special attention will be given to documenting the key phases of education. Here both quantitative and qualitative evidence will be used to complement each other in examining current educational practice. However, before turning to these phases of education we need to examine the structure of educational systems in the UK.

EDUCATIONAL SYSTEMS IN THE UK

The educational arrangements that exist in the UK tend to be considerably over-simplified.

Indeed, it is relatively common for writers to refer to one single British educational system which, in reality, does not exist.[14] In fact, three educational systems exist alongside each other within the UK: England and Wales, Scotland and Northern Ireland. The basic structures are broadly similar, as shown in figures 2.1, 2.2 and 2.3 which chart the main phases of education and the principal examinations that are available within each system.

In the UK control over the education system is exercised by central government, but the control of schooling is maintained through four separate ministries. The Department of Education and Science deals with all sectors of education in England, while the Welsh Office Education Department is concerned with schools, higher and further education (excluding universities) in Wales. In Scotland it is the Scottish Education Department that has responsibility for schools and further education, while schools and further education in Northern Ireland are the responsibility of the Department of Education in Northern Ireland.

Within the three educational systems there is some broad pattern of uniformity which has been brought about by concurrent legislation for the four component countries. The major legislation that governs the pattern of education in each country today was introduced at the end of the Second World War. In England and Wales it was the 1944 Education Act that established the basic structure of the educational system, while similar legislation resulted in similar systems for Scotland and Northern Ireland. The general educational trends in England and Wales have been followed in Scotland and Northern Ireland. Significant features have included the development of policies relating to higher education in the 1960s, the raising of the school leaving age in the early 1970s and the campaign for the provision of nursery schools in the 1970s. Such parallel developments that have occurred have been explained by the cultural and political links that exist in the UK, but they are also related to the concept of parity: that is that there should be parity of provision throughout Great Britain and Northern Ireland.[15]

While there are broad similarities between the systems there are also some differences, for the educational systems of the UK are characterized by weak central control. In these terms, they are examples of decentralized educational systems where local education authorities may innovate within the broad framework established by central government.[16] Nevertheless, the majority of children attend primary school from the age of five and transfer to secondary school at the age of eleven, except in Scotland where the age of transfer is twelve and in those local authorities in England and Wales that have adopted First Schools and Middle Schools.[17] However, the type of primary school attended may vary in size according to the community that is served, with one teacher, one-room schools in remote rural communities[18] in contrast to the large multi-cultural inner city schools that may exist in Birmingham, Wolverhampton and London where multi-ethnic communities are located.[19] Further differences exist in terms of who controls the schools. In some localities it will be the Church rather than the local authority which controls the schools. The main religious denominations to provide schools are the Church of England and the Roman Catholic Church (especially in centres of dense Catholic population and in Northern Ireland). It is usual for similar educational provision to be made in denominational and non-denominational schools apart from religious education which is in accordance with the teaching of the particular church. In England, Wales and Scotland there may be some interaction between pupils and teachers

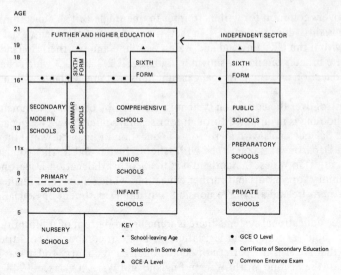

Figure 2.1   The Educational System of England and Wales

Notes:
1 First and Middle Schools have not been shown on this figure.
2 Further and Higher Education includes colleges of further education, technical colleges, colleges of higher education, polytechnics and universities.
3 This figure is not intended to show the proportion of schools in the educational system. For example, the comprehensive school predominates in secondary education.

Source: Adapted from R. Bell and N. Grant, *Patterns of Education in the British Isles* (London 1977), p. 212.

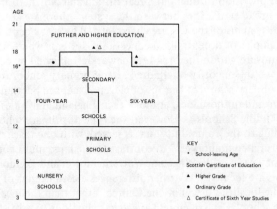

Figure 2.2   The Scottish Educational System

Notes:
1 Further and Higher Education includes further education colleges, central institutions (broadly equivalent to polytechnics), colleges of education and universities.
2 There are also some independent schools whose age structure is similar to those shown in figure 2.1.

Source: *Ibid*, p. 213.

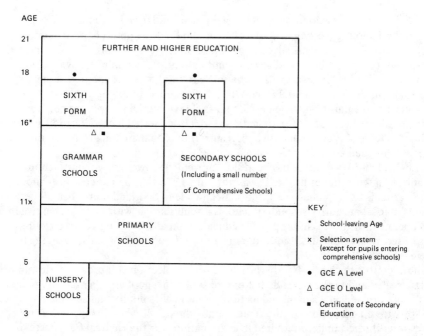

AGE

FURTHER AND HIGHER EDUCATION

KEY

*   School-leaving Age

x   Selection system
(except for pupils entering
comprehensive schools)

●   GCE A Level

△   GCE O Level

■   Certificate of Secondary
Education

Figure 2.3   The Educational System in Northern Ireland

Notes:
1 The pattern of further and higher education is similar to that for England and Wales.
2 Within Northern Ireland there is a strong voluntary sector of primary and secondary schools.

Source: Adapted from M. Sutherland, 'Education in Northern Ireland', in R. Bell, G. Fowler and K. Little (eds), *Education in Great Britain and Northern Ireland* (London 1973), p. 25.

from these various schools, while in Northern Ireland, Catholic and Protestant schools operate within systems that have little contact with each other.[20]

Secondary schools, whether they are comprehensive or part of the selective system, can be controlled by the local authorities or by the churches (again this is markedly the case in Northern Ireland). While tripartite, that is separate grammar, technical and modern schools were established following the post Second World War legislation, a campaign against selection according to academic ability resulted in a gradual shift towards the reorganization of secondary education along comprehensive lines in England, Wales and Scotland. At first, such schemes were experimental, being allowed as special cases in the 1950s in rural authorities such as Westmoreland (now part of Cumbria) and urban authorities such as Coventry and London which had insufficient secondary school accommodation following excessive bomb damage during the Second World War.[21] These authorities won concessions from Conservative governments who allowed experimental schemes in comprehensive secondary education from the mid-fifties. It was these initial schemes alongside political and parental pressure that influenced local authorities to consider a comprehensive system of secondary education.

When the Labour government took office in 1964 'all the pointers were in one direction, away from the local advocated road of diversity by means of broad divisions into separate types of school, and towards unification of the administrative system allowing for a genuine diversity within the single school'.[22] The Labour government did not legislate on secondary school provision, but allowed a variety of different patterns of comprehensive organization to be developed, as shown by the suggestions contained in circular 10/65[23] (circular 600 in Scotland) which requested local education authorities to submit schemes for comprehensive reorganization. The main long-term solutions that were recommended are shown in figure 2.4.

In England and Wales there has been slow movement towards secondary school reorganization with the result that it was not until 1978 that 85 per cent of school age children attended comprehensive schools. Meanwhile in Scotland more than 99 per cent of pupils in local authority secondary schools attend schools with a comprehensive intake and 83 per cent of these schools provide education on an all-through basis covering all stages of secondary education. Indeed, only a few schools admit pupils according to academic ability.[24]

A stark contrast exists in Northern Ireland where selection still predominates. In both the state sector and in the Catholic sector two types of school are maintained: grammar schools that provide an academic education for more able pupils; and secondary schools which provide an education for the remainder of the pupils who are regarded as being unable to reach the standard required in examinations for the General Certificate of Education (GCE). Indeed, writing in 1983, Murray and Osborne indicate that 'there are a very few "comprehensive" schools which combine both features'.[25] The result is that pupils in the grammar schools have a considerably greater opportunity to obtain academic qualifications compared with their peers in other secondary schools.

There are distinct differences in the secondary school examinations available in the three educational systems. In England and Wales pupils are entered for ordinary and advanced level examinations of the GCE which are taken at the ages of sixteen and eighteen respectively. In addition, since 1965, pupils can also be entered for the Certificate of Secondary Education (CSE) at the age of sixteen. While similar examinations are taken in Northern Ireland, it has been argued by Murray and Osborne that the CSE has had little impact on that country (at least up until 1975).[26] Meanwhile in Scotland a different pattern of examining exists. National examinations are conducted by the Scottish Certificate of Education (SCE) Examination Board. Here, pupils are presented for the SCE Ordinary Grade Examinations in their fourth year of secondary schooling[27] and for the Higher grade examinations in their fifth or sixth year. Finally, the Certificate of Sixth Year Studies is open to pupils who have successfully completed the Higher grade examinations. However, there is no equivalent to the CSE examination for Scottish pupils. Although some schools have established links with English CSE boards, this is disapproved of by some regional education authorities and forbidden by Strathclyde, the largest authority. Such diversity, both in terms of patterns of schooling and examinations in the secondary school sector in the different countries and between the three educational systems, creates problems in terms of the presentation of data and comparisons that might be drawn.[28] Thus, in subsequent sections of this chapter, attention will be drawn to the country or countries, system or systems to which the data apply.

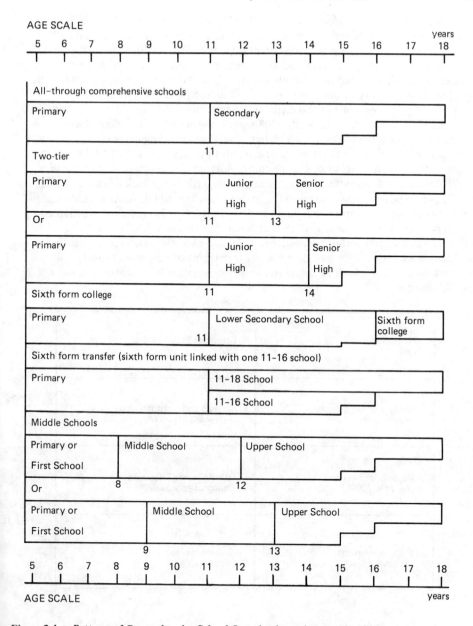

AGE SCALE

| 5 | 6 | 7 | 8 | 9 | 10 | 11 | 12 | 13 | 14 | 15 | 16 | 17 | years 18 |

All–through comprehensive schools

| Primary | | Secondary |

Two-tier   11

| Primary | | Junior High | Senior High |

Or   11   13

| Primary | | Junior High | Senior High |

Sixth form college   11   14

| Primary | | Lower Secondary School | Sixth form college |
    11

Sixth form transfer (sixth form unit linked with one 11–16 school)

| Primary | | 11–18 School |
| | | 11–16 School |

Middle Schools

| Primary or First School | Middle School | Upper School |

Or   8   12

| Primary or First School | Middle School | Upper School |

    9   13

AGE SCALE

| 5 | 6 | 7 | 8 | 9 | 10 | 11 | 12 | 13 | 14 | 15 | 16 | 17 | 18 | years |

Figure 2.4   Patterns of Comprehensive School Organization Advocated in 1965

Note: In 1965 the school-leaving age was 15; hence the pattern shown in this figure.

Source: Based on Department of Education and Science, *The Organization of Secondary Education* (Circular 10/65) (HMSO 1965).

Beyond the secondary schools there are broadly similar structures for further and higher education. In England and Wales higher education is provided in a local authority sector by colleges of higher education and polytechnics. The 1970s witnessed considerable changes in higher and further education outside the universities, with mergers and closures taking place among institutions in the local authority sector. In particular, the complete disappearance of colleges of education on the basis of closures and amalgamations has been one of the major features of the period between 1970 and 1980, summarized in figure 2.5. In the early 1980s some restructuring has taken place in universities, polytechnics and colleges of higher education providing degree level courses. Meanwhile in Scotland the fourteen central institutions provide courses of degree standard alongside those provided by the universities in all the countries concerned.[29]

This brief portrait has attempted to establish the basic framework of education in the UK and to point towards some of the main similarities and differences that exist in the four countries and three educational systems in the UK. However, all are marked by considerable diversity at local level with different patterns of schooling between authorities and within authorities. Furthermore, there are differences in the resources provided by local education authorities and the patterns of education provided in different parts of the UK. It is, therefore, to an examination of educational resources that we now turn.

1970	1980
Polytechnics (30)	Polytechnics (30)
Colleges of Education (Approx. 155)	Colleges and Institutes of Higher Education (Approx. 70)
Major Establishments (Approx. 700)	Other Further Education Colleges (Approx. 500)
Evening Institutes (Approx. 6500)	Evening Institutes (Approx. 5300)

Figure 2.5 The Changing Pattern of Further Education in England and Wales, 1970-80

Source: Derived from L.M. Cantor and I.F. Roberts, *Further Education To-day: A Critical Review* (London 1983) figure 1.1, p. 5.

RESOURCES FOR EDUCATION

We have already noted that the decentralized character of the educational systems allows considerable freedom for the local authorities to interpret the ways in which they will provide education and the resources they will devote to it. Accordingly, the geographical area in which children are located may well influence their educational opportunities as well as their educational achievements. In particular, this section considers the relationship between educational resources and educational disadvantage at the level of local authorities and schools.

To make comparisons between local education authorities measures are required to take account of the varying sizes of different localities. Mortimore and Blackstone[30] have indicated that two measures are traditionally used. First, basic educational expenditure can be broken down according to the number of pupils. This is usually done for each sector of education and results in a unit cost. Drawing on data from the educational estimates for 1980–81, Mortimore and Blackstone were able to calculate the 'top ten' and 'bottom ten' authorities in the primary and secondary school sectors in England and Wales. As table 2.3 indicates, there is considerable variation between local authorities. For example, in the primary sector the Inner London Education Authority (ILEA) was spending 61 per cent more than the national average, while Wolverhampton was spending 18 per cent more. Meanwhile, Trafford was spending 9 per cent below the national average and Dudley 17 per cent less. For secondary pupils a similar pattern was found, whereby the ILEA spent 52 per cent more than the national average, while Wakefield spent 17 per cent less. Another point which is clear from table 2.3 is the extent to which there is overlap between the provision in the primary and secondary sectors, as six authorities were in both 'top ten' groups, while there were three in both 'bottom ten' groups.

A second measure of the difference between local education authorities can be obtained using the pupil/teacher ratio; that is the number of full-time equivalent pupils to one qualified teacher. In table 2.4 data are provided on the 'top ten' and 'bottom ten' authorities in England and Wales. The average primary pupil/teacher ratio for England and Wales was 22.3 in 1980–81 while the average secondary pupil/teacher ratio was 16.1. As table 2.4 indicates, there is some considerable overlap between high-spending authorities and those with low pupil/teacher ratios. However, as Mortimore and Blackstone warn, a low pupil/teacher ratio cannot be taken as an indicator of educational quality. But, we might ask, to what extent do these variations in local education authority provision of resources contribute to the variation in the educational attainment of children from different social class backgrounds? Such a question has been addressed by Byrne, Williamson and Fletcher.[31] They maintain that there are three propositions that underlie their socio-spatial model of educational attainment. First, that social classes are viewed as relationships between groups that are differently placed in terms of rewards in society. Secondly, that the relationships between classes are based on control and domination and finally, that the rewards which the social classes have are spatially distributed[32] and include real income which is broadly defined to include educational provision. Within this framework Byrne, Williamson and Fletcher consider whether there is a significant degree of socio-spatial inequality in the educational system of England and Wales and whether it can be assessed in terms of differential outcomes. On the basis of a

Table 2.3   Education Estimates, 1980–1 (England and Wales)

Unit costs – net expenditure

Primary	£	Secondary	£
Top ten			
ILEA	703	ILEA	959
Haringey	630	Brent	808
Brent	616	Haringey	796
Ealing	594	Harrow	790
Powys	583	Manchester	775
Newham	580	Powys	756
Dyfed	572	Newham	744
Newcastle	537	Hounslow	744
Richmond	520	Barking	736
Wolverhampton	515	Ealing	735
Bottom ten			
Trafford	395	Solihull	565
Cornwall	394	Oldham	565
Stockport	393	Stockport	564
St Helens	391	Hereford & Worcester	563
Tameside	388	Suffolk	551
Somerset	388	Kirklees	549
Lancashire	384	Northants	547
Northants	380	Bradford	536
Lincolnshire	379	Dudley	532
Dudley	362	Wakefield	524
Average for all LEAs	436	Average for all LEAs	629

Based on: Chartered Institute of Public Finance and Accountancy (CIPFA) (1980), Education Estimates 1980–1.

Source: J. Mortimore and T. Blackstone, *Disadvantage and Education* (London 1982), p. 60.

statistical analysis in which measures of the socio-spatial system (the socio-economic status of the population, the environment, local authority policy, resources and provision) were related to educational attainment (measured in terms of the staying on rate) they were able to conclude that there were interconnections between educational provision, environmental conditions and educational attainment and that there was an absence of 'territorial justice'. Indeed, they maintain that school inputs help to account for differences in educational attainment.

Meanwhile, other studies in the UK have examined educational resources at the school level. First, we turn to a comparison of the resources of mixed and single-sex schools by Byrne.[33] Secondly, to a comparison of resources in Catholic and non-Catholic schools together with their curricula implications in Northern Ireland and finally, to comparisons of the resources in non-academic as opposed to academic departments in a comprehensive school.

Table 2.4   Pupil/teacher Ratios, 1980–1 (England and Wales)

Primary		Secondary	
Top ten			
ILEA	16.7	Brent	13.0
Wolverhampton	17.1	ILEA	13.5
Newham	17.4	Barking	13.5
Dyfed	17.4	Waltham Forest	13.8
Powys	17.8	Newcastle	14.0
Bradford	17.9	Wolverhampton	14.2
Brent	18.0	Haringey	14.2
Haringey	18.3	Harrow	14.2
Newcastle	18.6	Rochdale	14.4
Gwynedd	19.2	Barnet	14.4
Bottom ten			
Bromley	24.3	Kent	17.2
Stockport	24.3	Essex	17.2
West Sussex	24.3	Norfolk	17.2
Hampshire	24.4	Dyfed	17.2
Tameside	24.4	Calderdale	17.3
Oxfordshire	24.5	Gloucestershire	17.3
Sutton	24.8	Devon	17.4
Wirral	24.8	Derby	17.4
Hereford & Worcester	25.0	Warwickshire	17.6
Dudley	25.3	Somerset	17.8
Somerset	25.3		
Lincolnshire	25.3		
Average for all LEAs	22.3	Average for all LEAs	16.1

Based on: Chartered Institute of Public Finance and Accountancy (CIPFA) (1980), Education Estimates 1980–1.

Source: J. Mortimore and T. Blackstone, *Disadvantage and Education* (London 1982), p. 62.

In a study of 133 mixed and single-sex schools, Byrne draws attention to the way in which the provision of resources is a potential source of discrimination between the sexes. She found that almost all girls' schools were deficient in science laboratories and that while boys had the use of laboratories girls had to take science lessons in classrooms.[34] In addition, she found that in all but four schools the distribution of material resources for options reflected assumptions about the subsequent roles of girls and boys.[35] Indeed Byrne concluded that the discrimination she found in the distribution of resources was less a case of negative conscious discrimination, but more a question of the acceptance of inherited and unexamined social and educational assumptions about girls.

Meanwhile in Northern Ireland various commentators have considered the differences that exist in the conditions and facilities of Catholic schools and state schools. In particular, it is argued that conditions and facilities in Catholic schools are inferior to those in other state schools.[36] Indeed, it is argued that because the Catholic community has to help fund its own schools, this may result in lower standards of provision in the Catholic sector with larger classes, fewer grammar school places and, in turn, lower levels of achievement among the pupils. However, Darby[37] has indicated that there is no evidence to suggest that Catholic schools are less successful than state schools. Nevertheless, Murray and Osborne have noted on the basis of data from pupils in Catholic and state schools in Northern Ireland that Catholic pupils are less likely than state school pupils to have obtained passes in science and craft subjects, as shown in table 2.5. On the basis

Table 2.5   Proportion of 'O' level and 'A' level GCE Passes Gained in Science and Craft Subject Areas by Boys, all Boards, 1971 and 1975 in Northern Ireland

	Percentage					
	1971			1975		
	Roman Catholic	Protestant	Total	Roman Catholic	Protestant	Total
Ordinary Level						
Science[1]	29	71	100	26	74	100
Crafts[2]	42	58	100	29	71	100
Advanced Level						
Science[3]	22	78	100	23	77	100
Crafts[2]	58	42	100	26	74	100

Notes:
1 Science at Ordinary Level included: Physics, Chemistry, Biology, Botany, Zoology, Physics with Chemistry and General Science.
2 Craft at Ordinary and Advanced Levels included: Woodwork, Metalwork, Technical Drawing, Geometrical and Engineering Drawing.
3 Science at Advanced Level included: Physics, Chemistry, Biology, Botany and Zoology.

Source: Derived from tables 7.12 and 7.13 in R.C. Murray and R.D. Osborne, 'Educational Qualifications and Religious Affiliation' in R.J. Cormack and R.D. Osborne (eds), *Religion, Education and Employment: Aspects of Equal Opportunity in Northern Ireland* (Belfast 1983), p. 144.

of these data the authors conclude that it seems likely that these differences in subject passes are the result of a number of factors including available resources. Indeed, Murray and Osborne suggest that the voluntary schools may have been less able to secure funds to finance the more expensive facilities required for these subjects. Furthermore, such subjects require specialist teachers and, 'since fewer pupils leave the voluntary schools with the 'A' level passes that will enable them to acquire the appropriate degrees or other qualifications in science or technology, this creates a vicious circle because of the practice in Northern Ireland that both school systems are staffed almost entirely by people of the appropriate denomination, usually people who are themselves the products of the system'.[38] Furthermore, they argue that the Roman Catholic value system may result in there being less sympathy for science subjects.[39] Accordingly, the relative under-performance of Catholic pupils in craft and science subjects is in part attributed to the lack of resources in terms of buildings, specialist equipment and teachers.

In studying a co-educational Roman Catholic comprehensive school in England, Burgess examined the way in which resources were distributed between departments within the school.[40] In particular, he compared the resources that were available for academic as opposed to non-academic departments. Here he found that while academic subjects such as English, modern languages and science had specialist facilities, the Newsom department[41] for non-academic pupils had none. Indeed, there was only one classroom for Newsom work which was originally equipped for another subject and teachers often had to borrow rooms from other subject areas. Accordingly, the physical resources in terms of rooms and specialist equipment were not similar to the resources available for academic work. In this sense, Burgess maintains that the resources for Newsom teaching were not conducive for pupils to work. Indeed the headmaster of the school supported Burgess' view that the department's facilities were less good than those available in other parts of the school. In addition, the Newsom department unlike other departments had no full-time teachers as they were 'on loan' from subject departments. This was a further example of the department's lack of status and pointed to the inequality that existed between academic and non-academic areas of the curriculum in terms of the resources available.

The evidence that has been drawn upon in this section highlights the way in which resources available in local education authorities and in schools highlight basic inequalities. At the level of the local education authority, differences in provision indicate the way in which geographical location may influence patterns of attainment. Meanwhile, at the level of the school, basic provision of resources may result in differences in the education of boys and girls, academic and non-academic pupils and, in the case of Northern Ireland, Catholic and Protestant pupils. In these terms, the social context of education influences the level of educational attainment that can be achieved. The resources that are available for education, therefore, need to be considered in interpreting levels of attainment in different phases of education, the issue to which we now turn.

THE PRE-SCHOOL PHASE

For children below the age of five, organized educational provision comes from attendance at nursery schools, playgroups and day nurseries, although only nursery schools are under the direct control of the Department of Education and Science in England and Wales. Nursery education has traditionally been seen as a way of promoting equality of educational opportunity. However, it was not until the Plowden Report[42] was published on primary education that a new impetus was given to the provision of nursery schooling as the committee argued that such provision was desirable in terms of education, health and welfare. Indeed, the committee advocated that 90 per cent of four year olds and 50 per cent of three year olds should be provided with nursery schooling. In the early 1970s the White Paper *Education: A Framework for Expansion*[43] supported the Plowden view that nursery education should be provided to assist the social and educational circumstances of all young children. Indeed, it expressed a desire to see the development not only of nursery schools but also playgroups. As a result of this recommendation a modest development took place in nursery schooling so that by the late 1970s 53 per cent of all four year olds and 15 per cent of all three year olds were being educated in maintained schools. However, this was far short of the Plowden recommendations. During the 1970s the proportion of children attending nursery or primary schools, playgroups or day nurseries rose from 17 per cent to 40 per cent in 1979. The official statistics for attendance at nursery school between 1971 and 1979 for England are presented alongside data from the *General Household Survey* for Great Britain in table 2.6. Both sets of data indicate that in England and in Great Britain there was a broadly similar increase in nursery school attendance. In addition, these data can be complemented by data derived from the *General Household Survey 1979* on the proportion of under fives attending playgroups or day nurseries, as shown in table 2.7.

Table 2.6   Children Aged 2–4 Years Attending Nursery/Primary Schools, 1971–9

Year	Percentage		Base
	DES[1] England	GHS[2] Great Britain	
1971	14	10	1,826
1972	16	12	1,852
1973	18	14	1,639
1974	19	15	1,505
1975	21	18	1,551
1976	24	19	1,513
1977	24	19	1,386
1978	25	25	1,278
1979	27	21	1,156

Notes:
1 The Department of Education and Science figures are based on age at 1st January each year.
2 The *General Household Survey* figures are derived from interviews that take place throughout the year and attendance rates are based on the child's age at the time of interview.

Source: Office of Population Censuses and Surveys, *The General Household Survey 1979* (HMSO 1981), p. 104.

In Northern Ireland there were also similar moves to extend nursery education. Indeed, in 1972 the Education and Libraries Order singled out nursery education as an educational priority for it argued that those responsible for education should secure the provision of nursery schools or classes in other schools. In 1971, 18.4 per cent of children aged two to four were attending schools of some kind in Northern Ireland, while in England and Wales only 14 per cent of children attended nursery or primary schools and in Scotland only 5.1 per cent of such children attended. However, in contrast to other parts of Great Britain most of this provision was in primary schools. Indeed, Darby[44] reports that in 1973 there were only twenty-three nursery schools in the province, a situation that resulted in only 0.7 nursery school places for every one thousand of its population in comparison with Scotland that had 3.2 places. Clearly, in all parts of the UK there has been a demand for nursery school provision, which has been partly provided by local authorities which have slowly expanded nursery education, but we might ask:

Table 2.7   Proportion of Under Fives Attending Playgroups/Day Nursery in Great Britain, 1971-9

Year	Percentage	Base
1971	11	2,916
1972	13	2,927
1973	13	2,614
1974	18	2,359
1975	16	2,418
1976	16	2,341
1977	24	2,127
1978	21	1,916
1979	29	1,928

Source: Office of Population Censuses and Surveys, *The General Household Survey 1979* (HMSO 1981), p. 104.

what might be expected from such provision?

A number of commentators[45] have indicated that the expansion of nursery education might help to promote equality of educational opportunity by exposing all children to a similar environment during the day, by compensating some children for the inadequacies of their home background, by releasing all women from the care of young children for part of the day, by allowing poor and deprived women to work and by increasing the resources provided for the non-selective part of the educational system. However, to assess the extent to which nursery schools have begun to meet these expectations we have to see which children attend and what their family backgrounds are. *The General Household Survey* for 1979 reports that in Great Britain 89 per cent of four year olds were receiving day care other than by a parent, while 44 per cent attended nursery or primary school. However, the proportion receiving day care was not significantly higher among children from one parent families. Indeed, only 14 per cent of children from one parent families attended nursery school, as did 19 per cent of children whose mothers worked full-time. A further set of data on the day care of children under five from different socio-economic groups are summarized in table 2.8.

Such data point to a number of trends that cast doubt on the fact that equality has been achieved in pre-school provision. It is striking that 57 per cent of the children of professional, employers and managers groups received some kind of day care or education. Indeed, the children of these groups were more likely to attend playgroups and day nurseries than the children of the semi-skilled and unskilled manual group. Certainly, this accords with the view that playgroups are a middle-class response to the lack of nursery school places, although there is some evidence to suggest that there has been some small movement away from their middle-class origins.[46] However, Finch[47] has argued that playgroups have tended to remain middle class as there is usually a reluctance on the part of poor families to use them,[48] as they cannot cater for the childcare needs of working women[49] and because they are essentially a voluntary association with a predominantly middle-class base.[50]

However, we might ask what is being provided in nursery education. Does it confer an advantage on those children who have access to it? Blackstone[51] has indicated that there is relatively little evidence to suggest that nursery education confers academic advantage.

Table 2.8　Day Care of Children Under Five, by Type of Facility Used and Socio-economic Group of Father in Great Britain, 1979

Type of facility used	Socio-economic group of father[2]									Total	
	Professional, employers and managers		Intermediate and junior non-manual		Skilled manual and own account non-professional		Semi-skilled and unskilled manual and personal service				
	%		%		%		%			%	
Nursery or primary school	12		13		14		12			13	
Playgroup, day nursery	40		28		27		24			30	
Individual other than parent:											
other member of household	1		1		1		1			1	
relative outside household	4	9	5	8	9	12	8	13		7	11
neighbour, friend	1		2		2		4			2	
childminder	1		0		1		1			1	
other	3		0		0		0			1	
Total receiving day care	57		43		47		45			48	
Not receiving day care	43		57		53		55			52	
Base = 100%	453		332		689		363			1,837	

Notes:
1　Children in households containing more than one family with children under five have been excluded.
2　The socio-economic group of the head of household has been used where the father was not a member of the household.

Source: Office of Population Censuses and Surveys, *The General Household Survey 1979* (HMSO 1981), p. 108.

Indeed in their longitudinal study based on a national sample, Douglas and Ross[52] found that for children who had attended nursery school there was no long term advantage. While at the age of eight the nursery school children performed better than the control group, they found that by the age of eleven they had lost this advantage and by the age of fifteen they had fallen behind. However, Blackstone has argued that children do gain experience from nursery education which socializes them so that they are ready to mix with peers and adults other than their parents on joining an infant school. A study by Woodhead[53] indicates that nursery school experience results in the development of perceptual skills. However, when the performance of children from different social backgrounds was examined it was found that they all made gains, with the result that the gap between the advantaged and disadvantaged remained. Once again, a follow-up of children in the infant school indicated that initial gains were not maintained. On this basis we might consider what form the socialization process takes by examining accounts that focus on the activities in the nursery school classroom where gender socialization has been found to be a particular feature of social life.

There are relatively few accounts of what happens in classrooms with young children. Nevertheless, there has been considerable research on the influence of the toys and books that are provided in these classes.[54] Delamont[55] has commented how working class children who attend a day nursery or nursery school may get access to educational toys. However, on the basis of examining catalogues for educational toys and the toy section of two further catalogues she concludes that many of the toys and games on offer provide girls with passive, home-centred, non-scientific, non-technical roles compared with boys.

It is not merely the resources in the classroom that suggest sex differences, for Delamont[56] draws on the unpublished work by Clem Adelman in an English nursery school class to illustrate the distinctions between teacher interaction among boys and girls. In a nursery class Adelman reports the following comments directed at girls:

Teacher: What a horrid shout. Look pretty, don't shout. Who are you?
Girl: I am Norah, of course.
Later,
Girl: I am going to sit near you.
Teacher: Oh lovely, I would love you to sit by me. Would you like this . . .?
Girl: No thank you.
Teacher: You are just so beautiful. What do you do Jane?
Girl: I just do the housework.
Teacher: What sort of work?
Girl: Help clear up.[57]

In turn, Delamont reports how girls were also praised for their hair, clothes and names, while no similar comments were made to boys in the data Adelman collected. Such data might lead us to conclude that if nothing else, attendance at nursery school does socialize children into the sex differentiated world that they will encounter throughout their school careers.

THE PRIMARY SCHOOL PHASE

When introducing a survey of curricular differences for boys and girls the Department of Education and Science remark that in the primary school, although 'there is virtually no distinction made between boys and girls in the time-tabling of nursery and infant schools and classes, nevertheless boys and girls do behave differently . . . and are expected to behave differently.'[58] Indeed, some of the distinctions that have been noted in nursery schools are further reinforced through the socialization process that occurs among girls and boys in infant and junior schools. Some organizational procedures, such as the division of classes into single sex work groups and the division of names by sex on the school register, reinforce social divisions based on sex in the contemporary primary school classroom. However, there are further clues to sexual divisions both in terms of implicit and explicit aspects of school organization.

Within primary schools the majority of teachers are female. Indeed, table 2.9 indicates that women constituted 76 per cent of the teaching force of primary schools in England and Wales in 1980, but that more men became headteachers. Only 42 per cent of the available headships in primary schools in England and Wales in 1980 were held by women and only 6.4 per cent of women primary school teachers were heads. In contrast, men held 58 per cent of headships and 30 per cent of male teachers in primary schools were heads. Furthermore, although women were more likely to hold other positions of responsibility within primary schools, it was men who held a greater proportion of posts from Scale 3 upwards in relation to their numbers. Despite the predominance of women over men in primary schools in terms of numbers, it is men who have the most powerful positions. Accordingly, women who teach in primary schools are less likely to be appointed as headteachers than their male colleagues.[59]

Table 2.9   Full-time Teachers in Maintained Primary Schools in England and Wales: Grade Analysed by Sex, March 1980

	Men	Women
Headteachers	13,309	9,635
Deputy headteachers	7,784	11,932
Second masters/mistresses	208	371
Senior teachers	12	7
Scale 4	100	89
Scale 3	4,970	10,045
Scale 2	13,079	61,688
Scale 1	5,496	55,850
Total	44,958	149,617

Source: Department of Education and Science, *Statistics of Teachers in Service in England and Wales 1980* (HMSO 1980).

The distinctions between men and women and boys and girls in everyday life are further reinforced through the primary school curriculum. For example, King reports a discussion between a teacher and her class on the topic of 'christening' which results in the teacher reinforcing the notion of gender differentiation when a girl volunteers some information:

Teacher: Now Karina?

Karina: When you sometimes you got to a christening you can see which is a boy and a girl cause a girl has long dress and a boy has a short dress.

Teacher: Either a short dress or a little short suit. What colour do we say for a boy as a rule?

Pupil: White.

Pupil: Blue.

Teacher: Blue for a boy and what for a girl?

Pupils: White.

Pupil: Green! Green!

Teacher: White or?

Pupils: Pink.

Teacher: Pink! Pink! That's right.[60]

In these circumstances, it is the teacher who directs the pupils' comments in the area of gender differentiation and reinforces 'correct' answers while ignoring those answers that are judged to be incorrect.

However, it is not merely discussions which occur in primary school classrooms that have the potential to transmit messages about sex, race and social class within our society. For example, King discusses the ways in which socially approved worlds are introduced to pupils through the reading materials that are available. Indeed, King's analysis of the *Ladybird* series used in many infant schools in the UK notes how the central characters, Peter and Jane, engage in socially approved behaviour which is moderately adventurous but not dangerous. Furthermore, the characters engage in teacher approved activities outside school where they are supported by adults who adopt a middle-class life style. Similarly, King found that the *Gay-Way* series also used to introduce pupils to reading in the infant school transmits similar messages. Such an account supports Lobban's[61] analysis of six reading schemes that were widely used in Britain. She found that the texts presented pupils with a world in which the sexes were consistently different and where women occupied inferior positions in terms of social status. Her analysis also indicated that men were often the central characters and were given a greater range of roles, while women and girls were often placed in roles within the home as the wider world was preserved as a male domain. On the basis of this evidence Lobban concluded that these reading schemes reinforced traditional sex stereotyping where women were seen in domestic roles, while men were dominant and decisive and engaged in active roles. The result is that such curriculum materials transmit a picture of a gender differentiated world into which pupils are socialized.

A further area of the basic primary school curriculum that transmits a variety of hidden messages to its pupils is mathematics. As Hilary Burgess[62] demonstrates, it is usual for teachers to rely on a textbook or series of textbooks to transmit this area of the primary curriculum. One of the most widely used series of mathematics textbooks in UK[63] primary schools is the series entitled *Mathematics for Schools*[64] which is commonly known to the pupils and teachers as 'Fletcher Mathematics'. However, as Hilary Burgess reveals, the Fletcher scheme which can be used throughout the primary school does not merely transmit knowledge about mathematics. Her analysis of the pupils' books reveals that men were frequently depicted as occupation-holders while women (other than teachers) were portrayed as housewives and mothers. Indeed, in the series of seven infant school books and ten junior school books she found only one woman (apart from teachers) as an occupation-holder, in a scene in which she was portrayed as a waitress. However, Burgess argues that it is not only the illustrations that emphasize a stereotypical role; she demonstrates how the authors' mathematical problems, examples and comments also reinforce views about men and women. For example, she shows how in questions about shopping in a supermarket, pupils were asked why more men shopped between 1.00pm and 2.00pm and why fewer women shopped then than at any other time. She points out how the authors comment that 'men are most likely to shop during the lunch-break'. Such evidence highlights the fact that sex stereotyping is also a part of the mathematics curriculum.

In turn, Hilary Burgess indicates how this well-known mathematics scheme also transmits certain messages about race. She remarks:

> Fletcher mathematics is also lacking in representation of different ethnic groups, for while a very few children have names such as Delroy, Mario, Cy and Rashid, who are representative of children from different cultures, the illustrations lack a similar representativeness. Here, not a single adult represented in the series, male or female, could be described as belonging to a culture other than English. For an Asian, West Indian or any other child belonging to different ethnic groups, what message is being given concerning their future adult role?[65]

On this basis we need to consider the extent to which curriculum materials may successfully transmit images of society and in so doing, socialize pupils into a highly differentiated world regardless of their teachers' expectations.

Similar evidence on the content of the mathematics curriculum has been noted by Weiner, and by Walden and Walkerdine,[66] with the result that Weiner considers that sexist textbook materials may be a factor affecting the attitude and performance of girls in mathematics. There are now a number of surveys comparing the performance of boys and girls, not only in mathematics but across the whole of the primary school curriculum. Traditionally, much was written (in the days when the eleven plus examination was commonly used by local education authorities for secondary school selection about the differences in the eleven plus scores of boys and girls. The girls' scores were often so much higher than those for boys in English, mathematics and IQ tests that the sexes were assigned different 'pass' marks. The result was that girls had to achieve higher marks than boys to obtain a grammar school place. Yates and Pidgeon, for example, argued that girls performed better due to physical maturation and therefore different pass marks had to be used, otherwise:

> If the pass marks are made equivalent for the two sexes the number of girls admitted to grammar schools will, in most areas, substantially exceed the number of boys. In view of the fact that these differences exist at the age of eleven and that there is considerable uncertainty as to when and to what extent they eventually disappear, the most satisfactory course . . . to adopt would seem to be to treat boys and girls separately for the purpose of allocation to secondary school.[67]

In these terms, the good performance of girls was explained away by two of the most influential designers of educational tests.

Similar trends in the performance of girls compared with boys in primary schools in Britain are provided by Douglas in a national survey of academic ability and attainment in primary school.[68] The tests that were used showed that girls were slightly superior to boys at the age of eight and eleven years in each social class. However, the middle-class boys improved between the ages of eight and eleven with the result that they had nearly caught up the girls by the age of eleven, while boys from the manual working class were as far behind the girls at eleven as they were at eight. Douglas found that reading and vocabulary tests were the only valid basis for comparing changes in achievement by boys and girls during the primary school years. The girls had higher scores at the age of eight and eleven, although at eleven these were less marked. Furthermore, on the basis of teachers' judgements more boys were outstandingly bad at reading and fewer were outstandingly good. Finally, Douglas shows how girls got more grammar school places than boys.

Some of Douglas' results, especially on reading ability, have been repeated in subsequent surveys. In the survey of primary schools in England by Her Majesty's Inspectors[69] tests were given to over 5,000 primary school children. On the BD reading test, it was found that girls obtained a higher mean score than the boys which was statistically significant. Meanwhile, in Scotland a study by Maxwell[70] with 2,500 pupils in Scottish primary schools produced similar results, as at the age of nine it was found that girls had a higher level of reading and language attainment than boys, although this was not the case at the age of eleven.

While distinctions can be made between boys and girls in reading and language, there is not such a clear-cut difference between the sexes concerning mathematical ability. The data obtained by Douglas[71] show that girls had higher average scores than boys in an arithmetic test at the age of eleven, although middle-class boys surpassed the performance of middle-class girls, while manual working-class boys were below manual working-class girls. Meanwhile, in the primary school survey from the Inspectorate it is reported that in the mathematics test (age corrected to 11 years 2.5 months) 'there was no statistically significant difference in the total scores achieved by boys and girls'.[72] However, data from the Assessment of Performance Unit (APU) primary mathematics survey have been able to discriminate between the types of mathematical exercises at which boys and girls succeed. The APU found that girls tended to perform better at computation tasks, while boys do slightly, but not significantly, better in other subcategories: length, volume and capacity, rate and ratio.[73] Thus, by the end of primary school there is no significant difference between boys and girls. We might ask, however: how do race and social class influence primary school performance?

As Alan Little[74] has indicated, there are only a limited number of studies that provide data on the comparative performance of white and black children. Using data from surveys conducted by the ILEA, Little reports that by the end of their primary schooling, the children of New Commonwealth immigrants in the ILEA have been found to have a reading age one year below the national norm for their age group. At the end of primary schooling ILEA pupils were banded into three groups (top 25 per cent, middle 50 per cent, bottom 25 per cent) on verbal reasoning, English and mathematics. He reports that the percentage of immigrant pupils fully educated in the UK who were placed in the upper quartile were as shown in table 2.10 during the years 1966, 1968 and 1971.

On the basis of these data, Little indicates that the percentage of immigrant children in the upper band is half what should be expected and half what indigenous children achieve. However, on the basis of evidence on children from different ethnic backgrounds who are placed in the upper bands and who were fully educated in the UK, he shows that Asians who have completed all their primary education in the UK appear to do as well as the indigenous population in the ILEA (see table 2.11).

Table 2.10   Percentage of Immigrant Pupils Fully Educated in the UK Placed in the Upper Band on Transfer to Secondary School in the ILEA, 1966–71

	Verbal reasoning	English	Mathematics
1966	12	13	14
1968	10	12	12
1971	13	12	12

Source: A. Little, 'Education and Race Relations in the United Kingdom' in J. Megarry, S. Nisbet and E. Hoyle (eds), *World Yearbook of Education* (1981), p. 136.

Table 2.11   Percentage of Pupils Fully Educated in the UK Placed in the Upper Band on Transfer to ILEA Secondary School in 1968

	Verbal reasoning	English	Mathematics
West Indian origin	7.2	9.2	7.4
Asian origin	21.1	19.3	20.2
Indigenous	19.8	25.0	22.9

Source: *Ibid.*

West Indians, however, not only under-perform in relation to the indigenous population, but also below social disadvantaged sections; a finding that has been substantiated by other investigators. For example, in the Educational Priority Study in the ILEA[75] Barnes reports on the gap in performance between black pupils and socially disadvantaged whites when comparing performances in the English Picture vocabulary test at levels 1 and 2 (in the infant and junior schools). He found that pupils in the Educational Priority Area performed five points below the national norm at the infant level and nine points below the national norm at junior level; secondly, that West Indians performed thirteen points below the national norm at infant level and fifteen points at junior level. Such evidence points to the underperformance of black pupils in English primary schools which has been substantiated in other studies.[76] However, underperformance in the primary school does not just occur among pupils from different ethnic groups, but also among pupils from different social classes.

The evidence available on social class and educational attainment in the primary school has traditionally focused on the results in the eleven plus examination. However, the National Child Development Study by Davie, Butler and Goldstein[77] has examined different levels of attainment among infant and junior age children in Great Britain in reading and arithmetic. The test scores by parents' social class are shown in table 2.12. These data show the relationship between social class and attainment at the age of seven and point to the differences in reading ability between social class I and social class V, whereby a child from social class V was six times as likely to be a poor reader as a child from social class I. In particular, social classes I and V are distinguished from the other middle and working classes respectively. The lowest percentage of poor readers were in social class I and the highest percentage of pupils with poor scores were in social class V; both being trends that hold implications for subsequent school performance.

Table 2.12 Reading and Arithmetic Attainment Test Scores of Seven-year-old Children by Father's Social Class in Great Britain (percentages)

| | Registrar General's Social Class | | | | | | |
	I	II	III(N)	III(M)	IV	V	ALL
Grouped Southgate Reading test scores							
0 – 20	8	15	14	30	37	48	29
21 – 28	37	39	43	41	38	34	39
29 – 30	54	47	43	29	25	17	32
Grouped problem Arithmetic test scores							
0 – 3	12	19	19	30	34	41	29
4 – 6	38	39	43	42	42	37	41
7 – 10	50	42	38	28	24	22	31
N = 15,496							

Notes: Whole sample included those without father or social class information.

Based on data derived from tables A165 and A168 in R. Davie, M. Butler and H. Goldstein, *From Birth to Seven* (London 1972).

Source: I. Reid, *Social Class Differences in Britain*, 2nd edn, (London 1981), p. 215.

Further data on how the differences in attainment between the social classes develop in the primary school can be derived for Great Britain from the longitudinal studies by Douglas[78] on a cohort of children born in 1946 and from Davie, Butler and Goldstein's study.[79] In Douglas' study pupils were tested on intelligence, reading, vocabulary and sentence completion tests at the age of eight and similar tests, including arithmetic, at the age of eleven. As table 2.13 indicates, at each age there is a gradient in test scores according to social class. In addition, there is a greater increase in test scores for the middle class as opposed to the manual working class in the junior school years.

These results were also substantiated by Davie, Butler and Goldstein in their study. They found that at the age of eleven children whose fathers were in non-manual occupations were about one year ahead of those in social classes III manual and IV, who

Table 2.13　Average Test Scores of Children in Each Social Class at the Ages of Eight and Eleven Years

	Social Class			
	Upper Middle	Lower Middle	Upper Manual Working Class	Lower Manual Working Class
Eight year tests				
Picture intelligence	56.13	52.73	50.17	48.82
Reading	56.74	53.45	49.86	47.80
Vocabulary	58.33	53.88	50.19	47.63
Sentence completion	57.30	53.79	49.83	48.02
Eleven year tests				
Non-verbal ability	57.03	54.31	50.25	47.99
Verbal ability	57.43	54.32	50.12	47.78
Reading	57.54	54.01	49.89	47.52
Vocabulary	59.18	54.81	50.33	47.36
Arithmetic	57.18	54.43	49.86	47.30

Note: Douglas' definitions of social class categories are as follows:
Upper Middle Class
　The father is a non-manual worker, and
　a) both parents went to secondary school and were brought up in middle-class families, or
　b) both parents went to secondary school and one parent was brought up in a middle-class family, or
　c) both parents were brought up in middle-class families and one parent went to secondary school.
Lower Middle Class
　The rest of the non-manual workers' families.
Upper Manual Working Class
　The father is a manual worker and
　either the father or mother or both of them had a secondary school education, and/or one or both of them were brought up in a middle-class family.
Lower Manual Working Class
　The father is a manual worker, and
　both the father and the mother had elementary schooling only, and both the father and the mother were brought up in manual working class families.

Source: J. W. B. Douglas, *The Home and the School* (London 1964), p. 185.

in turn were 0.4 years ahead of social class V. They report that these differences were in addition to those found at the age of seven (see table 2.12) with the result that the overall differences at the age of eleven were 1.9 years for the non-manual child and 1.1 years for the manual child in terms of reading ability. Meanwhile, in arithmetic they found that the average difference was 1.1 years between the non-manual child and the child from social classes III manual and IV and 6.6 years between the latter and social class V.

The results indicate that there are considerable differences between pupils based on social class and that this is increased by modes of school organization such as streaming.[80] However, it is now relatively rare to find rigid streaming in the primary school.

Indeed, the primary school survey for England,[81] conducted between 1975 and 1977, found that only 3 per cent of classes for seven year olds, 10 per cent of classes for nine year olds and 17 per cent of classes for eleven year olds were streamed by ability. Accordingly, the question arises about the extent to which school organization affects social class differences in achievement. The research by Barker Lunn indicates how teachers over-estimate the ability of pupils from social classes I, II and III and under-estimate the ability of pupils from classes IV and V. This suggests that the pattern of social differentiation which occurs in the primary school will continue even with less structured modes of school organization and, as Nash has shown,[82] pupils will continue to be aware of their positions and their status in the primary school classroom.

The data that have been reviewed on primary schools have focused on the way in which schools differentiate their pupils according to sex, race and social class at the same time as transmitting the basic curriculum. The evidence shows a consistent tendency for pupils within particular social categories to perform less well than others. Such circumstances call for an explanation from social and educational researchers. Among sociologists much work has been done on this area of study, focusing upon factors associated with the family, the child and the schools. Indeed, Mortimore and Blackstone[83] have subdivided the factors involved in disadvantage and under-attainment into home-based factors, including family size, health and housing; cultural factors, including language and parental attitudes; and school factors, such as the extent to which teacher expectations operate as a self-fulfilling prophecy in the treatment of pupils in the classroom.[84] Here, we might consider the extent to which the trends that have been identified, together with their underlying processes, continue as pupils move into secondary education.

THE SECONDARY SCHOOL PHASE

The last twenty years have witnessed considerable changes in state secondary education as local authorities have adopted a comprehensive mode of school organization. The pattern of secondary school organization is reflected in table 2.14 which shows that the percentage of pupils attending comprehensive schools in England in 1965-66 was only 8.9 per cent. This rose to 34.4 per cent in 1970-71, doubling to 68.8 per cent in 1975-76, after which it climbed steadily to 81.4 per cent in 1979-80. Similar trends are to be found in Wales and Scotland although in both countries there has been a greater move towards an all-embracing comprehensive system. Meanwhile, Northern Ireland shows a consistent pattern in terms of retaining the selective system through a strong grammar school lobby and a strong voluntary sector.

With the development of the comprehensive system there has been a corresponding increase in the size of schools. As Baron notes,[85] no longer does the traditional English secondary school consist of 400 pupils with twenty or so teachers, as shown in table 2.15. With the growth of large schools many authorities have set about attempting to break down the number of pupils in these schools into smaller, more manageable units. Among the approaches that have been used are the division of schools into lower, middle and upper sections as a means of decentralization and a house and departmental system to subdivide the pastoral and academic activities of these schools.[86] Whatever the

Table 2.14　Pupils in Public Sector Secondary Education by School Type and Country 1965-6 to 1979-80

	1965-6		1970-1		1975-6		1977-8		1978-9		1979-80	
	000s	%	000s	%	000s	%	000s	%	000s	%	000s	%
England												
Maintained secondary schools												
Middle deemed secondary	–		55	1.9	223	6.0	258	6.7	266	6.9	267	6.9
Modern	1,454	55.1	1,121	38.0	574	15.5	386	10.0	328	8.5	262	6.8
Grammar	660	25.0	544	18.4	285	7.7	196	5.1	163	4.2	143	3.7
Technical	73	2.8	38	1.3	15	0.4	12	0.3	12	0.3	11	0.3
Comprehensive	262	9.9	1,017	34.4	2,544	68.8	2,956	76.8	3,062	79.1	3,147	81.4
Other	189	7.2	178	6.0	60	1.6	44	1.1	41	1.1	37	1.0
Total pupils	2,639	100.0	2,953	100.0	3,700	100.0	3,851	100.0	3,872	100.0	3,866	100.0
Wales												
Maintained secondary schools												
Middle deemed secondary	–		–	0.1	–		–		–		–	
Modern	70	39.3	43	22.3	16	6.8	11	4.5	5	2.2	6	2.7
Grammar	53	29.5	29	15.4	10	4.3	8	3.2	4	1.5	4	1.5
Comprehensive	50	28.3	112	58.5	208	88.5	222	92.0	232	96.0	230	95.5
Other	5	2.7	7	3.7	1	0.4	1	0.3	1	0.3	1	0.2
Technical	–	0.2	–		–		–		–		–	
Total pupils	178	100.0	191	100.0	235	100.0	242	100.0	242	100.0	241	100.0
Scotland												
Public sector secondary schools												
Selective	–		89	28.3	4	1.1	1	0.2	1	0.2	1	0.1
Comprehensive	–		184	58.7	349	87.6	376	92.5	385	93.8	394	96.1
Part Comprehensive/Part Selective	–		41	13.0	45	11.3	29	7.3	25	6.0	15	3.7
Total pupils	271		314	100.0	398	100.0	406	100.0	410	100.0	410	100.0

Northern Ireland
Public sector secondary schools

	1965-6		1970-1		1975-6		1977-8		1978-9		1979-80	
	000s	%	000s	%	000s	%	000s	%	000s	%	000s	%
Secondary intermediate	37	73.5	84	87.7	103	89.3	106	89.2	106	89.0	106	88.7
Grammar	10	20.0	11	11.8	12	10.7	13	10.8	13	11.0	13	11.3
Technical intermediate	3	6.5	–	0.5	–	–	–	–	–	–	–	–
Total pupils	*51*	*100.0*	*96*	*100.0*	*115*	*100.0*	*118*	*100.0*	*119*	*100.0*	*119*	*100.0*

Source: Department of Education and Science, *Education Statistics for the United Kingdom 1982 Edition* (HMSO 1982), p. 12.

Table 2.15 Size of Secondary Schools in the UK, 1979-80

	Size of Pupil Population											
	25 and under	26 to 50	51 to 100	101 to 200	201 to 300	301 to 400	401 to 600	601 to 800	801 to 1000	1001 to 1500	1501 and over	Total
Number of Schools	9	11	29	87	211	375	1046	1026	986	1438	353	5571

Source: Derived from Table 8, Department of Education and Science, *Education Statistics for the United Kingdom 1982 Edition* (HMSO 1982), p. 10.

approach, large numbers of teachers have been required, many of whom have been paid additional allowances for their responsibilities within the school system. The numbers of teachers employed in state secondary schools in England and Wales in 1980, together with their grade and sex, are shown in table 2.16.

Table 2.16　　Full-time Teachers in Maintained Secondary Schools in England and Wales: Grade Analysed by Sex, March 1980

	Men	Women
Headteachers	4,310	838
Deputy headteachers	5,387	2,465
Second masters/ mistresses	1,201	1,849
Senior teachers	5,311	1,216
Scale 4	22,140	6,270
Scale 3	33,979	19,399
Scale 2	33,585	31,426
Scale 1	29,417	47,213
Total	*135,330*	*110,676*

Source: Department of Education and Science, *Statistics of Teachers in Service in England and Wales* (HMSO 1980).

As in primary schools we find that men are proportionately more likely to hold senior posts. For although women represented 45 per cent of the secondary school teachers they only held 16 per cent of the secondary school headships. Indeed it is noticeable that women are under-represented in all senior secondary school positions above scale 3. This could be partly a reflection of the fact that women do not apply for senior posts in large numbers or, as a recent Equal Opportunities Commission (EOC) report indicated, when they do the selection procedures favour men.[87] The result is that not only are women's career prospects less in comparison with men, but so are their financial rewards (see table 2.17).

Table 2.17　　Full-time Secondary School Teachers in the UK: Sex and Average Salary, 1979–80

	Total teachers	Average salary
Male	155,000	£6,604
Female	127,000	£5,784

Note: The data on average salary exclude Scotland.

Source: Department of Education and Science, *Education Statistics for the United Kingdom 1982 Edition* (HMSO 1982), derived from table 20, p. 21.

As well as financial disadvantage, Byrne has argued that there is a further disadvantage to women being absent from senior positions in schools. She states that:

It is crucial that both girls and boys actually *see* women in leadership, management, government, making decisions in their daily lives, if we are to break the cycle of under-achievement. As long as children see men taking the top posts, decisions, and higher pay . . . children will believe what they see . . .[88]

However, the bulk of the evidence still points to differentiation among male and female staff in state secondary schools.

A more widespread trend that has been noted is the way in which schools differentiate their pupils. Sociologists have not only collected statistical data on these trends, but have also obtained detailed observations from pupils and former pupils. For many pupils external examinations are a key feature and a key problem in secondary schools:

The problem is that schools still need to concentrate on exams, because paper qualifications still count for something. (Geoff Clark, aged 18, Bodmin, Cornwall)

I hate the idea of exams but that's the only way you can get by. You have to play with the system. You don't have to agree with it, but you have to accept it a bit. If you rebel against it all the time you won't get anywhere and all you'll do is damage yourself. It won't change *them*. (Jo Chadwick, aged 17, Callington, Cornwall)

Half of us were clever and half of us weren't. At first I wanted to be clever and I used to listen to the teacher; but as time went on I used to sit further towards the back to be with my friends. (Catherine Crowe, aged 17, Warley, West Midlands)

Each of these statements recorded by White and Brockington[89] highlights a consumer's view of education, a view that emphasizes the way in which differentiation by examination is a crucial process in secondary schooling. It was Lacey,[90] in a study of a northern grammar school, who indicated the importance of differentiation and polarization. By differentiation he referred to the process by which students are ranked according to criteria that make up the academically oriented value system of the grammar school, while polarization was the process by which the school dominated culture is opposed by an anti-group. Similar kinds of processes have been identified by Hargreaves in a secondary modern school[91] and by Ball who found that there was a process of academic and behavioural differentiation among band one pupils in a comprehensive school.[92]

The process by which pupils are differentiated is also highlighted in studies that discuss aspects of the curriculum. For example, Keddie's[93] study of the way in which teachers attribute differences to A, B, and C stream pupils in a comprehensive school results in fourth year pupils being given access to different kinds of subject knowledge. She found that the curriculum materials that were provided for A stream pupils were intellectual' and 'abstract', while for C stream pupils, lessons were composed of 'real' material based on 'stories'. The result was that pupils were given differential access to curriculum knowledge; a situation that holds implications for opportunities in public examinations and post-school opportunities.

This point has been made by school leavers in studies by Hargreaves, Woods, Furlong, Corrigan and Burgess.[94] While several of these accounts (by Hargreaves and by Woods) are with secondary modern pupils, the study by Burgess deals with an urban co-educational

Roman Catholic comprehensive school. In each case pupils report that their school work (especially in the fourth and fifth year) is dull, repetitive and boring, where 'nothing' is learned. However as Burgess' informants indicate, the main point of comparison is not between different kinds of knowledge but between examination and non-examination work. Burgess' study involved an analysis of the Newsom department for pupils who were regarded as the 'less willing' and 'less able' members of the fourth and fifth year. Here, he found that the curriculum which the teachers constructed was an alternative to that provided in subject departments. Projects, practical work and relatively little written work was the routine adopted. While the teachers saw the courses they provided in first aid, mothercraft and home economics as real teaching, the pupils had other views. Burgess reports the views of two girls, Jenny and Sarah, in the following terms:

> *Jenny:*   We just go in and they [the teachers] just don't seem to care about anything. We can do what we like and when I can do just what I like, I don't like it. When we leave school people are going to be asking what we learnt in the last year. Gonna have to tell them we never did nothing really. You know things like first aid, mothercare, home economics. We can't really say we did a lot 'cos we never.

These remarks were echoed by many pupils who saw that the course with which they were provided involved little work. They were just passing time by 'doing nothing'. The position was summed up by Sarah when she remarked:

> People say to us 'Why are you so dull?' and we say 'Yes we're so dull because we don't learn anything, *we don't even take exams and things*' [my emphasis]. All Newsom is for is the dumb people who are thick.

Here, Newsom work was defined as 'doing nothing'. It was a course where pupils claimed they did not learn anything and where they had no opportunity to take examinations. The Newsom pupils made comparisons between 'proper' subjects such as history and geography that, in their terms, involved learning and examination work, and the Newsom course that was seen in adverse terms. These views were summed up in a conversation between Burgess and two pupils who claimed to be doing nothing at school.

> *R.B.:*   You do nothing?
> *Terry:*   No, not much.
> *R.B.:*   Surely you do something?
> *Terry:*   No just sit around and do woodcarving. I also do art but well art's taking a CSE.
> *Malcolm:* Well you done a lot in Newsom in the fourth year didn't you? Cooking and woodwork and metalwork.
> *Terry:*   I didn't do metalwork, I got chucked out. I don't reckon much to Newsom but the rest of the school is all right. If you're taking an 'O' level course it's all right. The teachers are pretty good then but when you're in Newsom it's just a mess around. It's a wasted two years.
> *R.B.:*   Why is it a wasted two years?
> *Terry:*   Because I'm achieving nothing am I? You come to school to achieve something like the kids trying to get their 'O' levels and their CSEs while we are just sitting around watching the world go by.

These remarks highlight the significance that is attached to examination work in the secondary school even by pupils who are outside such arrangements. Indeed, learning, achievement and 'good' teachers were all equated with examination work. In turn, these comparisons point towards basic inequalities that exist in the school curriculum where some pupils can and others cannot follow subjects for examinations. However, we might consider questions relating to the access that pupils have to curriculum subjects in secondary schools, and comparisons in examination performances by sex, race and class, given the central importance that is attached to subjects and examinations in the secondary school curriculum.

Nominally all subjects in the secondary school curriculum are available to pupils regardless of their sex. However, the HMI survey on secondary education in England[95] reported in 1979 that the opportunities to study craft subjects and science subjects were different for boys and girls. In craft subjects it was found that differentiation involved woodwork and/or metalwork for boys and home economics and/or needlework for girls. As table 2.18 indicates, this division existed in 19 per cent of the mixed schools included in the sample of 365 schools that were studied, while in 20 per cent of the schools such divisions operated but were not prescribed. Overall, differentiation in craft subjects occurred in practice in over 65 per cent of the 365 schools.

Similarly, in the case of science subjects the survey findings revealed differences in terms of the number of science subjects followed by boys and girls (table 2.19) and the science subjects studied (table 2.20). These data show that girls do substantially less science than boys, a trend that has also been confirmed by Kelly in examining data for Scotland.[96] However, there are differences, not just in the number of science courses but also in the particular subjects followed.

The main trends indicate that more boys than girls take physics, while more girls than boys take biology. This pattern has been identified by Kelly and her colleagues[97] concerning the importance of distinguishing between biology and the physical sciences, and reflects the evidence in the DES survey on curricular differences between boys and girls[98] where it was found that, despite 70 per cent of the girls in the fourth and fifth year having an opportunity to study physics in these years, only 17 per cent actually took the subject. The question that sociologists and educational researchers have addressed is why these patterns occur[99] and the extent to which they need to be kept in mind when interpreting examination results.

In 1979–80 just over one in four seventeen year olds had obtained at least five 'O' levels (or their equivalent) at school, while one in six left school with at least one 'A' level (or the equivalent for Scotland). The basic attainments of school leavers are summarized in table 2.21 which shows an increase in the numbers of children obtaining GCE ordinary level or its equivalent in the 1970s. This pattern may, in part, be attributed to the policy decision to raise the school leaving age to sixteen in 1972.[100] However, against such data a number of key questions need to be posed about the proportions of boys and girls and pupils from different socio-economic groups who succeed in public examinations.

Table 2.22 allows us to examine the trends that occur in subject areas. There is a tendency for girls to be more widely represented in arts and social science subjects, while boys are more involved with mathematical, scientific and technical subjects. Indeed, they are caught up in a vicious spiral as the trends that are marked out at 'O' level are

Table 2.18   Differentiation by Sex in Craft Subjects by Type of School (England)

| | Number of schools | | | | All schools | |
| | Type of school | | | | | |
Type of differentiation	Modern	Grammar	FR[1] Comprehensive	RR[2] Comprehensive	Nos.	Percentages
Prescribed by sex in mixed schools	28	5	28	8	69	19
Operating but not prescribed	31	2	31	10	74	20
Single sex schools	29	38	18	10	95	26
Wholly open choice	33	7	71	16	127	35
Totals	121	52	148	44	365	100

Notes:
1   Full ability range comprehensive.
2   Restricted ability range comprehensive.

Source: Department of Education and Science, *Aspects of Secondary Education in England* (HMSO 1979), p. 15.

Table 2.19 Numbers of Science Subjects Studied by Boys and Girls in Secondary Schools in the Fourth and Fifth Years in England

	Percentage of pupils	
	Boys	Girls
Year 4		
No. of subjects studied		
0	9	16
1	49	60
2	32	19
3 or more	10	5
Year 5		
No. of subjects studied		
0	9	18
1	50	60
2	31	18
3 or more	10	4

Note: Data are based on 204 schools.

Source: Department of Education and Science, *Aspects of Secondary Education in England* (HMSO 1979), derived from table 8a, p. 166.

Table 2.20 Science Subjects Studied by Boys and Girls in Secondary Schools in the Fourth and Fifth Years in England

	Percentage of pupils	
	Boys	Girls
Year 4		
Physics	51	13
Chemistry	31	19
Biology	32	60
Integrated and General Science	21	15
Other science	7	4
Year 5		
Physics	48	10
Chemistry	29	16
Biology	31	58
Integrated and General Science	23	15
Other science	7	4

Source: Department of Education and Science, *Aspects of Secondary Education in England* (HMSO 1979), derived from table 8b, p. 167.

Table 2.21 Attainments of School Leavers as a Percentage of the Relevant Population[1] in the UK, 1970–1 and 1979–80

Percentages

	1970–1			1979–80		
	Boys	Girls	Total	Boys	Girls	Total
As a percentage of the relevant population[1]						
17 years at 31 August						
1 or more GCE 'A' level or equivalent[2]	18	15	17	17	17	17
5 or more A to C awards[3] at GCE 'O' level or equivalent[4]	6	8	7	8	10	9
15 years at 31 August						
GCE 'O' level or equivalent:						
1 to 4 A to C awards[4]	16	17	17	24	28	26
1 or more D to E awards[5]	11	9	10	32	30	31
No GCE/SCE qualifications	44	44	44	16	13	14

Notes:
1 Based on population aged 17 for 5 or more 'O' levels and above, and aged 15 for other qualification levels.
2 Including Scottish equivalent – SCE 'H' grade.
3 Including Scottish equivalent – SCE 'O' grade.
4 Equivalent to standard of a former pass and including CSE grade 1 passes.
5 Including CSE 2 to 5 grades.

Source: Department of Education and Science, *Education Statistics for the United Kingdom 1982 Edition* (HMSO 1982), p. iv.

Table 2.22   GCE 'O' Level Passes (A to C Grades Only) and GCE 'A' Level Passes by Sex and Selected Subjects (Summer Examinations) in England and Wales, 1979

	'O' Level		'A' Level	
	Boys	Girls	Boys	Girls
Technical Drawing	27,670	761	2,162	39
Physics	79,046	26,309	30,899	7,187
Computer Science	5,784	2,185	1,196	287
Chemistry	56,337	31,621	23,420	10,561
Economics	15,502	9,407	19,350	8.744
Mathematics	108,140	75,091	29,107	9,516
Geography	64,578	48,449	15,073	10,561
History	43,124	44,708	13,990	14,236
Biology	50,456	74,272	13,553	15,272
French	40,746	61,258	7,141	13,572
German	12,040	18,628	2,270	4,704
English Literature	63,940	103,779	14,604	33,651
Sociology	5,197	15,913	1,996	5,605
Domestic subjects	608	33,063	21	3,977
English Language	126,410	171,668	–	–

Based upon Department of Education and Science, *Statistics of Education, Volume 2 School Leavers* (HMSO 1979), tables 28 and 29 and figures supplied by the Welsh Office for Wales.

Source: Equal Opportunities Commission, *Gender and the Secondary School Curriculum* (Manchester 1982), derived from figures 2.1 and 2.2 in the statistical appendix

reinforced at 'A' level, all of which are factors that will influence the post-school destinations of school leavers and the jobs that they may follow.

The data that are available for Northern Ireland (tables 2.23 and 2.24) confirm a similar trend. However, there is a further difference here between Catholic and Protestant pupils. As Murray and Osborne suggest,[101] stereotyping may be more widespread in Catholic than Protestant schools given the value systems that are related to the Catholic faith.

While these data on secondary school examinations tell us something of the differences between the sexes, they are only part of the story. What, for example, are the experiences of black pupils in public examinations? An ethnographic study by Mary Fuller[102] of black girls in a London comprehensive school reports that there is little evidence on the way in which sex and race may influence academic achievement. In addition, evidence is only available from a number of small-scale studies at school level or with one or more local education authorities.[103] For example, Fuller's work indicates that the black girls whom she studied were aware of a double subordination through being women and through being black. The girls she studied were determined not to accept the 'facts' of subordination as, for them, acquiring qualifications was perceived as an important part of schooling. However, there are different patterns of achievement for Asians and West

Table 2.23 Subject Distribution of 'O' Level Passes, all Schools, all Boards Northern Ireland, 1971 and 1975 (per cent)

Subject grouping	1971				1975			
	Roman Catholic		Protestant		Roman Catholic		Protestant	
	Boys	Girls	Boys	Girls	Boys	Girls	Boys	Girls
English Language and Literature	23	30	22	26	21	27	22	27
Languages (Latin, Greek, French, German, Irish, Russian, Spanish & Italian)	22	26	10	17	19	20	9	16
Mathematics, (Mathematics, Additional Mathematics, Pure Mathematics)	19	12	21	15	18	11	20	14
Science (General Science, Physics, Chemistry, Biology, Physics with Chemistry, Botany, Zoology)	14	6	21	12	14	8	22	13
History/Geography (History, Economic History, Ancient History, Geography)	12	13	15	16	14	12	16	16
Art/Music/Religious Education	3	6	5	6	9	14	5	7
Crafts (Woodwork, Metalwork, Technical Drawing, Geometrical and Engineering Drawing)	4	–	5	–	3	–	5	–
Other subjects	2	7	1	7	2	8	1	6

Note: Columns may not exactly total 100 due to rounding.

Source: R. C. Murray and R. D. Osborne, 'Educational Qualifications and Religious Affiliation' in R. J. Cormack and R. D. Osborne (eds), Religion, Education and Employment: Aspects of Equal Opportunity in Northern Ireland (Belfast 1983), p. 142.

Table 2.24 Subject Distribution of 'A' Level Passes, all Schools, all Boards, 1971 and 1975 (per cent)

Subject grouping	1971				1975			
	Roman Catholic		Protestant		Roman Catholic		Protestant	
	Boys	Girls	Boys	Girls	Boys	Girls	Boys	Girls
English Literature	11	23	8	20	11	23	8	20
Languages	20	27	8	21	17	24	6	20
Geography/History	22	22	23	23	29	21	23	21
Mathematics	22	9	24	8	14	6	19	8
Science	21	11	33	16	23	10	36	19
Crafts/Domestic Science	2	2	1	5	1	2	3	5
Art/Music/ Religious Education	2	6	3	6	5	12	4	8
Other subjects	–	–	–	–	–	2	1	–

Notes:
1 Northern Ireland Board only.
2 Columns may not exactly total 100 due to rounding.

Source: R. C. Murray and R. D. Osborne, 'Educational Qualifications and Religious Affiliation' in R.J. Cormack and R.D. Osborne (eds), *Religion, Education and Employment: Aspects of Equal Opportunity in Northern Ireland* (Belfast 1983), p. 143.

Indians in public examinations. Taylor's study of the secondary schooling of Asians and whites in Newcastle[104] concludes that there was a higher level of educational achievement among Asians than English boys. Meanwhile, in a study of a 16+ cohort of Asian boys in Leicester, Singh also found that their achievement in 16+ examinations was no worse than their white peers. Similarly, Brooks found there was little difference between white and Asian educational performance.[105] However, just as there were differences between West Indian pupils and white pupils in the junior school so this continues into secondary education. In a survey of eight multi-racial schools in an outer London borough, Little[106] reports that at 'O' level/CSE the average number of passes was 4.2 for white pupils and 1.0 for West Indian pupils.

Such findings are reinforced by statistical data that were specially collected for the Rampton inquiry[107] into the education of children from ethnic minority groups. To establish the extent of West Indian pupils' academic under-achievement, data were collected on the ethnic origin of school leavers in six LEAs that included approximately half the school leavers from ethnic minorities in England. In CSE and 'O' level English it was found that in the six LEAs studied 9 per cent of West Indians obtained 'O' level passes A to C or CSE grade 1, compared with 21 per cent of Asians and 29 per cent of other leavers, while in mathematics it was found that 5 per cent of West Indians obtained 'O' level passes A to C or CSE grade 1 compared with 20 per cent for Asians and 19 per cent for other leavers. Similar trends are found when comparing all CSE and 'O' level achievements and all 'A' level achievements (see table 2.25).

At CSE and 'O' level only 3 per cent of West Indians, compared with 18 per cent of Asians and 16 per cent of other school leavers, obtained five subjects graded A to C at 'O' level or grade one CSE. Furthermore, this is reinforced at 'A' level where only 2 per cent of West Indians obtained one or more passes at 'A' level. Such evidence points to the fact that West Indian pupils are under-achieving in schools with the result that the Rampton Committee concludes:

> Many West Indian pupils are under-achieving in relation to their peers, not least in obtaining the examination qualifications needed to give them equality of opportunity in the employment market and to enable them to take advantage of the range of post school opportunities available.[108]

But how might we account for such under-achievement? A recent review of disadvantage in education by Mortimore and Blackstone points, like the Rampton Committee, to factors within the educational system and beyond it.[109] The Rampton Committee indicated that the main reasons for under-achievement among West Indians were the lack of pre-school provision and linguistic difficulties[110] alongside school factors, especially matters concerning the content of the curriculum and the process of schooling.[111] Such factors bear a marked resemblance to the ways in which under-achievement has been explained among working-class pupils in the school system for they also show marked levels of under-achievement in secondary schools.

Much of the material that is available concerns the performance of pupils in maintained grammar schools rather than comprehensive schools. Accordingly, this section utilizes data from the longitudinal study by Douglas and his colleagues[112] and the study by Halsey, Heath and Ridge of 10,000 adult men in England and Wales.[113] Douglas, Ross and Simpson report on the progress of their sample in secondary schools where they show

Table 2.25   CSE, 'O' Level and 'A' Level Achievements Among School Leavers in Six Local Education Authorities in England

| | Leavers in 6 LEAs | | | All maintained school leavers in England (%) |
	Asians %	West Indians %	All other leavers %	
CSE and 'O' level				
No graded results (includes those not attempting examinations)	19	17	22	14
At least 1 graded result but less than 5 higher grades	63	81	62	66
5 or more higher grades	18	3	16	21
'A' level				
No 'A' level pass	87	98	88	87
One or more 'A' level pass	13	2	12	13
Total (number)	527	799	4,852	693,840

Source: A. Rampton, *West Indian Children in Our Schools* (HMSO 1981), tables C and D, p. 8.

the relationship between social class and those obtaining 'good' 'O' level certificates (defined as four passes including three from English language, mathematics, science and a foreign language) and those obtaining general certificates (defined as at least one 'O' level pass and any number and combination of passes in subjects other than those which constitute a 'good' certificate). The main trends are shown in table 2.26.

The social class inequalities that were found in the primary school were magnified by the secondary school. In particular, Douglas, Ross and Simpson draw attention to the pupils from manual backgrounds who became particularly handicapped through early leaving and poor examination performance. While the manual working-class pupils do attain 'O' level certificates, only a relatively small proportion obtain good certificates.[114] Halsey, Heath and Ridge draw attention to the fact that it is not just social class origins and success in examinations that have to be considered, but the relationship between social class and the proportion of pupils staying on at school (see table 2.27). The most striking feature is the drop-out of working-class pupils at the minimum school leaving age. However, it is also apparent that for those who survive there is a great degree of similarity in the examination success rates of different classes. On this basis, Halsey and his colleagues conclude that at 'O' and 'A' level those working-class pupils *who survive* compete on equal terms with pupils from other social classes. Nevertheless, by that stage the class differentials are very wide as the boy from the working-class family is more likely to drop out of school at the minimum school leaving age, less likely to continue into the sixth form and less likely to enter higher education. Indeed throughout the pupils' school careers there is a persistent class difference in survival rates and, therefore, inequality is increased. However, we now require further data about the performance of girls as well as boys in a secondary school system where the school leaving age has been

Table 2.26   Proportions of Children Staying at School and Gaining Certificates, Related to Ability and Social Class, in Great Britain

Social class		Percentage table Ability at 15 years				
		60 and over	55-59	50-54	45-49	44 and less
% Completing Session 1961–62						
Middle	(Upper	97	93	86	69	40
	(					
	(Lower	94	79	59	36	17
Manual	(Upper	90	67	35	22	6
	(					
	(Lower	80	46	27	12	3
% Starting Session 1962–63						
Middle	(Upper	90	82	71	42	20
	(					
	(Lower	78	52	37	20	8
Manual	(Upper	67	43	20	10	3
	(					
	(Lower	50	20	12	4	2
% Gaining Good Certificates						
Middle	(Upper	77	33	11	4	–
	(					
	(Lower	60	18	6	–	–
Manual	(Upper	53	15	2	1	–
	(					
	(Lower	37	9	3	–	–
% Gaining General Certificates						
Middle	(Upper	94	79	54	27	20
	(					
	(Lower	87	59	38	13	1
Manual	(Upper	86	45	17	5	–
	(					
	(Lower	69	31	12	2	–

Note: For the way in which Douglas defines social class categories see table 2.13.

Source: J. W. B. Douglas, J. M. Ross and H. R. Simpson, *All Our Future* (London 1968), p. 216.

raised to sixteen. This suggests that, hypothetically, pupils have the chance of taking public examinations, but does this increase educational opportunity and lead to improved chances in the labour market and in the higher reaches of the educational system?

Some clues are provided in the *General Household Survey* which gives data on the highest qualifications obtained by socio-economic groups and by sex in Great Britain.

Table 2.27 Social Class and School Examinations in England and Wales

Father's social class	1 Percentage staying on until 16 or later	2 Percentage obtaining School Certificate or 1 or more O-levels	3 Column 2 as a proportion of column 1 (O-level success rate)	4 Percentage staying on until 18 or later	5 Percentage obtaining Higher School Certificate or 1 or more A-levels	6 Column 5 as a proportion of column 4 (A-level success rate)
I, II (N = 1,072)	70.0	58.1	0.83	28.2	26.9	0.93
III, IV, V (N = 2,475)	32.6	24.2	0.74	7.7	6.9	0.90
VI, VII, VIII (N = 4,482)	26.8	11.8	0.71	3.0	2.8	0.93

Note:
The classes are defined as follows:

I Higher grade professionals, administrators, managers and proprietors) The Service
II Lower grade professionals, administrators and managers. Supervisors and higher grade technicians.) Class

III Clerical, sales and rank-and-file service workers) The
IV Small proprietors and self-employed artisans. The 'petty bourgeoisie') Intermediate
V Lower grade technicians and foremen. The aristocracy of labour) Class

VI Skilled manual workers in industry) The
VII Semi- and unskilled manual workers in industry) Working
VIII Agricultural workers and smallholders) Class

Source: A. H. Halsey, A. F. Heath and J. M. Ridge, *Origins and Destinations: Family Class and Education in Modern Britain* (Oxford 1980), based on table 8.12, p. 142.

Table 2.28 Socio-economic Group by Highest Qualification Level Attained by Sex: Economically Active Persons Aged 25–69 not in Full-time Education in Great Britain, 1979 and 1980 Combined

Highest qualification level attained	Socio-economic group							Total
	Professional	Employers and managers	Inter-mediate non-manual	Junior non-manual	Skilled manual and own account non-professional	Semi-skilled manual and personal service	Unskilled manual	
	%	%	%	%	%	%	%	%
Degree or equivalent								
Males	67	11	25	3	0	0	0	9
Females	66	6	14	1	2	0	0	4
Total	67	10	19	1	1	0	0	7
Higher education below degree level								
Males	17	14	26	7	4	1	0	8
Females	10	16	43	2	2	1	0	8
Total	16	15	36	3	4	1	0	8
GCE 'A' level or equivalent								
Males	5	10	11	9	7	3	1	7
Females	2	5	4	3	3	1	0	2
Total	4	9	7	5	6	2	1	5
GCE 'O' level or equivalent/ grade 1 CSE								
Males	5	19	13	19	12	7	3	12
Females	9	16	10	20	9	7	2	12
Total	6	19	11	20	11	7	2	12

Table 2.28 (continued)

Highest qualification level attained	Socio-economic group							
	Professional	Employers and managers	Intermediate non-manual	Junior non-manual	Skilled manual and own account non-professional	Semi-skilled manual and personal service	Unskilled manual	Total
	%	%	%	%	%	%	%	%
CSE other grades/commercial qualifications/apprenticeship								
Males	2	10	5	9	19	7	3	12
Females	3	9	5	20	11	6	5	11
Total	2	10	5	17	18	7	4	11
Foreign or other qualifications								
Males	3	5	5	6	4	4	3	4
Females	2	6	3	5	3	4	2	4
Total	3	5	4	5	4	4	2	4
No qualifications								
Males	2	31	16	47	55	78	90	48
Females	9	42	21	49	71	81	90	59
Total	3	33	19	48	57	80	90	52
Base = 100%								
Males	858	2,367	968	1,201	5,297	1,870	482	13,043
Females	126	571	1,294	3,003	720	2,444	1,044	9,202
Total	984	2,938	2,262	4,204	6,017	4,314	1,526	22,245

Source: Office of Population Censuses and Surveys, *General Household Survey 1980* (HMSO 1982), p. 123.

Table 2.28 brings together some of the trends which have been discussed in this section. The higher the social class the smaller the percentage without any qualifications and the larger the numbers with 'O' level (or equivalent), 'A' level and degrees. There is certainly a marked division between those in non-manual and manual occupations with respect to the proportion who obtained educational qualifications and who survived in the educational system. Furthermore, while there is little difference in the percentage of men and women who achieved at CSE and 'O' level, there are considerable differences at 'A' level and at degree level. In addition, there are more women without any qualifications. Such evidence would suggest divergencies in terms of the social class and sex of those individuals who pursue higher and further education in the UK.

DESTINATIONS AFTER SCHOOL

The main destinations of school leavers in England during 1979 are shown in table 2.29. Such data indicate that over 80 per cent of boys and 70 per cent of girls do not proceed to any form of further or higher education. However, of those who do proceed to such courses, the data indicate that more boys than girls take degree courses and more girls than boys are involved in teacher training. More boys than girls take HND and OND courses while girls are the main attenders in nursing and secretarial courses. In this section we examine some of the main trends in further and higher education, once more focusing on differentiation by sex, race and social class.

As can be seen from table 2.30 more men than women enter universities in the UK. The numbers of male and female undergraduate students have risen steadily over the years but despite some relative increase, women still only account for just over one-third of the undergraduate population. Furthermore, within subject groups men and women are not equally represented as shown in table 2.31.

Indeed, the pattern of subject differentiation that we noted earlier continues into higher education,[115] where women are under-represented in science and mathematics but over-represented in arts, languages and education. In the current economic climate of the early 1980s, with cuts in public expenditure and cuts in universities, especially in arts and social science subjects, together with an increase in places in science and engineering, it is doubtful if we shall witness a major increase in the number of women gaining entry to science subjects in universities, given their lack of qualifications in these areas of study.

In terms of postgraduate study the picture is much the same with women constituting just over one-third of the postgraduate population in UK universities where they are concentrated in arts subjects, especially education and languages (see table 2.32).

As one of the demands for appointment to posts in higher education is the possession of a higher degree it comes as no surprise that the majority of posts at every level in universities in the UK are held by men (as shown in table 2.33) and that men are even more likely to occupy the senior posts.[116] Indeed, if we turn to other sectors of higher education we find similar trends in terms of the proportion of women who are attending degree courses (see table 2.34) and, in turn, in the numbers of women to be found teaching within these institutions.

The evidence points to a situation whereby women are under-represented in higher education, a situation that might, in part, be anticipated given the nature of the educational process at other points in the educational system. However, we might in

Table 2.29   Destination of School Leavers by Sex, England, 1979

	No. of boys 000s	Percentage of boys	No. of girls 000s	Percentage of girls
Degree courses	32.7	8.7	21.6	6.0
Teacher training	0.8	0.2	3.1	0.9
HND/HNC	1.4	0.4	1.0	0.3
OND/ONC	1.8	0.5	1.3	0.4
Catering	1.7	0.5	4.2	1.2
Nursing	0.1	–	5.4	1.5
Secretarial	0.1	–	17.4	4.8
GCE 'A' levels	7.6	2.0	8.5	2.3
GCE 'O' levels	5.0	1.3	6.3	1.7
Other further education courses	13.6	3.6	24.1	6.7
Temporary employment	3.5	0.9	2.6	0.7
Other employment	308.8	81.9	264.8	73.5
All leavers	377.1	100.0	360.3	100.0

Note: This table includes those whose destinations were not known.

Source: Department of Education and Science, *Statistics of Education, Volume 2 School Leavers* (HMSO 1979), table 11, pp. 26–7.

Table 2.30   Full-time UK Domiciled Undergraduate Students Analysed by Sex, 1975–6 to 1980–1

	1975–6	1979–80	1980–1
Men (000s)	125.2	137.5	139.6
Women (000s)	70.8	87.2	92.2
Women as percentage of total	36.1	38.8	39.8

Source: University Grants Committee, *University Statistics 1980 Volume I Students and Staff* (Cheltenham 1982), derived from table C, p. 7.

turn consider the extent to which higher education continues the selective process which began lower down in the educational system.

As far as ethnic minorities are concerned, very little is known about their participation in higher and further education, mainly because the statistical data are not available, apart from the Rampton report whose survey indicated that 3 per cent of Asians and 1 per cent of West Indians took degree courses. Sociologists have yet to focus on questions about their participation rates compared with students from indigenous backgrounds who come from similar social classes and hold equivalent qualifications. In the early 1980s only small-scale studies, such as Tomlinson's intensive investigations of eight black women students in higher education, are available.[117] Nevertheless, as more ethnic minority children are British born it is considered that their experiences will be the subject of sociological studies of educational opportunity, alongside those that focus on social class.

We have already noted how there is a relationship between social class and education.

Table 2.31 Subjects Studied by Undergraduates in UK Universities in 1980–1, Analysed by Domicile and Sex

Subject Group	Total 000s	Percentage of total who were:		
		Home men	Home women	Overseas
Education	3.7	28	62	10
Medicine, Dentistry and Health	27.9	55	40	5
Engineering and Technology	36.8	76	6	19
Agriculture, Forestry, Veterinary Science	5.1	62	36	2
Biological and Physical Sciences	57.8	64	30	7
Administrative, Business and Social Studies	59.9	54	39	7
Architecture and other Professional and Vocational Studies	4.2	61	30	9
Languages, Literature and Area Studies	32.7	31	66	3
Arts, other than languages	23.0	44	52	5
All subjects	251.2	56	37	8

Source: University Grants Committee, *University Statistics 1980 Volume I Students and Staff* (Cheltenham 1982), derived from table E, p. 7.

Table 2.32 Subjects Studied by Postgraduate Students in UK Universities in 1980–1, Analysed by Domicile and Sex

Subject Group	Total 000s	Percentage of total who were:		
		Home men	Home women	Overseas
Education	8.7	41	44	15
Medicine, Dentistry and Health	3.6	34	21	45
Engineering and Technology	6.4	40	4	55
Agriculture, Forestry and Veterinary Science	1.1	30	15	55
Biological and Physical Sciences	10.8	55	14	31
Administrative, Business and Social Studies	10.3	37	25	38
Architecture and other Professional and Vocational Studies	1.4	36	28	37
Language, Literature and Area Studies	2.8	37	29	34
Arts, other than languages	2.4	47	25	28
All subjects	*47.5*	*42*	*23*	*35*

Source: University Grants Committee, *University Statistics 1980 Volume I Students and Staff*, (Cheltenham 1982), derived from Table E, p. 7.

Table 2.33　　Full-time Academic Staff in UK Universities by Level of Post and Sex, 1980-1

	Men	Women	Total
Professors	4,469	121	4,590
Readers and senior lecturers	8,775	602	9,377
Lecturers and assistant lecturers	22,278	4,101	26,379
Others	2,463	1,283	3,746
Total	37,985	6,107	44,092

Source: University Grants Committee, *University Statistics 1980 Volume I Students and Staff* (Cheltenham 1982), derived from table 25, p. 51.

Is this relationship maintained in higher education? Basic data on higher education were collected by the Robbins Committee[118] who conducted a survey of children born in the years 1940-1. Table 2.35 summarizes the data that were collected on the highest course of education by father's occupation. It is apparent that those children with a father with a professional background had a greater chance of a university education than those whose fathers were skilled, semi-skilled or unskilled manual workers. In fact, those with a professional background had a thirty-three times greater chance of reaching higher education than those with a semi- or unskilled manual background.

Further evidence on the social origins and attributes of university students in Great Britain is available in a survey of graduates conducted by Kelsall, Poole and Kuhn. In particular, their evidence from graduates who obtained degrees in 1960 provides a similar picture to other studies in terms of the composition of university graduates by sex and social class. On the basis of their data it is apparent that children of middle-class origin have a greater chance of becoming university graduates than those who are working class. It is also evident that a larger proportion of women than of men are from a middle-class background.[119]

However, this evidence was gathered before the expansion of higher education and the implementation of the Robbins principle that opportunities should be provided for all young people who are qualified in terms of ability and attainment. Recent evidence from the Universities Central Council on Admissions demonstrates that young people from non-manual classes, rather than manual classes, continue to gain admission to university (see table 2.36).[120] In addition, Edwards and Roberts[121] have shown that men from social class I had a 58 per cent chance of entering university compared with 38 per cent of women from the same social class.

Changing policies for higher education, including the policy of some universities to recruit 'mature' students, may change the social class composition of those who are admitted. This was one of the initial aims in establishing the Open University[122] and we might expect a different pattern in terms of the class composition of their students. Table 2.37 shows an increase in the recruitment of women and a decrease in the number of teachers and lecturers who became Open University students during the 1970s. Nevertheless, there are still more students from non-manual rather than manual occupations, following the general pattern shown in table 2.36 which summarizes the main trends in higher education during the period 1956-79. Indeed, the data for the UK reveal

Table 2.34 School Leavers Enrolling on Degree Courses by Sex and Type of Educational Establishment, England and Wales, 1975–6 to 1978–9

	1975–6			1976–7			1977–8			1978–9		
	No. of Boys	No. of Girls	% Girls	No. of Boys	No. of Girls	% Girls	No. of Boys	No. of Girls	% Girls	No. of Boys	No. of Girls	% Girls
University	27,130	15,610	36.5	26,630	16,880	38.8	29,070	17,580	37.7	28,980	18,820	39.4
Polytechnic	4,300	2,120	33.8	4,990	2,940	37.1	4,650	3,050	39.6	5,020	3,130	38.4
Others	430	660	60.6	800	820	50.6	700	990	58.6	700	1,070	60.4
Total	31,860	18,390	36.6	32,420	20,640	38.9	34,420	21,620	38.6	34,700	23,020	39.9

Based on: DES, *Statistics of Education, Volume 2 School Leavers 1975*, table 13, 1976–79, table 11; Welsh Office (1977–9 figures)

Source: EOC, *Gender and the Secondary School Curriculum* (Manchester 1982), table 2.4 in the statistical appendix.

Table 2.35   Highest Course of Education by Father's Occupation for Children Born in Great Britain, 1940–1

Father's occupation	Percentage					
	Higher education			'A' level or SLC[1]	Other post school or 'O' level	No post school or 'O' level/ SLC[1]
	Full-time		Part-time			
	Degree	Other				
Higher professional	33	12	7	16	25	7
Management, other professional	11	8	6	7	48	20
Clerical	6	4	3	7	51	29
Skilled manual	2	2	3	2	42	49
Semi/Unskilled manual	1	1	2	1	30	65
All children[2]	4	3	4	3	40	47

Notes:
1 SLC is the Scottish School Leaving Certificate.
2 All children includes those whose fathers' occupations were not known/whose fathers were unoccupied or dead.

Source: Robbins, *Higher Education Appendix One* (HMSO 1963), derived from table 2, p. 40.

a similar pattern during this period, whereby those individuals from social classes I and II take the greatest share of places, while individuals from social classes IV and V are barely represented.

Some of the trends that have been found to exist in higher education also occur in the non-advanced sector of further education. For example, in England, Wales and Scotland the pattern of course enrolment is such that women are found mainly in the arts and humanities subjects, while men enrol for courses in science and technology. At the same time, women predominate on adult and non-advanced further education courses (part-time and evening classes)[123] which may reflect patterns of accessibility. Yet in terms of training opportunities and day release courses, women have been under-represented; they constituted only 19 per cent of all young people who were released by their employers during working hours in England and Wales in 1979. In terms of social class background the limited evidence that is available confirms the broad patterns that have been identified in other sectors of education. Halsey and his colleagues,[124] drawing on their sample of adult men in England and Wales, indicate that 53 per cent of former grammar school pupils in the sample had received part-time further education, compared with 40.9 per cent of pupils who had attended elementary and secondary modern schools. Overall, there are low participation rates for women and ethnic minorities in further education. Indeed, the available evidence suggests that further education is not the alternative route or second chance of mobility for young people from the working class.[125]

But, we might ask, how do young people fare with their educational qualifications? How does the ultimate level of education influence patterns of employment and unemployment in the UK?

EDUCATION, EMPLOYMENT AND UNEMPLOYMENT

There has been a steady flow of sociological evidence to illustrate the relationship between education and employment and, in turn, the relationship between educational qualifications and employment given the number of occupations that are dependent upon qualifications. Indeed, Little and Westergaard maintained:

> As professionalization, bureaucratization and automation of work proceed, so access to occupations of the middle and higher levels increasingly demands formal educational qualifications.[126]

The evidence that was available in the 1961 Census indicates some link between the amount of education that individuals received and their occupational group. Those in the professional, employers and managers groups had received significantly more years of schooling than other groups, and there was a distinct difference between the educational experience of non-manual and manual groups. However, it is the achieved level of education which is significant here. The *General Household Survey* provides some data on the socio-economic groups of males and females in relation to the last school, college or university attended (see table 2.38).

Such data confirm the patterns of educational experience that have been suggested in earlier sections, whereby those in the professional, employers and managers and

Table 2.36   **Distribution of Children (1971) and Students in Higher Education (1956-79) by Social Class of Father**

	I	II	IIIN	IIIM	IV	V	N/C
			Percentages				
			Class				
1) Children aged 10-14 in 1971, GB	5.0	18.2	9.0	37.3	16.5	6.8	7.3
2) 'A' level pupils aged 18 in school & FE, FT, 1974, Eng.	20	40	12	18	8		2
3) Univ. entrants, FT, 1956, GB,							
Male	21	41	11	22	4	1	–
Female	26	45	9	16	2	1	–
All	22	42	11	20	4	1	–
4) Univ. students, FT, 1961/62, GB							
Male	17	40	12	19	6	1	5
Female	20	43	11	16	6	1	3
All	18	41	12	18	6	1	4
5) Univ. students by age, mid-1960s							
19 and under		64	11	21	4		–
20–22		71	8	17	4		–
23 and over		59	10	26	5		–
6) Univ. entrants, FT, 1979, UK	19.8	38.0	21.1	14.7	4.5	0.9	9.8
7) Teacher training students FT, 1961/62, GB							
Male	5	27	16	32	13	2	5
Female	8	35	14	28	8	2	6
All	7	33	14	29	9	2	6
8) AFE students, FT, 1961/62, GB	12	32	14	28	8	2	4
1961/62, GB							
PT day	6	20	16	39	12	4	3
PT evening	5	22	14	39	12	3	4
9) Poly. degree students, FT & PT, 1972/73, Eng.							
Male		46	19		26		10
Female		51	17		24		9
All	12	34	18	8	2	16	10
10) Poly. non-degree students, FT & PT, 1972/73	11	29	17	10	3	18	14
11) Poly. PT students, 1972/73, Eng.	9	23	19	12	4	18	15
The same, own occupation	9	38	29	2	0	15	7
12) Open Univ. PT entrants, 1971, UK	8	26	13	34	13	5	–
The same, own occupation	20	62	11	5	1	0	–

Table 2.36 (continued)

Based on (1) Census 1971 Household Composition Table 26; (2) G. Williams and A. Gordon, '16 and 18 year olds: attitudes to education', *Higher Education Bulletin*, vol 4, no. 1 (1975), pp. 26-37; (3) R. K. Kelsall, *Report on an Inquiry into Applications for Admission to Universities* (1957); (4), (7), (8) Robbins, *Higher Education Report Appendix 2B*, pp. 4, 72, 92, 128; (5) E. Hopper and M. Osborn, *Adult Students: Education, Selection and Social Control* (1975), table 4.8; (6) *Universities Central Council on Admissions Statistical Supplement 1978-9* Table E5; (9), (10), (11) J. Whitburn, M. Mealing and C. Cox *People in Polytechnics* (Guildford 1976) Tables 4.12, 4.A, 4.B, 6.7 and personal communication (students in (11) are also counted in (9) or (10)); (12) N. McIntosh, J. Calder and B. Swift, *A Degree of Difference: A Study of the First Year's Intake to the Open University of the United Kingdom* (Guildford 1976), p. 139.

Source: J.H. Farrant, 'Trends in Admissions' in O. Fulton (ed), *Access to Higher Education* (Guildford 1981), p. 85.

Table 2.37   Open University: Occupation of New Undergraduate Students, 1971–81

UK	Percentages		
Occupation	1971	1976	1981
Teachers and lecturers	40	27	20
Housewives	10	15	18
Technical personnel	12	11	12
Clerical and office staff	6	10	11
The professions and the arts	8	11	10
Shopkeepers, sales and services	3	4	5
Administrators and managers	5	5	3
Armed forces	2	3	3
Qualified scientists and engineers	6	4	3
In other employment	3	7	9
Not in employment	2	4	5
No information	2	–	–
Total new students (= 100%)	19.6	12.2	14.5

Note: These data relate to finally registered new students at the commencement of their studies.

Source: Central Statistical Office, *Social Trends 13* (HMSO 1982).

intermediate non-manual categories have had some experience of further or higher education in contrast to those in manual occupations.

Similar patterns are revealed in table 2.39 which shows the relationship between age, educational qualifications and occupational category for men and women. For both sexes it is found that those in the professional and in the intermediate non-manual categories have a tendency to possess higher educational qualifications, while junior non-manual workers are less likely to have higher educational qualifications although they possess some educational qualifications. Meanwhile, there is a tendency for skilled

Table 2.38 Socio-economic Group by Sex by Educational Establishment Last Attended Full-time
Economically active persons aged 25 to 69 not in full-time education, Great Britain, 1979 and 1980 combined

Educational establishment last attended full-time	Socio-economic group							
	Professional	Employers and managers	Intermediate non-manual	Junior non-manual	Skilled manual and own account non-professional	Semi-skilled manual and personal service	Unskilled manual	Total
	%	%	%	%	%	%	%	%
Males								
School	36	79	51	89	93	95	98	84
Polytechnic, college of further education, other college	24	14	32	9	6	4	2	10
University	40	8	16	2	0	0	0	6
Base = 100%	884	2,475	982	1,233	5,509	1,944	518	13,545

Females

School	23	70	37	83	91	94	97	80
Polytechnic, college of further education, other college	24	25	53	17	8	6	2	17
University	53	5	10	1	1	0	0	3
Base = 100%	127	578	1,284	3,016	720	2,463	1,050	9,238

All

School	34	77	43	84	93	95	97	82
Polytechnic, college of further education, other college	24	16	44	14	6	5	2	13
University	41	7	13	1	1	0	0	5
Base = 100%	1,011	3,053	2,266	4,249	6,229	4,407	1,568	22,783

Note: Colleges of further education include colleges of education in Scotland, Northern Ireland, and outside the UK, as well as former colleges of education in England and Wales.

Source: Office of Population Censuses and Surveys, *General Household Survey 1980* (HMSO 1982), table 6.1, p. 122.

Table 2.39　Socio-economic Group by Sex, by Age, by Highest Qualification Level Attained
Economically active persons aged 25 to 69 not in full-time education, GB, 1979 and 1980 combined

Age and highest qualification level attained	Socio-economic group						
	Professional	Employers and managers	Intermediate non-manual	Junior non-manual	Skilled manual and own account non-professional	Semi-skilled and unskilled manual and personal service	Total
	%	%	%	%	%	%	%
Males							
25–29 Higher education	89	33	56	18	10	1	23
Other qualifications	11	50	41	61	53	30	44
No qualifications	nil	16	3	21	37	68	33
Base = 100%	158	214	147	174	786	344	1,823
30–39 Higher education	87	28	61	14	6	1	21
Other qualifications	11	47	28	52	44	26	39
No qualifications	1	25	11	35	50	74	40
Base = 100%	272	726	324	291	1,520	548	3,681
40–49 Higher education	85	27	49	7	3	1	16
Other qualifications	14	44	36	43	40	19	35
No qualifications	1	29	15	50	58	80	48
Base = 100%	194	662	231	242	1,297	533	3,159
50–59 Higher education	77	21	38	6	1	1	12
Other qualifications	21	40	33	34	35	11	30
No qualifications	2	39	29	60	64	89	58
Base = 100%	168	585	193	325	1,236	606	3,113
60–69 Higher education	(49)	16	(20)	5	2	0	9
Other qualifications	(10)	39	(25)	27	31	10	26
No qualifications	(7)	44	(28)	68	67	90	65
Base = 100%	66	180	73	169	458	321	1,267

25–69 Higher education	84	25	50	10	4	1	17
Other qualifications	14	44	33	43	41	19	35
No qualifications	2	31	16	47	55	80	48
Base = 100%	858	2,367	968	1,201	5,297	2,352	13,043
Females							
25–29 Higher education	(26)	(12)	64	5	5	1	20
Other qualifications	(3)	(30)	29	70	40	31	45
No qualifications	(1)	(12)	7	25	54	68	34
Base = 100%	30	54	257	397	92	315	1,145
30–39 Higher education	(31)	25	65	3	7	1	15
Other qualifications	(5)	41	20	58	33	21	35
No qualifications	(2)	34	15	39	60	78	50
Base = 100%	38	162	422	854	208	970	2,654
40–49 Higher education	(17)	25	55	3	1	1	11
Other qualifications	(3)	30	20	46	25	13	27
No qualifications	(5)	45	25	51	74	85	62
Base = 100%	25	144	351	824	169	961	2,474
50–69 Higher education	(22)	17	43	2	2	1	7
Other qualifications	(8)	32	21	32	14	7	19
No qualifications	(3)	51	36	66	84	92	74
Base = 100%	33	211	264	928	251	1,242	2,929
All aged							
25–69 Higher education	76	22	57	3	4	1	12
Other qualifications	15	36	22	48	26	15	29
No qualifications	9	42	21	49	71	84	59
Base = 100%	126	571	1,294	3,003	720	3,488	9,202

Note: Higher education = qualifications above GCE 'A' level standard; other qualifications = qualifications at or below GCE 'A' level standard. The numbers of economically active women aged 60 to 69 are too small to show separately.

Source: Office of Population Censuses and Surveys, *General Household Survey 1980* (HMSO 1982), p. 124.

Table 2.40   Usual Gross Weekly Earnings, Hours Worked and Age by Highest Qualification Level Attained and Sex, Persons aged 20–69 in Full-time Employment in Great Britain, 1981

	Highest qualification level attained						
	Degree or equivalent	Below degree higher education	GCE 'A' level or equivalent	GCE 'O' level or equivalent CSE grade 1	CSE other grades/ commercial/ apprentice-ship	No qualifications	Total
Earnings							
Usual gross weekly earnings (index numbers total = 100)							
Males	154	126	109	104	96	91	100
Females	161	149	107	103	94	87	100
Median weekly earnings (£)							
Males (£)	187	153	133	127	116	110	122
Females (£)	131	121	87	84	77	71	82
Earnings of females relative to those of males (%)	70	79	65	66	66	64	67
Median hourly earnings (£)							
Males (£)	4.80	3.80	3.30	3.10	2.80	2.60	3.00
Females (£)	3.80	3.20	2.30	2.20	2.00	1.80	2.10
Earnings of females relative to those of males (%)	79	84	70	71	71	69	70
Hours							
Mean hours worked per week							
Males	40.8	41.0	41.8	43.5	43.4	44.3	43.2
Females	36.7	37.8	37.9	38.4	38.4	39.0	38.5
Mean hours of females relative to those of males (%)	90	92	91	88	88	88	89

Age

Mean age (years)

Males	38.4	37.7	33.7	35.6	41.9	44.2	40.5
Females	33.4	37.2	28.2	31.3	35.5	43.0	37.2

Source: Office of Population Censuses and Surveys, *General Household Survey 1981* (HMSO 1983), p. 133.

Table 2.41   Labour Market Status by Sex and Scottish Certificate of Education (SCE) Qualifications, Scotland, October 1980

	Job	Unemployed	YOP	Total	Unweighted N
	%	%	%	%	%
(a) Sex					
Males (%)	62	18	20	100	(1580)
Females (%)	59	19	21	99	(1488)
(b) SCE qualification					
Highers	79	13	8	100	(593)
4+ O grades (A–C)	78	12	10	100	(506)
1–3 O grades (A–C)	62	14	23	99	(964)
D–E awards at O grade	52	21	27	100	(334)
No SCE awards	45	28	28	101	(671)

Source: Based on table 1 in Brian Main and David Raffe, 'The 'Transition from School to Work' in 1980–81: A Dynamic Account', *British Educational Research Journal*, Vol. 9, No. 1 (1983), p. 61.

manual workers, both male and female, particularly in the younger age group to possess educational qualifications that can be obtained in schools and colleges. In contrast, non-skilled manual workers possess few qualifications regardless of the age group to which they belong, although this is more the case for women than for men.[127] Finally, when comparisons are made between those with and those without educational quali-fications, it is found that those with educational qualifications tend to earn more per week. Furthermore, the higher the level of qualification the greater the level of earnings (see table 2.40).

These data suggest that educational qualifications and experiences influence life chances.[128] However, questions might be asked about whether this relationship has been maintained, given the changing social and economic circumstances of the late 1970s and early 1980s. Youth unemployment has risen in Britain from 67,000 in January 1970 to 240,000 in January 1980 and was recorded at 425,000 in January 1981. In the second half of the 1970s the government response was in terms of the Job Creation Programme, the Work Experience Programme, the Youth Opportunities Programme (YOP) and, from September 1983, the Youth Training Scheme.

On the basis of a study of school leavers in the labour market in Scotland, Main and Raffe[129] have been able to explore the relationship between labour market status, sex and educational qualifications. As table 2.41 shows, fewer girls entered the labour market than boys, and those who did were less likely than boys to get jobs. Of those not in jobs about half of both the boys and the girls were on YOP courses.

The data on the relationship between educational qualifications and employment, unemployment and YOP places, indicate that those with Highers fared little better than those with O grades when it came to employment prospects. However, only one year separates these groups which may have some impact on employment possibilities. Never-theless, O grade results were strongly associated with getting a job, being unemployed or being on a YOP course, since, of those without jobs, it was found that young people with intermediate qualifications were most likely to be on YOP. Such data point towards the continued strong association between educational qualifications and employment. Main and Raffe speculate about the continued stratification of opportunities for school leavers, not only in terms of different job opportunities in employment and unemploy-ment, but in terms of the places available in the Youth Training Scheme (YTS) and prospects for future employment. Indeed, evidence from Barry and O'Connor[130] suggests that many employers who are sponsoring work experience schemes selected YOP trainees using similar criteria to those used for recruitment to permanent jobs. In these terms it seems likely that selection for YTS places will continue to be associated with educational qualifications. It would appear, therefore, that educational qualifications will continue to be a key variable in the transition not only from school to work, but from school to youth training schemes as well as into employment or unemployment.

CONCLUSION

Since the end of the Second World War there have been numerous changes in the struc-ture of state education provided in the UK. There have been changes in the provision of nursery education; 'new' methods of teaching have been adopted in the school system as project materials have been introduced into infant, junior and secondary schools; the selection system has largely been replaced by comprehensive schools; the school leaving age has been raised to sixteen; and more places are available for students to engage in further and higher education. As such, it would appear that there has been large-scale educational change, but, we might ask, what patterns and processes have occurred within the educational system? To what extent have different social groups benefited from these changes? In order to address these questions this chapter has focused on the different phases of education that are available in the UK. Inevitably some selection has taken place and the focus has been upon broad patterns that exist in the state educational system. The bulk of the data provided relate to Great Britain and to the educational system of England and Wales, although where data exist, specific reference has been made to Scotland and Northern Ireland. The overall pattern is based on distinct social divisions by gender, race and social class. Indeed, it could be argued that the divisiveness in education is cumulative with the result that the patterns established in pre-school and in the early years of schooling result in a series of selection processes which have a marked effect on the educational routes that can be taken in secondary, further and higher education. However, there is much work to be done by researchers, teachers and policy-makers who need to consider the steps that should be taken if we are to move to a school system that offers equality of educational opportunity for all. Some might argue that the comprehensive system of secondary education offers some solution to this dilemma. However, the evidence available to date[131] suggests that little has changed and the fundamental curriculum processes that occur within the school system need to be modified[132] if we are to see any changes in the basic pattern of those who succeed in the educational systems of England and Wales, Scotland and Northern Ireland.

Notes to Chapter 2

1   In writing this chapter I am indebted to Richard Brown for his editorial support and detailed comments on an earlier draft of this material. In addition, Hilary Burgess and Marie Stowell also provided many useful comments.

2   H. S. Becker, 'Comment' in M. Wax, S. Diamond and F. O. Gearing (eds), *Anthropological Perspectives in Education* (New York 1971), p. 10.

3   For a similar argument see S. Delamont, 'All Too Familiar? A Decade of Classroom Research', *Educational Analysis*, Vol. 3, No. 1 (1981), pp. 69-83.

4   For a comprehensive discussion on this topic see the papers in H. Silver (ed), *Equal Opportunity in Education* (London 1973).

5   A classic set of papers on this issue can be found in A. H. Halsey, J. Floud and C. A. Anderson (eds), *Education, Economy and Society* (New York 1961). For a series of more recent contributions see the papers in J. Karabel and A. H. Halsey (eds), *Power and Ideology in Education* (Oxford 1977).

6   For discussions of education and unemployment see D. Gleeson (ed.), *Youth Training and the Search for Work* (London 1983), esp. part 3; T. Rees and P. Atkinson, *Youth Unemployment and State Intervention* (London 1982), and B. Main and D. Raffe, 'The "Transition from School to Work" in 1980/81: A Dynamic Account', *British Educational Research Journal*, Vol. 9, No. 1 (1983), pp. 57-70. Meanwhile for ethnographic detail on the transition from school to work and school to unemployment for boys see P. Willis, *Learning to Labour* (Farnborough 1977) and for girls H. Roberts, 'After Sixteen: What Choice?' in R. G. Burgess (ed.), *Exploring Society* (London 1982), pp. 91-113.

7   There are vast numbers of papers within this tradition, many of which have concentrated upon state schools in England, although a Scottish independent school for girls has been studied by Sara Delamont. See, for example, S. Delamont, *Interaction in the Classroom* (London 1976); P. Woods and M. Hammersley (eds), *School Experience* (London 1977); P. Woods (ed.), *Teacher Strategies* (London 1980); and P. Woods (ed.), *Pupil Strategies* (London 1980).

8   The classic starting-point for this tradition can be found in M. F. D. Young (ed.), *Knowledge and Control: New Directions for the Sociology of Education* (London 1971). While sociologists have continued the theoretical debate in this field there are relatively few empirical studies although there has been some recent interest, as shown by I. F. Goodson, *School Subjects and Curriculum Change* (London 1982) that deals with rural studies; and I. F. Goodson and S. J. Ball (eds), *Defining the Curriculum* (Lewes 1984) that deals with a variety of academic and

non-academic aspects of the school curriculum.

9   O. Banks, 'The Sociology of Education, 1952-1982', *British Journal of Educational Studies*, Vol. 30, No. 1 (1982), pp. 18-31; and O. Banks, 'Sociology of Education' in L. Cohen, J. Thomas and L. Manion (eds), *Educational Research and Development in Britain 1970-1980* (Windsor 1982) pp. 43-54.

10 See, for example, the papers in R. Dale, G. Esland and M. Macdonald (eds), *Schooling and Capitalism: A Sociological Reader* (London 1976).

11 See, for example, E. Byrne, *Woman and Education* (London 1978); R. Deem (ed.), *Schooling for Women's Work* (London 1980); S. Delamont, *Sex Roles and the School* (London 1980); D. Spender, *Invisible Women: the Schooling Scandal* (London 1982); and for an overview of the sociology of education that identifies gaps in the field in respect of the education of girls and women see S. Acker, 'No Woman's Land: British Sociology of Education 1960-1979', *Sociological Review*, Vol. 29, No. 1 (1981), pp. 77-104.

12 See, for example, Delamont, *Sex Roles, op. cit.*

13 The focus of attention will be upon state education as the influence of the independent sector has been documented elsewhere in this volume in the chapter on 'Elites and Privilege' by Philip Stanworth. However, this should not be taken to imply that independent schools are not of interest to sociologists and educational researchers. For recent work on independent schools see, for example, G. Walford (ed.), *Sociological Perspectives on the Public Schools* (Lewes 1984); and for a project that compares state and independent schools see L. Stenhouse, 'Library Access, Library Use and User Education in Academic Sixth Forms: An Autobiographical Account', in R. G. Burgess (ed.), *The Research Process in Educational Settings: Ten Case Studies* (Lewes 1984), pp. 211-33.

14 For a recent article that equates the English educational system with British education see G. W. Roderick and M. D. Stephens, 'The British Education System 1870-1970', in G. Roderick and M. Stephens (eds), *The British Malaise, Industrial Performance, Education and Training in Britain Today* (Lewes 1982), pp. 11-29; and for critical commentary see R. G. Burgess, 'Exploring Frontiers and Settling Territory: Shaping the Sociology of Education', *British Journal of Sociology*, Vol. 35, No. 1 (1984), pp. 122-37.

15 For a discussion on parity of provision between Northern Ireland and other parts of Great Britain see J. Darby, 'Educational Provision in Northern Ireland', *The Northern Teacher*, Vol. 12, No. 4 (1977), pp. 3-12.

16 For discussions of the implications of weak central control see M. S. Archer, *The Social Origins of Educational Systems* (London 1979). However, some commentators have argued that attempts are being made to establish greater central control. See, for example, D. Lawton, *The Politics of the School Curriculum* (London 1980); and B. Salter and T. Tapper, *Education, Politics and the State* (London 1981).

17 First and Middle Schools involve children's primary education being subdivided from either 5 to 8 and from 8 to 12, or 5 to 9 and 9 to 13. For a discussion of the educational processes and the practice of these schools see the papers in A. Hargreaves and L. Tickle (eds), *Middle Schools: Origins, Ideology and Practice* (London 1980).

18 For a discussion of rural education in the UK (especially in Wales) see R. Nash,

Schooling in Rural Societies (London 1980).

19   For a discussion of education in multi-racial Britain see A. Little, 'Educational Policies for a Multi-Racial Britain' in B. Simon and W. Taylor (eds), *Education in the Eighties: The Central Issues* (London 1981), pp 55-76.

20   This pattern relates to the historical development of the school system, the details of which are discussed in J. Murphy, *Church, State and Schools In Britain 1800-1970* (London 1971). For a discussion on the influence of religion on schooling in Northern Ireland see, for example, J. Darby, 'Divisiveness in Education', *The Northern Teacher* (Winter 1973), pp. 3-8; and R. C. Murray and R. D. Osborne, 'Educational Qualifications and Religious Affiliation' in R. J. Cormack and R. D. Osborne (eds), *Religion, Education and Employment: Aspects of Equal Opportunity in Northern Ireland* (Belfast 1983), pp. 118-45.

21   For a discussion of the comprehensive movement in England and Wales see, for example, D. Rubinstein and B. Simon, *The Evolution of the Comprehensive School* (London 1971); and C. Benn and B. Simon, *Half Way There* (Harmondsworth 1972). For a local study that focuses on Coventry see G. C. Firth, *Comprehensive Schools in Coventry and Elsewhere* (Coventry 1963); and G. C. Firth, *Seventy Five Years of Service to Education* (Coventry 1977).

22   Rubinstein and Simon, *op. cit.*, p. 93.

23   Department of Education and Science, *The Organization of Secondary Education* (HMSO 1965).

24   Scottish Information Office, *Scottish Education Factsheet 15* (Edinburgh 1983).

25   Murray and Osborne, *op. cit.*, p. 125.

26   *Ibid.*, p. 124.

27   Scotland is due to move to a common system of examinations at 16+ in Autumn 1984. This will involve the phasing out of the Ordinary Grade Examination which will be replaced by a Scottish Certificate of Education for children of all abilities. For a discussion of this new scheme see M. O'Connor, 'Every Child in Scotland will be able to take this exam', *The Guardian* (25 October 1983). Similarly, England and Wales are to have a General Certificate of Secondary Education to replace 'O' level and CSE. It is to be awarded from 1988.

28   For a discussion of some of the problems of comparing educational data, especially concerning public examinations, see R.G. Burgess, 'Education' in R.G. Burgess (ed.), *Key Variables in Social Investigation* (London forthcoming).

29   In 1979-80 there were 45 universities in the UK: 34 in England, 1 in Wales, 8 in Scotland and 2 in Northern Ireland. In Northern Ireland a new university is about to be created by amalgamating the New University of Ulster with Ulster Polytechnic.

30   J. Mortimore and T. Blackstone, *Disadvantage and Education* (London 1982).

31   See D. S. Byrne and W. Williamson 'Some Intra-regional Variations in Educational Provision and their Bearing Upon Educational Attainment, the Case of the North East', *Sociology*, Vol. 6, No. 1 (1972), pp. 71-87; and D. S. Byrne, W. Williamson and B. Fletcher, *The Poverty of Education* (London 1975).

32   For a discussion of this point see G. Taylor and N. Ayers, *Born and Bred Unequal* (London 1969).

33   E. M. Byrne, 'Inequality in Education – Discriminal Resource-allocation in Schools', *Educational Review*, Vol. 27, No. 3 (1975), pp. 179-91.

34 For a discussion of a lack of specialist resources for girls, see the results of the survey of secondary schools in England reported in Department of Education, *Aspects of Secondary Education in England* (HMSO 1979).

35 Byrne reports that in many institutions differences in facilities for girls and boys were explained in terms of the fact that teachers considered it would be boys rather than girls who had to earn a living.

36 See Darby, 'Divisiveness', *op. cit.*

37 *Ibid.* and J. Darby, *Conflict in Northern Ireland: The Development of a Polarized Society* (Dublin 1976).

38 Murray and Osborne, *op. cit.*, p. 131.

39 For a similar analysis in respect of Catholic schools in England, see J. O'Brien, 'Science and Catholic Education', *Catholic Teacher's Journal*, Vol. 9 (1966), pp. 16-17.

40 R. G. Burgess, *Experiencing Comprehensive Education: A Study of Bishop McGregor School* (London 1983).

41 Newsom was a department which the school's headmaster considered provided courses for pupils for whom the maximum expectation of success in public examinations seemed likely to be three CSE grade fives or less.

42 Department of Education and Science, *Children and their Primary Schools* (HMSO 1967), esp. pp. 291-343.

43 *Education: A Framework for Expansion* (Cmnd. 5174) (HMSO 1972).

44 Darby, 'Educational Provision', *op. cit.*

45 See, for example, T. Blackstone, *A Fair Start* (London 1970); A. H. Halsey, *Educational Priority: EPA Problems and Policies* Vol. I (HMSO 1972); P. Lodge and T. Blackstone, *Educational Policy and Educational Inequality* (London 1982), esp. pp. 88-112.

46 See, for example, B. Plowden 'The Playgroup Movement: a Cycle of Opportunity', in Pre-school Playgroups Association, *Focus on the Future of Playgroups* (London 1973); and J. Finch, 'Dividing the Rough and the Respectable: Working Class Women and Preschool Playgroups' in E. Gamarnikov, D. Morgan, J. Purvis and D. Taylorson (eds), *The Public and the Private* (London 1983), pp. 106-17.

47 Finch, *op. cit.*

48 For further discussion see S. Shinman, *A Chance for Every Child? Access and Response to Pre-School Provision* (London 1981).

49 See the data from the General Household Survey. Office of Population Censuses and Surveys, *The General Household Survey 1979* (HMSO 1981), pp. 104-8.

50 For discussion on the middle-class character of voluntary associations, see C. Pickvance, 'Voluntary Associations' in R. G. Burgess (ed.), *Key Variables in Social Investigation* (London forthcoming).

51 Blackstone, *op. cit.*

52 J. W. B. Douglas and J. M. Ross, 'Subsequent Progress of Nursery School Children' in *Educational Research*, Vol. 7 (1964), pp. 83-94; and for further discussion on the longitudinal study, see J. W. B. Douglas, *The Home and the School* (London 1964).

53 M. Woodhead, *Intervening in Disadvantage: A Challenge for Nursery Education* (Slough 1976).

54 See, for example, the accounts of action research projects promoting pre-school

education and discussed in Mortimore and Blackstone, *op. cit.*

55 S. Delamont, *Sex Roles and the School* (London 1980), pp. 14-7.

56 *Ibid.*, pp. 35-6.

57 Extract from Adelman's material, reported in Delamont, *Sex Roles, op. cit.*, p. 35.

58 Department of Education and Science, *Curricular Difference for Boys and Girls* (HMSO 1975), p. 2.

59. For further discussions on women teachers and promotion see R. Deem, *Women and Schooling* (London 1978), the survey by the National Union of Teachers reported in NUT/EOC, *Promotion and the Woman Teacher* (London 1980); and W. Roy, *Teaching Under Attack* (London 1983), esp. pp. 78-95.

60 R. King, *All Things Bright and Beautiful? A Sociological Study of Infants' Class-rooms* (Chichester 1978), pp. 45-6. For methodological commentary on this study see R. King, 'The man in the Wendy House: Researching Infants' Schools' in R. G. Burgess (ed.), *The Research Process in Educational Settings: Ten Case Studies* (Lewes 1984).

61 See G. Lobban, 'Presentation of Sex Roles in British Reading Schemes', *Forum for the Discussion of New Trends in Education*, Vol. 16, No. 2 (1974), pp. 57-60; and G. Lobban, 'Sex Roles in Reading Schemes', *Educational Review*, Vol. 27, No. 3 (1975), pp. 202-10.

62 H. M. M. Burgess, *An Appraisal of Some Methods of Teaching Primary School Mathematics*, unpublished MA dissertation, University of London, Institute of Education (1983).

63 The use of mathematics schemes in the UK is discussed in P. Reynolds, 'Teaching Mathematics in Primary and Middle Schools' in M. L. Cornelius (ed.), *Teaching Mathematics* (London 1982), pp. 17-35.

64 H. Fletcher et al., *Mathematics for Schools* (London 1979) (2nd edition) is a set of books for teachers and pupils in infant and junior schools and is accompanied by a parents' manual. For a critical commentary on the scheme see H. M. M. Burgess, *op. cit.*, esp. ch. 2.

65 H. M. M. Burgess, *op. cit.*, p. 63.

66 G. Weiner, 'Sex Differences in Mathematical Performances: A Review of Research and Possible Action' in R. Deem (ed.), *Schooling for Women's Work* (London 1980), pp. 76-86; and R. Walden and V. Walkerdine, 'Girls and Mathematics: The Early Years', *Bedford Way Paper* No. 8, University of London, Institute of Education (1982).

67 A. Yates and D. Pidgeon, *Admission to Grammar Schools* (London 1957), pp. 168-9.

68 The main evidence is provided in Douglas, *op. cit.*, a report on the ability and attainment of primary school children which is part of a longitudinal study of 5,386 children born in the first week of March 1946. For a methodological comment on this study see J. W. B. Douglas, 'The Use and Abuse of National Cohorts' in M. D. Shipman (ed.), *The Organization and Impact of Social Research* (London 1976), pp. 3-21.

69 Department of Education and Science, *Primary Education in England: A Survey by HM Inspectors of Schools* (HMSO 1978).

70 J. Maxwell, *Reading Progress from 8-15* (Slough 1977).

71   Douglas, *op. cit.*
72   DES, *Primary Education, op. cit.*, p. 166.
73   D. D. Foxman et al., *Assessment of Performance Unit: Mathematical Development Primary Survey Report No. 1* (HMSO 1980).
74   See A. Little, 'Education and Race Relations in the United Kingdom' in J. Megarry, S. Nisbet and E. Hoyle (eds), *World Yearbook of Education* (London 1981), pp. 129-43.
75   J. Barnes, *Educational Priority, Volume 3 Curriculum Innovation in London's Educational Priority Areas* (HMSO 1975).
76   See, for example, A. Little, 'Performance of Children from Ethnic Minority Backgrounds in Primary Schools', *Oxford Review of Education*, Vol. 1, No. 2 (1975), pp. 117-35. In addition, C. Mabey, 'Black British Literacy', *Educational Research*, Vol. 23, No. 2 (1981), pp. 83-95, has reported on the results of an ILEA literacy survey of the reading attainment of black pupils. She found that black British reading attainment was significantly lower at the age of eight compared with other groups and contributed to their under-achievement; a situation that she considers can be explained in terms of social deprivation, linguistic handicaps, teacher expectations and pupil self-image.
77   R. Davie, M. Butler and H. Goldstein, *From Birth to Seven* (London 1972).
78   Douglas, *op. cit.*
79   Davie, Butler and Goldstein, *op. cit.*
80   See, for example, B. Jackson, *Streaming: An Educational System in Miniature* (London 1964); and J. Barker Lunn, *Streaming in the Primary School* (Slough 1970). However, sociologists have now questioned aspects of the methodology used in such studies; especially concerning the interpretation of test scores and the meaning that can be attached to the concepts of 'ability' and 'attainment'. For a critical review of this evidence see P. Robinson, *Perspectives in the Sociology of Education* (London 1981), esp. chs. 4 and 9.
81   Department of Education and Science, *Primary Education, op. cit.*
82   R. Nash, 'Camouflage in the Classroom' in J. Eggleston (ed.), *Contemporary Research in the Sociology of Education* (London 1974), pp. 245-50.
83   Mortimore and Blackstone, *op. cit.*, pp. 24-102.
84   The literature is extensive on each of these areas. General references have therefore been provided which give guides to fields of study so that more specific studies can be followed up. On family/home factors see the papers in M. Craft, J. Raynor, L. Cohen (eds), *Linking Home and School* (3rd edn.) (London 1980). On linguistic factors see the papers in B. Bernstein, *Class, Codes and Control*, Vols. 1 and 3 (London 1971, 1975). On schools see the literature reviewed in P. Woods, *Sociology of the School: an Interactionist Viewpoint* (London 1983).
85   G. Baron, 'The English Notion of the School', unpublished paper, University of London, Institute of Education (1955).
86   For approaches used see Benn and Simon, *op. cit.*; and for a discussion of decentralization in comprehensive schools see E. Halsall, *The Comprehensive School* (Oxford 1973). On the operation of the House system see E. Richardson, *The Teacher, the School and the Task of Management* (London 1973); and R. G. Burgess, *Experiencing Comprehensive Education, op. cit.*, esp. pp. 52-83.

87   See EOC, *Formal Investigation Report: Sidney Stringer School and Community
      College, Coventry* (Manchester 1983). For further discussion of promotion and the
      woman teacher see NUT/EOC, *op. cit.*; and on women as headteachers, see R. G.
      Burgess, 'Headship: Freedom or Constraint?' in S. J. Ball (ed.), *Comprehensive
      Schooling: A Reader* (Lewes 1984).

88   E. Byrne, *Women and Education* (London 1978), p. 212.

89   R. White and D. Brockington, *Tales Out of School* (London 1983), p. 41.

90   C. Lacey, *Hightown Grammar: The School as a Social System* (Manchester 1970).

91   D. H. Hargreaves, *Social Relations in a Secondary School* (London 1967).

92   S. J. Ball, *Beachside Comprehensive: A Case Study of Secondary Schooling*
      (Cambridge 1981).

93   N. Keddie, 'Classroom Knowledge' in M. F. D. Young (ed.), *Knowledge and
      Control: New Directions for the Sociology of Education* (London 1971), pp. 133-
      60.

94   Hargreaves, *Social Relations, op. cit.*; P. Woods, *The Divided School* (London
      1979); V. Furlong, 'Interaction Gets in the Classroom: Towards a Study of Pupils
      Knowledge' in M. Hammersley and P. Woods (eds), *The Process of Schooling*
      (London 1976), pp. 160-70; Corrigan, *op. cit.*; R. G. Burgess, *Experiencing Com-
      prehensive Education, op. cit.*, especially part two; and R. G. Burgess, 'It's Not a
      Proper Subject: It's Just Newsom' in I. F. Goodson and S. J. Ball (eds), *Defining
      the Curriculum* (Lewes 1984).

95   Department of Education and Science, *Aspects of Secondary Education in
      England: A Survey by HM Inspectors of Schools* (HMSO 1979).

96   See A. Kelly, 'Choosing or Channelling?' in A. Kelly (ed.), *The Missing Half: Girls
      and Science Education* (Manchester 1981), pp. 123-38.

97   See the essays in A. Kelly (ed.), *ibid.*

98   Department of Education and Science, *Secondary Education, op. cit.*

99   See the essays in part one of Kelly, *op. cit.*

100   Department of Education and Science, *Raising the School Leaving Age to Sixteen*
      Circular 8/71 (HMSO 1971).

101   Murray and Osborne, *op. cit.*

102   M. Fuller, 'Black girls in a London Comprehensive School' in R. Deem (ed.),
      Schooling for Womens Work (London 1980), pp. 52-65.

103   See, for example, G. Driver, *Beyond Underachievement* (London 1980).

104   J. H. Taylor, *The Halfway Generation: A Study of Asian Youths in Newcastle-
      upon-Tyne* (Slough 1976).

105   See D. Brooks and K. Singh, *Aspirations Versus Opportunities: Asian and White
      School Leavers in the Midlands* (Walsall 1978).

106   Little, 'Education and Race Relations', *op. cit.*

107   A. Rampton, *West Indian Children in Our Schools: Interim Report of the
      Education of Children from Ethnic Minority Groups* (HMSO 1981).

108   *Ibid.*, p. 10.

109   Mortimore and Blackstone, *op. cit.*

110   For a similar discussion concerning Black British children see Mabey, *op. cit.*; and
      for similar comments on children of working-class origin in the English school
      system see the work reported in Bernstein, *op. cit.*

111 On inequality in the school curriculum see M. Shipman, 'Curriculum for Inequality' in R. Hooper (ed.), *The Curriculum: Context, Design and Development* (Edinburgh 1971), pp. 101-6; and M. Shipman, 'The Limits of Positive Discrimination' in M. Marland (ed.), *Education for the Inner City* (London 1980), pp. 69-92.

112 J. W. B. Douglas, J. M. Ross and H. R. Simpson, *All Our Future* (London 1968).

113 A. H. Halsey, A. F. Heath and J. M. Ridge, *Origins and Destinations: Family, Class and Education in Modern Britain* (Oxford 1980); and for a critical review of this study, see T. Blackstone in *The Times Higher Education Supplement* (18 January 1980).

114 For a discussion of the way in which social class background influences examination success in Scottish schools see A. C. Ryrie, 'Social Class Examination Success and School Differences', *Scottish Education Review*, Vol. 13, No. 1 (1982), pp. 36-43.

115 The pattern is broadly similar in polytechnics in the UK. See the data provided in Central Statistical Office, *Social Trends* 13 (HMSO 1980), p. 45.

116 For an account that provides a similar view see R. Szreter, 'Opportunities for Woman as University Teachers in England since the Robbins Report of 1963', *Studies in Higher Education*, Vol. 8, No. 2 (1983), pp. 139-50.

117 See S. Tomlinson, 'Black Women in Higher Education – Case Studies of University Women in Britain' in L. Barton and S. Walker (eds), *Race, Class and Education* (London 1983), pp. 66-80; and for further comments on the absence of data see A. Little and D. Robbins, 'Race Bias' in D. Warren-Piper (ed.), *Is Higher Education Fair?* (Guildford 1981), pp. 57-79; and M. Craft and A. Craft 'The Participation of Ethnic Minority Pupils in Further and Higher Education', *Educational Review*, Vol. 25, No. 1 (1983), pp. 10-19.

118 Robbins, *Higher Education* (HMSO 1963).

119 R. K. Kelsall, A. Poole and A. Kuhn, *Graduates: The Sociology of an Elite* (London 1972) esp. table 1, p. 178.

120 UCCA, *Statistical Supplement to the Seventeenth Report 1978-1979* (Cheltenham 1980).

121 E. G. Edwards and I. J. Roberts, 'British Higher Education: Long Term Trends in Student Enrolment', *Higher Education Review*, Vol. 12 (1980), pp. 7-43.

122 See J. Tunstall, *The Open University Opens* (London 1974), esp. part 3.

123 For a study in this area that focuses on the workings of class, gender and patriarchy in women's popular education, see R. Deem, 'Gender, Patriarchy and Class in the Popular Education of Women' in S. Walker and L. Barton (eds), *Gender, Class and Education* (Lewes 1983), pp. 107-21.

124 Halsey, Heath and Ridge, *op. cit.*

125 See D. Raffe, 'The "Alternative Route" Reconsidered: Part-time Further Education and Social Mobility in England and Wales', *Sociology*, Vol. 13, No. 1 (1979), pp. 47-73; R. M. Blackburn, A. Stewart and K. Prandy, 'Part-time Education and the "Alternative Route"', *Sociology*, Vol. 14, No. 4 (1980), pp. 603-14; and the papers in D. Gleeson (ed.), *Youth Training and the Search for Work* (London 1983), esp. part 2.

126 A. Little and J. Westergaard, 'The Trends of Class Differentials in Educational Opportunity in England and Wales', *British Journal of Sociology*, Vol. 15, (1964),

pp. 301-16, quotation on p. 303.

127   For a discussion of the way in which working-class pupils get working-class jobs
      together with an ethnographic study of the school to work transition for boys, see
      Willis, *op. cit.* For a discussion of these trends among a sample of school leavers in
      Bradford see Roberts, *op. cit.*

128   For a discussion of the relationship between education and social mobility see the
      chapter on 'Work' by Richard Brown in this volume together with the associated
      references.

129   B. Main and D. Raffe, 'The Transition from "School to Work" in 1980/81: A
      Dynamic Account', *British Educational Research Journal*, Vol. 9, No. 1 (1983),
      pp. 57-70.

130   J. Barry and D. O'Connor, 'Costs and Benefits of Sponsoring the Unemployed',
      Employment Gazette (March 1983), pp. 113-16.

131   Ball, *op. cit.*; and R. G. Burgess, *Experiencing Comprehensive Education, op. cit.*

132   See D. H. Hargreaves, *The Challenge for the Comprehensive School* (London
      1982); and L. Stenhouse, 'The Legacy of the Curriculum Movement' in M. Galton
      and B. Moon (eds), *Changing Schools . . . Changing Curriculum* (London 1983),
      pp. 346-55.

3
Work

Richard K. Brown

INTRODUCTION

'What do they do?' remains the most illuminating question to ask about someone met for the first time. It is illuminating precisely because a man's or a woman's work, or the fact that they do not need to or cannot work, is indicative of so much else about their social situation and their likely life experiences. Even now, when we enjoy a shorter working week and longer holidays than our forefathers, most adults in the United Kingdom probably spend between a fifth and a quarter of every year at work outside the home – nearly a third of their waking hours – and domestic work, voluntary and other work consume a varying amount of time in addition. This sort of quantitative importance, however, is not the only or even the main reason for considering work in the context of a discussion of UK society. Its significance for society and its members is much more complex, but before considering the possible areas of interest in work in a little more detail it will be helpful to try to distinguish (and make use of) some of the definitions which 'work' can be given.

Even a brief consideration of the writing on this subject will reveal a wide variety of approaches. There is no agreement among social scientists as to the definition and significance of 'work'. One source of difficulty lies in the fact that 'work' cannot be used unambiguously as referring to certain activities. In attempting to distinguish 'work' from 'leisure', for example, Parker has argued that it is necessary to use the two 'dimensions' of 'time' and 'activity' to provide an adequate definition of 'work' (and of 'leisure'). He has suggested, therefore, that 'work is an activity that is carried on under conditions in which there are normally demands with respect to time and place and in which effort is directed to the production of goods and services . . . work contributes something which others are willing to pay for (or for which others would have to be paid if one did not do it oneself) . . .'[1]

In contrast, Jaques has stressed the psychological, decision-making, responsibility-taking characteristics of work. He has emphasized the need to get away from physical definitions – such as the reference to effort – and has defined 'psychological work' as the 'exercise of discretion within prescribed limits in order to reach a goal or objective'. This remains very broad, however, and he delimited one type of 'psychological work' by reference to the economic and social context in which it is performed; 'economic work' is 'all work whose designated goal is part of the social network connected with the creation and distribution of goods and services' for sale, and thus excludes housework, do-it-yourself, and so on. 'Economic work' can be divided into 'entrepreneurial work' and 'contractual employment work', which 'does not carry the responsibility for setting goals or objectives', and this further distinction obviously implies an economic and social system with certain characteristics.[2]

Developing an approach based on Marx, Braverman also stressed the goal-directed nature of human work and the importance of where the power to set goals is located. 'Human work is conscious and purposive, while the work of animals is instinctual . . . at the end of every labour process, we get a result that already existed in the imagination of the labourer at its commencement.' But in the case of human work 'the unity of conception and execution may be dissolved' so that an individual's ability to work ('his power to labour over an agreed period of time') may be sold to an employer. In the resulting 'labour process', however, the worker may not share his employer's goals, and so the employer has to try to exercise control in order to ensure that his purposes are realized: that the right quantity and quality of work is actually done in what, from the employer's point of view, is the appropriate period of time.[3]

Even these three examples indicate both certain common points of reference and important differences in understanding and emphasis. For our purposes *work* can perhaps best be regarded as a very general, all-embracing term, used to refer to all those physical and mental activities which are aimed to transform natural materials into a more useful form, to improve human knowledge and understanding of the world, and/or to provide or distribute goods and services to others, in whatever context such activities are carried out. As such it obviously includes housework and many other activities carried out in what the actors would regard as 'non-work' time; and some concentration of the focus of attention is necessary if the discussion in this chapter is to be manageable.

Such a limitation is indicated by the conventional answer to the 'what do they do?' question; this would usually refer to a person's job or *occupation*, or — if they had no occupation, paid or unpaid — to the fact that they were retired or unemployed or in full-time education. An occupation is a socially structured and socially recognized set of work activities, the carrying out of which produces goods and/or services for which others would be willing to pay or would have to pay if they were not provided voluntarily. It therefore implies both a place in the social division of labour—and in highly industrialized societies like our own this is very complex, so that there are thousands of more or less distinct occupations—and a potential or actual place in the market for goods and services.

Most of the discussion of work and occupations in the past has been concerned with what might be termed the 'formal economy', work which is publicly remunerated by wages, salaries or profits. In recent years, however, it has been pointed out that this is to ignore all domestic work, on which as many woman (and man) hours may be spent as on conventional work, and also other activities which provide goods or services even though they are not officially noticed. In a helpful exploration of these issues Gershuny and Pahl distinguished between the 'formal' and 'informal' economies, and suggested that the latter covered three areas of work:[4]

1. *Household economy*: production, not for money, by members of a household and predominantly for members of that household, of goods or services for which approximate substitutes might otherwise be purchased for money.
2. *Underground, hidden or black economy*: production, wholly or partly for money

or barter, which should be declared to some official taxation or regulatory authority, but which is wholly or partly concealed.

3. *Communal economy*: production, not for money or barter, by an individual or group, of a commodity that might otherwise be purchasable, and of which the producers are not principal consumers.

Domestic work in the 'household economy' clearly performs an essential function in enabling 'formal' economic activity to take place, and its official and academic neglect, until recently, reflects the subordinate position accorded to women in our society and the unjustifiably low evaluation given to areas of work for which they carry by far the largest responsibility. Opinions differ as to the economic importance and social significance of the 'hidden' and 'communal' economies, and especially as to whether such activities are becoming more important at a time when rates of unemployment are high and technological developments are expected by some to reduce opportunities for 'formal' employment in the future. It will not be possible to pursue such debates further here, nor to discuss domestic work. The discussion which follows will, indeed, be almost entirely concerned with the nature and characteristics of the *occupational structure* of British society, which as we shall see below is a highly complex topic in its own right. In following the discussion, however, it is important to remember that it does neglect certain types of work which are undoubtedly of importance for a complete understanding of the economic and social system, and that 'work' is being used to refer to the more limited sets of activities which are recognized and recorded as belonging to the 'formal' economy.

The work people do within the 'formal' economy is rewarded by their receiving payment. They are therefore necessarily involved in exchange relations with others, and the nature of these relations is a crucial characteristic of their work-related social situation. Some may work as employers, or as independent artisans or self-employed professionals whose relations with their customers or clients need not extend beyond the actual period of the exchange. For the majority in our sort of society, however, 'work' means employment — a continuing relationship with an employer carrying out such activities as they direct and under their control in return for a wage or salary. The *employment relationship* is therefore of central importance in a discussion of work in UK society and we shall consider it more fully in the section on the rewards and deprivations of work.

In recent years there has been some tendency among social scientists to pay less attention to work and to see it as less important for an understanding of highly industrialized societies. This may reflect the degree of technological mastery over the physical world which men apparently possess, so that in such societies problems of material want and scarcity can be seen — unjustifiably — as merely residual; it may reflect, too, the fact that rising standards of living have given many the opportunity to develop their interests and lives outside work in 'leisure' activities, at the same time as the repetitive and fragmented nature of much of the work which helps to make such standards of living possible reduces any intrinsic value work might have had for them; and indeed, much work is often so opaque that it is not obvious even to those who do it, and still less to outside observers, exactly what part their occupation plays in the economic and social system as a whole.

Thus, in some versions of 'post-industrial society' theory, for example, much greater emphasis is placed on the control and expansion of knowledge than on the control and expansion of production for an understanding of future developments.[5] Other social scientists have argued that work is no longer 'a central life interest' for most people, that it is merely something done in order to make enough money to 'live' properly in one's non-working hours, and has no value and significance for them in itself.[6] In some contributions to current debates about social stratification, too, an emphasis has been placed on cultural sources of deprivation or privilege, minimizing the significance of the possession or lack of material, and work-related, resources.[7]

I do not wish to claim that work has exactly the same significance for an understanding of our society and of the experiences of those who are members of it as it had a century ago. There have, of course, been considerable changes, though by no means all in the same direction. Attempts to remove work from a central place in an analysis of modern society, however, are at best premature and probably entirely mistaken.

In the first place work is important because without it there would be no human society. Whatever else it may include, work also refers to those activities in a society which enable essential material needs to be met. For this reason it has central social and cultural significance in all societies. The ways in which work is organized, however, the social relations surrounding it, and the social meanings attributed to it can vary enormously both within and between societies. Indeed it may be helpful to consider work in a variety of ways: the occupational structure and the social relations of production are central elements of the social structure, and are also ones which provide varying opportunities and/or constraints to the individual members of a society; and work is a set of activities and social relations which are invested with important meaning and significance, both socially and individually.

In the case of the United Kingdom, for example, the development of a capitalist industrial society from the middle of the eighteenth century onwards meant far-reaching changes in the social organization of work and the social relations of production. The division of labour and the nature of work tasks were transformed as ownership of the means of production was concentrated in the hands of a few who employed, as 'free' wage labour, formerly more economically independent workers. The subsequent growth in size and concentration of the ownership and control of units of production and administration, and their consequent bureaucratization, meant that more and more work was carried out within an employment relationship, in the company of others with similar tasks and in a similar situation, and where the control of the ultimate 'employer' was exercised through an extensive hierarchy of managers and supervisors.

As Weber more than perhaps anyone else has emphasized, the Industrial Revolution itself, and the subsequent developments in industrialized societies, were dependent on and also embodied and reinforced certain distinctive values relating to work.[8] These emphasized the intrinsic importance and value of work and the obligation of all to work hard and to the best of one's ability; and the desirability of the rational organization of work, free of traditional and personal restraints, to attain given ends. Labour was to be regarded as a commodity to be bought and sold without regard to the character or needs of the labourer, and work was to be organized to maximize efficiency and productivity, not to provide interesting and rewarding tasks, or opportunities for participation or control by the workers. In the early years of the factory system of production much attention was devoted by employers to inculcating an appropriate work ethic and an acceptance of these values,[9] and powerful mechanisms of socialization and communication currently exist to ensure that obligations to work are internalized.[10]

Work therefore has meanings which are given to it by dominant groups in a society and which serve the interests of the powerful. To a greater or lesser extent these may be accepted and internalized by individual members of the society, but they do not exhaust the possible meanings work may have for an individual, nor the range of 'subordinate' value systems which may co-exist in the same society. In a valuable and insightful discussion of the meaning of work, Fox has suggested that there are 'two great alternative meanings' of work for the individual: as an activity of 'central importance to his personality development and life fulfilment' or as 'little more than a tiresome necessity in acquiring the resources for survival or for what he may define as the real living which he begins as work ends'.[11] The objective necessity of work for the survival of human society means that the second, instrumental, view of work must always have some part in the meaning of work for many if not all members of any society. However, it is clear, notably from studies of those without work such as the retired and the unemployed, that work almost always means more than this narrow instrumental view would suggest. In his discussion, for example, Fox describes eight ways in which work can be important to the individual in addition to its importance as a source of income. It provides opportunities to relate to society, and opportunities for interaction with others; it sustains status and self-respect, and offers a sense of personal identity; it structures the passage of time and distracts from private worries, fears and disappointments; and it provides scope for the satisfaction of 'achievement', and offers the possibility of identifying with a transcendent cause.[12] Jahoda provides a similar list:[13]

> ... an analysis of employment as an institution makes it possible to specify some broad categories of experience, enforced on the overwhelming majority of those who participate in it: the imposition of a time structure, the enlargement of the scope of social achievement into areas less emotionally charged than family life, participation in a collective purpose or effort, the assignment by virtue of employment of status and identity, and required regular activity. These categories of experience ... follow necessarily from the structural forms of modern employment.

It is obviously very difficult to explore on a large scale and in quantitative terms these ways in which work may be significant to an individual, but it is important to keep them in mind as possibilities when considering the more tangible, and often very restricted rewards, and costs, of working.

Work is important to an individual not just in ways of which he or she may be aware, however, but also because the work people do — their occupations — are the most important influences on the life chances of them and their families. When it comes to considering income, health, educational opportunity and achievement of children, liability to accident, to unemployment and redundancy, rates of infant and adult mortality and morbidity, and many other social characteristics, it is occupational categories which reveal the clearest patterns of difference. Indeed for this reason most discussions of 'social stratification' or 'social class' in contemporary Britain are based on occupational categories.[14] Such work-related inequalities of condition and opportunity exist even though those affected may not always be aware of them or may consider them unacceptable.

This is not to argue, of course, either that occupational categories are a satisfactory basis for discussion of 'social class' or that life chances are solely related to occupation. Occupational categories provide little help, for example, in identifying the 'owners of the means of production' from the non-owners, or the 'propertied' from those who lack property, which Marx and Weber in their rather different ways saw as the basic divisions in the class structure in capitalist societies.[15] There are, too, other powerful influences on life chances. As this and other chapters in this volume demonstrate, differences of gender, race and age are related to inequalities of condition and of opportunity, in some areas reinforcing those related to work and occupation and in others cutting across them. In addition there are considerable regional differences within Britain, though they may be accounted for partly by the different industrial and occupational composition of the various regions.[16] Those who have investigated housing markets have argued that housing 'classes', determined by their differential access to the means of accommodation, do not correspond to occupationally based classes, because of the allocation of public housing in terms of administrative rather than market criteria, and because of discrimination on the grounds of colour or ethnic origin.[17] Similarly in studies of educational opportunity and achievement a number of factors, such as size of family, social origin of the mother, parental interests, and the nature of the school, which are not straightforwardly related to the occupation of the parents, can be influential on the outcomes of educational process.[18] Many of these additional factors, however, are modifications of the central influence and importance of occupation, or are mediated through occupational differences.

In the following sections we shall pursue some of these concerns with work in more detail and attempt to describe and understand the current situation in Britain. We shall consider first of all the changing occupational structure of British society and the ways in which occupations can be classified to indicate similarities of social situation and life chances. Then we shall look at the costs and rewards of work, particularly for those in employment, including both the more obvious material rewards and the less tangible privileges and deprivations associated with various types of occupations. Finally, the question of the occupational opportunities open to different social groups must be considered to see how access to particular types of work and employment is structured. In this context social origins and social mobility, educational qualifications and aspects of the workings of the labour market will be seen to be of considerable importance.

THE CHANGING OCCUPATIONAL STRUCTURE

Highly industrialized societies are characterized by an extensive and complex division of labour. The variety of jobs which men and women do is extremely large. The most comprehensive indices of this are the lists of job titles used by Census and other authorities in their coding of occupations for official statistics or other administrative purposes; for example, the current Office of Population Censuses and Surveys *Classification of Occupations* lists approximately 23,000 occupational titles, classified into 161 occupational groups.[19] Any attempt to describe the occupational structure of a society must therefore categorize and classify the variety of men's and women's work in some way. All forms of categorization are both arbitrary (to some extent at least) and likely to conceal as well as reveal significant differences and similarities between occupations.[20] Such problems can be partly overcome by considering a variety of approaches, and in this section we shall consider several types of classification, which can be roughly ranged along a continuum from the 'non-evaluative' (or less evaluative) to the more 'evaluative'.

By 'non-evaluative' I mean those sets of categories which refer, so far as this is ever possible, to objective characteristics of the job or occupation. The occupational structures of societies differ, for example, in terms of the distribution of the working population between different industries or economic sectors (groups of related industries). The working population can be differentiated too in terms of its members' economic status; slavery and other forms of unfree labour no longer exist in most industrialized societies, but there are significant differences in the social and economic situation of employers, the self-employed, employees, and unpaid family workers, and their relative proportions have changed over time. Thirdly, there is the possibility of grouping occupations in terms of the similarities in the type of work done, whatever may be the economic status of the persons concerned or their industrial location; in this case we can describe groups of occupations as 'manual or non-manual'; as 'clerical', 'technical', 'managerial', and 'professional'; and more evaluatively, as 'skilled' or 'unskilled'.[21]

'Evaluative' schemes pose rather more problems but can be much more revealing. They involve grouping and ranking occupations in terms of some judgement of their desirability, standing or prestige, judgements which are made either by the administrator or investigator, or by a sample of members of the population in question. As examples of the first type of evaluation we have the Registrar General's allocation of all occupations to one of five (or more recently six) 'social classes', based on 'general standing within the community of the occupation concerned', and to one of sixteen (sometimes seventeen) 'socio-economic groups' based on differences in status and skill. Because of the apparent arbitrariness of these categorizations some investigators have asked a sample of redundants to grade occupations, and have then attempted to create their own scales; or have created scales based on the pattern of social relationships of a large sample of respondents.[22]

The main advantage of evaluative schemes for our purposes is that they may group occupations in a way which takes account of a number of their socially relevant concomitants, such as their level and type of rewards, their social standing, the education, training and skills needed, and so on. Although no set of occupational categories can be regarded as a straightforward division of the population into 'classes' as the sociologist would understand that term, schemes of occupational grading probably come closest to grouping together those with similar 'life chances'.[23] They are therefore the best available basis for exploring the differential impact of work for men's and women's lives and social situations in our society.

It is not my intention to provide a detailed description and analysis of the changing occupational structure of Britain. Such accounts are already available and involve considering in detail the ways in which sources and classifications of data have changed over time.[24] But a brief historical background will be helpful in putting the subsequent discussion into perspective.

Occupational Classifications

During the past 140 years — the period for which detailed and moderately reliable statistics are available — not only has the absolute size of the economically active population grown as a result of the overall increase in population, from just under 7 million in Great Britain in 1841 to over 25 million in 1981, but the activity rate (roughly speaking the proportion of those old enough to work who are actually working) has also increased from 50 per cent in 1841 to 61 per cent in 1981.[25] Whereas up until 1931 this increase occurred for both men and women, since then the increased proportion of women in employment, and especially of married women, has more than compensated for the declining proportion of adult men who are economically active. The increased participation rate on the part of married women appears to have halted, but up until the late 1970s it more than compensated for the growing proportions of men who have been retired, and of men and women who were full-time students. As table 3.1 shows, the absolute number of men who are economically active has fallen since 1961 whereas the number of women has grown throughout the post-war period and particularly during the 1950s and 1970s. The other major change over this period is, of course, the increase in the number of unemployed, particularly men, an increase which has been particularly great in the period since 1971, and which will be considered further below.

The industrial distribution of the labour force (including employers and workers on their own account) shows considerable change over the same period. In 1851 22 per cent of the economically active population in Great Britain were engaged in agriculture, forestry and fishing; by 1911 this proportion had fallen to under 8 per cent; a further sixty years later, in 1971, the proportion was less than 2 per cent. In contrast the proportion in manufacturing industry (including gas, electricity and water) has remained fairly constant at 40 per cent, nearly 35 per cent and nearly 40 per cent in these same three years; and the major growth has occurred in the 'service industries' (but excluding building and construction — about 6 per cent of the labour force) which have grown in size almost without interruption — 29 per cent in 1851, 45 per cent in 1911 and 51 per cent in 1971. None of the economic sectors so far mentioned includes 'mining and quarrying', in which employment reached a peak of over 7 per cent of the labour force in 1921 to decline to less than 4 per cent in 1951 (when there were still nearly 700,000 miners) and less than 2 per cent in 1971.[26]

These overall figures conceal some important intra-sectoral changes. Within manufacturing, for example, more than 12 per cent of the occupied population were employed in the textile industries in 1841 and 8 per cent in clothing and footwear, proportions which had only fallen slightly by 1911; in 1971, however, textiles accounted for approximately 2.5 per cent of the occupied population and clothing and footwear for 2 per cent. In contrast the group of industries described, in the 1911 categorization, as 'metal manufacture, machines, implements, vehicles, previous metals etc.' has employed a greatly increasing proportion of the labour force — 6 per cent in 1841, 10.5 per cent in 1911 and about 19 per cent in 1971. Within the service sector, too, there have been changes of a similar magnitude: a marked decline in employment in private domestic and other services, from 19 per cent of the labour force in 1841 and over 14 per cent in 1911 to 8 per cent (in 'miscellaneous services') in 1971; and a steady growth of the proportion in commercial and financial activities and in public administration.[27]

Table 3.1 Economic Activity in the UK, 1951-81[1] (thousands)

	Total				Males				Females			
	1951	1961	1971	1981[2]	1951	1961	1971	1981[2]	1951	1961	1971	1981[2]
Population aged 15 and over (16 and over in 1981)	38,899	40,373	42,127	43,700	18,336	19,159	20,080	20,900	20,562	21,214	22,047	22,800
Economically Active												
Employees in employment	20,970	22,825	22,122	21,198	13,767	14,661	13,715	12,264	7,203	8,164	8,407	8,935
Self-employed (with or without employees)	1,798	1,760	1,909	1,856	1,469	1,427	1,534	1,485	329	332	375	371
Total in civil employment	22,768	24,585	24,031	23,054	15,236	16,088	15,249	13,749	7,532	8,496	8,782	9,306
Unemployed	207	287	724	2,681	139	208	618	1,918	68	78	106	763
Total civilian labour force	22,974	24,871	24,755	25,735	15,375	16,297	15,867	15,667	7,600	8,575	8,888	10,069
H.M. Forces	835	474	368	334	812	459	353	317	23	15	15	17
Total working population	**23,809**	**23,345**	**25,123**	**26,069**	**16,187**	**16,756**	**16,220**	**15,984**	**7,623**	**8,590**	**8,903**	**10,086**
Total working population as a percentage of population aged 15/16 and over	*61*	*63*	*60*	*60*	*88*	*87*	*81*	*76*	*37*	*40*	*40*	*44*

Notes:
1 Figures for June each year.
2 Estimates.

Source: 1951 and 1961: *British Labour Statistics: Historical Abstract* (1971), pp. 220–2; 1971 and 1981: *Annual Abstract of Statistics, 119, 1983* (1983), pp. 8–9, 112; *Social Trends No. 13, 1983* (1982), p. 12.

Table 3.2   Employees in Employment by Industry in the UK, 1961–81 (thousands)

	1961 Total	1971 Total	1981 Total	1981 Males	1981 Females	1981 totals as % of all employees
Agriculture, forestry, fishing	710	432	360	270	89	1.6
Mining and quarrying	727	396	332	316	16	1.6
Manufacturing						
Food, drink, tobacco	793	770	632	385	247	
Chemicals, coal, petroleum products	499	482	432	320	113	
Metal manufacture	643	557	326	290	36	
Engineering & allied	3,654	3,615	2,739	2,171	568	
Textiles, leather, clothing	1,444	1,124	707	291	417	
Rest of manufacturing	1,508	1,511	1,202	873	329	
Total manufacturing	8,540	8,058	6,038	4,330	1,709	28.5
Construction	1,485	1,262	1,132	1,023	109	5.3
Gas, electricity, water	389	377	340	272	68	1.6
Services						
Transport & communication	1,678	1,568	1,440	1,164	276	
Distributive trades	2,767	2,610	2,635	1,180	1,455	
Insurance, banking, finance	684	976	1,233	577	656	
Professional & scientific	2,124	2,989	3,695	1,161	2,533	
Miscellaneous	1,819	1,946	2,414	1,017	1,397	
Public administration	1,311	1,509	1,579	954	625	
Total Services	10,382	11,597	12,996	6,053	6,942	61.3
All industries & services	22,233	22,122	21,198	12,264	8,934	100.0

Source: *Social Trends, No. 13, 1983* (1982), p. 54.

The detailed changes which have taken place in the UK between 1961 and 1981 are shown in table 3.2. Perhaps the most striking is the marked and relatively sudden decline in the number and proportion employed in manufacturing industry, which occurred during the 1970s. This decline has continued since 1981; in June 1983, in Great Britain, it was estimated that there were 5,378,000 employees in manufacturing industry, as compared with just under 6 million two years earlier, and they represented 26.5 per cent of all employees. During both the 1960s and the 1970s employment in the service sector grew, especially 'insurance, banking and finance', and 'professional and scientific' (e.g. education, health) and 'miscellaneous' (e.g. catering, personal services); these are all areas of work where relatively large numbers of women are employed, which, as we have seen is reflected in their participation rate. Since 1980 in fact the total number of men and women employed in the service sector has also declined.[28]

Clearly both the long term and the shorter term changes in the industrial distribution of the labour force, allied to technological and organizational changes within industries, have had significant consequences for the typical patterns of work experience and of social relations with employers and fellow employees. Similar longer term changes have occurred in all highly industrialized societies as mechanization and other technical and organizational developments allow greater productivity first in agriculture and then in the manufacture of goods. The more recent changes in part reflect the continuation of this process in manufacturing industry and its extension to some service industries. In part, however, the causes are more specific to the UK–recession, weakened position in the world economy; and in part the changes may reflect a more general 'new international division of labour' whereby manufacturing is increasingly being located in the less developed societies of the world where labour costs are much lower. Further rapid changes must be expected in the next decade or two as the full impact on employment is felt of the introduction of micro-electronic technology which is likely to be even greater in some service industries than in manufacturing.[29]

Thirdly, there have been some changes in the economic status of those who are economically active. At all dates since the First World War at least nine out of every ten members of the occupied population have been employees, but the proportion has grown slightly and since the Second World War the proportion who are self-employed, with or without employees, has fluctuated between 7 and 7.5 per cent (see table 3.1).[30]

Most interesting and relevant to our subsequent discussion are the changes in the occupational distribution of the labour force. Unfortunately the distinction between the industrial and occupational distributions of the labour force has only been embodied in Census statistics since 1921, and classifications have been changed at intervals since then, so that it is impossible to compile a continuous series of data classified on the same basis. It is however possible to suggest some of the more important of the changes which have taken place, and to indicate in a little more detail the ways in which certain occupations which are less affected by alterations in classification have grown or declined in importance.

The enormous absolute and relative increase in the numbers of non-manual workers is probably the most dramatic and important change in the occupational structure of Britain since the Industrial Revolution and the shift from agriculture to industry. It has a number of components.[31] Of the greatest quantitative importance are the growth in employment in 'clerical' occupations and the expansion of (broadly) 'commercial' occupations; the work situations and social relations of the former have been described and analysed by a number of sociologists, but the latter rather less socially distinct grouping appears so far to have attracted less interest.[32] A second important component of this shift into white-collar occupations is the growth of public employment from less than 6 per cent of the working population in 1901 to nearly 25 per cent in 1950 (in Great Britain) and nearly 30 per cent in 1978 (in the United Kingdom), a phenomenon which has attracted a lot of public comment in recent years. There has been a continuous growth in the absolute and relative numbers of national and local government employees since 1901, and in the last twenty-five years this has more than outweighed any decline in numbers in the armed forces and in the nationalized industries, so that public sector employment has continued to grow. Though these figures include many manual workers and professional employees, a large proportion are in clerical and administrative occupations.[33] Current governmental measures to 'denationalize' or 'privatize' some publicly owned industries and services will, of course, reduce public sector employment.

An especially significant increase has been that of the professions, because it is the occupations which have successfully established the claim to be 'professional' which have secured for their members the greatest control over conditions of work and autonomy on the job.[34] The attractions of 'professional' status mean that this label is more widely claimed than it is granted, and precise definitions of 'professional occupations' are impossible, but the general trend over the past century or so is clear. In addition to the considerable absolute and relative increase in the numbers of 'professionals' there have been significant changes in the internal composition of this category of occupations: the traditional 'professions' — clergy, lawyers and doctors — are a much smaller proportion of the total, as also are teachers, and the newer 'professions' based on science and technology have increased enormously; and the former more or less clear demarcation between men's and women's 'professional' work has been somewhat eroded though not eliminated.

A final important element in the absolute and relative increase in the number of non-manual workers is the growth of the 'administrative overhead' in industry, the proportion employed in managerial, administrative and technical occupations. This process has occurred in both manufacturing and service industry at least since the early years of this century, in Britain and in other highly industrialized societies. It reflects the growth of bureaucracy and the adoption of 'rational, scientific' management techniques as enterprises became larger and technologically more complex.[35] Between 1948 and 1981, for example, the proportion of administrative, technical and clerical workers in manufacturing industry in Britain increased from 16 per cent to 29.6 per cent of the total number of employees.[36] The growth in the sizes of the establishments and the enterprises within which people work also represents an important change in the *context* of work. In manufacturing industry in the UK there were 533 *establishments* recorded as employing 1,000 or more persons in 1935, and 908 in 1981; and in 1977 the 'Bullock Report' on industrial democracy suggested that there were over two thousand *enterprises* in the UK which employed more than 200 persons, of which 1,199 employed more than 1,000 and 157 more than 10,000.[37]

The overall impact of these changes for the period from 1911 to 1971 in Britain is shown in table 3.3.[38] The proportion in manual work has declined from nearly 75 per cent before the First World War to just under 55 per cent in 1971 and the numbers and proportion in white-collar work have grown correspondingly. The relative, and in 1971 absolute, decline in manual work has affected skilled, semi-skilled and unskilled workers. In contrast, in this sixty-year period when the total occupied population has grown by a third, the number of white-collar workers has grown three times, the number of clerks four times, and the number of higher professionals five times. However, it is important to note that these overall occupational shifts have had rather different implications for men and for women. Women are relatively under-represented in manual occupations and over-represented in white-collar work; as a corollary the proportion of men in manual work has fallen rather less than the proportion for the labour force as a whole, from over 73 per cent in 1911 to just under 61 per cent in 1971. On the other hand, within the two broad groupings of non-manual and manual work women are under-represented in the more skilled categories (managers and administrators, and higher professionals; skilled manual work) and over-represented in the less skilled, less responsible types of work; and

Table 3.3 The Occupied Population of Great Britain by Major Occupational Groups, 1911-71

Occupational Groups	Number of persons in major occupational groups (thousands)				Occupational groups as a percentage of the total occupied population (percentages)				Female workers as a percentage of all workers in each occupational group (percentages)			
	1911	1931	1951	1971	1911	1931	1951	1971	1911	1931	1951	1971
Employers and Proprietors	1,232	1,407	1,117	622	6.7	6.7	5.0	2.6	18.8	19.8	20.0	24.9
White-collar workers	3,433	4,841	6,948	10,405	18.7	23.0	30.9	42.7	29.8	35.8	42.3	47.9
(a) Managers and administrators	631	770	1,245	2,085	3.4	3.7	5.5	8.6	19.8	13.0	15.2	21.6
(b) Higher professionals	184	240	435	928	1.0	1.1	1.9	3.8	6.0	7.5	8.3	9.9
(c) Lower professionals and technicians	560	728	1,059	1,880	3.1	3.5	4.7	7.7	62.9	58.5	53.5	52.1
(d) Foremen and inspectors	237	323	590	736	1.3	1.5	2.6	3.0	4.2	8.7	13.4	13.1
(e) Clerks	832	1,404	2,341	3,412	4.5	6.7	10.4	14.0	21.4	46.0	60.2	73.2
(f) Salesmen and shop assistants	989	1,376	1,278	1,364	5.4	6.5	5.7	5.6	35.2	37.2	51.6	59.8
Manual workers	13,685	14,776	14,450	13,343	74.6	70.3	64.2	54.7	30.5	28.8	26.1	29.4
(a) Skilled	5,608	5,618	5,617		30.5	26.7	24.9		24.0	21.3	15.7	13.5
(b) Semi-skilled	6,310	6,044	6,124		34.4	28.7	27.2		40.4	42.9	38.1	46.5
(c) Unskilled	1,767	3,114	2,709		9.6	14.8	12.0		15.5	15.0	20.3	37.2
Total occupied population	18,350	21,024	22,515	24,370	100.00	100.00	100.00	100.00	29.6	29.8	30.8	36.5

Sources: Abbreviated from G. S. Bain, R. Bacon and R. Pimlott, 'The Labour Force' in A. H. Halsey (ed.), *Trends in British Society since 1900* (London 1972), p. 113; R. Price and G. S. Bain, 'Union growth re-visited: 1948–1974 in perspective', *British Journal of Industrial Relations*, Vol. 14, No. 3 (November 1976), p. 346; and C. Hakim, *Occupational Segregation*, Department of Employment Research Paper No. 9 (London 1979), p. 28. There are some minor differences between these sources. For an account of the definitions of the various categories and the way in which the original table was constructed, see G. S. Bain, *The Growth of White-Collar Unionism*, (Oxford 1970), esp. pp. 189–90.

with respect to some of these areas of work (managers and administrators; skilled manual workers) the situation has worsened rather than improved since 1911.[39]

The distributions of the occupied population in terms of industry, economic status and occupation indicate the broad long-term changes which have taken place in the occupational structure of the United Kingdom over the past century or more. Such sociographic and descriptive data do provide an important point of reference. The traditional area of work for most of the world's population for most of recorded history (work on the land) is of very minor importance, statistically, in the UK and has been for nearly a hundred years. Work for an increasing proportion of the population, indeed, no longer means manual labour — or even manual labour with the assistance of mechanical power — but the manipulation of symbolic materials in an office, or the processing, in some way or other, of people. Work for an increasing proportion is no longer concerned with the production or distribution of a material product, but with providing services. Even in extractive and manufacturing industry the heavy labour which was romanticized by the pre-Raphaelites, or captured more grimly and prosaically by many illustrators and engravers, is less important, and work for many involves making a minute contribution to a possibly unknown product in mass production or process industry.[40] The fascination of construction sites and men digging holes in the road is perhaps all the greater for its increasing rarity as a type of work.

Status Rankings

The more evaluative classifications build on the type of occupational categories included in table 3.3 to produce rankings either of the whole occupied population, or of heads of households and their families, which reflect other social characteristics. The Registrar General's classification of Social Class has been in use, in one form or another, since 1911. Originally introduced to show variations in infant mortality rates (that most sensitive indicator of standards of living), it has been used to identify a whole range of social differences in British society. The six categories currently in use are:[41]

  I   Professional, etc., occupations (including doctors, lawyers, chemists, and clergymen)
  II Intermediate occupations (including most managerial and senior administrative occupations, e.g. sales managers, authors, MPs, colliery managers, personnel managers, senior government officials, school teachers, farmers, physiotherapists, and nurses)
  III Skilled occupations
      (N) Non-manual (including typists, clerical workers, sales workers, sales representatives, and shop assistants)
      (M) Manual (including cooks, railway guards, plasterers, bricklayers, foremen packers, and foremen in the engineering and allied trades)
  IV Partly-skilled occupations (including barmen, bus conductors, canteen assistants, and telephone operators [but not supervisors who are III N])
  V   Unskilled occupations (including office cleaners and stevedores [but not foremen who are III M], lorry drivers' mates, and labourers)

The distribution of the population of Great Britain in 1971, in terms of these categories, is shown in table 3.4. This table is roughly comparable with the occupational

Table 3.4 Social Class Composition of People Aged 15 and Over, for Various Groups in Great Britain, 1971

Percentages and thousands

	Men only			Women only			Men and women aged 15 and over		
	Economically active	Retired	Economically active and retired	Married		Single widowed and divorced	Own occupation of economically active and retired	Head of family	Chief economic supporter
				Own[1] class	Husbands[2] class	Own[3] class			
	(1)	(2)	(3)	(4)	(5)	(6)	(7)	(8)	(9)
Percentage in each Social Class:									
I	5.2	3.0	5.0	0.9	5.3	1.2	3.6	5.1	4.9
II	17.8	19.1	18.0	16.2	19.8	19.2	17.8	20.0	19.8
III N	11.9	12.1	11.9	35.4	11.3	41.2	21.1	11.9	14.2
III M	39.0	34.2	38.5	10.0	39.0	10.8	28.4	37.9	34.8
IV	17.8	20.3	18.1	28.2	17.5	22.7	20.9	18.0	18.6
V	8.3	11.2	8.6	9.4	7.1	4.9	8.2	7.3	7.7
Total classified (=100%)	15,368	1,911	17,279	5,697	12,365	3,834	26,809	13,150	15,907
Total[4] unclassified	516	323	909	1,101	471	1,549	3,488	694	1,374
Total in Great Britain	15,884	2,304	18,188	6,797	12,835	5,383	30,367	13,844	17,281

Notes:
1 Economically active and retired married women by own social class.
2 Married women enumerated with their husband by the social class of husband including both the economically active and retired, and those economically inactive.
3 Economically active and retired single, widowed, and divorced women.
4 Unclassified persons: those for whom no occupation or inadequate information was reported in the Census. A large proportion of this group were out of work, retired, or inactive at Census date.

Based on: Census of Population, 1971, Economic Activity Tables

Source: *Social Trends*, No. 6 (HMSO 1975) p. 11.

distribution in table 3.3 in terms of the proportions classified in non-manual and manual work, but differs from it in so far as a much larger proportion of the occupied population are shown as skilled manual workers (Social Class III M). It also demonstrates that there are considerable differences in the 'Social Class' distributions of men and women; this means that there are many households in which husband and wife are in a different 'Social Class' if this is categorized on the basis of their own work. In fact this situation is the more common, and there are a considerable number of cases where the wife has the 'higher' 'Social Class' ranking.[42] Such differences necessitate some reservations about attempting to relate work to other social characteristics, when these are done on the assumption that households can be classified in terms of the husband's or even the head of the household's occupation. The distinction between Social Class I and II is also somewhat arbitrary; all major professional occupations are classified as I, but even higher administrative and managerial occupations are classed as II.

More recently the Census authorities have devised a separate classification of Socio-Economic Groups, with the intention of forming categories of people with similar 'social, cultural and recreational standards' and of producing a larger number of more sharply defined groups. The categories used, and the relationship between them and the Social Class categories, can be seen in table 3.5. Although there are important areas of overlap, the separation of workers in agriculture from other workers, and the use of employment status as a differentiating factor, make the relationship a fairly complex one.[43]

In the *General Household Survey* the Office of Population Censuses and Surveys has collapsed the sixteen Socio-Economic Groups into six ranked groupings which, it should be noted, are roughly comparable to the Registrar General's Social Classes. These groupings are used for the tabulation of some data to be presented below and the details are as follows:[44]

General Household Survey – Socio-Economic Groups

		Corresponding SEGs	Examples
1	Professional	3, 4	Doctors, lawyers, chemists, clergymen
2	Employers and Managers	1, 2, 13	Sales managers, MPs, colliery managers, personnel managers, senior government officials, farmers
3	Intermediate & junior non-manual	5, 6	Teachers, nurses, physiotherapists, sales representatives, clerical workers, typists, telephone operators, shop assistants
4	Skilled manual (including foremen and supervisors) including own account non-professionals	8, 9, 12, 14	Railway guards, foreman packers, foremen in engineering and allied trades, bricklayers
5	Semi-skilled manual and personal service	7, 10, 15	Cooks, canteen assistants, barmen, bus conductors
6	Unskilled manual	11	Lorry driver's mates, labourers, stevedores, office cleaners

Table 3.5   Economically Active Population by Socio-economic Group and by Social Class, GB, 1971

Socio-economic groups	Males	Females (thousands)	Percentage of total economically active by social class[1]						
			I	II	III	IV	V	Not classified	Total
1 Employers and managers (large establishments)	597	101		2.7	0.1				2.8
2 Employers and managers (small establishments)	1,231	316		4.9	1.1	0.1	[2]		6.2
3 Professional workers – self-employed	140	11	0.6						0.6
4 Professional workers – employees	660	76	2.9						2.9
5 Intermediate non-manual workers	886	1,011		6.9	0.7				7.6
6 Junior non-manual workers	1,896	3,408			19.2	2.0			21.2
7 Personal service workers	160	1,142		0.1	1.4	3.7			5.2
8 Foremen and supervisors – manual	564	55			2.5				2.5
9 Skilled manual workers	4,775	549			21.3				21.3
10 Semi-skilled manual workers	2,033	1,145				12.7			12.7
11 Unskilled manual workers	1,222	667					7.5		7.5
12 Own-account workers (other than professional)	710	176	1.0	2.0	0.4	0.2			3.6
13 Farmers – employers and managers	122	15	0.5						0.5
14 Farmers – own-account	131	21	0.6						0.6
15 Agricultural workers	242	59			0.1	1.1			1.2
16 Members of Armed Forces	240	12						1.0	1.0
17 Inadequately described occupations	276	375						2.6	2.6
Total economically active population	15,884	9,138	3.5	16.8	48.3	20.0	7.8	3.6	100.0

1   The titles of each social class are given as Professional (I), Intermediate (II), Skilled (III), Semi-skilled (IV) and Unskilled (V).
2   Less than 0.2 per cent.

Source: OPCS, *Census 1971: Economic Activity*, Part 4 (HMSO 1975), table 29 based on 10% sample results, reproduced in C. Hakim and W. R. Hawes, 'The Labour Force' in Open University, *Labour and Income* (Milton Keynes 1982), p. 34.

In devising these classifications of 'Social Class' and 'Socio-Economic Grouping' the Census office were using evaluative criteria to determine into which category any particular occupation was to be placed. The bases of the classifications were not exclusively or even mainly economic, but represented a synthesis of mostly implicit criteria such as the skill of the occupation and the education and/or training required for it, but also including – in the case of 'Social Class' at least – an assessment of how members of the society in general regarded the occupation, how they would rank it as compared with others. These assessments were, in a sense, second-hand and represented 'what the investigators thought other people would think' of an occupation. Such procedures obviously have severe limitations and as has been mentioned already this has led sociologists to attempt to develop occupational rankings which are empirically based either on the views expressed by samples of the population, or on the pattern of social relations of a large sample of respondents.[45] Such occupational rankings might be considered preferable to the official categories, but their use is more problematic than might be thought at first, and is in any case impractical in any discussion such as this one. It is more problematic because of the ambiguities about precisely what respondents are doing when they grade occupations. Are they assessing prestige, strictly defined as symbolic advantages and power, or are they evaluating jobs as more or less desirable in terms of a range of considerations?[46] It is impractical because the generally available official and national statistics have not been tabulated in these terms and cannot easily be so retabulated. Thus while acknowledging both the importance of developing more sociologically satisfactory ways of categorizing occupations, and the limitations of official classifications, our analysis will depend heavily on the official sets of categories. For discovering the broad differences in the costs and rewards of work – to which we now turn – they are indeed probably adequate.

THE REWARDS AND DEPRIVATIONS OF WORK

As we have seen, 'work' for most people in Britain means work as an employee. In the majority of cases, therefore, the nature of the employment contract is a crucial analytical point of reference in considering the rewards and deprivations arising from work. Before considering it in more detail, however, we need to discuss briefly whether the conditions and experience of work for those not dependent on an employer are likely to be very different from those of comparable employees.

Self-employment

Those who run their own business and employ others, or who are self-employed, comprised about 8 per cent of the occupied population of the UK in 1983. In terms of their industrial distribution, in 1979 they were numerically important only in agriculture, forestry and fishing (approximately 42 per cent of all occupied), in construction (approximately 24 per cent), in the distributive trades (approximately 11 per cent) and in 'miscellaneous services' (approximately 7.5 per cent).[47] In contrast, of all those working in manufacturing industry as a whole, only just over 1.5 per cent were employers or self-employed. The occupational distribution of employers and the self-employed presents a similar picture: they outnumber employees in the same occupations only in a very few cases – farmers, builders, shopkeepers, certain professional groups (lawyers, clergymen, dentists and chiropodists) and certain service occupations (watch repairers, shoe repairers, publicans, hotel keepers and restauranteurs) – and it is only in these and a few similar occupations that this category of workers is at all numerous in absolute terms.[48]

The sense of autonomy, of working for oneself, of running one's own business, is both the main differentiating characteristic of self-employment and the main attraction for those who aspire to such economic independence. In many cases the types of tasks which have to be performed – and the conditions under which they are performed – and the other rewards and deprivations of working are largely the same. The importance of autonomy and independence as an ideal, for many people in our society, should not, however, be underestimated. In recent years it has been explicitly encouraged by the government because the creation of small businesses has been seen as desirable in itself and in providing an important source of economic growth.

In official statistics the main differentiation made within the category of the self-employed is that between those with and those without employees. In a study of 'the entrepreneurial middle class' Scase and Goffee distinguish four sub-categories: the *self-employed*, formally employing no labour though they may depend on the unpaid services of their families; *small employers*, who work alongside employees but in addition perform administrative and managerial tasks; *owner-controllers*, singularly and solely responsible for the administration and management of their businesses; and *owner-directors*, who depend on managerial structures to supervise and control their business activities.[49] Autonomy and economic independence are important for the self-employed wherever they come on this continuum. Employers have the additional problems of depending on, and of supervising and controlling, the work of others, but, as businesses grow in size, they also have the prospects of unearned income and increased economic security from the accumulation of capital.

Thus the self-employed must be seen as a very heterogeneous category ranging from the independent artisan or small shopkeeper at one end, who obtains his or her independence at the probable cost of longer hours of work, similar or lower levels of earnings and considerably greater anxiety than a comparable employee;[50] to the 'propertied' directors of their own businesses at the other, not markedly different in respect of income or autonomy from the 'non-propertied' directors of comparable businesses whose ownership is in other hands.[51] To be independent, to have autonomy at work, is important subjectively and objectively as we shall see in discussing employment. However, when the majority of the self-employed and employers are compared to employees doing the same sort of work (i.e. self-employed professionals with employed professionals, small shopkeepers with managers of similar shops) the general patterns of their other rewards and deprivations from work are probably very similar. The major exceptions are probably the higher professionals and those with larger and growing businesses where economic independence can provide incomes and material benefits markedly greater than are normally available to comparable employees.

The Employment Contract

For the great majority of the occupied population in the UK work is regulated primarily by a contract of employment, an agreement to an exchange between the employer and the employee. The nature of the agreement is, however, very complex, especially as it is seen as also being typically surrounded by a variety of obligations and expectations which may not be formally specified. At its simplest it represents the exchange of payment for labour power, and in certain pieceworking and sub-contracting situations may involve little more than that. In all other situations and thus for almost all employees, however, the exchange necessarily involves the employee entering into a continuing relationship with the employer, a relationship in which she or he is placed in a position of subordination. Giddens has written: 'What really distinguishes capitalism as a form of economic system is that labour (power) *itself* becomes a commodity, bought and sold on the market.'[52] In contrast to the case with other commodities, however, the exchange of labour power cannot be instantaneous; what the employer obtains is the employee's *capacity to work*, and to make effective use of this he has to control and direct the activities of the employee whilst in his employment. From the employee's point of view, therefore, work involves not only the deprivations which result from the expenditure of physical and mental energy but also those incurred by the loss of autonomy to the authority of the employer. How this authority is exercised, the sorts of controls and direction to which the employee is subject, form part of the costs of working, though ones which it may be difficult to quantify.

For these reasons employment in capitalist societies like the UK must be regarded as involving an inherent coercive element. All those without sufficient wealth to provide for themselves without working are forced to sell their labour power to an employer in the labour market; and this necessarily involves entering a subordinate role in the employing organization, though the degree of subordination may vary considerably — some employees share in the exercise of authority. Control over the exercise and products of a man's labour are therefore lost. In return for his or her labour, of course, the employee receives the means of subsistence. In terms of conventional analyses there is a disagreement as to what would constitute a 'fair' return for work, as wages and salaries are clearly not just the product of market forces and cannot be legitimated in those terms. In terms of a Marxist analysis, in contrast, there can never be a 'fair' wage or salary in a capitalist society as the employer appropriates the 'surplus value' which is created by the employee over and above what is needed for his own maintenance and reproduction.[53]

Whether or not a Marxist analysis is accepted, many commentators accept the notion that employees in modern industrial societies suffer 'alienation'. They differ, however, in whether they see 'alienation' as inherent in the structure of work relations in capitalist and similar societies, or whether they see it as possible to modify or eliminate 'alienation' by appropriate changes in industrial organization and technology, but still within the same overall societal framework. Marx's original conception is well represented in the following passage:[54]

> In what does this alienation of labour consist? First, that the work is *external* to the worker, that it is not part of his nature, that consequently he does not fulfil himself in his work but denies himself, has a feeling of misery, not of well-being, does not develop freely a physical and mental energy, but is physically exhausted and mentally debased. The worker therefore feels himself at home only during his leisure, whereas at work he feels homeless. His work is not voluntary but imposed, *forced labour*. It is not the satisfaction of a need, but only a *means* for satisfying other needs. Its alien character is clearly shown by the fact that as soon as there is no physical or other compulsion it is avoided like the plague. Finally, the alienated character of work for the worker appears in the fact that it is not his work but work for someone else, that in work he does not belong to himself but to another person.

Such a conception of alienation contains, but should not be reduced to, reference to the psychological state of a particular actor or actors; it is more than a synonym for 'job satisfaction'. It encompasses as an essential element particular structural features of a society, whether or not the actors recognize them.[55]

This more wide-ranging view of 'alienation' implies two assertions: first, that something can be said in general about the nature of man and what he needs to realize his full potential, to be fully free; and secondly, that such needs cannot be met within the existing social arrangements of modern industrial society, particularly in its capitalist variants, but probably in most socialist ones also. Both these judgements have been challenged. Some writers have stressed the cultural determination and variability of what people want from their work so that it makes no sense, beyond a very trivial level, to talk of 'needs' or of 'man's essence'.[56] Other writers, operating with different conceptions of human needs or of man's nature, have argued for the possibility of meeting such needs or of realizing man's potential with only relatively minor changes to the organization and administration of work.[57] Thus considerations of work and the employment contract necessarily enter an area where there are basic philosophical disagreements which influence the conduct of research and the interpretations of its findings, and these should be borne in mind when considering the empirical evidence which is discussed below.

It is neither possible nor necessary to continue these debates here, but one implication of them for a discussion of the employment contract is that any consideration of the rewards and deprivations of work must be concerned with more than just the obvious financial rewards and should see subordination and loss of autonomy as a part of the costs of working which can also vary considerably between different work situations. Some would go further and stress that apparent sources of positive satisfaction in work are merely *relative* to the overriding deprivations of work in our sort of society. This is the position taken by Baldamus. He has pointed to the open-ended nature of the employment contract — pay may be specified but the content and intensity of work is not, and often cannot be. The employer therefore has to exercise control over his employees to secure appropriate levels of effort. 'Effort', Baldamus suggests, should be conceptualized as the deprivations of 'impairment', 'tedium' and 'weariness' arising from the work realities of unpleasant and damaging physical conditions, repetitive tasks and coercive work routines, and partially offset by the relative satisfactions of 'inurement', 'traction' and 'contentment'. As such, effort is both inherently subjective (only really known by those experiencing it) and empirically potentially unstable. Stability in the 'effort bargain', which determines the actual day-to-day working out of the relationship between pay and effort, is dependent on shared definitions of what constitutes a 'fair day's pay for a fair day's work', and these arise during socialization before entering work and more especially in the work place.[58]

Baldamus' analysis of the contract of employment is based on the case of the non-skilled worker who only has basic labour power to sell. Many employees, however, have skills, qualifications and/or experience to offer on the labour market, and/or do work where they carry considerable responsibility for reaching decisions. Wages and salaries, therefore, must be seen in many cases as payments for skill or compensations for carrying responsibility. As with effort, both these qualities are hard to define precisely and are subject to negotiation in practice. In the case of skill this is reflected in the frequent disputes and negotiations about differentials and the apportionment of work which occur in industry and elsewhere. In the case of responsibility Jaques has argued that an element of discretion is a characteristic of all employment work, that it becomes increasingly important as one moves up the organizational hierarchy, and that it can be measured in terms of 'time span' and is the essential factor to which 'fair' levels of pay should be related. The first two points are widely accepted, but the degree of responsibility expected, and the payment due for it are typically seen as matters for negotiation on the job, and are not regarded as something which can be objectively determined.[59]

The implications of the discussion in this section so far are that the employment contract necessarily involves elements of coercion and conflict; and that it contains inherent ambiguities or uncertainties over the contribution which the employer can legitimately expect from his or her employees. In turning to look at the rewards in detail we shall see that they too are far from straightforward.

As will be apparent from the above discussion, and as has been stressed by a number of writers, the relationship between employer and employee has central 'calculative' elements, though coercive and/or normative ones are normally also involved.[60] In our sort of society most labour is 'formally free', not legally coerced; and people work because they need to earn their means of subsistence and not primarily for idealistic reasons. The prime rewards for the employee are financial, and jobs are assessed in these terms. A comparison of relative advantages, even in these terms, however, is far from easy as earnings may include a number of components — basic pay, bonuses, overtime pay, shift allowances, and so on. Certainly basic wage rates and salary scales are not necessarily a good guide to the likely level of earnings at a particular point in time and, in the working life of any individual, do not necessarily reflect likely lifetime earnings nor the opportunities within a particular occupation or career for promotion, leading to higher earnings in the future.

Though pay is the most important reward from work it is by no means the only one, and this further complicates consideration of occupational rewards. Many employees receive fringe benefits — holidays with pay, sick pay, pensions, subsidized meals, car allowances or the use of a company car, accommodation allowances or housing at reduced rent, the perks of expense account lunches or the possibility of buying company goods or services at reduced prices, and so on. Systematic information about all these benefits does not exist, but it is possible to consider some of them in detail and their relationship to occupational categories.

It is more difficult to take account of rewards which cannot even potentially be quantified and expressed in money terms, yet there are such rewards which can be of considerable importance in many occupations. Some of them have already been referred to in the introduction in the brief discussion of the possible meanings of work: status and prestige among one's fellows at work and elsewhere; the gratifications deriving from doing work which is intrinsically interesting or which is seen as socially valuable, or which provides opportunities for achievement or personal development. Some jobs are seen as attractive because they are convenient (reasonable hours, a short journey to work) or clean, safe or secure, though such 'attractions' are perhaps better seen as the absence of deprivations than anything more positive.[61] All these less tangible rewards are normally encompassed within investigations of job satisfaction. Ideally such investigations recognize and try to take account of the variety of considerations which may enter into any overall synthesizing judgement about a job. It remains difficult, however, if not impossible without further information, to be sure of the meaning and significance of a general claim to be 'satisfied' or 'dissatisfied' with one's job, so that although we shall consider such evidence we must do so with caution. It must be remembered too that all such judgements are relative to the respondent's expectations and orientations; a work situation with apparently the same 'objective' characteristics may therefore be very differently evaluated by the same respondent at different points in time, or by different respondents at any one time.[62]

Finally, it is important to try to consider the degree of countervailing power typically possessed by an occupation which may enable workers to secure some control over their market and work situations, and so reduce their dependence on employers. In most cases such power derives from the collective organization of the relevant employees so that they can bargain with employers, and if necessary attempt to secure their aims by strikes or other forms of industrial action. The degree of organization in trade unions or professional associations is thus an important means by which the rewards from work may be increased and the deprivations contained. As has been stressed many times in the literature on trade unions, of course, this 'remedy' may prove as bad as − or worse than − the 'disease'; the occupational association may become oligarchically controlled and dominate the market and work situations of its members in as alien a way as did the employers.[63]

The basic deprivations of work have already been discussed − the physical and mental effort involved in working; the psychological costs of carrying responsibility; the costs in terms of effort and deferred gratifications involved in training and acquiring skills and qualifications. It will be apparent that they are very difficult, and probably impossible, to quantify systematically across a whole range of occupations. Some general indications of varying demands for effort can be inferred from information about hours of work, the incidence of shift working, of payment by results, and so on, which we shall consider in conjunction with data on pay. Certain other sources of deprivation are rather less problematic. The physical and social conditions of work differ in their consequences for the health of the employee, so that occupations can be compared in terms of their accident rates, and the likely health and life expectancy of their members. Secondly, occupations, and industries, differ in terms of the degree of job security they offer, though recent experience has indicated that this may change unexpectedly over time; rates of unemployment, the availability of alternative vacancies, the incidence of redundancy, can all, in principle at least, be compared.

A final problem must be mentioned, though it will prove less important than might be thought at first. Many of the characteristics mentioned are incommensurable − they cannot be assessed on the same scale, so that it is impossible to say, for example, that so much extra pay compensates precisely for certain dangerous working conditions. In theory it could become very difficult to make anything but rather impressionistic comparisons between occupations; in practice it is less so because, as we shall see, rather than higher rewards of one sort compensating for absence of other sorts of reward, or for particularly severe deprivations, occupations tend to be generally favoured or deprived in terms of many if not all indices.

In considering the detailed evidence a variety of comparisons will be possible. In some cases particular occupations or industries can be considered; in others only general types of work − skilled manual, for example, or professional; and in others only the basic comparison between manual and non-manual occupations will be possible.

Pay and Hours

The employment contract involves more than an exchange of work (or labour power) for pay, but the income they receive is the most important reward for most employees. We shall consider first the changes in relative earnings for the main occupational categories which have taken place during the present century, then go on to look at the most recent data for all employees in a little more detail, and finally discuss very briefly those at the two ends of the earnings continuum, the high- and the low-paid.

In the conclusion to his survey of changes in occupational structure and earnings in Great Britain between 1906 and 1960 Routh commented: 'The outstanding characteristic of the national pay structure is the rigidity of its relationships',[64] and as the summary of his findings (extended to 1978) in table 3.6 indicates, this is broadly true. Professional, managerial and supervisory employees earned more than manual workers in 1913-14, and continued to do so in 1978; men earned on average between 114 and 121 per cent of the average earnings for both men and women throughout the period, whilst the comparable range for women was consistently very much lower at between 58 and 68 per cent; skilled male manual workers (but not skilled women) consistently earned more than semi- and unskilled workers, whose percentages of average earnings were only slightly higher in 1978 than they had been before the First World War.

Even so there have been some important changes over the period as a whole. In the first place the degree of dispersion of male earnings has declined considerably, and this is reflected, for example, in the fact that whereas in 1913-14 a 'higher professional' earned on average more than three times as much as a skilled manual worker (£328 and £90 p.a. respectively), in 1978 the differential had been reduced to less than twice (£8,286 and £4,354 p.a.). More striking perhaps is the decline in the relative position of male 'lower professionals' and 'clerks', the latter grouping in particular receiving clearly lower earnings than male semi-skilled manual workers in 1978, although clerks had had almost identical average earnings to skilled manual workers until before the Second World War. Among women there were marked changes in the period from 1913-14 to 1922-4 when the non-manual groups and unskilled manual workers all improved their relative earnings considerably; these advantages were reduced as a result of changes in subsequent years; but the pay of clerical and manual women workers increased relatively more than the average in the 1970s to give them some relative improvement overall in the whole period.

In 1965 Routh attributed the relative stability of the pay structure to the very strongly held, even if intuitive, opinions that wage and salary earners have about the appropriate, 'just', pay for their occupations, and the efforts they therefore undertake to maintain or restore differentials. The stability of the overall structure of earnings in the long term is seen as the outcome of the 'almost constant state of change' which results from occupational groups' attempts to improve or regain their relative position in the pay hierarchy – attempts which have the effect of making any major restructuring very difficult.[65]

In 1983 there was also a clear general hierarchy of earnings (in terms of overall averages) which paralleled that reported by Routh for 1978 and earlier years; the most

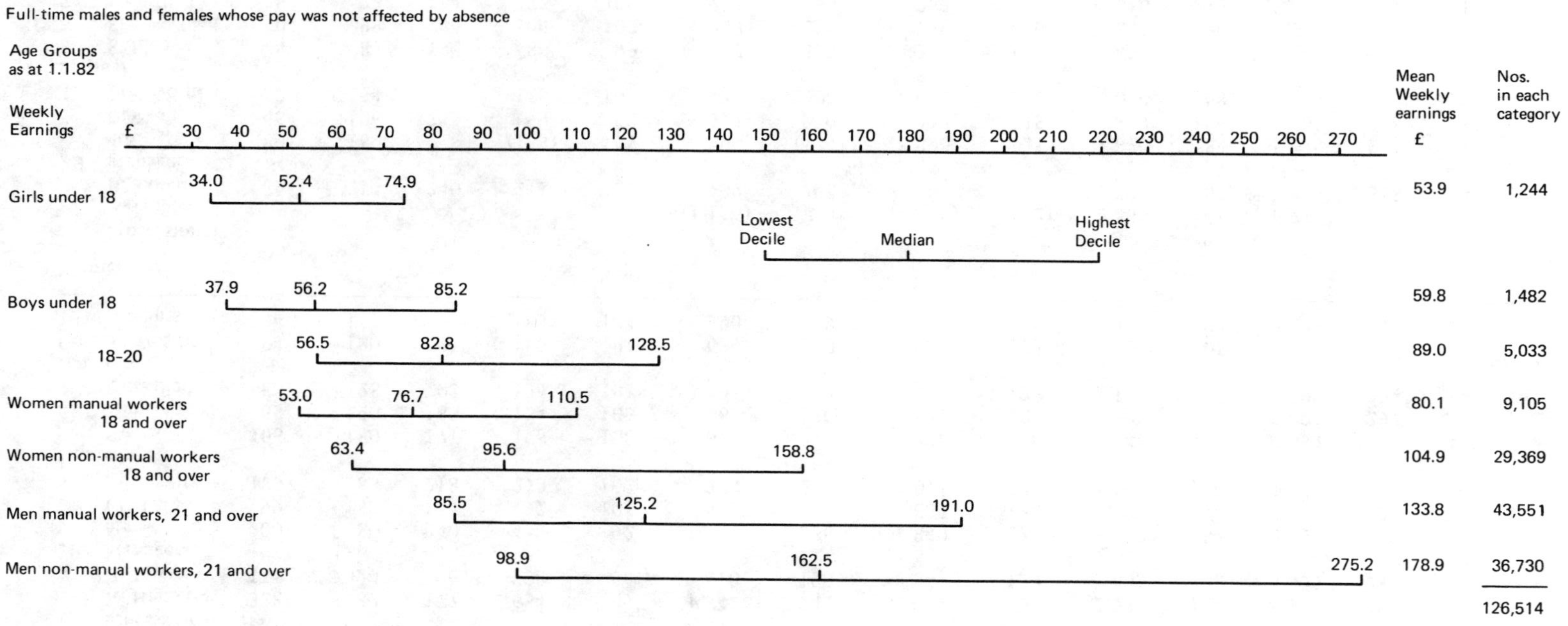

Full-time males and females whose pay was not affected by absence

Age Groups as at 1.1.82 / Weekly Earnings	£	Mean Weekly earnings £	Nos. in each category
Girls under 18	34.0 52.4 74.9	53.9	1,244
Boys under 18	37.9 56.2 85.2	59.8	1,482
18–20	56.5 82.8 128.5	89.0	5,033
Women manual workers 18 and over	53.0 76.7 110.5	80.1	9,105
Women non-manual workers 18 and over	63.4 95.6 158.8	104.9	29,369
Men manual workers, 21 and over	85.5 125.2 191.0	133.8	43,551
Men non-manual workers, 21 and over	98.9 162.5 275.2	178.9	36,730
			126,514

Scale (£): 30 40 50 60 70 80 90 100 110 120 130 140 150 160 170 180 190 200 210 220 230 240 250 260 270

Labels: Lowest Decile   Median   Highest Decile

Figure 3.1   Distribution of Gross Weekly Earnings in Great Britain, April 1982

Source: Department of Employment, *New Earnings Survey 1982*, Part E, Analyses by Region and Age Group (HMSO 1983), Tables 124 and 126, pp. E66-8, E72-4.

Table 3.6 Average Earnings in Great Britain, Seven Occupational Classes, Various Years, 1913–14 to 1978

	1913-14	1922-4		1935-6		1955-6		1960		1970		1978		Multiple of 1913-14
	£	£	% of 1913-14	£	% of 1922-4	£	% of 1935-6	£	% of 1955-6	£	% of 1960	£	% of 1970	
Men														
1 Professional														
A. Higher	328	582	177	634	109	1,541	243	2,034	132	2,928	144	8,286	283	26
B. Lower	155	320	206	308	96	610	198	847	139	1,885	223	5,435	288	35
2B Managers, etc.	200	480	240	440	92	1,480	336	1,850	125	3,400	184	8,050	237	40
3 Clerks	99	182	184	192	105	523	272	682	130	1,337	196	3,701	277	37
4 Foremen	123	268	218	273	102	784	287	1,015	129	1,669	164	4,685	280	38
Manual														
5 Skilled	106	180	171	195	108	622	319	796	128	1,440	181	4,354	302	41
6 Semi-skilled	69	126	183	134	106	469	350	581	124	1,289	222	3,827	297	55
7 Unskilled	63	128	203	129	101	435	337	535	123	1,154	216	3,390	294	54
Averages														
Current weights[1]	94	180	191	186	104	634	340	848[4]	134	1,707	201	4,786	280	51
1911 weights	94	177	138	185	104	590	319	746	126	1,445	194	4,241	293	45
Women														
1 Professional														
A. Higher						(1,156)		(1,525)	(132)	2,460	161	6,712	273	
B. Lower	89	214	240	211	99	438	208	606	138	1,224	202	3,892	318	44
2B Managers, etc.	(80)[2]	160		(168)	105	800	(524)	1,000	125	1,870	187	5,070	271	63
3 Clerks	45	106	235	99	93	317	320	427	135	839	196	2,730	325	61
4 Forewomen	57	154	270	156	101	477	306	602	126	1,014	168	3,214	317	56
Manual														
5 Skilled	44	87	198	86	99	317	369	395	125	677	171	2,246	332	51
6 Semi-skilled	50	98	196	100	102	269	270	339	126	645	190	2,356	365	47
7 Unskilled	28	73	261	73	100	227	280	283	125	610	215	2,275	373	81
Averages														
Current weights[1]	50	103	204	104	101	319	307	417[4]	131	824	198	2,691	327	54
1911 weights	50	103	205	104	101	307	295	402	131	731	182	2,516	344	50

Men and Women

Current weighted average[3]	81	157	194	162	103	531	328	704	133	1,385	197	3,961	286	49

Notes:
1. According to number of men and women in relevant class in nearest population census year.
2. Included in weighted average. Their exclusion lowers the average fractionally.
3. According to proportions in occupational classes in nearest census year until 1935–6; thereafter, proportion in total labour force.
4. Weights from Bain and Price, 'Union growth and employment trends in the UK, 1964–1970', *British Journal of Industrial Relations*, Vol. 10, No. 3 (November 1972), pp. 366–81.

Source: G. G. C. Routh, *Occupation and Pay in Great Britain, 1906–1979* (London 1980) reproduced in C. Hakim and W. R. Hawes, 'The Labour Force' in Open University, *Labour and Income* (Milton Keynes 1982), p. 54.

Table 3.7   The Earnings and Hours of Work of Male and Female Employees, in Full-time Employment, Manual and Non-manual in Great Britain, April 1983

Employees whose pay was not affected by absence	Full-time men aged 21 and over			Full-time women aged 18 and over		
	Manual	Non-manual	All	Manual	Non-Manual	All
Average Gross Weekly Earnings	143.6	194.9	167.5	87.9	115.1	108.8
of which: overtime payments	18.1	6.1	12.5	3.4	1.6	2.0
P.B.R. etc. payments	11.4	5.4	8.6	7.0	1.3	2.6
shift etc. payments	5.0	1.5	3.4	2.2	1.5	1.7
Distribution of Average Gross Weekly Earnings:						
10 per cent earned less than	91.2	106.3	96.3	57.9	69.1	65.6
50 per cent earned less than	138.4	176.1	150.3	84.1	104.7	98.8
10 per cent earned more than	204.5	300.2	255.0	122.2	172.4	166.2
Average Gross Hourly Earnings	326.5	503.4	399.1	224.3	310.0	288.5
excluding overtime	319.0	502.9	398.0	222.0	309.0	287.5
Average Weekly Hours	43.9	38.4	41.5	39.3	36.5	37.2
of which overtime hours	4.7	1.3	3.2	1.2	0.4	0.6
Distribution of Hours – percentage of employees:						
36 hours or fewer	1.8	24.0	11.7	17.8	35.4	31.2
36-40 hours	47.8	58.3	52.4	64.3	59.4	60.6
40-48 hours	29.8	13.2	22.4	14.2	4.5	6.8
more than 48 hours	20.6	4.5	13.5	3.7	0.7	1.4
Employees Who Received Overtime payments:						
percentage of employees	49.8	19.2	35.5	19.1	12.6	14.1
average payment per week	36.3	32.1	35.2	18.0	12.6	14.3
average overtime hours per week	9.3	6.2	8.5	6.0	3.2	4.0
Employees Who Received P.B.R. etc. payments						
percentage of employees	46.9	18.8	33.8	34.0	13.8	18.4
average payment per week	24.4	28.7	25.5	20.5	9.3	14.1

Employees Who Received Shift etc. payments

percentage of employees	25.1	7.3	16.8	14.3	11.7	12.3
average payment per week	£20.0	£21.1	£20.3	£15.2	£13.2	£13.8

Source: Department of Employment, *New Earnings Survey 1983* (London 1983), Part A, Streamlined Analyses and Key Analyses by Agreement, pp. A14–A16.

highly paid category was male non-manual workers, followed by male manual workers, female non-manual workers and female manual workers (table 3.7). Indeed if the figures for juveniles are included the earnings hierarchy continues with boys under 18 and girls under 18, in that order, forming the two lowest paid categories. Significantly boys aged 18 to 20 earn on average more than women in manual jobs (see figure 3.1). The differential between the average earnings of manual and non-manual male workers is clear, but smaller than that between men and women who average less than two-thirds as much as male earnings (though not entirely because of lower rates of pay). In the early 1970s this differential, and those between younger and adult workers, and between manual and non-manual workers, all narrowed somewhat. Since the 1970s the relative earnings of men and women and of younger and adult workers do not appear to have changed greatly, but the differentials between manual and non-manual workers have widened again.

Examination of the make-up of pay reveals further differences between the main categories. The differential in hourly rates of earnings between male manual and non-manual workers is markedly greater than the earnings difference (as it is to a much smaller extent for women), but the gap between the sexes narrows when hourly earnings are considered. This is because male manual workers work on average more than four hours a week longer than any other category, mostly but not entirely because of overtime; more than a fifth of all male manual workers worked more than 48 hours a week, whilst hardly any employees amongst the other groupings worked such long hours; and nearly half the male manual workers had their earnings augmented by overtime payments, as compared with fewer than a fifth in any other category. The other two sources of augmented earnings (and also, of course, of intensified demands for effort) — payment by results and shift payments — are also primarily of relevance for manual workers, though in this case a substantial proportion of women workers are involved as well, especially in working under incentive payment schemes.

Thus male manual workers work longer hours, and possibly under more intense demands for effort, to receive lower pay on average than male non-manual workers; and the same is true, but to a markedly lesser extent, for female employees. The difference between men's and women's earnings on the other hand is primarily a question of lower hourly rates of pay for women, but in the case of manual workers the effect of this is increased by the absence, for most women, of any overtime or shift payments.

The aggregate figures so far discussed conceal the great range of different levels and patterns of earnings received by specific occupational goupings. In the case of non-manual employees it is possible to compare both meaningful general categories ('professional', 'managerial', etc.) and certain specific occupations. The data show the way in which relative advantages tend to reinforce each other, rather than compensating for disadvantages: in the case of both men and women the more highly paid non-manual occupations work slightly shorter hours, and with few exceptions are less likely to be involved in working overtime, shifts and under payment by results. In the case of all the categories men earn more than women in the same occupational grouping; in cases where equal pay has been operative for some years, for example teaching, this is due to the fact that male teachers are on average older, and more likely to occupy posts of responsibility. Men in each case also work slightly longer hours, and are more likely to receive pay for overtime and payment by results. The pattern of shift working is less clear-cut, presumably because certain predominantly female occupations, such as nursing, are heavily involved in shift work.[66]

It is important to note that the non-manual category includes some substantial groupings of employees who are relatively low paid by any standard; clerical workers and, even more so, those involved in selling, both men and women, earn less than the average for all occupations. On the other hand the financial rewards of a 'professional' occupation are clear, relative to those of other non-manual employees of the same sex, and this is also the case for men in managerial occupations.

The patterns but not the levels of hours and earnings for manual employees are similar in many respects. For both men and women there are considerable differences in earnings between occupations at the top and the bottom of the hierarchy. Whatever their occupational category, however, men on average are clearly in an advantageous position compared with even the most highly paid women, and this is so whether gross, net or hourly earnings are considered. Relatively few categories of male manual workers averaged less than £120 per week in 1983 and only a quarter of all male manual workers earned less than £110 per week – whilst in only one category of female manual workers did earnings average more than £100 per week, and only just over a quarter of female manual workers earned as much as this. Men on average work longer hours and consequently receive overtime pay and in many cases shift pay. The distribution of payment by results is less clearly differentiated. In cases where the same occupational titles can be compared (inspectors and testers; repetitive assemblers; packers, etc. and storekeepers) women earn on average between two-thirds and three-quarters as much as men. Occupational categories largely or entirely specific to women (e.g. cleaners, sewing machinists, kitchen hands) are even less well paid.

The consistent and systematic differentials in pay between male and female manual workers should not be allowed to obscure the very considerable differences in levels of earnings for men in manual work. In many cases these differences reflect the responsibility attached to the position (as in the case of foremen) and in others the actual and/or successfully claimed skill of the job itself (e.g. electricians, fitters, printing-machine minders). The available data are not presented in terms of the skilled, semi-skilled and unskilled division, but in general the most highly paid manual occupations are those with skill and/or responsibility. In some cases, however, such as face-trained coal miners, high pay also compensates for the deprivations of shift work and working underground and for the extra effort of overtime and working under a bonus scheme. One effect of pay which compensates for overtime, shift work and working under payment by results is to increase the differential between the most and least highly paid manual occupations.[67]

The data reported in the *New Earnings Survey* do not permit very much to be said about those with very high earnings from employment, but they can be augmented with the information for a slightly earlier period which has been presented and discussed by the Royal Commission on the Distribution of Income and Wealth. The Commission estimated that in 1974–5 about 65,000 individuals in the UK had incomes from employment (including self-employment) of £10,000 or more, about 0.3 per cent of the recipients of total employment incomes at all levels; and if the distribution between the sexes parallels that for the previous year, almost all of them were men.[68] (£10,000 represents about £192 per week; in 1975 the *New Earnings Survey* reported average gross weekly earnings in Great Britain of £60.8 for men and £37.4 for women.)[69] Those with incomes from employment of £10,000 or more in 1974–5 probably represented about 30 per cent of all income units (married couples or single persons) with incomes of this size. In 1974 they were to be found primarily in manufacturing industry, and in insurance, banking, finance, etc., with substantial numbers also in the distributive trades. Occupationally the most important categories were general management (55 per cent of those earning £10,000 or more a year), and 'professional and related occupations supporting management and administration' (e.g. including lawyers, company secretaries, accountants, personnel managers, marketing and advertising managers, administrative civil servants and local government officers, and so on).

In a later report the Royal Commission gave detailed consideration to the incomes of the self-employed, who have a more unequal distribution of incomes than do employees and who include a relatively large number with high incomes, especially those in professional occupations and proprietors of companies. Incomes from self-employment in most cases must be considered to include a return on capital employed and a reward for taking risk, as well as rewards for employment.[70]

In contrast to the case with high pay, the earnings data do provide an indication of the extent and patterns of distribution of low pay. The definition of 'low pay' is, of course, contentious, being variously defined in terms of the level of supplementary benefits for a married man with two children, two-thirds of the average male manual worker's wage or of median male earnings (manual and non-manual), or those with pay which would place them in the lowest decile (10 per cent) of male manual workers.[71] The Low Pay Unit has argued that these various definitions converged on £90 per week (£2.25 per hour for a 40-hour week) as a reasonable cut-off point for low wages in April 1982. In terms of this criterion up to six and a half million adults working either full- or part-time could be considered low paid, a third of the adult workforce; if overtime is taken into account the figure is slightly lower (see table 3.8).

Whichever of these definitions of low pay is adopted, a number of clear generalizations can be made about the pattern of low pay. First, in terms of the overall dispersion of the earnings of full-time male manual workers the situation has scarcely changed at all since the end of the nineteenth century; indeed after some improvement in pay relative to median earnings in the mid-1970s the least well-paid male workers were worse off in 1982. Secondly, women, young people (and, to a lesser extent, older workers) and ethnic minorities are more likely to be low-paid than white male adults. Thirdly, whilst all the main occupational and industrial categories, and both manual and non-manual groupings, include some low-paid workers, they are disproportionately concentrated in certain occupations: selling, catering, cleaning, and farming and related activities; and in certain industries: for men, agriculture, the distributive trades, miscellaneous services (catering, cleaning, etc.) and – though not for non-manual workers – clothing and footwear; for women, textiles, clothing and footwear, distribution (especially non-manual women workers), professional and scientific services (health, education etc.) and miscellaneous services. The incidence of low pay among women and members of ethnic minorities is largely a reflection of their concentration in low-paid occupations and industries. Finally, although there is evidence to suggest that the actual individuals who are low-paid change quite rapidly, the overall distribution of earnings, and the social and industrial/occupational characteristics of the low-paid remain largely the same.[72]

Thus, though low pay has been shown to be frequently associated with low skill,

Table 3.8   Estimated Number and Proportions of Adult Workers earning Low Wages, GB, April 1982

	Including overtime		Excluding overtime	
	No. (million)	%	No. (million)	%
Full-time Males *(aged 18 and over)*				
Manual	0.9	16.4	1.4	25.0
Non-manual	0.4	8.5	0.4	9.9
All men	1.4	12.9	1.8	18.2
Full-time Females *(aged 18 and over)*				
Manual	0.7	71.9	0.8	76.1
Non-manual	1.5	43.2	1.5	44.4
All women	2.2	50.0	2.3	51.9
All full-time	*3.6*	*25.1*	*4.1*	*28.7*
Part-time Adults				
Men	0.2	33.7		
Women	2.3	64.6		

Note: Low Wages defined as less than £90 per week (£2.25 an hour for part-timers) in April 1982.

Source: C. Pond and S. Winyard, *The Case for a National Minimum Wage*, Low Pay Unit, Pamphlet No. 23 (London 1983), p. 10, based on Department of Employment data.

lower than average education and ill-health, such an 'explanation' would be to ignore the structural characteristics of low-paid employment and the vulnerable labour market position of many of those who are low-paid. Low pay is to be found especially in industries where many small labour intensive firms are in competition and where levels of unionization are low and collective bargaining weak or non-existent. Women, especially married women, young people, older workers and members of ethnic minorities are restricted in their opportunities for employment, especially but not only during periods of high unemployment, and are therefore disproportionately likely to be employed in such firms and industries, and in the less well-paid jobs in industries with generally higher levels of earnings.[73]

It is possible to summarize the above discussion of pay and hours by making a number of simplified summary statements: the evidence is that non-manual employees earn more than manual employees, even though they work shorter hours; men earn more than women; adults more than juveniles; and the skilled/qualified more than the unskilled/unqualified. We can add that when manual workers (and especially men) receive high earnings it is often associated with overtime, payment by results, and/or shift working. In addition, if lifetime earnings are considered, the advantages of the non-manual worker are further increased; though their average earnings are lower than those of manual workers until the late twenties (or younger for women), their earnings peak is not reached until the 40-49 age group, whereas manual workers reach their maximum earnings at a younger age and decline more rapidly.[74] Non-manual workers have the advantages, with reference to lifetime earnings, of increments and greater opportunities for promotion; manual workers suffer the disadvantages of declining physical strength and fitness, and thus declining ability in later years to increase their pay by working overtime or earning high bonus rates.

The explanation of the pattern of earnings is too complex to be explored here.[75] The Royal Commission on the Distribution of Income and Wealth has suggested that there are three main theories of wage and salary structures: (i) 'labour market' theories, which treat the structure of wages and salaries as being determined by market processes; (ii) 'human capital' theories, which regard the acquisition of knowledge and skills as an investment on which a return can be expected; and (iii) 'institutional' theories, which regard the influence of customary relativities, collective agreements, and government regulations as so pervasive that they transform the nature of the labour market. Such theories are not mutually exclusive.[76] Market forces cannot be discounted but the labour market does not operate in terms of perfect competition: employees may lack the information or the means to be mobile to better paying jobs; employers may discriminate; occupational organizations (professional associations, trade unions) may restrict entry and so increase the price of their labour; and some employers may be in a quasi-monopsony position in a local labour market. Similarly, earnings differentials do not precisely parallel differences in natural aptitudes, qualifications and experience; 'credentials' may be used to restrict entry to an occupation or to screen potential employees rather than because the qualifications are needed to perform the work; and the opportunity to acquire skills, or having acquired them to exploit them in the labour market, are not freely and equally available. Industries and occupations characterized by low earnings are typically weakly unionized; equal pay legislation appears to have brought some improvement in women's earnings; and customary differentials appear to have influenced the historic pattern of earnings; but there is considerable dispute as to whether collective organization and action can have more than a marginal or short-term effect on levels of pay. What does appear to be the case, however, is that other rewards than pay are very similarly distributed to pay itself.

'Fringe Benefits' and other Rewards from Work

In addition to their wage or salary almost all employees now receive additional 'benefits' from their work. Many of these have a real or notional money value, but others are more intangible. We will briefly review the distribution of these rewards, and then consider the 'costs' of work and the nature of the overall pattern which available information reveals.

The most comprehensive attempt to ascertain the position with regard to fringe benefits and other conditions of employment is still probably that of Wedderburn and Craig who in 1968 surveyed a random sample of establishments in manufacturing industry with 100 or more employees and received replies from nearly 450 of them.[77] Their findings show that with regard to all the benefits and conditions they investigated manual workers were less well placed than non-manual workers; and where there were significant differences in the conditions between types of non-manual worker, senior and middle management had superior conditions of employment to those of foremen, clerical workers and technicians. Thus, for example, operatives were less likely to receive sick pay, or pensions, or fifteen days or more holiday a year (or a choice of holiday dates), or time off with pay for domestic reasons; and they were more stringently regulated and sanctioned with regard to lateness, absence, and notice of dismissal. A minority of establishments, the exact number varying with the condition in question, had the same conditions for all grades of employee; others treated operatives less favourably than non-manual grades; and quite a substantial number had differences within the non-manual grades too. A later survey of 328 companies, by the British Institute of Management in 1976, showed a trend towards a reduction in differentials in fringe benefits between non-manual and manual employees, though it also reported that 'all aspects of discrimination against manual workers remain common'.[78] More comprehensive recent data are available about particular conditions of employment.

Holidays with Pay: The provision of paid holidays is much more widespread and more generous than it used to be. In 1951 two-thirds of the manual workers covered by national collective agreements or wages council awards received two weeks paid holiday a year (excluding public holidays); by 1974 fewer than 6 per cent of them received less than three weeks.[79] Table 3.9 shows the changes which have taken place in the provision of holidays with pay since 1970, though these overall figures, of course, conceal considerable differences in entitlement between specific occupations. Nevertheless in that year fewer than 7 per cent of manual workers and less than half of non-manual workers had four or more weeks holiday each year; by 1981 more than three-quarters of all manual workers and almost nine out of ten non-manual workers received this amount of paid holiday. However, although in general all categories of employee have become entitled to significantly longer paid holidays during this period, important differentials in entitlement remain: non-manual workers continue to receive longer holidays than manual workers, and within these two categories men continue to receive longer holidays than women. It is particularly ironic that those who conventionally carry the heavier burden of domestic and childcare duties should receive shorter holidays.

Sick Pay: Although the details of the provision are not available, the *General Household Survey* found that nearly three-quarters of full-time employees aged sixteen or over, men and women, were covered by sick pay arrangements of some sort in 1976. There was very little difference in the overall coverage for the two sexes, with women being in the slightly better position. The figures represented an overall improvement on the situation five years earlier when slightly fewer than two-thirds were so covered.[80] However, there were considerable differences in coverage between major occupational categories, ranging from 97 per cent of 'managers in large establishments' entitled to pay when sick, to only 56 per cent of skilled and semi-skilled manual workers (see table 3.10).

Pension Schemes: The probability of receiving an occupational pension varied even more widely; in 1979 only just over a fifth of all agricultural workers were covered by a private pension scheme of any sort, whereas more than half of all manual workers were, and more than four-fifths of intermediate grade non-manual workers, professional employees, and managers in large establishments (see table 3.10). Details are not available regarding the differences, if any, between men and women, but some years earlier, in 1972, it was clear that those employed in industries where public ownership was substantial (public administration, gas, water, electricity; mining; transport and communications; professional

Table 3.9 Paid Holidays of Manual and Non-manual Employees by Sex in Great Britain, 1970 and 1981

Percentage of employees entitled to annual paid holidays of duration:	1970				1981			
	Males		Females		Males		Females	
	Manual	Non-manual	Manual	Non-manual	Manual	Non-manual	Manual	Non-manual
Less than three weeks	29	10	32	20	3	2	4	2
3 and less than 4 weeks	64	42	63	49	10	7	18	9
4 and less than 5 weeks	} 7	49	} 5	32	68	49	64	57
5 weeks and over					{ 18	41	13	31

Source: condensed from *Social Trends 1983* (London 1982), p. 59. Original data are from the relevant New Earnings Surveys, and relate to full-time male employees aged 21 and over and full-time female employees aged 18 and over.

Table 3.10   Sick Pay and Occupational Pensions by Socio-economic Group in Great Britain, 1976 and 1979 (percentages)

Socio-economic group (Full-time employees aged 16 and over)	Get paid when sick 1976 %	Covered by private pension scheme 1979 %
Managers in large establishments	99	88
Managers in small establishments	95	60
Professional workers – employees	98	82
Intermediate non-manual	97	86
Junior non-manual	93	63
Personal service workers	75	37
Foremen and supervisors	87	71
Skilled manual workers	60	56
Semi-skilled manual workers	60	57
Unskilled manual workers	63	56
Agricultural workers	[67]	21
Averages { Males	77	–
Females	80	–
All groups	78	64

Source: *General Household Survey, 1976*, pp. 60-1; *GHS* 1979 data quoted in C. Hakim and W. R. Hawes, 'The Labour Force' in Open University, *Labour and Income* (Milton Keynes 1982), p. 38.

and scientific services) were more likely to be covered by occupational pension schemes. As in the case of sick pay schemes the coverage of occupational pensions increased during the 1970s.[81]

Job Satisfaction: Jobs vary widely in many other ways than those so far discussed. The content of the work may be varied and intrinsically interesting, or repetitive and boring; its mastery may demand long periods of training, or it may be picked up in a few hours; there may be opportunities to exercise discretion and take responsibility, or work activities may be minutely controlled and all significant decisions taken by others; the job may offer possibilities for self-development, leading perhaps to promotion to a more demanding and better-paid position, or it may offer nothing but the prospects of carrying out the same easily learned tasks for the rest of a working life. Whether the more desirable of these sets of characteristics are seen as positive rewards or merely relative satisfactions, they certainly contribute significantly to the experience of work of those in different occupations.

Unfortunately it is very difficult to assess a wide range of jobs in these terms, though more or less successful attempts have been made in the context of studies of particular workplaces or occupations.[82] An alternative is to try to obtain a summary measure of people's experience of their work through questions on job satisfaction, but this too presents certain difficulties. There appears, first of all, to be a tendency for a very high proportion of respondents to express satisfaction with their job, however unrewarding it may appear to be, and this may reflect the feeling that to admit dissatisfaction in such a context is to admit personal failure. Secondly, the source of the satisfaction with a job, and the meaning it has for the respondent, may vary very considerably between respondents, but this will not be apparent unless more, and more searching, questions are asked. Thirdly, satisfaction is always relative to expectations so that an expression of satisfaction or dissatisfaction may tell us more about the respondent's aspirations and orientation than about his or her work. Indeed job satisfaction studies can be regarded as providing a notable example of the limited horizons and standards of comparison of those in objectively deprived situations, of the tendency for aspirations to become tailored to experience so that what appears to the respondent as inescapable (in this case, say, a dead-end job) may be helped in fact to become so.[83]

The results of job satisfaction questions are not entirely useless however, especially if the variations within the respondent group are the focus of attention. The replies to the question asked every year between 1971 and 1980 by the *General Household Survey* indicate some decline in the overall very high level of reported job satisfaction between 1971 and 1977, and a slight increase since that date in the proportions claiming to be 'very' or 'fairly' satisfied. A strong relationship has been shown between expressed dissatisfaction and withdrawal from work by absence, or the intention to leave. Although the percentage differences are not great, expressed job satisfaction is generally higher for women than for men, for older people rather than younger (with the exception of the under-18s) and for part-time rather than full-time workers.[84] The pattern of job satis-faction between different socio-economic groups has been fairly stable over the years. As can be seen in table 3.11, managerial, supervisory and professional workers (and those in agriculture) appear the most satisfied, and manual workers the least, though, among men, only in the case of unskilled manual workers are fewer than 80 per cent reported to be 'very' or 'fairly' satisfied with their jobs; this slightly greater dissatisfaction amongst the unskilled does not apply in the case of women employees, where the occupational ranking in terms of job satisfaction is otherwise much the same, but the overall level of satisfaction is slightly higher, especially for part-time employees.

Absence: Opinions expressed in attitude surveys may be a poor predictor of behaviour, and in this connection data on absence from work provide an interesting check on expressions of satisfaction or dissatisfaction with a job. Absence statistics are, of course, also difficult to interpret because they include both 'voluntary' and 'involuntary' ab-sences and the conventional categories of reasons for absence cannot really be taken to reflect that distinction. Nevertheless, in aggregate absence statistics can be regarded as an approximate index of general levels of 'morale' — in this context implying identification with the purposes of the employing organization.

There are clear differences in the overall levels of absence between managerial, pro-fessional and supervisory employees on the one hand, and manual workers on the other, with junior non-manual and personal service workers occupying an intermediate position (see table 3.11). Much of this difference is attributable either to differences in absence due to illness or injury, reflecting in part the conditions of work of such employees, or to the greater propensity for skilled and semi-skilled manual workers (but not the unskilled) to be absent due to 'strikes, short-time and lay-offs' (mostly in fact short-time or lay-offs). Rates of absence have varied very little during the ten years since 1971. Women working full-time, but not those working part-time, tend to have slightly higher rates of absence due to illness or injury than men, but there is no overall difference between the sexes in reported absence.[85]

Table 3.11 Job Satisfaction and Absence by Socio-economic Group in Great Britain, 1980 and 1981

Socio-economic group (men aged 16–64; women aged 16–59)	Job satisfaction – 1980						Absence – 1981			
	Male (full-time)		Female (full-time)		Female (part-time)		Employees aged 16 and over absent in the previous week because of:			
	very satisfied	fairly satisfied	very satisfied	fairly satisfied	very satisfied	fairly satisfied	own illness or injury	strike/ short-time layoff	personal & other reasons	Total
	(percentages)						(percentages)			
Managers in large establishments	52	37	61	30	*	*	2	1	1	3
Managers in small establishments	51	37	50	37	*	*	2	1	2	5
Professional workers – employees	40	46	58	26	*	*	3	0	2	5
Intermediate non-manual +	38/46	42/44	52/49	37/40	56	36	3	1	2	6
Junior non-manual	39	43	40	45	52	38	4	1	1	7
Personal service workers	*	*	52	40	46	41	5	2	2	8
Foremen and supervisors (manual)	45	43	*	*	*	*	3	2	*	6
Skilled manual workers	37	46	36	51	39	45	5	4	2	10
Semi-skilled manual workers	37	45	39	45	49	38	6	6	2	13
Unskilled manual workers	35	42	48	41	*	*	7	1	1	9
Farmers, managers and agricultural workers	56	38	*	*	*	*	5	0	3	9
Total	40	44	44	42	50	39	4	2	1	8

* Sub-sample size too small

+ Ancillary workers/foremen and supervisors (non-manual)

Sources: *General Household Survey, 1980,* p. 104; *General Household Survey, 1981,* p. 111.

The Costs of Work

As we have seen, some of the most important rewards which can be derived from work (especially those which are inherent in the job itself) are not easily reported and compared. This difficulty is even greater when the attempt is made to compare the deprivations associated with different types of work, to look for example at the 'effort' involved in the effort bargain. The total 'costs' of working to the employee cannot be properly assessed. Some indications of them have already been discussed: hours of work, including overtime and shift work; the intensity of effort demanded in so far as this is transmitted through payment-by-results schemes. Two further aspects can also be considered with the same focus on occupational differences: the costs of work in terms of accidents and ill-health; and insecurity of employment and the liability of becoming, and remaining, unemployed.

Accidents and Ill-Health: The effects of work on the employee's physical and mental health are manifested in a variety of ways. Some occupations are obviously dangerous so that the risk of a severe or even fatal accident is high; some involve working in conditions which have a less immediately obvious but clearly observable, longer term effect on health, perhaps giving rise over time to a disabling disease, such as pneumoconiosis among miners. Even if such direct connections cannot be easily established, however, all occupations can be regarded as influencing, for better or worse, the health of those engaged in them. Thus morbidity and mortality statistics provide a good summary indication of the degree to which the conditions of work in an occupation, in a literal sense, affect the employee's life chances.

Considering first of all the published figures for fatal accidents, and major and other reported injuries in 1982 (table 3.12) it is clear that their distribution is very uneven between industries, ranging from 180 injuries of any sort per 100,000 employed (and a two in a million rate of fatal injuries) in 'insurance, banking and finance', to a hundred times as great a probability of injury (and twenty-two in a hundred thousand rate of fatal injuries) in 'mining and quarrying'. A breakdown of these figures in terms of occupational categories is not available, but it is notable that the two industries with clearly the worst record for injuries, especially fatal injuries, 'mining and quarrying' and 'construction', employ a relatively large proportion of manual workers, whilst the two industries with the best record are the predominantly white-collar industries, 'insurance, banking and finance' and 'professional and scientific services'. Although there are, of course, fluctuations in rates of accident and injury from year to year, and considerable variation within some of the categories shown, such as manufacturing industry, and transport and communications, the main outlines of the overall pattern change relatively little over time. As is the case with all statistics, published industrial accident and injury figures cannot be seen as unproblematic, and they have indeed been criticized for concealing the full extent to which those at work are liable to hazards likely to lead to loss of life or health.[86]

The best indication of the occupational distribution of liability to accident or ill-health is probably provided by more general statistics relating to mortality and the incidence of particular diseases and disabilities, though it is impossible to separate clearly the direct effects of work from the more general effects of different levels and patterns of living. There are, however, persistent differences in the standardized death rates for men

Table 3.12 Injuries to Employees Reported to the Health and Safety Commission in Great Britain, January–December 1982 (provisional)

Industrial classification	Number employed June 1982 (000s)	Fatal injuries	Fatal & major injuries	All injuries	Incidence rates for all injuries per 100,000 employees at risk
Agriculture, forestry & fishing	345	28	175	7,349	2,080
Mining and quarrying	325	73	1,132	38,328	11,850
Manufacturing	5,660	123	4,140	132,165	2,330
Construction	1,024	102	2,043	40,902	4,070
Gas, electricity & water	331	14	185	8,044	2,440
Transport & communication	1,363	50	564	18,041	1,330
Distributive trades	2,656	11	237	31,995	1,200
Insurance, banking, finance	1,300	3	11	2,346	180
Professional & scientific services	3,660	4	1,107	30,665	340
Miscellaneous services	2,496	17	544	27,204	1,120
Public administration & defence	1,496	13	1,041	45,409	3,040
Unclassified	–	30	1,290	5,551	
Total	20,656	468	12,469	367,999	

Sources: Nos. employed, *Employment Gazette*, Vol. 91, No. 9, September 1983, pp. 58-9; Health and Safety Commission, *Annual Report 1982-3*, p. 47.

of working age related to 'Social Class' (see table 3.13), and although expectations of life have, of course, improved in absolute terms over the period covered by the table, the relative differences widened until the most recent period. The fact that the differences in death rates are also observable for married women classified according to their husbands' occupations does imply that the differences are 'attributable not only to specific occupations but also to the life-styles and standards of living connected with them'.[87]

The *General Household Survey* provides systematic data about the occupational distribution of ill-health, though it relies on self-reported information. The relevant findings for 1981 (table 3.14) parallel those for earlier years in showing a clear 'class gradient' in the incidence and severity of both chronic and acute illness, with those in manual occupations (and especially semi- and unskilled manual work) having rates worse than average, and professional and (to a lesser extent) managerial employees having rates considerably better than average. The figures in table 3.14 cover men and women of all ages; the rates of illness vary considerably with age, but the 'class gradient' is observable when the age groups for those of working age are considered separately. These data, of course, can be complemented by reference to the information on absence due to illness or injury reported above, which show a similar pattern of differences according to occupational category (table 3.11).

Unemployment: Workers who sell their labour power in the market are dependent for their income on there being employers who wish to purchase their ability to work. In

Table 3.13 Standardized Mortality Ratios,[1] Adult Males Under 65 Years of Age by Social Class, England and Wales

Period	Social Class					
	I Professional etc.	II Intermediate non-manual	III Skilled manual(M)/ routine non-manual (N)		IV Semi-skilled manual	V Unskilled manual
1930–2 Men	90	94	97		102	111
1949–53 Men	86	92	101		104	118
1959–63 Men	76	81	100		103	143
			IIIN	IIIM		
1970–2 Men	77	81	99	106	114	137
Married Women	82	87	92	115	119	135

Note:
1 Standardized Mortality Ratios are death rates adjusted to take account of the age structure of each social class and to present them on a comparable basis. Married women (1970–2) are classified according to their husband's occupation.

Sources: 1930–63, Open University, *Inequality within Nations, Health and Inequality* (Milton Keynes 1976). Based on B. Preston, 'Statistics of Inequality', *Sociological Review*, Vol. 22, No. 2, 1974, pp. 103–17. 1970–2 C. Hakim and W. R. Hawes, 'The Labour Force' in Open University, *Labour and Income* (Milton Keynes 1982), p. 39. Based on *Social Trends No. 8* (London 1977).

Table 3.14 'Chronic' and 'Acute' Ill-health by Socio-economic Group in Great Britain, 1981

Socio-economic group	Chronic ill-health				Acute sickness	
	Reported long-standing illness		Reported limiting long-standing illness		Average number of restricted activity days per person per year	
	Males	Females	Males	Females	Males	Females
	(percentages)					
Professional	22	18	10	10	11.2	15.1
Employers and managers	26	26	14	15	15.3	20.9
Intermediate and junior non-manual	27	28	14	17	17.8	22.8
Skilled manual, and own account professional	29	28	16	17	20.0	21.7
Semi-skilled manual, and personal service	32	36	20	24	24.2	29.6
Unskilled manual	32	46	19	31	23.4	37.0
All	28	30	16	19	19.3	24.1

Source: *General Household Survey, 1981* (London 1983), pp. 142, 143, 145.

the early stages of industrialization this generally resulted in a very one-sided relationship, and periods of unemployment, due to cyclical changes in demand or to structural
changes in the economy which meant that particular workers were no longer required,
were the common experience of many men and women. Trade union organization and
action, and state intervention, have limited the extent to which employers can hire and
fire at will, and state action has reduced the financial hardship associated with redundancy and unemployment. Nevertheless the possibility of unemployment remains, as
it has always been, one of the risks faced by employees; job insecurity is one of the
potential costs of work. The likelihood of unemployment, however, and the chances of
obtaining another job both vary considerably for different types of employee.

For most of the first two and a half decades after the Second World War unemployment rates in the UK remained at less than 3 per cent of all employees (never more than
600,000 men and women) though rates were considerably higher in Northern Ireland
throughout this period, and in some of the regions of Britain. This was in marked contrast
to the inter-war period: in only one year between 1921 and 1939 did the annual average
percentage of insured workers unemployed in the UK drop below 10 per cent, and the
numbers of persons (insured and uninsured) registered as unemployed remained at over
a million from December 1922 until April 1940, reaching a peak of nearly three million
in January 1933.[88] Perhaps the most important change in the conditions and context of
work in recent years has been the dramatic increase in unemployment, which has begun
to make the early post-war period seem like the exception rather than the norm. From an
annual average of around 350,000 in the mid-1960s, the number of registered
unemployed in the UK rose to nearly 900,000 in 1972; after some recovery in 1973–4
it rose further to 1.4 million in 1977; and after a slight fall in 1979 rose rapidly to 2.5
million in 1981 and three million in 1982.[89] This last figure represents an unemployment
rate of more than 12 per cent. It excludes, however, those who do not register (many of
whom are married women), but includes as registered unemployed some who are not
actively seeking work. It has been estimated on the basis of the results of the Census,
the *General Household Survey* and the Labour Force Survey that the unregistered unemployed can be a considerable number (for example, 400,000 in 1981), but that they have
not increased at the same rate as registered unemployment, and that there may be as
many registered unemployed who are not actively looking for jobs.[90] Such a judgement
would be contested by some commentators. It is clear, however, that recent changes in
provisions for registration, and for counting the registered unemployed, have had the
effect of reducing the apparent level of unemployment; and that the figure would be
considerably higher without the various temporary employment schemes, especially for
young workers, which have been introduced by governments since the early 1970s; and
it is likely that the number of those in the population who would like to have paid
employment, and would seek it in conditions of full employment, is considerably greater
than the three million or so currently registered as unemployed.[91]

Relying on the official figures, however, it is possible to discuss the incidence and
impact of unemployment, and important to do so because they are not evenly spread.
Men are about twice as likely to be unemployed as women, though this may partly reflect
their different propensities to register. In the first few months of 1983 when the
seasonally adjusted rate of unemployment (excluding school-leavers) in the UK was
between 12.4 and 12.7 per cent, men had comparably defined rates of between 15 and

15.9 per cent, and women ones of between 7.8 and 8.3 per cent. Though the rates have of course changed over the years, the relative differences between the rates of male and female unemployment have remained much the same at least since the mid-1970s.[92] Rates of unemployment are also markedly higher than average for the young (24 and under, but especially the under 20s) and, in the case of men, for those aged 55 and over. On the other hand, studies of the flows into and out of unemployment suggest that young people have a high likelihood of becoming unemployed but the duration of their period of unemployment will be short, whereas the opposite is the case for those approaching retirement age.[93] Details of the duration of unemployment for different age groups and both sexes reflect this: at the end of 1982 and the beginning of 1983 when a third or more of the unemployed in the UK had been unemployed for a year or more (approaching 40 per cent of unemployed men and about a quarter of unemployed women), the comparable figures for those aged 55 and over were about half for both men and women, whilst the figures for those under 25 were less than the averages. As the level of unemployment has risen the proportion unemployed for a year or more has increased, as also has the probability of experiencing repeated, shorter spells out of work. Unemployment rates are also higher among ethnic minority groups, partly but not solely because of the higher proportion of young people among them.[94]

Of particular interest, however, is the incidence of unemployment for members of different occupational categories. Unfortunately, in allocating the unemployed to occupational categories Job Centres place them in the one most appropriate for finding a job and as a result many more are recorded in the 'general labourer' category than last held such a job or would regard that as their usual occupation. Nevertheless the data contained in table 3.15, which reflect this process, are useful in indicating the broad occupational incidence of unemployment; they can also be compared with unfilled vacancies notified to Job Centres, using the same categories, though in this case the Department of Employment estimates that only about a third of all vacancies are so notified. In September 1982 seven out of every ten of those registered as unemployed (and eight out of ten men) were manual workers, although the proportion in the economically active population as a whole is less than 60 per cent; and only just over half the notified vacancies (54 per cent) were for manual workers. Even if the notified vacancies are regarded as a third of all vacancies at the time, the latter comprise one vacancy for every eleven manual workers as compared with one for every six non-manual workers. Thus these figures indicate that not only are manual workers, especially among men, disproportionately likely to be unemployed, but they also have less chance of securing another job than non-manual workers.

These findings can be compared with those from the Census and from surveys. The distribution of men and women who were described as economically active in April 1981, between those in employment and those 'not in employment', is shown in table 3.16. ('Not in employment' is not, of course, identical to 'unemployed' and certainly not to registered unemployed.) In all categories women had lower rates of 'non-employment' than men, and for men especially, but in general for women also, those in manual work had higher rates than those in non-manual categories. Comparable findings have been reported from a study using unpublished data which showed that as overall unemployment doubled between June 1979 and June 1981 it affected those in different occupational categories in the same proportions (though those occupations

Table 3.15   Unemployment and Vacancies: Occupational Distributions in the UK, September 1982

Occupational category	Number unemployed			As % of total	Unfilled vacancies (000s)
	Male	Female (000s)	All		
Managerial and professional	223	106	329		16
Clerical and related	136	249	385		18
Other non-manual	72	123	195		18
All non-manual	*431*	*478*	*909*	*31*	*52*
Craft occupations etc.	387	29	415		18
General labourers	729	134	863		3
Other manual	576	190	766		41
All manual	*1,692*	*353*	*2,045*	*69*	*62*
Total	2,123	831	2,954	100	115

Source: *Employment Gazette*, Vol. 90, No. 11 (November 1982), p. 537.

Table 3.16 Socio-economic Groups Economically Active in and not in Employment in Great Britain, April 1981

	Economically active in employment (000s)			Economically active not in employment (000s)			Those not in employment as % of all economically active		
	Men	Women	Total	Men	Women	Total	Men	Women	Total
1 Employers & managers – large establishments	847	205	1,052	16	3	19	2	1	2
2 Employers & managers – small establishments	1,356	426	1,782	67	14	81	5	3	4
3 Professional workers – self-employed	144	14	157	2	–	2	1	–	1
4 Professional workers – employees	702	86	787	19	2	22	3	2	3
5 Intermediate non-manual workers	1,136	1,420	2,556	40	40	81	3	3	3
6 Junior non-manual workers	1,473	3,685	5,159	85	149	233	5	4	4
7 Personal service workers	178	1,201	1,379	26	53	78	13	4	5
8 Foreman and supervisors – manual	559	66	626	35	3	38	6	3	6
9 Skilled manual workers	4,090	392	4,482	451	32	483	10	8	10
10 Semi-skilled manual workers	2,107	1,028	3,135	266	89	355	11	4	10
11 Unskilled manual workers	906	665	1,571	218	21	239	19	3	13
12–16 Others (self-employed, those in agriculture etc.)	1,473	275	1,748	97	8	105	6	3	6
17 Inadequately described	547	411	958	439	314	753	45	43	44
All persons	15,518	9,874	25,393	1,762	727	2,489	10	7	9

Source: calculated from *Census 1981*, National Report, Great Britain, Part 2 (London 1983), p. 25.

connected with engineering, supervisors and craftsmen, showed a larger proportional increase). Thus the non-manual rate rose from 2.7 per cent in 1979 to 5.2 per cent in 1981, as compared with rates of 5.8 per cent and 12.3 per cent for manual workers at the same times.[95]

Trade Unions

Unemployment and its consequences provide only one example of the fundamental asymmetry of the social relations of unemployment; as Beveridge pointed out in 1944, an employer faced with a shortage of labour suffers inconvenience or loss of profit, but a person who cannot find employment faces a personal catastrophe. In the determination of the conditions of employment, individual employees on their own are relatively power-less compared to the employer. Organization into trade unions, or professional or other occupational associations, so as to be able to take collective action, creates a real possibility of exercising some control over the terms of the employment contract and the conditions of work. Though it will not be possible here to explore further the ways in which such possibilities are realized, through collective bargaining and other forms of action, it is important to see which categories of employee are organized into unions or other associations and may therefore be able to exercise such control.[96]

In 1892, when official statistics were first compiled, trade union membership totalled 1.5 millions (just over 11 per cent of the labour force); it grew rapidly just before and during the First World War, to more than 8 million members, declined to about half that number by the early 1930s, and grew during the Second World War to reach just over 9 million (45 per cent of the work force) in the United Kingdom in 1948.[97] As table 3.17 shows, for Great Britain there was very little increase in total union member-ship between 1948 and 1968, nor much change in its distribution, and as the total labour force grew by 2.5 million, union density (the percentage of potential union members who belong to a union) actually fell. In the decade since 1968, however, union membership grew substantially to exceed 12.5 million members (nearly 54 per cent of the labour force) in 1979 (and over 13 million in the UK). Since that year, membership has declined sharply and by the end of 1981, after the loss of one and a quarter million members altogether in the UK, it had declined to the position reached in 1975. These losses occurred particularly in manufacturing industry and construction, and paralleled the decline in employment in these sectors.[98] All these figures do not include certain organizations (e.g. some professional associations and staff associations) which, although they do not meet the official criteria defining a trade union, may well act to improve and protect the market and work situations of their members, but it will not be possible to consider them further here.[99]

During the first two decades after the Second World War union membership was much more common among male employees than female, and among manual workers than white-collar workers. Though the number of white-collar workers who were members of a union increased by nearly a million between 1948 and 1968 this did not quite keep pace with the growth in white-collar employment. Between 1968 and 1979, however, union density among women workers increased by over 40 per cent to reach 39.5 per cent, three-fifths of the density among men; and union density among white-collar workers (many of them, of course, women) grew by more than a third to almost 70 per

Table 3.17 Trade Union Membership, Potential Union Membership, and Union Density in Great Britain, 1948–79

	1948			1968			1979		
	Union membership	Potential membership	Density	Union membership	Potential membership	Density	Union membership	Potential membership	Density
	000s	000s	%	000s	000s	%	000s	000s	%
Total	9,118	20,270	45.0	9,693	22,703	42.7	12,702	23,687	53.6
Male	7,468	13,485	55.4	7,428	14,452	51.4	8,866	13,979	63.4
Female	1,650	6,785	24.3	2,265	8,251	27.5	3,837	9,708	39.5
Manual workers	7,056	14,027	50.3	6,637	13,322	49.8	7,578	12,035	63.0
White-collar workers	2,062	6,243	33.0	3,056	9,381	32.6	5,125	11,652	44.0
Sector									
Public sector	3,279	4,637	70.7	3,661	5,537	66.1	5,190	6,297	82.4
Manufacturing	3,720	7,290	51.0	4,138	8,286	49.9	5,157	7,386	69.8
Manual	3,567	6,124	58.2	3,808	6,140	62.0	4,235	5,274	80.3
White-collar	154	1,167	13.2	330	2,146	15.4	923	2,112	43.7
Construction	611	1,326	46.1	472	1,571	30.1	520	1,415	36.7
Agriculture, forestry, fishing	224	989	22.7	131	517	25.4	86	378	22.7
Private services	665	4,578	14.5	768	6,042	12.7	1,215	7,284	16.7

Source: R. Price and G. S. Bain, 'Union Growth in Britain: retrospect and prospect', *British Journal of Industrial Relations*, Vol. 21, No. 1 (March 1983), pp. 49, 51, 52.

cent of the comparable figure for manual workers.

The density of union membership also varies considerably between industries and industrial sectors (table 3.17), and with the size of establishment. The public sector is the most densely organized; manufacturing industry has above average union membership for manual workers; but white-collar workers in manufacturing industry, and employees in the primary sector, and especially in private sector services, are very weakly organized. The primary sector includes agriculture, and the last grouping includes distribution and miscellaneous services which, as we have seen, contain large numbers of low-paid workers. The more detailed figures of membership by industry show that in 1979 unionization was virtually complete in coal-mining, in the public utilities, in the transport industries and in national and local government, and very high, especially among manual workers, in most manufacturing industry, ranging from 28 per cent of all workers in leather and leather goods to over 98 per cent in cotton and man-made fibres. In most, but not all cases, union density had increased since 1948 and especially since 1968. In contrast the service industries show a very much more uneven pattern, with in some cases negligible union membership.[100]

One structural characteristic which affects the industry figures is size of establishmen Price and Bain have argued that 'the available evidence suggests that establishment size is a virtual determinant of unionization'; and that 'the influence of establishment size is almost certainly a major reason for the low density levels . . . in construction, agriculture, and private sector services, which are all dominated by small undertakings.'[101] As we have seen, the average size of establishments has increased over the years which is on factor contributing to the overall growth of unionization.

The question of whether unions can really affect their members' levels of earnings, or whether market forces operate more or less regardless of union organization, has aroused a good deal of controversy among economists.[102] It may well be that certain structural characteristics of employment in the low-paid industries (e.g. small firm size) give rise to both levels of earnings and low union membership density; similarly, structural conditions may lie behind the low levels of unionization, and the poor levels of pay, for women, who are in any case relatively heavily concentrated in the low-paid industries; what can be said, however, is that in addition to their low pay and poor conditions of employment workers in these industries also lack the organizational means to take collective action to improve their situation.

The picture revealed by the data considered in this whole section is a complex one, and it is made more complex by the variations in the ways in which the statistics are categorized. Nevertheless a clear overall pattern can be discerned. In terms of almost all the criteria considered — pay, hours, fringe benefits, job satisfaction, health, job security — the non-manual worker is more highly rewarded and suffers fewer deprivations than t manual worker; and with the exception of one or two considerations, notably recorded unemployment, men are better placed than women. Within these overall categories certain further differences are apparent. Among non-manual workers it is particularly those in professional, and, perhaps to a lesser extent, managerial occupations who appea to have the most favourable conditions of employment (except with regard to the chances of earning the very highest salaries, where top managerial positions have the advantage); and certain non-manual occupations — 'clerical' and 'selling' — have a balance of rewards and deprivations which is similar to that of many manual workers ar worse than that of some of them. Among manual workers there is a general tendency for the more skilled to be better rewarded/less deprived, and in some respects, health for example, for the unskilled to have a considerably worse record than the skilled and semi-skilled. Thus a clear class gradient remains, and the indications are that it is not changing very rapidly. Further, as we have just seen, many of the more disadvantaged workers — women, those in private sector services — are only weakly organized in trade unions and so less able to take action to improve their situations.

OCCUPATIONAL ALLOCATION — CHOICE AND CONSTRAINT

Thus far we have examined the changing occupational structure of Britain and the pattern of deprivations and rewards associated with particular types of work. We have seen that the distribution of work-related rewards and deprivations is such that a rough hierarchy of occupations emerges, in which certain categories of employment offer relatively high pay and good conditions for doing work which must be regarded as less depriving than that for which lower levels of pay and fewer other benefits are received. This hierarchy is not clear-cut, and the ranking of any particular occupational grouping might vary a little depending on which characteristics were most emphasized. Nevertheless there is undoubtedly a systematic pattern of work-related inequalities.

The differentials which exist can be assessed in a variety of ways and according to a variety of criteria. For some they may seem entirely justified as providing incentives for achievement, and/or rewards for the exercise of skill or the carrying of responsibility.[103] For others they may seem unjustified, whether or not they act as such incentives, in terms of basic beliefs and values about human equality. One important consideration, however, which is likely to affect most people's evaluation of these inequalities, is the nature of the allocation process which determines how particular positions in the structure of occupations are filled. Is the process of occupational allocation more or less random; or meritocratic, with allocation in terms of abilities or achievement? Is there equal opportunity to be unequal; or is the process one which is structured to favour those who are initially privileged in terms of family of origin, or some other criterion? Discussion of such questions necessitates a brief consideration of the patterns of social mobility, and of the ways in which the operation of the labour market tends to channel particular categories of people into particular types of work, as well as reference to the account of education (see chapter 2).

Social Mobility

Social mobility studies investigate the relationship between the social status (primarily based on occupation) of children and their parents. Until relatively recently the most comprehensive source of information about social mobility in Britain was derived from studies carried out by Glass and his colleagues in the late 1940s.[104] On the basis, in particular, of the evidence from a large scale survey it was argued that there was a relatively high degree of self-recruitment in Britain, especially at the two ends of the social scale, that most mobility was fairly short-range, and that the middle of the occupational hierarchy was characterized by a 'buffer zone' so that movement either way over the fundamental line of cleavage between manual and non-manual occupations, although not infrequent, would tend to be short-range.[105]

The Glass study, and these arguments derived from it, have come under severe criticism, and more recent work has demonstrated that the situation is not as clear-cut as this. Data for England and Wales, and for Scotland, show that for men (both studies excluded women) there is still a considerable measure of self-recruitment, especially at the two ends of the occupational scale, so that in particular a large proportion of male manual workers are the sons of manual workers – about 70 per cent in England and Wales (see tables 3.18 and 3.19), and over 75 per cent in Scotland. On the other hand, the upper socio-economic groupings have recruited a substantial proportion from manual worker origins. This upward mobility is a consequence of the growth in the numbers in professional, administrative and managerial occupations, which we have already noted, but the fact that such positions have been filled in substantial, though by no means equal, proportions by manual as well as non-manual workers' sons certainly undermines any notion of a 'buffer zone', or of the relative closure of the upper occupational status groups.[106]

Though no comparable enquiries have been carried out into women's social mobility, Heath has used available data to consider their patterns of occupational and 'marital' mobility (the latter means comparing the woman's father's status with that of her husband). The concentration of women's employment in lower level white-collar work and semi- and unskilled manual work (and their exclusion from most higher professional and managerial, and skilled manual jobs) leads to a situation where women as a whole have inferior opportunities for occupational mobility compared to men. However, single women who have been able to concentrate on a career have better chances than men of upward mobility and of access to at least lower level professional and managerial work. The labour market segregation of women into lower white-collar jobs means that the chances of women from manual workers' homes obtaining non-manual work are better than those of men, and that very few women from a non-manual background are downwardly mobile into manual work.[107]

In past discussions of social mobility it has been assumed that the main mechanism for upward mobility in recent decades has been the educational system. The professionalization of occupations and the growing size and bureaucratization of organizations, it was argued, led to the recruitment of employees on the basis of formal qualifications; and the expansion of educational opportunities with the introduction of secondary education for all after the Second World War, and the subsequent growth of higher education, enabled at least some of those with ability from less privileged backgrounds to obtain the necessary qualifications for a high status job. At the same time it was argued that whereas in the past able individuals from humble origins had been able to improve their position by building up their own business or working their way up from the shop or office floor even without formal qualifications, these opportunities had been severely diminished by the same process of professionalization and bureaucratization which favoured mobility through the educational system.[108] In fact in the recent study of social mobility in England and Wales it was found that a substantial proportion of those who were upwardly mobile (and indeed of those who maintained the occupational status of their family of origin) had had experience of lower status work at an earlier stage of their work history; they had obtained their present situation at least in part by gaining advances

Table 3.18   Social Mobility, England and Wales, 1972; 'inflow' – Class Composition by Class of Father[a] at Respondent's Age 14

Father's[1] class[3]	Respondent's class[3] (1972)								
	I	II	III	IV	V	VI	VII	N	%
	Percentages[2] by column								
I	25.3	12.4	9.6	6.7	3.2	2.0	2.4	680	7.9
II	13.1	12.2	8.0	4.8	5.2	3.1	2.5	547	6.4
III	10.4	10.4	10.8	7.4	8.7	5.7	6.0	687	8.0
IV	10.1	12.2	9.8	27.2	8.6	7.1	7.7	886	10.3
V	12.5	14.0	13.2	12.1	16.6	12.2	9.6	1,072	12.5
VI	16.4	21.7	26.1	24.0	31.1	41.8	35.2	2,577	30.0
VII	12.1	17.1	22.6	17.8	26.7	28.0	36.6	2,126	24.8
N	1,230	1,050	827	687	1,026	1,883	1,872	8,575	
%	14.3	12.2	9.6	8.0	12.0	22.0	21.8		

Notes:

1   Or other 'head of household'. The two basic questions in the 1972 inquiry from which the data of the table derive were: 'What is your job now?' – following on several questions on earlier occupations; and 'What was your father's (or other head of household's) job at that time (i.e. at respondent's age 14)?' – following on several other questions about respondent's family circumstances at that age.

2   These percentages exclude farmers and smallholders, who would be allocated to class IV and class VII respectively.

3   The Classes were defined as follows: I. Higher-grade professionals, administrators; managers in large establishments; large proprietors; II. Lower-grade professionals; higher-grade technicians; lower-grade administrators; managers in small establishments; supervisors of non-manual employees; III. Routine non-manual (clerical) employees; sales personnel; other rank and file service workers; IV. Small proprietors; self-employed artisans; non-professional 'own account' workers; V. Lower-grade technicians; supervisors over manual workers; VI. Skilled manual wage-workers; VII. Semi- and unskilled manual wage-workers.

Source: J. H. Goldthorpe, *Social Mobility and Class Structure in Modern Britain* (Oxford 1980), p. 44.

Table 3.19   Social Mobility, England and Wales: 'outflow' – Class Distribution of Respondents by Class of Father[1] at Respondent's Age 14

Father's[1] class[3]	Respondent's class[3] (1972)								
	I	II	III	IV	V	VI	VII	N	%
				Percentages[2] by row					
I	45.7	19.1	11.6	6.8	4.9	5.4	6.5	680	7.9
II	29.4	23.3	12.1	6.0	9.7	10.8	8.6	547	6.4
III	18.6	15.9	13.0	7.4	13.0	15.7	16.4	687	8.0
IV	14.0	14.4	9.1	21.1	9.9	15.1	16.3	886	10.3
V	14.4	13.7	10.2	7.7	15.9	21.4	16.8	1,072	12.5
VI	7.8	8.8	8.4	6.4	12.4	30.6	25.6	2,577	30.0
VII	7.1	8.5	8.8	5.7	12.9	24.8	32.2	2,126	24.8
N	1,230	1,050	827	687	1,026	1,883	1,872	8,575	
%	14.3	12.2	9.6	8.0	12.0	22.0	21.8		

Notes:
1 See note 1, Table 3.18
2 See note 2, Table 3.18
3 See note 3, Table 3.18

Source: J. H. Goldthorpe, *Social Mobility and Class Structure in Modern Britain*, (Oxford 1980).p. 48.

during their working life. In addition, analysis of different cohorts in the sample showed that those born more recently had, as expected, had apparently greater chances of direct entry into upper status groups (presumably through educational channels), but these increased chances were not 'counter-balanced' by a decline in the likelihood of upward mobility through 'work-life' advance.[109]

Thus, data on social mobility can provide some indication of the overall dimensions of occupational allocation in Great Britain, but leave a number of questions for further exploration. Occupational allocation for men, and for women, is neither completely random nor completely determined by the occupational status of the father; it is therefore important to see how the mechanisms of allocation both provide opportunities (within limits) and confer advantages on those already privileged, and place constraints on those already relatively deprived. The two questions of particular importance are the extent to which social origins can confer educational advantages which can then be used to secure more highly rewarded jobs; and how far the operation of the labour market creates or reinforces inequalities of opportunity.

The relationship between social origins, education and occupation has been explored in chapter 2. As will be apparent from that discussion the educational system is far from strictly 'meritocratic' in its effects. Quite apart from the continued existence of fee-paying schools, which allow educational advantages to be bought by those with sufficient income, processes of selection and streaming, and geographical and other inequalities in resources lead to a distribution of opportunities which on the whole favours those who come from the more economically privileged backgrounds; and the assumptions of teachers, administrators, parents and — as time goes on — increasingly the children themselves, about the academic potential and occupational opportunities of particular categories of children, are a further constraint. Many from less privileged backgrounds clearly do succeed in using educational opportunities to be upwardly occupationally mobile, but they have to overcome handicaps on the way which are sufficient to block those with somewhat less ability, or less determination, or less luck. Though it is far from perfect, there is a clear relationship between educational qualifications and occupation, such that the better the qualifications the more rewarding the job.[110] By the time any individual enters the labour market, therefore, the chances of a rewarding career are determined to a considerable extent. It remains to be seen in what ways the operation of the labour market modifies this picture.

The Labour Market

Although there are some very valuable contributions to it,[111] there is no wholly adequate sociological account of the labour market in the UK. This section will certainly not fill that gap but has a more limited purpose. The basic conception of the labour market in neo-classical economics is one which sees behaviour in it as rational and individualistic, with the underlying processes reflecting the workings of supply and demand, income and price.[112] Such a conception, which with modifications and extensions can, of course, become very complex and sophisticated, carries the implications that the market for labour may reflect, perpetuate and even increase inequalities derived from other sources (those individuals with greater skills, more experience and/or better qualifications will get more highly rewarded jobs than those with lesser capacities), but that its operation does not in itself create such differences. The crucial question for our purposes, therefore, is whether there are characteristics of the labour market, unacknowledged by such conventional approaches, which mean that in practice it places certain individuals, or categories of persons, at a relative advantage or disadvantage, advantages and disadvantages which may become cumulative over a lifetime.

First of all, it is important to establish that the labour market is not one but a large number of partially overlapping markets. Labour markets are fragmented geographically, and industrially and occupationally. For some occupations there may be an effective national, or even international, market in the sense that jobs are advertised nationally or more widely and applicants may come from anywhere in the area covered by those advertisements. Most labour markets are more restricted than that; and most potential applicants for jobs are very restricted as to the geographical area in which they can seek work. Quite apart from the social costs of having to move home, the economic costs of moving house and the sheer difficulty of obtaining alternative accommodation may restrict 'choice' of employment to the positions available in the local area. Hence rates of unemployment may vary quite widely by region for lengthy periods of time.

Labour markets are fragmented occupationally in terms of the skills and qualifications which are a prerequisite for certain work. Such lines of division may be deepened and/or added to by the actions of employers, for example in customarily seeking employees only from certain sections of the population; and of collectivities of employees, for example in the successful claims of trade unions or professional associations to preserve certain areas of work for their members, or for those with certain attributes, regardless of whether or not others, non-members or without those attributes, could do it. The ways in which the labour market is affected by collective action, of employees and employers, is a further crucial respect in which it departs from the neo-classical atomistic model. Collective bargaining over pay and other terms and conditions of employment is, of course, the most obvious way in which this is manifested, and as we have seen, it is essential to take this into account in discussing earnings differentials. Few individuals, other than top executives in large companies and chairmen of nationalized industries, are able to bargain individually with employers as to the rate at which they are to be paid; but some occupational groups have far greater power and resources in the labour market than others, and greater possibilities of improving and protecting their terms and conditions of employment, at least in the medium term.

In terms of a discussion of occupational allocation, however, the more important limitations on the neo-classical view of the labour market are those which are critical of the primacy given to rational individual 'choice'.[113] Effective choice requires that jobs be available and that those seeking work within a particular section of the labour market are not all wanting the same scarce jobs. Individuals' preferences, or 'orientations to work', should differ and a suitable range of desirable types of work should be available. In times of full employment some workers appear to have been able to find work which matched their orientations, for example, securing high pay even at the cost of increased effort,[114] but this is far from generally the case. 'Choice' also requires that workers know which jobs have which characteristics and what attributes they need to obtain them. Available information about jobs is often limited, and it is costly in terms of time as well as money to obtain more, if this is possible at all; limited information clearly makes rational choice very difficult for the ordinary job seeker. Workers who move between obs to try and find one which suits them are likely to find that their 'choice' of work quickly becomes restricted because many employers place considerable emphasis on motivational factors (e.g. stability and reliability) in recruiting workers, especially the non-skilled, and are therefore less likely to hire those whose employment record shows a lot of changes of job.

Quite apart from the restrictions caused by high levels of unemployment, the extent to which workers can 'choose' is restricted by their own attributes or lack of them (in general, the fewer qualifications or less experience, the less the choice) and by their lack of information about jobs, and lack of awareness of potential employers' criteria for selection (and possibly of ability to meet them). In many cases there may also be limitations on job seekers' control over occupational allocation due to characteristics of the recruitment process. In some occupations and/or industries the process tends to be very 'formal' and bureaucratic: posts are advertised in known and public ways and stated universalistic criteria are relevant for appointments and promotions (broadly true, for example, in education and in national and local government). Elsewhere the labour market may operate much more 'informally' and unpredictably, with particularistic criteria like kinship links, religious affiliation, or membership of the right clubs, of relevance in getting a job. Recruitment has often been carried out in this way for managerial posts in many small and medium-sized organizations, for example, and for manual work on the docks or in parts of the construction industry.

In addition to these sources of constraint, employers may discriminate against certain categories of employee, sometimes with no apparent rationale at all, but often on the basis of assumptions about the likely attributes and behaviour of certain categories of persons. Married men with young families, for example, are often preferred to young single men and older men, because their commitment to steady work is seen as greater; men may be preferred to women, or whites to coloured, because they are seen as more reliable and/or more productive. If, as in the case of discrimination on grounds of gender or colour, the (white, male) employees who benefit from these processes share the employers' 'tastes', and are more or less aware of the benefits such discrimination brings them, this will reinforce such patterns of recruitment and the restrictions on opportunities for others which they create.[115]

In the last two decades particular attention has been given to a further important set of constraints on processes of occupational allocation: those arising from the creation of internal labour markets, and from the associated development of labour market segmentation. In large organizations the majority of posts may be filled from within, so that external recruitment is normally only necessary for the basic grades of, say, manual worker, clerk and management trainee. The allocation of the more senior and better-rewarded positions is confined to those who are already working in the organization. It has been argued that this is particularly likely to occur in large, capital intensive (and quasi-monopolistic) organizations where reliability in the operation of expensive plant is specially important, and the skills needed are best acquired on the job (and the employing organization can afford to offer job security, and 'generous' pay and fringe benefits). The development of such internal labour markets, however, has beneficial consequences for the employer and for existing employees; it creates a degree of 'employment dependence' for those employees who have been promoted to positions with augmented rewards for length of service and the taking of responsibility which they would lose if they moved to another employer, and it gives existing employees chances of more highly rewarded jobs without competition from those outside the organization. As a corollary it means that those outside seeking work are often restricted to choosing between employers, each of whom is recruiting at a basic grade, with opportunities for subsequent advancement which may appear very uncertain and imprecisely specified.[116]

The development of internal labour markets has been seen as a key aspect in more general processes of labour market segmentation whereby opportunities for employment are divided between a primary sector of relatively well paid secure jobs, mostly in larger organizations, and a secondary sector of poorly paid insecure jobs. Some of the latter may be found in large firms and used by them to cope with fluctuations in demand, but many are in small firms dependent on larger organizations and/or in highly competitive industries, where there is great instability of demand and strong downward pressure on labour costs. Attempts to establish empirically such a model of a dual labour market have not been altogether successful in Britain.[117]

A simple division into two sectors needs modifications. Some skilled and qualified workers may be able to secure continuous well-rewarded employment without becoming dependent on any one employer; they represent an 'independent' primary sector in contrast to the 'subordinate' primary sector of the employer dependent.[118] Other workers with no special skills have been able to obtain relatively secure, even if poorly paid, work, especially in the public sector. Nevertheless the linking of the notion of the internal labour market with certain assumptions about the different ways in which employers will recruit for primary as compared with secondary jobs has provided valuable insights into patterns of women's employment.[119] More generally, if labour markets are segmented to any extent in some of the ways suggested, then clearly this will restrict the possibility of 'choice' of occupation on the part of job seekers. In particular, those who find themselves in the secondary sector, for whatever reason – ill-health, for example, or reluctance to be tied down to one employer, or due to discrimination on grounds of gender or colour – may well find it very difficult to escape from the vicious circle of low skills and an unsuitable employment record leading to low pay in insecure employment. In so far as the security and rewards of the primary sector employees depend, in part at least, on the existence of a secondary sector to take up variations in demand, labour market segmentation is also a way of dividing the working class and reducing the likelihood of collective action to improve the position of the lower paid.

Thus labour markets operate in ways which are clearly well removed from providing all employees with chances of competing for the more desirable and more highly rewarded jobs. 'Choice' is restricted by barriers to geographical and occupational mobility, and by highly imperfect information about opportunities. Employers can and do discriminate against certain categories of worker. Initial qualifications and point of entry into a highly fragmented labour market are important influences on future opportunities and the relative advantages and disadvantages so acquired are likely to be reinforced rather than mitigated as further work experience is gained. Inequality of rewards and conditions is part of the structure of a highly fragmented, segmented labour market; chance may partly determine allocation within it; and movement from more deprived to more highly rewarded sectors can be difficult if not impossible, so that further inequalities are created by the operation of the labour market itself. British society is not closed, but nor is it completely open, and whatever other justifications may be offered for the existing pattern of work-related inequalities, they cannot be defended as being rewards to those who are successful in a competition in which all have equal chances.

CONCLUSION

The nature and consequences of the division of labour have always been major questions of interest to social scientists. For some, like Adam Smith, the increase in the division of labour was a fundamental cause of economic growth and the possibility of the greater welfare of mankind; for others, as in some of the writings of Marx, its virtual abolition appeared to be a prerequisite for real human freedom. It is perhaps with the work of Durkheim, however, that analysis of the problems of the division of labour is most notably associated.[120] For Durkheim the central question was whether, and if so how, social cohesion and social solidarity could be maintained in societies with an increasingly complex division of labour. He argued very forcefully that organic solidarity based on the interdependence of those who have differentiated functions, would and should develop. In his discussion of 'abnormal forms', however, he acknowledged three other possibilities: an 'anomic' form of the division of labour in which there was inadequate normative regulation of economic life for solidarity to develop; the 'forced' division of labour in which individuals were constrained to undertake certain tasks, there was no 'harmony between individual natures and social functions', and 'social inequalities' did not 'exactly express natural inequalities'; and the situation where there is too much specialization, 'each employee is not sufficiently occupied' and 'operations are carried on without any unity'.[121]

In this chapter we have been concerned with aspects of the division of labour in contemporary Britain, and in the light of the evidence which has been discussed would have to conclude that the situation resembles Durkheim's 'abnormal' forms more closely than his ideal type of organic solidarity. For very many in our society their role in the division of labour is one which is forced on them by the constraints of their upbringing, education and lack of opportunity in the labour market; there is no consensus as to the appropriate distribution of obligations and rewards as between different classes and categories of occupations whose situations are so unequal; and there is not only a 'social' but also a 'detailed' division of labour which Braverman, for example, regards as the special product of capitalist society,[122] which leaves the workers performing only a fragment of a whole task.

It can, indeed, be argued that both anomie and alienation characterize the division of labour in Britain; an absence of normative consensus leading to disorder, as for example in industrial relations; and persistent inequalities of condition and of opportunity which constrain individuals in unacceptable ways and make any attempt to establish normative agreement difficult if not impossible.[123] At the moment there are no agreed remedies for such problems, nor any immediate prospects of their solution. In the last few years the rapid growth in unemployment has increased the degree of inequality by creating a large minority of the relatively deprived even as those in employment have seen their real incomes rise. Behind the present continuing level of unemployment, however, there are further questions, which may shortly have to be faced, about the future place of paid work in highly industrialized societies like our own. If the development of micro-electronic technology means that much existing work can be done automatically, or with far less labour, what place will work have in our society in the future? And what will be the consequences for social cohesion and individual identity of a situation where spending a major part of an adult lifetime in employment is no longer a normal expectation? It is perhaps too soon to see whether these more radical predictions will be fulfilled, but examination of work in UK society as it is now — including proper acknowledgement of the far from satisfactory nature of the work many men and women currently have to do — seems an essential base from which these or other questions can be discussed.

Notes to Chapter 3

1   S. R. Parker, R. K. Brown, J. Child, M. A. Smith, *The Sociology of Industry* (London 1972), pp. 173-5; see also S. R. Parker, *Leisure and Work* (London 1983), pp. 1-12, 18-32.
2   E. Jaques, *Equitable Payment* (Penguin edn. 1967), pp. 52-5; see also W. Brown and E. Jaques, *Glacier Project Papers* (London 1965), esp. chs. 3 and 4.
3   H. Braverman, *Labor and Monopoly Capital* (New York 1974), pp. 46-58. For yet another, very perceptive, approach to work, see E. C. Hughes, *Men and their Work* (New York 1958).
4   J. I. Gershuny and R. E. Pahl, 'Britain in the decade of the three economies', *New Society* (3 January 1980), pp. 7-9; see also the discussion in M. Jahoda, *Employment and Unemployment: A Social-Psychological Analysis* (Cambridge 1982), esp. ch. 2.
5   Notably in D. Bell, *The Coming of Post-Industrial Society* (Penguin edn. 1976).
6   See R. Dubin, 'Industrial workers' worlds — a study of the "central life interests" of industrial workers', *Social Problems*, Vol. 3 (January 1956); see also J. H. Goldthorpe et al., *The Affluent Worker — Industrial Attitudes and Behaviour* (Cambridge 1968), esp. chs 2 and 7.
7   Such an interpretation has been made of some of the work of B. Bernstein, for example, *Class, Codes and Control*, Vol. 1 (London 1971); and of the concern with cycles of transmitted deprivation, see, for example, K. Joseph, 'The Cycle of Deprivation' in E. Butterworth and R. Holman (eds), *Social Welfare in Modern Britain* (Glasgow 1975), pp. 387-93; and Community Development Projects, *Gilding the Ghetto* (London 1977).
8   M. Weber, *The Protestant Ethic and the Spirit of Capitalism* (London 1930); and *General Economic History* (New York 1961), esp. ch. 30.
9   R. Bendix, *Work and Authority in Industry* (New York 1963), esp. chs 2 and 4; S. Pollard, *The Genesis of Modern Management* (London 1965), esp. ch. 5; E. P. Thompson, 'Time, work discipline and industrial capitalism', *Past and Present*, Vol. 38 (1967), pp. 56-97.
10 See, for example, W. Baldamus, *Efficiency and Effort* (London 1961), esp. ch. 8; and R. Hyman and I. Brough, *Social Values and Industrial Relations* (Oxford 1975).
11 A. Fox, 'The meaning of work' in G. Esland and G. Salaman (eds), *The Politics of Work and Occupations* (Milton Keynes 1980), pp. 139-91. See also R. Williams, 'The meanings of work' in R. Fraser (ed.), *Work: twenty personal accounts*

(Penguin edn. 1968), pp. 280-98.

12 A. Fox, *op. cit.*, pp. 168-72.

13 M. Jahoda, *Employment and Unemployment: A Social-Psychological Analysis*
    (Cambridge 1982), p. 59.

14 See, for example, I. Reid, *Social Class Differences in Britain – a source book*
    (London 1977), p. 15: 'Social class is a grouping of people into categories on the
    basis of occupation.' For an analysis based on a quite clearly different approach
    see J. Westergaard and H. Resler, *Class in a Capitalist Society* (London 1975).

15 See T. B. Bottomore and M. Rubel (eds), *Karl Marx – selected writings in
    Sociology and Social Philosophy* (London 1956), pp. 178 *et seq.*; H. H. Gerth and
    C. W. Mills, *From Max Weber* (London 1948), p. 182.

16 I. Reid, *Social Class Differences in Britain*, pp. 65-70.

17 J. Rex and R. Moore, *Race, Community and Conflict* (Oxford 1967).

18 J. W. B. Douglas, *The Home and the School* (London 1967); D. S. Byrne,
    W. Williamson and B. Fletcher, *The Poverty of Education* (London 1975).

19 In addition to the OPCS *Classification of Occupations*, the Department of
    Employment has produced its own comprehensive occupational classification,
    CODOT (*Classification of Occupations and Directory of Occupational Titles*),
    HMSO 1972, which has an index of 11,000 job titles which are grouped into
    eighteen broad divisions. The Department of Employment's *List of Key Occu-
    pations for Statistical Purposes* (KOS) arranges about 400 occupations into the
    same eighteen divisions which are used, for example, for the *New Earnings Survey*.

20 The difficulties involved in categorizing occupations are reflected in the vagaries
    of official classifications. The Classification of Occupations introduced by OPCS
    in 1980 was fundamentally revised from, and incommensurable with, that used for
    the 1961, 1966 and 1971 Censuses, which was itself a considerable revision of the
    classification used in 1951. The 1980 classification was intended to be broadly
    compatible with a condensed version of KOS. For a discussion of some of these
    problems, and employment statistics generally, see N. K. Buxton and D. I. Mackay,
    British Employment Statistics – a guide to sources and methods (Oxford 1977);
    C. Hakim and W. R. Hawes, 'The labour force' in *Labour and Income*, Statistical
    Sources D291, The Open University (Milton Keynes 1982), pp. 6-61; R. Hyman
    and B. Price, 'Labour statistics' in J. Irvine, I. Miles and J. Evans (eds), *Demystify-
    ing Social Statistics* (London 1979), pp. 222-36.

21 Some of the problems involved in using even these apparently straightforward
    categories are discussed in G. S. Bain and R. Price, 'Who is a white collar
    employee?', *British Journal of Industrial Relations*, Vol. 10, No. 3 (1972),
    pp. 325-39; and P. Sadler, 'Sociological aspects of skill', *British Journal of
    Industrial Relations*, Vol. 8, No. 1 (1970), pp. 22-31.

22 A. Stewart, K. Prandy and R. M. Blackburn, *Social Stratification and Occupations*
    (London 1980), esp. pt. 1.

23 But see the valuable discussion by T. Nichols, 'Social class: official, sociological
    and Marxist' in J. Irvine et al. (eds), *Demystifying Social Statistics* (London 1979),
    pp. 152-71.

24 See Buxton and Mackay, *op. cit.*, and Department of Employment, *British
    Labour Statistics: Historical Abstract 1886–1968* (HMSO 1971); A. H. Halsey (ed.)

Trends in British Society since 1900 (London 1972), esp. pp. 97-128; D. C. Marsh, *The Changing Social Structure in England and Wales, 1871-1961* (London 1965), esp. pp. 1-164; G. G. C. Routh, *Occupation and Pay in Great Britain, 1906-1979* (London 1980); Ministry of Labour, *Occupational Charges 1951-1961*, Manpower Studies No. 6 (HMSO 1967); R. Knight, 'Changes in the Occupational Structure of the Working Population', *Journal of the Royal Statistical Society*, Vol. 130, Pt. 3 (1967), pp. 408-22.

25   Department of Employment, *British Labour Statistics: Historical Abstract 1886-1968* (HMSO 1971), p. 195; *Census 1981*, National Report, Great Britain, Pt. 1, (HMSO 1983), p. 52. These figures are based on the total population above the age of 10 in 1841 and above the minimum school-leaving age of 16 in 1981. The activity rates for those of working age, 16-65 for men and 16-60 for women, are, of course, higher, being approximately 78 per cent (91 per cent for men and 63 per cent for women) in the United Kingdom in 1979, see *Social Trends 1983* (HMSO 1982), p. 51.

26   C. Clark, *The Conditions of Economic Progress* (London 1957), esp. pp. 510-20; *Social Trends 1983*, p. 54.

27   *British Labour Statistics: Historical Abstract* (London 1971), p. 195; *British Labour Statistics Yearbook, 1974* (London 1976), pp. 170-1.

28   Department of Employment, *Employment Gazette*, 91, No. 9 (September 1983), p. 58.

29   See, for example, F. Froebel, *The New International Division of Labour* (Cambridge 1980); B. Jones, *Sleepers, Wake! Technology and the future of work* (Brighton 1982); and T. Forester (ed.), *The Microelectronics Revolution* (Oxford 1980).

30   See also G. G. C. Routh, *Occupation and Pay in Great Britain 1906-1979* (London 1980).

31   See the account in G. D. H. Cole, *Studies in Class Structure* (London 1955), esp. pp. 50-77.

32   See D. Lockwood, *The Blackcoated Worker* London 1958); K. Prandy, A. Stewart and R. M. Blackburn, *White-Collar Work* (London 1982).

33   B. Abramowitz and V. F. Eliasberg, *The Growth of Public Employment in Great Britain* (Princeton 1957), p. 25; *Social Trends, No. 10, 1980* (London 1979), p. 124.

34   See the discussion in T. J. Johnson, *Professions and Power* (London 1972); and G. Esland, 'Professions and professionalism' in G. Esland and G. Salaman (eds), *The Politics of Work and Occupations* (Milton Keynes 1980). In addition to the relevant Census volumes, details of the growth of numbers in 'professional' occupations can be found in M. J. Woolgar, 'The Growth of the Clergy as a Profession in England and Wales', unpublished PhD thesis (University of Leicester 1960), esp. p. 41; A. M. Carr-Saunders, D. Caradog Jones and C. A. Moser, *A Survey of Social Conditions in England and Wales* (Oxford 1958), pp. 108-11. See also tables 3.3 and 3.5.

35   See R. Bendix, *Work and Authority in Industry* (New York 1956), esp. ch. 4; and S. Melman, *Dynamic Factors in Industrial Productivity* (Oxford 1956). For discussion of the relationship between size of organization and proportions of

administrative and clerical employees see D. S. Pugh and D. J. Hickson, *Organ-izational Structure in its Context* (Farnborough 1976), esp. ch. 5.

36   *British Labour Statistics, Historical Abstract*, p. 408; *Annual Abstract of Statistics, 119, 1983* (London 1983), p. 119.

37   *British Labour Statistics, Historical Abstract*, p. 408; *Annual Abstract of Statistics 1983*, p. 131; *Report of the Committee of Inquiry on Industrial Democracy* (Bullock Report), Cmnd. 6706 (London 1977), p. 5.

38   Comparable figures for 1981 were not available but recent data for England, based on a sample survey and categorized in less detail, can be seen in table 3.16.

39   For a more detailed discussion of the differentiation of men's and women's work in Britain see C. Hakim, *Occupational Segregation*, Department of Employment Research Paper No. 9 (London 1979).

40   See F. D. Klingender, *Art and the Industrial Revolution* (London 1968); and N. Hedges and H. Beynon, *Born to Work* (London 1982).

41   *Social Trends, No. 6, 1975* (London 1975), p. 29.

42   *Ibid.*, p. 12.

43   The relationship has been made even more complex by the revision of the *Classification of Occupations* in 1980 (which forms the basis from which 'Social Classes' and 'SEGs' are derived). The post 1980 figures for Classes or SEGs do not refer to the same clusters of occupations as those based on the 1970 or earlier Classifications.

44   *Social Trends*, No. 6, 1975 (London 1975), p. 30.

45   See, for example, J. H. Goldthorpe, *Social Mobility and Class Structure in Modern Britain* (Oxford 1980), esp. pp. 39-42; and A. Stewart, K. Pandy and R. M. Blackburn, *Social Stratification and Occupations* (London 1980), esp. pt. 1.

46   See the discussion in J. H. Goldthorpe and K. Hope, 'Occupational grading and occupational prestige' in K. Hope (ed.), *The Analysis of Social Mobility – methods and approaches* (Oxford 1972).

47   *Social Trends, No. 13, 1983* (London 1982), p. 55, and *Employment Gazette*, Vol. 91, No. 9 (September 1983), pp. 58-9.

48   *British Labour Statistics Yearbook, 1974* (London 1976), pp. 228-30.

49   R. Scase and R. Goffee, *The Entrepreneurial Middle Class* (London 1982), esp. pp. 23-7. See also the contributions to F. Bechhofer and B. Elliott (eds), *The Petite Bourgeoisie* (London 1981), and F. Bechhofer et al., 'The petit bourgeois in industrial society', *Archives Européennes de Sociologie*, Vol. 17 (1976), pp. 74-99.

50   F. Bechhofer and B. Elliott, 'An approach to the study of small shopkeepers and the class structure', *Archives Européennes de Sociologie*, Vol. 9 (1968); F. Bechhofer et al., 'Small shopkeepers: matters of money and meaning', *The Sociological Review*, Vol. 22, No. 4 (1974).

51   T. Nichols, *Ownership, Control and Ideology* (London 1969).

52   A. Giddens, *The Class Structure of the Advanced Societies* (London 1973), p. 84.

53   For further discussion see B. Wootton, *The Social Foundations of Wage Policy* (London 1955); J. E. King, *Labour Economics* (London 1972); R. Hyman and I. Brough, *Social Values and Industrial Relations* (Oxford 1975); T. Nichols (ed.), *Capital and Labour* (Glasgow 1980); and the references cited by King, Hyman and

Brough, and Nichols.

54   T. B. Bottomore and M. Rubel (eds), *Karl Marx – Selected Writings in Sociology and Social Philosophy* (London 1956), pp. 169-70, quoted from the Economic and Philosophical Manuscripts of 1844.

55   For further discussion see J. E. T. Eldridge, *Sociology and Industrial Life* (London 1971), esp. pt. 3; S. Lukes, 'Alienation and Anomie' in P. Laslett and W. G. Runciman (eds), *Philosophy, Politics and Society* (Oxford 1967), pp. 134-56.

56   See, for example, J. H. Goldthorpe et al., *The Affluent Worker–Industrial Attitudes and Behaviour* (Cambridge 1968), pp. 178-80.

57   F. Herzberg et al., *The Motivation to Work* (New York 1959); C. Argyris, *Personality and Organization* (New York 1957); V. H. Vroom and E. L. Deci (eds), *Management and Motivation* (Penguin edn. 1970).

58   W. Baldamus, *Efficiency and Effort* (London 1961).

59   E. Jaques, *Equitable Payment* (Penguin edn. 1967); for a different conceptualization, see T. Lupton and D. Gowler, *Selecting a Wage Payment System* (London 1969).

60   These concepts are discussed in A. Etzioni, *A Comparative Analysis of Complex Organizations* (New York 1961); see also the important discussion of A. Fox, *Beyond Contract: Work, Power and Trust Relations* (London 1974); and the reservations in P. R. D. Corrigan, 'Feudal Relics of Capitalist Monuments', *Sociology*, Vol. 11, No. 3 (September 1977).

61   W. Baldamus, *Efficiency and Effort*, esp. pt. 2; this view appears close to the notion of 'hygiene' factors developed by Herzberg.

62   For a selection of writings on this topic see M. Weir (ed.), *Job Satisfaction* (Glasgow 1976); for a brief discussion of major approaches, see P. Warr and T. Wall, *Work and Well-being* (Penguin edn. 1975); for a recent review of empirical studies see R. K. Brown, M. M. Curran and J. M. Cousins, *Changing Attitudes to Employment?* Department of Employment Research Paper, No. 40 (London 1983).

63   An introduction to the literature on trade union government can be found in J. A. Banks, *Trade Unionism* (London 1974), esp. pt. 3; and in J. Hemingway, *Conflict and Democracy* (Oxford 1978), esp. ch. 1; see also T. Lane, *The Union Makes Us Strong* (Arrow edn. 1974).

64   G. G. C. Routh, *Occupation and Pay in Great Britain 1906–1960* (Cambridge 1965), p. 147.

65   *Ibid*, p. 150.

66   Department of Employment, *New Earnings Survey 1983*, Part A, Streamlined Analyses and Key Analyses by Agreement (London 1983), tables 8 and 9, pp. A49-A62.

67   *Ibid.*

68   Royal Commission on the Distribution of Income and Wealth, *Report No. 3, Higher Incomes from Employment*, Cmnd. 6383 (HMSO 1976), pp. 7-12.

69   Department of Employment, *New Earnings Survey 1975*, Part A (HMSO 1975), p. A5.

70   Royal Commission on the Distribution of Income and Wealth, *Report No. 8, Fifth Report on the Standing Reference*, Cmnd. 7679 (HMSO 1979), pp. 227-39. See also RCDIW, *Report No. 3*, pp. 29-35.

71   See C. Pond and S. Winyard, *The Case for a National Minimum Wage*, Low Pay
     Unit pamphlet No. 23 (London 1983), pp. 8-10; and also F. Field (ed.), *Are Low
     Wages Inevitable?* (Nottingham 1976).
72   Royal Commission on the Distribution of Income and Wealth, *Report No. 6, Lower
     Incomes*, Cmnd. 7175 (HMSO 1978); *Department of Employment Gazette*, Vol. 85,
     No. 1 (January 1977), pp. 22-3.
73   C. Pond and S. Winyard, *op. cit.*, pp. 15-22.
74   *New Earnings Survey 1983*, Part A, pp. A63-A66.
75   In addition to the works by Wootton, King, and Hyman and Brough cited above
     (note 53), see A. B. Atkinson, *The Economics of Inequality* (Oxford 1975);
     Open University, 'Income and Inequality' in *Patterns of Inequality* (Milton Keynes
     1976); and G. G. C. Routh, 'Interpretations of pay structure', *International
     Journal of Social Economics*, Vol. 1, No. 1 (1974), pp. 13-39.
76   Royal Commission on the Distribution of Income and Wealth, *Report No. 8*,
     pp. 44 *et seq*.
77   D. Wedderburn and C. Craig, 'Relative deprivation in work' in D. Wedderburn (ed.),
     Poverty, Inequality and Class Structure (Cambridge 1974), pp. 141-64; details of
     the sample are reported in D. Wedderburn, 'The conditions of employment of
     manual and non-manual workers' in Social Science Research Council, Conference
     Proceedings, *Social Stratification and Industrial Relations*, mimeo (Cambridge
     1969), p. 30.
78   E. Wigham, 'Industry still divided by the colour of the collar', *Times Business
     News* (9 March 1976).
79   *British Labour Statistics Yearbook 1974*, p. 125.
80   See C. Hakim and W. R. Hawes, 'The Labour Force' in *Labour and Income*, D291
     Statistical Sources, Open University (Milton Keynes 1982), p. 38; and the
     General Household Survey for the relevant years.
81   C. Hakim and W. R. Hawes, *op. cit.*, p. 38; *General Household Survey 1972*, p. 140.
82   See, for example, J. H. Goldthorpe et al., *The Affluent Worker: Industrial
     Attitudes and Behaviour* (Cambridge 1968); D. Wedderburn and R. Crompton,
     Workers' Attitudes and Technology (Cambridge 1972); H. Beynon and R. M.
     Blackburn, *Perceptions of Work – variations within a factory* (Cambridge 1972);
     R. M. Blackburn and M. Mann, *The Working Class in the Labour Market* (London
     1979); K. Prandy et al., *White-Collar Work* (London 1982).
83   See R. Blauner, 'Work satisfaction and industrial trends in modern society' in
     R. Bendix and S. M. Lipset (eds), *Class, Status and Power* (London 1966),
     pp. 473-87.
84   See R. K. Brown, M. M. Curran and J. M. Cousins, *Changing Attitudes to Employ-
     ment?*, Department of Employment Research Paper No. 40 (London 1983), esp.
     pp. 28-9.
85   *General Household Survey 1981* (HMSO 1983), pp. 86-8, 111-4.
86   See, for example, P. Kinnersley, *The Hazards of Work* (London 1973); and
     T. Nichols and P. Armstrong, *Safety or Profit: industrial accidents and the
     conventional wisdom* (Bristol 1973).
87   C. Hakim and W. R. Hawes, *op. cit.*, p. 38; see also B. Preston, 'Statistics of
     inequality' in *Sociological Review*, Vol. 22, No. 1 (1974), pp. 103-18, who argues

that some but not all the differences between 'classes' can be attributed to causes of death specific to certain occupations, and argues against the possibility that poor health determines social class rather than the opposite.

88 *British Labour Statistics, Historical Abstract 1886-1968*, pp. 306-10, 324. For a discussion of the problems of measuring unemployment and interpreting unemployment statistics see W. R. Garside, *The Measurement of Unemployment* (Oxford 1980), and C. Hakim and W. R. Hawes, *op. cit.*, pp. 39-45.

89 *Employment Gazette*, Vol. 91, No. 9 (September 1983), p. 522; and earlier years. For excellent detailed discussions of unemployment see B. Showler and A. Sinfield (eds), *The Workless State* (Oxford 1981); and A. Sinfield, *What Unemployment Means* (Oxford 1981).

90 'The unemployed', *Employment Gazette*, Vol. 91, no. 6 (June 1983), pp. 265-7.

91 *Employment Gazette* (September 1983), p. 54, reported that 540,000 people were assisted by special employment and training measures at the end of July 1983 and that this meant that 330,000 were in jobs, training or early retirement rather than claiming benefit.

92 *Employment Gazette* (September 1983), pp. 522-3.

93 J. Stern, 'Who becomes unemployed?', *Employment Gazette*, Vol. 91, No. 1 (January 1983), pp. 21-3; 'Unemployment flows: new statistics', *Employment Gazette*, Vol. 91, No. 8 (August 1983), pp. 351-8.

94 See C. Hakim and W. R. Hawes, *op. cit.*, p. 44.

95 D. Deaton, 'Unemployment' in G. S. Bain (ed.), *Industrial Relations in Britain* (Oxford 1983), pp. 241-3.

96 For further discussion of trade unions and industrial relations see G. S. Bain (ed.), *Industrial Relations in Britain* (Oxford 1983), and G. Palmer, *British Industrial Relations* (London 1983).

97 R. Price and G. S. Bain, 'Union growth in Britain: retrospect and prospect', *British Journal of Industrial Relations*, Vol. 21, No. 1 (March 1983), pp. 46-68.

98 'Membership of trade unions in 1981', *Employment Gazette*, Vol. 91, No. 1 (January 1983), pp. 26-8.

99 For a discussion of the problems of defining a trade union see G. S. Bain and R. Price, *Profiles of Union Growth* (Oxford 1980), pp. 1-12, 13-15.

100 See R. Price and G. S. Bain, *op. cit.*, esp. pp. 54-5.

101 R. Price and G. S. Bain, 'Union growth revisited: 1948–1974 in perspective' in *British Journal of Industrial Relations*, Vol. 14, No. 3 (November 1976), p. 348; see also G. S. Bain, *The Growth of White Collar Unionism* (Oxford 1970).

102 For a recent discussion of determinants of pay levels see D. Marsden 'Wage Structure' in G. S. Bain (ed.), *Industrial Relations in Britain* (Oxford 1983), esp. pp. 266-7.

103 This type of argument is a central feature of the 'functionalist theory of stratification'; see R. Bendix and S. M. Lipset (eds), *Class, Status and Power* (London 1967), pp. 47-96.

104 D. Glass (ed.), *Social Mobility in Britain* (London 1954).

105 See the discussion, and further references, in A. Heath, *Social Mobility* (Glasgow 1981), esp. pp. 30-4 and ch. 2; J. H. Goldthorpe, *Social Mobility and Class*

Structure in Modern Britain (Oxford 1980), esp. ch. 2; and G. Payne, G. Ford and C. Robertson, 'A reappraisal of Social Mobility in Britain' in *Sociology*, Vol. 11, No. 2 (May 1977), pp. 289-310.

106   J. H. Goldthorpe, *op. cit.*; G. Payne, G. Ford and C. Robertson, 'Changes in occupational mobility in Scotland' in *Scottish Journal of Sociology*, Vol. 1, No. 1 (November 1976), pp. 57-79.

107   A. Heath, *Social Mobility* (Glasgow 1981), pp. 107-36.

108   The evidence for both parts of this argument has been questioned; see D. J. Lee, 'Class differentials in educational opportunity and promotion from the ranks' in *Sociology*, Vol. 2, No. 3 (September 1968), pp. 293-312; E. Thorpe, 'The taken-for-granted reference: an empirical examination' in *Sociology*, Vol. 7, No. 3 (September 1973), pp. 361-76; T. Noble, 'Intragenerational mobility in Britain: a criticism of the counterbalance theory' in *Sociology*, Vol. 8, No. 3 (September 1974), pp. 475-83; see also A. Stewart et al., *Social Stratification and Occupations* (London 1980), esp. pt. 3.

109   J. H. Goldthorpe, *op. cit.*, pp. 54-63.

110   For recent data see 'Qualifications and the labour force', *Employment Gazette*, Vol. 91, No. 4 (April 1983), pp. 158-64, which presents information from the 1981 Labour Force Survey.

111   See, for example, R. M. Blackburn and M. Mann, *The Working Class in the Labour Market* (London 1979), esp. ch. 1; and J. M. Cousins, *Values and Value in the Labour Market*, Working Papers in Sociology No. 9, Department of Sociology and Social Policy (University of Durham 1976).

112   See A. H. Amsden (ed.), *The Economics of Women and Work* (Penguin edn. 1980), esp. pp. 11-38; Blackburn and Mann, *op. cit.*; and Part IV, 'The Labour Market' in G. S. Bain (ed.), *Industrial Relations in Britain* (Oxford 1983).

113   See the discussion and empirical findings in Blackburn and Mann, *op. cit.*

114   The best known example of this is probably J. H. Goldthorpe et al., *The Affluent Worker-Industrial Attitudes and Behaviour* (Cambridge 1968). See also R. K. Brown, 'Sources of objectives in work and employment' in J. Child (ed.), *Man and Organization* (London 1973), pp. 17-38.

115   For recent discussion, see K. Mayhew and J. Addison, 'Discrimination in the labour market' in G. S. Bain (ed.), *Industrial Relations in Britain* (Oxford 1983), pp. 311-35.

116   See R. D. Barron and G. M. Norris, 'Sexual divisions and the labour market' in D. L. Barker and S. Allen (eds), *Dependence and Exploitation in Work and Marriage* (London 1976), pp. 47-69; and M. Mann, *Workers on the Move* (Cambridge 1973).

117   See Barron and Norris, *op. cit.*; and N. Bosanquet and P. B. Doeringer, 'Is there a dual labour market in Great Britain?' in the *Economic Journal* (June 1973), pp. 73-91.

118   For discussion of this distinction, and of segmentation as applied to the USA, see D. M. Gordon, R. Edwards and M. Reich, *Segmented Work, Divided Workers* (Cambridge 1982).

119   See Barron and Norris, *op. cit.*

120   E. Durkheim, *The Division of Labour in Society* (New York 1964). See also

the discussion in J. E. T. Eldridge, *Sociology and Industrial Life* (London 1971), pp. 73-91.

21 *The Division of Labour in Society*, pp. 376-7, 389.

22 H. Braverman, *Labor and Monopoly Capital* (New York 1974), esp. pp. 70-84.

23 See the discussion in A. Fox and A. Flanders, 'The reform of collective bargaining: from Donovan to Durkheim', *British Journal of Industrial Relations*, Vol. 7, No. 2 (July 1969), pp. 151-80; and J. H. Goldthorpe, 'Social Inequality and Social Integration in Modern Britain' in D. Wedderburn (ed.), *Poverty, Inequality and Class Structure* (Cambridge 1974), pp. 217-38.

4
Women and the Division of Labour

Hilary Wainwright

Most sociology is in one way or another a response to social movements and conflicts. Either it is a reaction to social struggles and instabilities, providing ideological defences of the established order; or it is driven by such struggles to search critically into the social relationships that lie behind everyday experience. The sociology of sex and gender is no exception to this connection between social theory and social movements. Until the growth of the women's liberation movement in the late 1960s, sociologists showed little curiosity in the social relations that lie behind the unequal position of men and women.[1] The different social positions of men and women were more or less taken for granted.[2] Different branches of sociology, the sociology of the labour market, of the family, of education etc., might occasionally include the *effects* of these differences in their studies. But the differences in social position themselves were rarely considered valid subjects of sociological inquiry. Women's active resistance to the inequality and oppression of these differences has produced new demands on sociology, on its writers, teachers and students. These demands seek to harness the explanatory power of social theory in order to strengthen the political power of the women's movement. This chapter is itself one small response to these demands. I hope it helps towards meeting them.

This absence in sociology of any concerted study of sex and gender reflected the apparent naturalness — until recently — of differences and divisions between men and women in everyday social experience. And this, in turn, is at root a result of the division of labour between men and women; in particular the division between waged labour and domestic labour. In an economy in which a person's capacity to work is bought and sold in exchange for a wage, labour which is performed on the basis of personal and emotional relations rather than on the basis of monetary exchange is not recognized as labour. Consequently women's work in caring for children and husbands does not appear as necessary labour; it appears as a natural part of family life rather than the product of a particular social organization of production and reproduction. Domesticity is seen as an inherent part of being a woman. Domestic labour appears as a choice to which women are by nature drawn. It is quite conceivable within this framework that individual women occasionally make different choices and develop more masculine tendencies. Domesticity can then be discarded as a woman enters a male-dominated world, in which, barring a few areas of male prejudice, she can be equal. In this way the inequalities facing women have appeared to be the inequalities they face when they enter the world of men; there has been no need to explain why this world is a 'man's world'!

Not only does the separation of domestic from wage-earning labour appear natural, it also reduces the recognition of women as autonomous individuals and thereby makes the inequality of their position *vis-à-vis* other individuals less noticeable. Women have seemed merely 'different' and 'complementary'. They have appeared as part of a male-defined social unit, the family. The basis for individuality, the condition for identifying inequalities, is thus veiled, like the sexual division of labour itself, by the exchange basis of all labour except domestic labour. Being defined as a wage-earner, in the past, present or future (a woman buys commodities, but she does so with her husband's wage) is a condition of social recognition as an independent individual. Women, outside, or partially outside, these relations consequently appear only as secondary parts of a 'man and wife' entity.

Why should these assumptions and appearances now be challenged on a wide scale? A full answer will not be clear until the end of this chapter, when we will have examined women's participation in waged labour in detail. However the consequence of these trends stands out clearly: the naturalness of women's responsibility for domestic labour is now experienced by women themselves as increasingly contradictory to their situation as wage-earning workers (although this does not necessarily entail that the two sets of institutions, the family and the labour market, are in conflict). A consequence of this experience is that the way in which domestic labour is organized is now being resisted, transformed and subjected to close theoretical scrutiny. It is slowly and sometimes painfully being disentangled from the emotional relations which hitherto concealed its economic character. For the first time large numbers of married women are earning their own wages, not because of exceptional and temporary circumstances, as during the two World Wars, not on an occasional 'pin-money' basis, and not in conditions where extended families could lighten their domestic burden. In Britain the proportion of married women working grew from 10 per cent in 1931 to 22 per cent in 1951, 42 per cent in 1971 and to 50 per cent in 1980.[3] Their capacity to work is sold to employers or to the state, and little of it is left to be given automatically, as an act of love and care, to the cherishing of husbands and children. Domestic labour has thus come to be regarded as a burden, as work. The problem of how to reduce and how to reorganize domestic labour consequently faces every married woman, in differing degrees. And in the resulting process of evaluating all the partial and *ad hoc* alternatives, the personal, gender-based nature of this labour becomes increasingly apparent. At first it became a problem to re-solve or argue about in individual families. But a problem so widely shared could not be contained as a private dilemma. It became a problem which concerns the social organ-ization and the social division of labour. Furthermore, as women increasingly consider themselves to be individuals with a permanent future outside the home, and thereby gain in self-confidence, they are demanding equality with other workers and are questioning the assumptions of domesticity and dependence which lie behind the inequalities.

As these changes in the position of women come up against the sexual division of labour and reveal it as a set of fundamental social relations, so a greater theoretical understanding of women's inequality becomes possible, and new political initiatives and pressures are created. In order to highlight the significance of these changes this chapter will start by criticizing those definitions of women's inequality which do not recognize the under-lying sexual division of labour. Secondly, we will describe the different forms this division takes and the different consequences it has. Thirdly, we will identify the links between these and the present social organization of domestic labour and trace their historical development. In the course of this analysis, and more directly at the end, we will examine

in detail the tendencies which erode, modify or reinforce private domestic labour and
the inequalities it produces or makes possible.

PUBLIC EQUALITY, PRIVATE DEPENDENCE

Campaigns and movements around the needs and demands of women are nothing new.
What *is* new about the modern women's movement is that it is attacking relations
between the sexes at a more fundamental level than ever before. Previous movements
fought against the prejudice that domestic obligations should not exclude women from
equal rights as a citizen or as a worker. The women's movement today is questioning the
very basis of these domestic obligations. However, the legislative effect of its campaigning
has, so far, been mainly to extend the rights of women on the more traditional basis,
without providing material support for alternatives to the present sexual division of
labour.

John Stuart Mill, the liberal reformer and writer, was a particularly notable advocate
of equal rights, but based on the existing sexual division of labour. In his time he was in
the forefront of demands for women's right to vote, but at the same time he argued:

> When the support of the family depends not on property, but on earnings, the
> common arrangement, by which the man earns the income and the wife superintends
> the domestic expenditure, seems to me in general the most suitable division of labour
> between two persons. In an otherwise just state of things, it is not, therefore, I think,
> a desirable custom that the wife should contribute by her labour to the income of
> the family.[4]

The majority of suffragette supporters similarly took for granted women's role in the
rearing of children and the organization of the home. Their argument was that this role
should not justify the exclusion of women from the political and legal gains won for
men in the development of parliamentary democracy; women's specific contribution to
the life of the nation gave them every right, they argued, to participate in the decisions
concerning the government of the nation. It is therefore not surprising to find suffragette
literature that combines the glorification of motherhood with demands for political
equality. The problem of sexual equality was seen solely as a matter of political and
legal rights. The presence of deeper inequalities, rooted in the nature of the family and
in the sexual division underpinning the family's relation to production, was scarcely
perceived.[5]

Recent legislation, particularly the Sex Discrimination Act (1975) and the Equal Pay
Act (1970), in certain respects represents the logical culmination of this tradition. On the
one hand these Acts extend the principle — although not the full reality[6] — of equal
rights, from the political institutions which concerned the early campaigners to economic
institutions. Their *intentions* stop at this. They do not directly challenge, or provide the
conditions for reorganizing domestic labour. And in fact other legislation, covering social
security, pension rights and taxation, positively reinforces a family model based on the
male breadwinner. On the other hand, the *implications* of the Equal Pay Act and the
Sex Discrimination Act are far more subversive to the economic position of women in
the family and therefore to the sexual division of labour than were the political demands

and reforms of the nineteenth and early twentieth centuries. The provisions of these recent reforms accede to the principle of women being equal competitors in the labour market, with an equal right of access to training for this market, and to the principle of women being buyers, creditors and property-owners in their own right. The widespread acceptance and expectation of such equality, encouraged and given legitimacy by legislation, conflicts with the assumptions behind domestic labour and the position of dependence on which it is based. To be an equal competitor in the labour market implies being free of all obligations and hindrances that interfere with selling one's capacity to work to the highest bidder. To be an individual consumer implies economic independence. All this conflicts with, even though it does not directly challenge, the idea that women are naturally responsible for the home. By contrast, previous reforms concerning political equality were quite compatible with women's distinct and separate domestic labours. Women could be politically equal while remaining economically and socially dependent. The above legislative reforms, by contrast, have raised expectations of economic and social equality and independence, without creating the conditions to make it possible.

THE FACTS OF INEQUALITY

A description of the extent and nature of inequality in the labour market, in education and training, and in relation to the tax and social security system, will show how much more is necessary than legislative extensions of women's public rights, in order to undermine the sexual division of labour.

Sociology of Class

Before considering the statistics available it is important to note the inability of most sociological analyses of inequality to identify, let alone understand, the relation of women to class. The weakness lies in the way that such analyses implicitly start from the relation of the family rather than of the individual to the productive process.[7] There is some sense in this, for two reasons. First, it is the family which guarantees the continuity of social classes through generations. Secondly, in a large number of families a woman's status and wealth are determined primarily by the class position of her husband. But this tendency to subsume the family into class denies the possibility that the organization of the family and its relation to production might itself create a pattern of inequality within and across classes. This weakness is characteristic of sociologists who, in analysing class, limit themselves to documenting the extent of the divisions and inequalities rather than identifying the social relations involved in the productive process and the position of each class or social group within them.[8] The latter approach would consider the fact that it is the *individual* worker who enters the labour market to be an important distinguishing feature of a capitalist economy. Such a starting-point would then leave open, as an explicit problem for analysis, the question of how the organization of the family related to class divisions.

What then is the position of women within the class divisions of British capitalism? There is little to be said about sex inequalities as far as ownership of capital is concerned. Primarily for reasons of tax and inheritance women have an almost equal share in the

Table 4.1   Economic Activity Rate by Age and Sex in Great Britain, 1961–79

	15-19	20-24	25-44	45-59/64	60/65+	All ages
	Age					
	Percentages					
Married women						
1961	41.0	41.3	33.1	32.6	7.3	29.7
1966	43.6	43.5	41.8	46.3	12.1	38.1
1971	41.6	45.7	46.4	53.4	14.2	42.2
1975	51.9	54.3	55.1	59.6	13.4	47.9
1977	54.7	59.0	59.1	61.9	12.3	50.4
1979	50.8	57.6	58.8	60.9	10.0	49.6
Non-married women						
1961	73.2	89.4	84.8	70.5	12.1	50.6
1966	68.4	86.7	84.2	72.8	12.9	49.2
1971	57.2	81.2	80.4	73.4	11.0	43.7
1975	60.2	77.0	79.2	73.1	8.9	41.8
1977	62.7	78.0	78.9	71.8	7.3	42.1
1979	63.2	79.3	78.4	70.9	5.4	42.5
All women						
1961	71.1	61.8	40.3	41.4	10.0	37.3
1966	66.5	61.6	47.3	52.0	12.6	42.2
1971	55.9	60.1	50.6	57.4	12.4	42.7
1975	59.4	64.0	58.3	62.3	10.8	45.7
1977	62.0	67.7	61.9	63.8	9.5	47.4
1979	62.3	68.3	61.9	62.9	7.4	46.9
All men						
1961	74.6	91.9	98.5	96.8	25.0	86.0
1966	70.6	92.6	98.2	95.1	23.5	84.0
1971	60.9	89.9	97.9	94.5	19.4	81.4
1975	65.8	88.9	97.7	93.9	15.3	80.6
1977	67.9	89.0	97.8	92.7	13.4	79.8
1979	68.5	89.7	97.4	91.2	10.2	78.6

Source: *Social Trends* (1982)

ownership of wealth: they owned about 40 per cent of all private wealth in 1980. This property is rarely controlled by the woman: it is family property, invested by the husband. Here we will focus on the sexual division of labour amongst those who have to sell the capacity to labour in order to live.[9] It is in the relation of the working class, broadly defined, to production and reproduction that the sexual division of labour has historically been rooted.

The starting-point for analysing this division of labour must be the entry, unprecedented in peace-time, of women into the labour market during the course of the post-war boom. Between 1881 and 1951 the percentage of women in the work force aged 15 and over was relatively stable, ranging between 25 per cent and 27 per cent, with higher fluctuations during the two World Wars. In the course of the 1950s the conditions of full employment and relatively high growth produced selected labour scarcities and drew back into the labour force – at lower levels of the job hierarchy – many of the women who after the war had been squeezed out and encouraged to return to domesticity. The extent and speed of this process amongst married women is illustrated in table 4.1 and contrast markedly with the static, if not slightly declining, trend amongst unmarried women and all men. The explanation for the slight decline in the latter two groups is presumably due to the impact of growing unemployment. Married women have been less severely affected for reasons we will discuss later.

Table 4.2 describes this growth in terms of the changing ratio of male to female employees:

Table 4.2   Population and Labour Force in Great Britain, 1911–81

| | (thousands) | | | | |
| | Population | Labour force | | Percentage of total labour force | |
		Male	Female	Male	Female
1911	40,831	12,927	5,424	70	30
1921	42,769	13,656	5,701	71	29
1931	44,795	14,790	6,265	70	30
1951	48,918	16,007	7,419	68	32
1968	53,781	16,322	8,936	65	35
1973	55,900	16,200	9,400	63	37
1974	56,000	15,700	9,400	60	40
1980	55,900	16,000	10,300	57	43
1981	56,300	16,000	10,100	58	42

Source: 1911–68 figures from G. A. Philips and R. T. Maddock, *The Growth of the British Economy* (London 1973); 1973–4 figures from Government Statistical Service, *UK in figures* (HMSO June 1975); 1980–81 figures, *UK in figures* (HMSO 1982).

The central feature to note about this rapid increase of women in employment is that it is the increase in married women working which has accounted for all of the increase from 1966 onwards (see table 4.3).

Table 4.3   Proportion of Women Workers Married in Great Britain, 1951–81

1951	43%
1961	53%
1971	62%
1981	64%

Source: Department of Employment, *Gazette* (1982).

Table 4.4 shows the activity rates of women according to the ages of their children.

A second central feature of the increase in women's employment is the high proportion of women entering part-time jobs. All the figures cited include both part-time and

Table 4.4   Working Women with Children in Great Britain (including married women and women alone with dependants)

| | Absolute numbers with | | Percentage of total | |
	children 0-4 (with or without 5-15)	children 5-15	female workforce 0-4	5-15
Working full-time	140,750	764,205	1.5	7
Working part-time	372,223	1,415,007	4	30
Economically inactive	1,726,954	1,411,531		

full-time workers. The number of female part-time workers (working 30 hours or less a week) has increased both absolutely and as a proportion of all female workers. In 1951 13 per cent of all working women worked part-time; in 1965 17.8 per cent; in 1970 18.5 per cent; in 1973 20.6 per cent; in 1975 22.6 per cent; and in 1981 nearly 40 per cent. Table 4.5 shows the absolute increase and the comparison between female part-time workers and the very small numbers of male part-time workers:

Table 4.5   Numbers of Male and Female Part-time Workers, 1951–81

Year	Men	Women
1951	47,000	784,000
1961	172,900	1,882,000
1966	372,000	2,748,000
1971	572,000	3,152,000
1981	361,624	3,543,329

Source: *Census of Population*, 1971 and 1981.

How far does this mass entry of married women into paid employment herald the end of the sexual division of labour?

Until the influence of the women's liberation movement focused attention on the position of women once they had entered the labour force, there was a rather over-optimistic tendency to assume that entry into paid work was itself an indicator of increasing equality between men and women. The most developed sociological expression of this optimism lies behind some of the arguments of Young and Wilmott's *The Symmetrical Family*. At one point, in trying to demonstrate a contemporary trend towards 'marital symmetry', they say: 'It was not a man's place to do women's work any more than the other way round. All that now has changed. Wives are working outside the home in what is much less of a man's world than it used to be.'[10] In fact, the evidence seems to indicate that the occupational sphere is only no longer a man's world in the minimal sense that women are also present. It remains a man's world in the more significant sense that, with few exceptions, women are still confined to a specific place within it, and, except in some professional sectors, the trends do not seem to be moving away from this segregation. The sexual division of labour has not been undermined as women have entered the labour force; in general, it has only been extended beyond the boundaries of the family. The statistics below must be examined, not merely as a verification of this point but also as clues to whether this problem is merely one of a time-lag, now to be speeded up by the Sex Discrimination Act, or whether the nature of women's involvement in the labour force has historically become moulded around the division between domestic and wage-earning labour.

The Labour Market and the Sexual Division of Labour

What features of women's position within the labour market would indicate whether there was a process of *accommodation* – albeit with important tensions and instabilities – or a process of *erosion* between the new mass presence of women in the paid labour force and the traditional division of labour? An erosion would tend to be the dominant process only if the cultural and material nature of women's paid labour overtly conflicted with the relations of private domestic labour. Here we will distinguish between, on the one hand, the relations within the job market and the question of whether these conflict or extend the sexual division of labour; and on the other hand, the responses of women themselves to the new needs they experience and the new expectations they develop. This distinction is necessary because it might well be that the institutions of the job market and the state mainly accommodate to sexual divisions, while at the same time women are developing forms of resistance precisely because of the subjective contradictions involved in this accommodation to the sexual division of labour.

What then are the cultural and material relations that underpin the present sex-based organization of domestic labour? An interweaving of economic and emotional dependence is the foundation. The nature of women's unpaid work flows from this. Carried on in isolation, it is in theory a labour of care and devotion to particular individuals; in fact it is a major contribution to the economy and to society. But its separation from the economy and its basis in personal relations means that it is not seen as professional, skilled or a source of status. The power relations of sex and gender flow from the same source. It is not that women lack all power, but rather that their direct power and control is limited to the informal sphere of the family. Power in the formal worlds of politics and economics lies on the other side of the division of labour. Until recently it has been only the occasional individual who has had the resources to change sides.

How far has women's mass entry into paid labour involved women in direct conflict with this traditional role? The following table describes in a very general way the position of women within the job structure.[11]

Table 4.6 Economically Active Women by Socio-economic Group in Great Britain

	Females (1)	Total (2)	(1) as % of (2)
Professional	9,687	93,680	10.3
Intermediate occupations	192,600	521,629	36.9
Skilled non-manual	380,473	553,329	68.8
Skilled manual	79,177	614,888	12.9
Partly skilled	206,002	454,828	45.3
Unskilled	66,612	160,019	41.6

Source: *1981 Census*, Economic Activity Tables.

In order to examine this in more detail we will explore separately all the possible ways in which the dramatic increase in the proportion of married women who earn a wage might undermine the division of labour. First, what does women's job situation imply for the idea of direct personal care as an intrinsically female labour. Table 4.7 indicates that for a large number of women (the majority) their labour both outside and within the home is characterized by an entrenched sexual bias: a bias which is reflected in the fact that it is women, almost exclusively, who do the work that involves the direct servicing of people's immediate needs.

Table 4.7   Predominantly Female Occupations in Great Britain

	Thousands	
	All persons	Women
90% or over female occupations		
Hand and machine sewers, embroiderers	238	230
Nurses	432	394
Maids, valets, etc.	443	428
Canteen assistants	304	293
Typists, secretaries, etc.	770	759
75% and under 90% female occupations		
Shop assistants	969	786
Charwomen, sweepers and cleaners	522	456
Kitchen hands	122	100
Office machine operators	177	153
Hairdressers, etc.	159	124
Telephone operators	107	89
60% and under 75% female occupations		
Clerks and cashiers	2,475	1,546
Waiters and waitresses	113	82
Primary and secondary teachers	496	318
Packers and labellers, etc.	183	121
Bartenders	103	73

Source: Annual Census of Employment (June 1974)

If we now look at particular professions we find that a similar situation prevails in teaching. In spite of the fact that in January 1974 61.6 per cent of qualified teachers in all public sector and assisted schools in the UK were women, the higher the grade of teacher — that is the greater the administrative and intellectual content of the job — the smaller the number of women (see tables 4.8 a and b).

Figures for the medical profession reveal the same situation; the nearer a job is to the direct process of caring for people's immediate needs, the higher the concentration of women.[12] (See table 4.9).

The small proportion of skilled jobs held by the 37.6 per cent of women workers who are manual workers (see table 4.6) is a further illustration of the way in which the development and application of skills totally distinct from those connected with domesti labour is the exception to the norm. As the following figures indicate, it occurs either in

Table 4.8a   Percentages of Various Grades of Teachers who are Women, Maintained Primary and Secondary Schools in England and Wales, 1965–74

	Lowest Grade Scale 1 or equivalent	Highest Grade Scale 5 or equivalent
1965	77.0	20.0
1969	75.1	20.6
1974	71.7	n.a.

Source: Department of Education and Science, *Statistics of Education* 1974, Vol. 4, table 23; 1969, Vol. 4, table 21; 1965, Part II, table 59.

Table 4.8b   Percentages of Women Teachers in Primary and Secondary Schools in England and Wales, 1979

1979	Lowest Grade Scale 1 or equivalent	Highest Grade Scale 5 or equivalent
Secondary	59.6	32.4
Primary	90.7	61.2

Source: *Statistics of Education* (1980).

Table 4.9   Female Hospital, Medical and Dental Staff[1] in England, September/October 1974

	(1) Female	(2) Total	(3) Col. (1) as a % of col. (2)
Hospital nursing staff[2]	269,145	301,849	89.2
Hospital medical staff[3]	4,407	27,576	16.0
General medical practitioners	2,975	21,531	13.8
Hospital medical consultants	894	10,603	8.4
General dental practitioners	1,020	11,023	9.3

Notes:
1. Total staff including part-time, honorary, etc. staff
2. Includes registered, student, enrolled, pupil and other nursing staff
3. From consultant down to pre-registration house officers (plus a few other staff). Figures exclude 'paragraph 94' appointments – mainly GPs acting as part-time medical officers at convalescent homes, general practitioner, maternity hospitals or other hospitals, or carrying out occasional work in the Blood Transfusion Service

Source: *Health and Personal Social Services Statistics for England* (1975), tables 3.4, 3.13, 3.20, 3.28.

trades where from the historical transition from home to factory production women have been long established as skilled workers, as in textiles, or in trades where their physical attributes (e.g. manual dexterity) are a significant advantage given the existing technology of the industry, as in instrument and electrical engineering.

Table 4.10   Female Manual Workers in Great Britain, by Industry and Occupational Position

Industry	Percentage of total women full-time workers who are manual		Women as percentage of all workers in the category	
	1976	1982	1971 skilled	unskilled
Food, drink and tobacco	62.8	68.5	18.1	30.7
Chemicals	46.3	47.4	9.1	29.6
Mechanical engineering	60.0	32.4	2.9	20.2
Instrument engineering	26.8	55.6	23.4	42.8
Electrical engineering	65.1	61.1	20.2	41.2
Vehicles	52.2	43.0	2.7	16.3
Textiles	81.5	80.6	43.7	31.8
Paper, printing, publishing	49.7	42.8	25.5	33.5
Transport and communications	20.3	24.6	1.2	14.1
Distributive trades	12.3	12.0	13.0	44.1

Sources: *New Earnings Survey* (1976), tables 56, 57; *1971 Census* Economic Activity, Part IV, table 33; *New Earnings Survey* (1982).

Table 4.10 shows the static nature of the situation – with if anything the segregation of women's work becoming more marked – and available information does not indicate any change. Census figures for 1966 and 1981 show that there has been a gradual decline in the proportion of skilled manual workers as a whole who are women, from 24 per cent in 1911 to 14.7 per cent in 1966, and 12 per cent in 1980. At the same time there has been a steady rise in the proportion of unskilled manual workers who are women (15.5 per cent in 1911, 27.5 per cent in 1966, 41 per cent in 1981) and, in particular, in the proportion of sales and shop assistants who are women (35.2 per cent in 1911 to 58.7 per cent in 1966). The following figure provides a vivid demonstration of the concentration of women workers in a narrow band of service occupations.

From these statistics it should be clear that the mass increase of women in paid labour has not involved the majority of women in forms of labour that clash with the women's traditional domestic role. Entry into the labour market has not enabled women as a social group to become separated sufficiently from domestic labour so as to break down the traditional divisions between masculinity and femininity. Rather this division is reproduced on the extended terrain of the labour market. So long as the pressure towards domestic labour becoming 'sex neutral' remains so weak, there will be little impetus to consider the present organization of domestic labour as historical rather than 'natural'. Yet this is a pre-condition for the conscious reorganization of domestic labour

The extent of women's involvement in jobs through which they hold, or share, control over any form of social organization is similarly too minimal to clash with the characteristic impotence of domestic labour. The small areas where women do have some degree of control are those in which, as in domestic labour, they control the organization of children and other women. The situation in teaching is one of the best illustrations. Table 4.11 shows the percentage of female heads of primary schools and mixed secondary

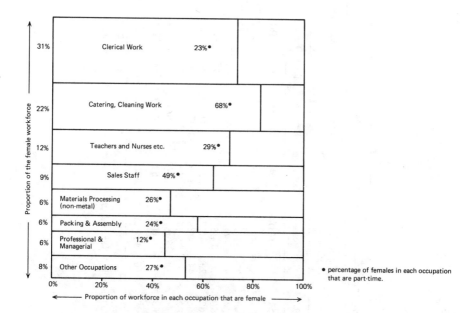

Figure 4.1   Occupations of Women Workers

Percentage of part-time women of all women in each major female occupation

Source: *New Earnings Survey* (1979 and 1980)

Table 4.11   Women Heads of Schools, England and Wales, 1966–75

	Percentages	
	Primary	Mixed secondary
January 1966	47.3	2.6
January 1970	42.9	4.7
January 1975	42.2	6.3

Note: Excludes those teachers in nursery schools, special schools and immigrant centres.

Sources: *Statistics of Education* (1975), Vol. 1, table 14; (1970), Vol. 1, table 13; (1966), Vol. 1, table 12.

schools over the last ten years.

The absence of a clash between the conditions of women's paid work and the basic lack of power in their domestic situation is not merely an example of the way in which the sexual division of labour extends into the labour force. It is also a product of the

Table 4.12 Women in the Unions

Figures in brackets show how many women there would be if they were represented according to their share of the membership

Union	Membership			Executive members		Full time officials		TUC delegates	
	Total	Female	%	Total	Female	Total	Female	Total	Female
APEX Professional, Executive Clerical, Computer	150,000	77,000	51	15	1(8)	55	2(28)	15	4(8)
ASTMS (Technical, Managerial)	472,000	82,000	17	24	2(4)	63	6(11)	30	3(5)
BIFU (Banking, Insurance Finance)	132,000	64,000	49	27	3(13)	41	6(20)	20	3(10)
GMWU (General & Municipal)	956,000	327,000	34	40	0(14)	243	13(83)	73	3(25)
NALGO (Local Govt Officers)	705,000	356,000	50	70	14(35)	165	11(83)	72	15(36)
NUPE (Public Employees)	700,000	470,000	67	26	8(17)	150	7(101)	32	10(22)
NUT (Teachers)	258,000	170,000	66	44	4(29)	110	17(73)	36	7(24)
NUTGW (Tailor & Garment)	117,000	108,000	92	15	5(14)	47	9(43)	17	7(16)
TGWU (Transport & General)	2,070,000	330,000	16	39	0(6)	600	6(96)	85	6(14)
USDAW (Shop, Distributive Allied)	462,000	281,000	63	16	3(10)	162	13(102)	38	8(24)
Totals	6,022,000	2,265,000	38	316	40(150)	1,636	90(640)	418	66(174)

All figures are approximate, and the most recent that were available in November 1980. Taken from *Hear this, brother*, by Anna Coote and Peter Kellner, New Statesman Reports, No. 1 (1980).

inherent lack of democracy in the way in which work, in the public sector and the private sector, is organized. Only a very small minority of men or women share in determining the organization of resources, machines, labour and culture. For the majority of men the family is the only situation which is not alien and outside the realm of their control. For an even greater number of women there is only a small area within the family which offers any possibility of control. Moreover the organizations which in theory are fighting for greater power by workers over the conditions and organization of their work have not done much, with regard to either their own structures or the demands they fight for, to transform the situation. Table 4.12 indicates the lack of any concerted effort by trade-union organizations to reverse the bias against women sharing power. Women trade-unionists, however, have begun to demand a position of power within their trade unions. They have had some success in unions such as NUPE and parts of the TGWU where there are large concentrations of women members and where the leadership is responsive to a more active, aware membership.

Material Dependence

The central pillar on which the sexual division of labour has previously rested is material dependence. It is this which makes personal relations between men and women, relations of power and subordination. Women's entry into paid labour has added to the joint income and occasionally this gives women more control over how the family wage is spent, but it has not altered the fundamental dependence. The majority of working women do not earn what the TUC has calculated to be a 'living wage'.

Table 4.13   Average Earnings of Men and Women in Great Britain, 1977–81

(1) Average hourly earnings excluding overtime

Aged 18+	1977(£)	1978(£)	1979(£)	1980(£)	1981(£)
Male	1.75	1.98	2.27	2.73	2.97
Female	1.09	1.23	1.38	1.70	1.88
Difference	0.66	0.75	0.89	1.03	1.09
Women's earnings as % of men's earnings	62.3%	62.1%	60.7%	62.3%	62.6%

(2) Average gross weekly earnings including overtime

Aged 18+	1977(£)	1978(£)	1979(£)	1980(£)	1981(£)
Male	79.4	90.3	104.5	124.5	133.1
Female	45.0	51.1	57.1	70.5	76.9
Difference	34.4	39.2	47.4	54.0	56.2
Women's earnings as % of men's earnings	56.7%	56.6%	54.6%	56.6%	57.8%

Source: *New Earnings Survey* Part B (1982).

Before examining the reasons for this difference in earnings it is important to note that the averages used in table 4.13 conceal wide discrepancies, ranging from the chemical industry where women's rate was 96 per cent of men's rate, down to completely un-organized and relatively isolated groups of women, such as cinema employees, who receive only just over 60 per cent of men's average rate.

In spite of the 1970 Equal Pay Act, or rather because of all its loopholes, employers have a large repertoire of techniques that allow them to avoid significantly altering pay differentials. First, they can further consolidate the industrial apartheid between men and women by redefining men's jobs; for example, male shop assistants have been found to be described in company books as 'management trainees' so that comparison with female shop assistants is ruled out. The first report by the Office of Manpower Economics, published in 1972, gives further examples:

> In one company, 80 per cent of employees were women engaged on work similar to that of men rated as semi-skilled; they were, however, paid a rate below that for unskilled men. The costs of meeting equal pay within the existing job and pay struc-ture were considered by management to be prohibitive. With the acceptance of trade union representatives who are concerned about male unemployment in the area, it is therefore now separating men and women into distinct categories of jobs.
>
> For example, the machine shop has had a female day shift and a male night shift: men are now being recruited for day work and women are being transferred to other departments. The more technical inspection jobs are being allotted to men and women are being transferred to simple inspection tasks; central packing is becoming a male area, line packing is reserved for women; work in the finishing and paint shops and in the stores is to be a male preserve; this also applies to sign-writing, even though many women are considered to be more skilful at this. White-collar jobs are to be graded into three grades: the lower one predominantly women, the middle one mixed and the upper one predominantly for men. As a result of this reorganization it is expected that by the end of 1972 very little of the work undertaken by women will be even broadly similar to that of men.[13]

For the majority of women anti-discrimination legislation has made little difference. It makes illegal all attempts to bar women explicitly from certain jobs. But the major pro-portion of job separation that renders the Equal Pay Act inadequate is not the result of explicit discrimination: employers do not need to tax their ingenuity when, as we have seen, women's position in the labour market is already firmly entrenched. An extensive study carried out in the late 1970s, of 25 firms covering 37 groups of workers, found only two cases of women doing the same or broadly similar work to men and therefore qualifying for equal pay.[14]

Job evaluation, which is not compulsory under the Act, does little either to overcome this lack of comparability, or to thwart employers who regrade techniques. In fact it can provide a pseudo-scientific rationalization for management's regrading. Service payments are another way in which employers can ensure that men will earn more than women for the same or a similar job: large extra payments or bonuses for long unbroken service with the firm almost inevitably exclude the majority of the six and a half million working mothers in Britain who have stopped and restarted work at some point. Overtime and shift supplements provide another means of maintaining earnings differentials.

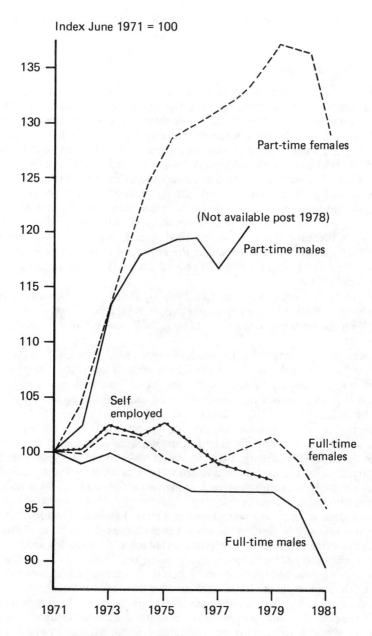

Index June 1971 = 100

Figure 4.2   **Trends in Employment, 1971–81**

Note:

Figures for full-time males 1979–81 assume part time rate unchanged.

Source: *Employment Gazette* (July 1982); Annual Census of Employment reports, DE Gazette.

This use of women as a 'reserve pool of labour' is increasing as a proportion of all workers.

The State and Domestic Labour

Given the absence of any automatic tendency for women's paid employment to modify directly the assumptions and material relations justifying domestic labour, it is not surprising that neither the state nor employers have considered the need to reorganize domestic labour, nor have the union leaderships attempted actively to fight for any reorganization. The present situation should be contrasted with the one period, the Second World War, when labour requirements did briefly conflict with the requirements of domestic labour. The government then encouraged local authorities to set up over one hundred new nurseries and in some areas subsidized restaurants, in order to reduce the amount of time that women spent on housework so that they could become industrial workers. But this was not the beginning of any permanent change in the organization of housework. When the war ended and men returned from the armed forces in search of employment, the majority of nurseries and all the subsidized restaurants were closed down. Between 1949 and 1970 the numbers of local authority day nurseries had declined from 903 to 435.

Employers rarely feel any compulsion to fill this gap. Their use of women as a pool of flexible labour as distinct from a permanent part of the skilled or semi-skilled labour force depends on the existence of women's domestic obligations. Factory-based nurseries are rare.

Those aspects of welfare benefits that concern women further consolidate the position of dependence that underpins domestic labour. Four areas of legislation – Supplementary Benefits, National Insurance, taxation, and student grants – are particularly important ways in which the state supports this dependence and discriminates against life-styles that attempt to achieve relationships based on material independence.

Supplementary Benefit regulations discriminate against women who are living with a man but who want to be financially independent. If a woman is married or if she is proved to be 'cohabiting' with a man then she cannot make an independent claim for Supplementary Benefit. The man she is assumed to be dependent on has to claim for them both as a unit. They receive the rate for a married couple and this is significantly lower than the rate for two single people.[15]

The Supplementary Benefits handbook makes it clear that evidence which shows that the man is not financially supporting the woman is not accepted as conclusive evidence that they are not living as 'man and wife'. Other evidence, such as sharing accommodation, sharing the same bedroom, having a long-lasting relationship, can be sufficient to establish 'cohabitation' and therefore restriction to the married couple rate of benefit. Thus, the regulations are based on the assumption that a woman who is living with a man, or is married to him, should be supported by the man. The practical consequences of the regulations often have the effect of turning this value judgement into a reality. Women with children in particular are trapped within relationships of dependence by these regulations; on the one hand they cannot achieve a degree of independence by going out to work because of the lack of childcare facilities, and on the other hand they cannot have the relationships that they choose without the continual threat of having

Table 4.14   Education and Day Care of Children Under Five: Maintained and Registered Places, 1961–81 (thousands)

	England and Wales						Great Britain	United Kingdom
	1961	1970	1976	1979	1980	1981	1981	1981
Children under 5 in maintained schools								
Nursery schools								
– all day	21	16	15	16	16	15	19	22
– part day	3	18	35	37	37	37	66	67
Primary schools								
– all day	181	228	321	263	259	263	273	292
– part day	3	29	117	158	161	167	167	167
Total	208	291	488	474	473	482	525	548
Maintained or registered day care places								
Maintained day nurseries								
– all day	} 22	} 22	27	28	29	28	32 }	} 37
– part day		2	3	3	3	3	4	
Registered nurseries								
– all day	} 18	} 20	27	24	25	23	23 }	} 456
– part day		229	369	386	390	382	425	
Registered child minders								
– all day	} 14	} 48	65	69	73	72 }	108	111
– part day		37	20	32	39	33		
Total	54	358	511	542	559	541	592	604

Source: *Department of Health and Social Security, Welsh Office Department of Education and Science, Scottish Education Department, Social Work Services Group, Department of Health and Social Services N. Ireland, N. Ireland Department of Education.*

their only source of independent income taken away.

National Insurance legislation also assumes that the married woman should be dependent on her husband's income. These assumptions have not significantly changed over the quarter of a century since William Beveridge recommended that the man should make contributions on behalf of himself and his wife as a team. However, one innovation is that married women have the option of buying their own stamps; though this is not in fact an option for independence. In spite of the fact that a married woman who opts for her own stamps pays the same contribution as a single woman, she receives less than three-quarters the amount of Sickness and Unemployment Benefit paid to a single woman. For many women it is difficult even to achieve this token of independence since staying at home to look after her children does not entitle a woman to have stamps credited to her — it is not considered to be work. She has to pay for the stamps each week, even though looking after children makes it very difficult, under present conditions, to earn a wage. A woman who opts to buy her own stamps may find a further obstacle to independence when she reaches retirement age. Even if she has paid for the full number of stamps for as long as thirty years she will still not have contributed enough to draw a pension on her own insurance and she will have to make do with a married woman's pension, which is significantly less than a single woman's.

The present taxation system financially favours those who are married as compared with those who are unmarried, whether the latter are sharing accommodation or living alone. In doing so it sustains materially the idea that the married woman performs the housework while the man is the main wage-earner. The married man receives an allowance which helps him to 'keep' his wife at home while compensating for the loss of her potential earnings. It is possible to be taxed as two single people, but this is only financially beneficial for two people if their joint income is over a certain amount; otherwise the married woman's income is treated as part of the husband's.

The philosophy of dependence prevails even in the student grants system. A woman student married to a non-student is assumed to be dependent on her husband; consequently she receives a lower grant than an unmarried student. This is not merely an economic calculation on the part of the state about the costs involved in shared living accommodation. The fact that this does not apply to male students married to working wives reveals the official assumption that for the woman marriage means economic dependence.

These various aspects of the material and legislative reinforcement of marriage and women's dependent position within it, cannot be understood merely as survivals of Victorian morality. They must be seen in the context of the importance of women's private domestic work to the present economy. The comments of William Beveridge in recommending his plan for social security still underly the state's relation to the family, with only minor modifications to accommodate women's partial entry into paid work.

> In any measure of social policy in which regard is had to facts, the great majority of married women must be regarded as occupied on work which is vital though unpaid, without which their husbands could not do their paid work and without which the nation could not continue. In accord with the facts the Plan for Social Security treats married women as a special insurance class of occupied persons and treats man and wife as a team. . . .

The attitude of the housewife to gainful employment outside the home is not and should not be the same as that of a single woman. She has other duties . . . . Taken as a whole the Plan for Social Security puts a premium on marriage in place of penalising it . . . In the next thirty years housewives as Mothers have vital work to do in ensuring the adequate continuance of the British race and of British ideals in the world . . . [16]

EXPLAINING THE SEXUAL DIVISION OF LABOUR

Its Continuation in each Generation

How does the sexual division of labour reproduce itself and what are its historical origins? The problem has four main aspects. First, the way in which family relations based on this division give men and women a sexual identity, an interpretation of their own biology around a sharp polarization between masculinity and femininity. Secondly, the way that the education system prepares the majority of women for the future job market on the assumption that 'homemaking' will be their primary obligation. Thirdly, the dependence of employers on a secondary labour market, a reserve force. Finally, the fact that there is no impetus for the state or employers to concern themselves with domestic labour beyond ensuring that a sufficient supply of labour power reaches the market.

This chapter tries to show the way that the institutions in which social power and resources are concentrated are integrated into and dependent on the daily preservation of the sexual division of labour. Towards the end of this chapter we will demonstrate that this process is not smooth, harmonious or stable; however the point in this section is that within the existing institutions of modern British capitalism the dominant tendency is to *reproduce* sexual divisions — even if these are in new forms with new ideologies. All erosions are therefore the product of counter-institutions and relationships which have to fight *against the grain* and mobilize alternative sources of power in order to survive.

Women's Conception of Themselves

When a girl joins the education system, when she becomes involved in a network of personal relations, when she gets a job, when she gets married and tries to combine her domestic obligations with her job outside the home, she is not simply the passive victim of an enforced division of labour. Women have absorbed, unconsciously and consciously as part of their self-conception, a cultural interpretation of their biological distinctiveness as women. It is this which provides the basis for their active complicity in their own subordination. The processes whereby this complicity takes place have not yet been clearly understood. All that can be attempted here is a résumé of the argument so far. Until the mid-fifties research on the formation of sexual identity was dominated by the debate over the relative importance of natural and social determinants of femininity and masculinity. Much of this debate centred around the seminal work of Margaret Mead[17] which analysed societies in which the characteristics normally associated with masculinity and femininity did not coincide in the 'normal' way with the biological division between

the sexes. More recent research within social psychology, for example the work of
R. Hartley, H. A. Moss and J. Kagan,[18] has followed up Mead's stress on the social
determination of masculinity and femininity with detailed studies of the possible
mechanisms involved.

The question that is being investigated is how relationships within the family transmit
the norms underpinning the sexual division of labour in such a way that the majority of
girls slip unconsciously into them. In general the research summarized below does not
pose the problem so explicitly. The most well-known approach points to the ways in
which sex stereotypes are learned through the differential treatment of girls and boys
from babyhood. From a sample of American mothers H. A. Moss shows that there is a
significant difference between the way in which mothers hold and cuddle sons compared
with daughters. Ruth Hartley develops a typology of different treatment which includes
manipulation (e.g. different forms of dress, different degrees of 'fuss'), canalization
(e.g. being encouraged to play with different types of toys), verbal appellation (e.g. being
praised and punished for different sorts of behaviour) and activity exposure (e.g. suggestions for different chores or forms of play); Lois Murphy shows evidence of mothers
giving boys far more autonomy that girls. And there are many other studies that examine
further aspects of differential treatment through which the little boy or girl learns what is
expected from him, or her: what it means to be male or female.

These processes of learning through differential treatment are certainly important.
The powerlessness of the child makes him or her their helpless victim. But there are a
number of weaknesses in the accounts of these processes in so far as they attempt to
provide theories on the formation of sexual identity solely in terms of this learning
process.

In part, this is a consequence of failing to examine the effect of the mother's general
social position on the way in which the mother/child relationship transmits the sexual
division of labour. Certain links between the division of labour, specifically the general
social context of the mother/child relationship, and the emotional content of family
relations are fairly obvious. The mother's separateness from, or weak connection with,
social life and her consequent lack of autonomy, means that she tends to seek her own
fulfilment, her own identity, through her child – and her husband. The father, on the
other hand, relates to the child as an autonomous individual with a consequent distance
from the child's character and needs. This affects fundamentally the nature of the child's
emotional relationship with each of the two parents. And it is primarily through this
relationship that a child initially develops its sense of identity and therefore its responses
to the division of labour. By failing to take full account of emotions in the formation of
self-identity, studies based on learning theory do not come to grips with the deeply-
rooted nature of sexual identity. To explain sexual identity in terms of social learning is
like explaining objects that are attached to each other without identifying the glue. The
nature of the emotional relations within the family provides the glue through which
the learning process sticks and has significance. This can be illustrated by looking at the
process of socialization in reverse, that is the process of self-conscious change in, and
reconstruction of, a woman's social identity. The idea of the gradual learning of a social
role by association and models tends to imply that once that role is consciously rejected
all aspects of the identity that went with it can equally consciously be stripped off. It
does not account for the persistence of unconscious but powerful processes producing

feelings and emotions highly conducive to passivity and subservience, however consciously some of the subordinate roles have been rejected.

The slowness, until recently, with which women have come to challenge in practice their place as unpaid labour in the home and as low-paid labour in the factory, is partly a result of the way that domestic labour is unconsciously intertwined with emotions and feelings. Housework appears as a labour of love, an expression of care and concern. Questioning this labour would seem to imply the undermining of a woman's emotional relationships. The attitude can only be changed if emotions and feelings are separated from the requirements of housework. Only then will the economic function of house-work become clear and the need to organize it on a non-sex basis become a possibility. The 'unlearning' of roles has rarely proved to be sufficient. Understanding the initial formation of these emotions rather than merely how models and norms are learnt is therefore central to understanding how women themselves reproduce the relations of their oppression.

Freud has probably come nearest to identifying the structures which produce the child's early emotional relations, although he certainly does not relate them to women's position in the division of labour. Freudians explain the formation of the female identity in terms of the way in which the initial emotional attachment that all infants have towards their mother, in the present structure of the nuclear family, must necessarily change for cultural reasons as the child grows up. The relationships involved in this change are described as the Oedipus complex. In the case of the girl this involves the culturally enforced repression of her desire for her mother and the culturally induced transfer of her sexual attention to her father. This transfer involves a repression, or rather a transformation, of her unconscious desire for a penis into a socially acceptable form, that is into the desire for a husband and a baby. In the course of this transfer the girl, who like the boy has a combination of passive and active impulses, brings to the fore her passive impulses, her impulses to live through others, and represses her active impulses to control and participate in the outside world. By this process her female identity at a conscious and, perhaps more important, unconscious, level is formed.

Of course there are complexities in this theory that cannot be discussed now. Although Freud may be an important starting-point for solving the problem of how women become mentally prepared for their social destiny he does not provide the whole answer. As feminists have pointed out, he went in several false directions.[19] A particular-ly important question is how far the relationships that Freud identifies are a product of the particular family structure and culture of modern capitalist society. When Freud referred to the repression and transferences involved in these relationships as culturally induced he used culture in the broadest sense of human civilization. Detailed studies of differential socialisation could usefully complement the more Freudian emphasis on the studying of infants' emotional responses to their first pattern of human inter-relation-ships. Different forms of play encouraged for boys and girls, different characteristics praised or condemned, and the different use of language to boys and girls, probably all provide clues to the precise mechanisms whereby definitions of what is socially unaccep-table — so crucial to the Freudian theory of repression — enter consciousness.

EDUCATION AND THE SEXUAL DIVISION OF LABOUR

The relationship between education and the sexual division of labour can best be understood in terms of the general purpose of the education system in preparing each generation for the social division of labour as a whole. This process of preparation can be broken down into three important components: the way the education system trains the future labour force in basic skills such as literacy and numeracy and gives them some grounding in scientific and humanistic knowledge in order to prepare them for learning more occupationally specific skills; the way in which fifth and sixth forms, colleges of further education, polytechnics, technical colleges and universities meet the needs of the occupational structure more specifically by providing specialised guidance and teaching; finally, the way that, at all levels, the education system provides ideological support for the division of labour, and for institutions like the state and the family which guarantee and reproduce this division. The mechanisms of this general ideological support include the content of curricula, the organization of teaching, discipline, and forms of selection. In all these ways the distinct destinies of girls and boys within the division of labour are reflected and actively reinforced.

However, education's role in producing generations of women who, as mothers, teachers, nurses, housewives, social workers, service workers and secretaries, will perform the tasks of socialising the young, caring for the sick, the old and exhausted, is not without contradictions. There is not necessarily a harmonious relationship between the needs of the family and domestic labour, and the requirements of employers and of the state. For example, the declining rate of a real increase in expenditure on the Welfare State in the last few years, and changes in the organization of welfare facilities, have put more of a burden on the family and therefore on the housewife, e.g. for the care of the old and the handicapped. Within the lower levels of the education system the indirect effect of this has been pressure for more time and resources to be spent on developing domestic science teaching; on the other hand the needs generated by industrial reorganization and technological advances for selective increases in non-manual skilled labour have produced a demand for more scientifically and mathematically skilled women, and thus for more equal resources to be allocated to training such women. In many schools two distinct images of women are therefore beginning to emerge. A further contradiction arises from historical factors that have produced schools and colleges partially in conflict with the division of labour: for example, the feminist energies of education reformers like Frances Buss and Emily Davies achieved a standard of education for middle class girls in the early twentieth century almost equal to their brothers.[20] Many of these reformers' achievements have been undermined, but their heritage is partly responsible for the conflict between expectations engendered by a relatively egalitarian ethos in the higher levels of the education system and the reality of limited job opportunities. This conflict has been one cause of an increasing consciousness of their secondary position among women within higher education.

These and other contradictions will be looked at in more detail in the course of analysing the different levels of the relationship between education and the sexual division of labour.

EDUCATION IN BASIC SKILLS AND KNOWLEDGE

In 1864 the first Schools Enquiry Commission asked if girls were capable of learning Latin and mathematics. In the early twentieth century the headmistress of one of the most advanced centres for girls' education, Manchester Girls' Grammar School, said: 'Mathematics should be kept at a minimum for girls, it does not underlie their industries as it does so many of the activities of men.'

Comparable judgments have an active influence in present-day education. They are, for instance, reflected in the subjects chosen by, or for, girls for their 'A' levels (see table 4.15).

Table 4.15　GCE 'A' level Subject Choice by Boys and Girls School Leavers During the Academic Year 1978–79[1] (thousands)

	Boys	Girls
Science		
Mathematics	33.08	11.91
Physics	28.13	7.07
Chemistry	22.56	9.90
Biology, botany or zoology	13.53	15.95
Other science subjects (e.g. building construction, geology, metalwork, technical drawing or woodwork)	5.43	1.03
Social science		
Geography	15.81	11.16
Economics, English economic history, British constitution	18.25	8.55
General studies	17.44	12.60
Vocational subjects (including domestic & commercial)	1.16	4.66
Other social science	1.29	3.79
Arts		
English	14.01	29.57
History	13.94	15.47
French	5.38	13.62
Other modern languages	2.69	6.86
Classics	1.18	1.98
Religious knowledge	0.93	2.69
Art, craft or music	6.38	9.54
Other arts	0.15	0.13
Total:		
Physical and natural sciences	104.73	46.86
Social sciences	53.93	40.76
Arts	44.66	79.86
Total numbers of leavers	203.22	167.48

[1] Excluding leavers from special schools.

Source: Extracted from *Statistics of Education* (1980).

When girls do turn to science the majority of them take biology, the science with the least abstract and the most humanistic image. Further evidence is provided by the statistics of those sitting the General Certificate of Education examination at 'O' level in 1972: 164,000 girls took biology but only 88,000 took physics and chemistry, whereas 88,000 boys took biology and 285,000 took physics and chemistry. However, the combined pressures brought about by the growing involvement of women in social production and the growing confidence of girls and women in their right to equal opportunities, have begun, however unevenly, to undermine some of these discrepancies. The percentage increases in tables 4.16 and 4.17 indicate that the gap between boys and girls passing GCE examinations in scientific subjects is diminishing.

The explanation of continuing – though diminishing – sexual differences lies in a combination of girls' own conceptions of their femininity and future aspirations, the assumptions and expectations of many of their teachers and parents, and the prevailing images of love and marriage reflected in the media and popular culture, together with the institutional constraints of restricted curricula, inadequate science teaching, and the channelling of any available facilities and resources into domestic science and home economics. The last aspect of the explanation, which concerns government education policy, can only be fully understood in the context of the needs of industry, the general pattern of which will be analysed in the next section.

In the first element in this explanation one sees the consequences of the formation of the female identity discussed in the last section. Many studies have revealed that girls are particularly prone to 'under-achievement' in relation to their measured IQ. This under-achievement tends to come to the fore during puberty. Before puberty girls tend to do better than boys, especially in linguistic/verbal subjects but also in mathematical subjects. This greater achievement is itself probably related to the initial formation of female identity in the sense that girls' tendency towards passivity and conformity will make them more attentive pupils than boys, who are likely to have developed stronger tendencies towards aggression and autonomy. Around puberty many girls find themselves in the situation of wanting to do well academically but having a sneaking feeling that intellectual dominance in relationships with men contradicts their femininity; or, less crudely, they experience a conflict between the active autonomous impulses of work and achievement and the passive impulses of traditional sexual relationships. The momentum of emotions whose basis has been structured in early socialization tends to drive women towards sexual relationships of subordination. Thus intellectual effort appears as an obstacle to emotional satisfaction. The other half of this process is of course male socialization and the male's desire, however unconscious, to dominate and prove himself *vis-à-vis* women.

The majority of girls are aware that attempts to keep up with boys do not provide any escape from the dreary destiny of unskilled, low-paid work. Romance, marriage, jobs connected with the world of femininity – hairdressing, boutiques, secretarial work – seem to offer the best option. An illustration of this can be seen in a study carried out in the early sixties on the attitudes to work and marriage of 600 adolescent girls. This showed that in the age range of 14–17 the vast majority had no ambition or goal other than marriage and homemaking. In essays about their future lives, 90 per cent wrote of marriage, while 53 per cent mentioned paid work as something that their husbands would oppose or as a way of saving money to buy a house. There is, however, strong evidence

Table 4.16   CSE and GCE Examinations: Results at GCE Ordinary level, percentage increase 1974–79

Summer examination	Percentage increase 1974–79
English language	
Boys	13.8
Girls	21.0
Total	17.8
English literature	
Boys	11.1
Girls	14.9
Total	13.4
History	
Boys	8.6
Girls	2.5
Total	5.4
French	
Boys	8.3
Girls	13.1
Total	11.1
German	
Boys	19.5
Girls	26.3
Total	23.5
Art	
Boys	12.3
Girls	11.2
Total	11.6
Other art subjects	
Boys	13.9
Girls	18.4
Total	16.7
Mathematics	
Boys	29.5
Girls	40.7
Total	33.6
Physics	
Boys	37.3
Girls	62.6
Total	42.8
Chemistry	
Boys	28.7
Girls	57.5
Total	37.7
Biology	
Boys	24.8
Girls	18.2
Total	20.8
Other science or technical subjects	
Boys	21.5
Girls	1.5
Total	18.5
Economics	
Boys	18.1
Girls	42.5
Total	28.6

Table 4.16 (continued)

Summer examination	Percentage increase 1974–79
Geography	
Boys	12.8
Girls	1.6
Total	7.7
Other social science or vocational subjects	
Boys	28.4
Girls	28.7
Total	28.6
All subjects	
Boys	19.8
Girls	20.9
Total	20.4
Total arts	13.9
Total science and technology	30.4
Total social science/vocational	19.8

Source: Examinations boards survey.

Table 4.17   CSE and GCE Examinations: Passes at GCE Advanced level, percentage increase 1974–79

Summer examination	Percentage increase 1974–79
English literature	
Boys	−8.6
Girls	6.5
Total	1.3
History	
Boys	−3.8
Girls	2.3
Total	−0.8
French	
Boys	28.0
Girls	10.2
Total	16.0
German	
Boys	3.6
Girls	25.6
Total	17.3
Art	
Boys	8.2
Girls	−2.1
Total	2.0
Other arts subjects	
Boys	8.9
Girls	12.2
Total	10.9

Table 4.17 (continued)

Summer examination	Percentage increase 1974–79
Mathematics	
Boys	26.3
Girls	40.9
Total	29.6
Physics	
Boys	22.9
Girls	27.8
Total	23.8
Chemistry	
Boys	29.5
Girls	40.1
Total	32.6
Biology, botany and zoology	
Boys	13.4
Girls	36.1
Total	24.5
Other science or technical subjects	
Boys	−3.6
Girls	68.8
Total	3.2
Economics	
Boys	21.6
Girls	74.2
Total	35.6
Geography	
Boys	2.5
Girls	0.2
Total	1.5
General studies	
Boys	51.9
Girls	55.6
Total	53.4
Other social science or vocational subjects	
Boys	50.2
Girls	43.6
Total	45.6
All subjects	
Boys	17.4
Girls	21.3
Total	19.1
Total arts	4.2
Total science and technology	26.4
Total social science/vocational	30.6

Source: Examinations boards survey.

that among girls with the possibility of obtaining a career there is greater resistance to the female stereotype. We shall return to this crucial explanation of women's continued complicity in their subordination. It has far-reaching implications for trends towards divergence between the position of women with the realistic prospect of individual careers and the position of women likely to become part of an undifferentiated mass work force.

Girls have their traditional aspirations reinforced, or their resistance to stereotyped choices constrained, by severely restricted curricula. Sometimes this is a result of explicit assumptions about what is relevant for girls and what for boys. In many mixed schools the timetable is organized so that girls do needlework or domestic science while boys do metalwork or woodwork. Other restrictions, particularly in girls' schools but also in mixed schools, are due to a serious shortage of adequate facilities and teaching staff for mathematical courses. In 1972 the ILEA Standing Committee on Careers Opportunities for Girls reported the evidence presented to them on this problem: 'In most schools there are difficulties in the recruitment of maths and science teachers and although girls' schools may be particularly affected, we noted that girls in some mixed schools also suffered when it came to the allocation of scarce resources. There are very few girls' schools equipped with any form of workshop facilities other than for needle-craft and home economics.'

In 1973 a study was carried out by HM Inspectorate which looked at the extent to which curricular differences and customs contributed to the inequality of opportunity for boys and girls. The prevailing picture was that traditional assumptions were being worked through the curricular patterns of secondary schools; and that there was support and acceptance of these patterns by the majority of teachers, pupils and parents.

The significance of this sexual differentiation in the learning of basic skills is not only that it prepares the way for a more rigid division of learning within specialized training; it also has a direct bearing on the occupational division of labour. Lack of mathematical competence is a major obstacle to wider job choices for women because of the range of jobs closed to those without 'O' level maths. These closed options now include not only the sciences but many branches of commerce, administration and even the social sciences. The careers ruled out by not having 'O' level mathematics include; accountancy, architecture, advertising, astronomy, banking, biochemistry, cartography, computer programming, dentistry, economics, engineering, horticulture, laboratory technology, land management, market research, optics, park administration, patent work, the Post Office (technical), printing, the police, radiography, statistics, surveying, textile technology and town planning. The role of the educational system in nourishing the sexual division of labour thus becomes all too clear when one sees that the number of girls who have this key to wider opportunities is only half the number of boys.

TRAINING FOR FUTURE WORK

We have seen that sexual differentiation is particularly marked in the lower streams of the education system. This is partly because within the division of labour the likely destiny of children is more apparent at the lower level. This is one indication of a pattern in which the degree of sexual differentiation varies directly with the extent to which parts of the education system are integrated with the occupational structure. Where the function of education is directly tied to an occupation, sexual differences are most extreme. For example, in the case of day-release courses – which is the most widespread form of industrially-backed part-time education – only 13.3 per cent of the students for 1970–1 were women, and this figure has increased only a few percentage points over the last ten years. Of the 16–19 age group of employees 40 per cent of men and only 10 per cent of women at present obtain release from employment for further education. Only 4 per cent of all those released from employment for part-time courses are women. Table 4.20 indicates this asymmetry in relation to apprenticeships. (The actual entry figures are down because of the raising of the school-leaving age.)

This lack of training, education facilities, and encouragement closes the trap which restricts the majority of women to the unskilled low-paid job market described in the first section. This in turn reinforces the sexual division of labour in the home. Wages are so low that going out to work does little to reduce woman's economic dependence on her husband. The nature of the work is either an extension of housework or is completely without interest and so in many cases it does little to change a woman's attitude towards her home.

Within full-time further education the situation is not much better. From the 1970–2 statistics of the London and Home Counties Regional Advisory Council for Further Education it would seem that the trend towards diminishing sexual differences – which the DES optimistically infer from the GCE results – is not carried through into further education. Girls are still concentrated in traditional areas and there is no sign of a move across to science/technology-based subjects. In the *Schools Council Working Paper* No. 45 on the education of 16 to 19-year olds there is clear evidence of the direct pressure of the poor job market in producing this situation. This points to the fact that in areas where women form the majority of students, as in OND Business Studies, the education on these courses is often adapted to the lower level or work opportunities for girls: 'It is noteworthy that in many colleges girls taking OND in Business Studies are expected to acquire shorthand and typewriting skills. This suggests that the colleges do not expect these young women to be offered managerial openings and therefore advise them to take the secretarial skills in order to get into business at the level of personal assistant rather than trainee manager. . . .'[21]

At the highest level there has been a very slight increase in the proportion of women getting into university but it is significantly below what would be expected on the basis of the sex distribution of 'A' level grades. Analysis of the annual statistics for London 'A' level exams shows a higher percentage of girls in the top three grades and yet fewer girls with three 'A' levels go to university compared with boys.

Table 4.18 indicates the continuation in higher education of the pattern of differentiation of subject choice, in relation to secondary education.

The extent to which education is predominantly a female option is clearly reflected in these figures. A teacher writing about her experience of one of these colleges vividly describes the main theme of their culture: 'My college, like most, had academic pretensions but underlying and undermining it was an environment which cocooned you securely from any real mental effort. Right from the beginning we accepted that marriage would be on the agenda long before a teaching job. Student culture, from 'freshers week' and the emphasis on that all too familiar song 'How do you feel when you marry your

Table 4.18   School Leavers during Academic Year 1978–79

Destination of leavers	Boys					Girls				
(i) Age at 31 August 1978	15	16	17	18 and over	Total	15	16	17	18 and over	Total
Leavers entering										
Degree courses	0.05	1.35	26.23	5.08	32.72	0.02	0.92	18.66	1.97	21.57
Teacher training courses	–	0.01	0.66	0.11	0.78	0.08	0.08	2.66	0.25	3.06
HND/HNC courses	–	0.03	1.00	0.39	1.42	–	0.02	0.92	0.08	1.02
OND/ONC courses	1.18	0.46	0.13	–	1.78	0.99	0.20	0.07	–	1.26
Catering courses	1.39	0.11	0.15	0.03	1.67	3.52	0.44	0.28	–	4.24
Nursing courses	0.03	0.02	–	–	0.05	4.18	0.66	0.50	0.02	5.36
Secretarial courses	0.13	–	–	0.01	0.14	13.70	1.82	1.71	0.12	17.36
GCE A level courses	4.28	1.08	2.00	0.25	7.61	5.70	1.08	1.60	0.15	8.54
GCE O level	4.44	0.43	0.14	0.01	5.02	5.69	0.46	0.15	0.01	6.31
Other further education courses										
Science and engineering	2.88	0.55	0.72	0.12	4.27	0.77	0.21	0.64	0.02	1.64
Education social studies and professional courses	2.07	0.41	1.31	0.20	3.98	8.72	1.26	1.60	0.07	11.65
Arts	1.26	0.30	1.15	0.08	2.80	2.45	0.70	2.19	0.16	5.50
Miscellaneous and other courses	1.73	0.40	0.32	0.06	2.51	4.07	0.53	0.58	0.09	5.28
All full-time further education	19.46	5.15	33.80	6.34	64.75	49.88	8.39	31.59	2.94	92.80
Temporary employment pending entry to										
Degree courses	0.05	0.52	2.06	0.11	2.74	–	0.26	1.78	0.05	2.09
Teacher training courses	–	–	0.01	0.01	0.02	–	0.02	0.06	–	0.07
Other courses	0.20	0.18	0.38	0.02	0.78	0.07	0.09	0.32	–	0.48
Total	0.25	0.70	2.45	0.14	3.54	0.07	0.37	2.16	0.05	2.65
Employment	234.69	23.53	19.06	2.30	279.58	185.92	27.75	20.49	1.59	235.75
Destination not known	20.35	3.30	4.39	1.11	29.15	21.32	3.65	3.63	0.54	29.14
All leavers	274.75	32.68	59.70	9.89	377.02	257.20	40.16	57.87	5.11	360.34

(ii) Age at 31 December 1978

	School leaving age	Others aged 16	17	18 and over	Total
All leavers	180.70	108.82	50.08	29.43	377.02
	176.42	108.57	52.72	22.64	360.34

(iii) Age on leaving school

	School leaving age	Others aged 16	17	18 and over	Total
All leavers	188.51	100.64	33.15	59.72	377.02
	169.08	99.33	38.98	52.95	360.34

Source: Sample survey, *Statistics of Education* (1980).

Table 4.19   Analysis by Type of Employment Entered and Age of Entry (thousands)

		Males				Females			
		15	16	17	Total	15	16	17	Total
Apprenticeship or learnership to skilled occupation (including pre-apprenticeship training in employment)	1973	5.9	51.0	9.1	66.0	0.6	3.3	1.1	5.0
	1972	52.2	40.7	7.3	100.2	14.0	3.0	1.0	18.0
	Difference	−46.3	+10.3	+1.3	−34.2	−13.4	+0.3	+0.1	−13.0
Employment leading to recognized professional qualifications	1973	0.1	1.6	1.6	3.3	0.1	2.2	1.7	4.0
	1972	0.5	1.3	1.5	3.4	0.3	2.0	1.6	3.9
	Difference	−0.4	+0.3	+0.1	−0.1	−0.2	−0.2	+0.1	+0.1
Clerical employment	1973	0.8	10.2	6.6	17.8	5.1	40.6	16.6	62.3
	1972	3.3	8.9	6.2	18.4	29.3	33.9	15.1	73.6
	Difference	−2.5	+1.3	+0.6	−0.6	−24.2	+6.7	+1.5	−16.0
Employment with planned training, apart from induction training, not covered above	1973	2.3	13.2	4.9	20.4	1.2	8.2	3.0	12.4
	1972	26.4	12.1	4.1	42.6	30.7	7.0	2.7	40.5
	Difference	−24.1	+1.1	+0.8	−22.2	−29.5	+1.2	+0.3	28.1
Other employment	1973	5.9	20.9	6.2	33.1	3.5	15.1	4.7	23.3
	1972	68.7	19.9	5.7	94.3	69.3	13.9	4.3	87.5
	Difference	−62.8	+1.0	+0.5	−61.2	−65.8	+1.2	40.4	−64.2
Total	1973	15.0	96.9	28.6	140.5	10.5	69.4	27.2	107.0
	1972	151.2	82.9	24.8	258.9	143.6	59.9	24.8	228.2
	Difference	−136.2	+14.0	+3.8	−118.4	−133.1	+9.5	+2.4	−121.2

Source: Department of Employment, *Gazette* (May 1974).

Table 4.20   Apprentice Trainees, Great Britain

Total	807,672
Men	621,101
Women	186,571
Women – single, widowed or	
divorced	155,465
– married	31,106

Source: *Census National Report*, 1981.

ideal . . .' to the spoon-banging crescendo like some primitive initiation rite, only emphasized it more strongly.[22] The implications are backed up by a survey of the attitudes of female teachers by the National Institute of Industrial Psychiatrists. They found that the majority of women thought that men were better in authority, fairer, more patient and generally more respected. One third of the sample admitted they thought that men were generally superior. In the light of this it comes as no surprise that teachers tend to reinforce sex roles.

EDUCATION AND THE IDEOLOGY OF SEXISM

When a girl goes to school her vague consciousness of what it means to be a girl is developed into a concrete shape by the models presented of her future destiny. They include reading-books where boys always appear to have the monopoly of adventure and naughtiness, where adult women are engrossed only in housework and never appear in the world of work and activity outside the home (other than shopping); science textbooks which in their illustrations show a few pictures of girls doing things like tending plants, stroking kittens or blowing bubbles and numerous pictures of boys demonstrating 'energy' by chopping wood, kicking footballs and having pillow fights, or using torches, magnifying glasses and other technical instruments. They include, too, the structure of the school itself in which women are almost invariably in subordinate positions to men: women are the assistant teachers, secretaries, auxiliary workers, cooks and cleaners; men are most frequently the headmasters, the heads of departments.[23]

The strength of these models of behaviour and aspiration does not derive from their being consciously taught as the ways in which girls ought to behave. Their power lies in the appearance that they present of the complete naturalness and inevitability of women's secondary position. There appears to be no way out except to refuse to identify with one's own sex. A partial solution therefore for girls who react negatively to the limp and passive bystanders or the happy plastic figures doing the washing up, is to identify with the active, interesting images of the opposite sex. But to be a tomboy is to be in limbo. A girl is expected to 'grow out of it', and consequently is not related to herself as she is and wants to be, but only to the hints of femininity that fit into what she ought to be. On the other hand boys will not easily accept her. It is a solution she knows can never work. Apart from this ambiguous solution the shape of the images that most girls absorb appears to point to becoming a wife and mother as the main goal in life. There are very few reading-books for children, even among the newest series, that present different images of girls.

The idea that women's present subordinate position is natural and inevitable is not, in general, consciously constructed to inculcate sex roles. Most writers probably think they are presenting real life; in fact a lot of effort has gone into making children's reading-books more realistic by not restricting them to a middle-class life-style. But they are still only presenting an idealized form of the real situation of women, and are not describing the contradictions. And it is only an awareness of these contradictions which can give girls the tools with which to construct an alternative. The fact that women *do* get out to work, that women *do* organize against low pay and bad conditions, that there *are some* women doctors, scientists, politicians, artists and poets, that girls *do* feel like having adventures, and taking the initiative, all provide holes in the smothering blanket of domesticity.

Women and the Economy

Earlier in this chapter the position of women within the labour market was presented in terms of what is in effect a dual market. The main point of this description was to show the ways in which the chief feature of women's paid work did not directly clash with the sexual division of labour. The analysis went on to show how the socializing institutions through which social values regarding the division of labour are acquired and skills and capacities are learnt, reflect and reinforce this. The relation of the state to the family guarantees it materially. Is it the cultural and official reinforcement of women's role which prevents a general erosion of accepted attitudes? Or is there a sense in which modern capitalist industry also depends on and sustains the dual labour market? If this is the case, the cultural and political processes already traced have a strong material basis, not easily weakened, as far as the majority of women are concerned, by egalitarian cultural pressures stemming from the formal granting of equal economic and legal rights.

In order to understand the present distribution and the future of women as wage labourers, we must not be content with the relatively equal situation of some women (despite their dual role as domestic labourers) in parts of the professional sector. Instead, we should identify those features of a capitalist economy which thrive on the sexual division of labour and thereby endorse it. Only in this way will it be possible to explain why women are concentrated in certain sectors of the economy and to evaluate fully the strength of processes tending to erode women's unequal position.

There are two main processes which are relevant: capitalism's tendency to create a section of the labour force which is sufficiently manoeuvrable to be easily expelled from employment during periods of recession or of increased capital intensity, and to be drawn rapidly into employment when there is fresh investment and new sections of industry are opened up; secondly, the tendency towards a dual economy in which the large, corporate, high labour-cost sector comes to *depend* on, rather than to squeeze out, small firms running on low labour costs, producing components and acting as subcontractors to the large corporations.

To consider the first: in the past capital has relied on agricultural labour, immigrants, or a high rate of native male unemployment to provide the necessary surplus labour. In the course of the post-war boom these sources reached their political and economic limits. And yet the need for new sources of labour grew fast; particularly for new ndustries, new services and new administrative extensions to the production process for which no existing section of the labour force was available or trained. The expansion of he welfare state, combined with the increased revenue which the state gained from the expansion of the economy, led to an unprecedented growth in the need for clerical and other service workers throughout government departments. A similar demand for clerical and administrative workers increased with the growing need of large corporations to monitor, plan and control the production process as its size and complexity grew and as he processes of coordination, skill and planning had been transferred from the shop loor to the office.[24] The growth in advertising and related marketing processes which has followed the increased power of the large corporations reinforced this need. Along with this growth in the service and clerical sectors there has been a simultaneous mushooming of new light industries, made possible by the technological advances preceding nd during the expansion of the economy. These light industries needed a rapid influx of unskilled and green labour which could be easily fitted into the new assembly-line echniques unacceptable to many workers in the traditional industries. Moreover this abour force had to be expendable. Corporate investors rarely considered new plants to be permanent. Plants were subject to changes in multinational plans and possibilities, or were highly tactical operations geared to utilizing government subsidies and ready o move at the slightest sign of trouble or greener fields elsewhere. And even if a plant vas stable the technology utilized within it was not. New combinations of machinery nd labour need to be continually tested and, in the eyes of management, the 'Luddite' estrictive practices of the unions would hold back progress.

Married women, with initially low wage expectations, negligible traditions of organization, no established work customs and with an alternative life to return to, provided the ideal work force.

If capitalism were a stable economic system this basis on which married women have been drawn in to meet capital's new labour needs during the boom period would not produce any strong tendency towards reinforcing the division of labour. Married women would develop high wage expectations and become strongly organized in the same way as other groups who have acted as sources of surplus labour in England, such as exgricultural workers, Irish and, increasingly, Asian and West Indian workers. But given he increasingly lengthy periods of recession which periodically and unpredictably afflict he capitalist economy, the sexual division of labour provides a unique advantage to apitalism. No other group is so well situated from capital's point of view. The sexual division of labour and the ideology that justifies it ensures that women are not dependent or their subsistence on wage labour. Among workers in a capitalist society they are unique n having access to a means, or a partial means, of livelihood on the basis of social elations other than economic exchange relations. It is almost as if capitalism was able to preserve a rural economy for workers to return to, and could yet make use of them whenever necessary. The situation of 'guest-workers' in France and Germany is the earest equivalent.[25]

The unique feature of married women as wage labourers has become increasingly mportant in a context where employers face growing uncertainty combined with uccessful attempts by unions to raise the cost of redundancies. The Redundancy Payment Act, the Employment Protection Act, and the successful occupation of actories during the early 70s, all contribute in different ways. In this context the

advantage of employing women is that they can work part-time. In consequence
the costs and problems of making redundancies are evaded. This is becoming more
attractive as the size of investment projects and the growing uncertainty of general
economic conditions increases the risks facing the multinational companies. Not sur-
prisingly there has been a significant growth in the number of part-time married women
workers. The Counter Information Services report, *Women Under Attack*, describes it
as follows:

> Between 1961 and 1971 full-time employment (both sexes) in the manufacturing
> sector fell by 405,000, while part-time employment increased by 85,000. In the year
> June 1971 to June 1972 full-time male employment in all industries fell by 106,000,
> and full-time female employment fell 14,000. Part-time female employment, however
> rose 120,000 in the same period. Obviously employers have become willing to employ
> part-time workers, and part-time women workers in particular, at times when full-
> timers are losing their jobs and there is plenty of full-time labour available on the mar-
> ket. This is not to say that part-time women are not susceptible, in employment
> terms, to market cycles. In the manufacturing industries they numbered 470,000 in
> September 1973, rising to 504,900 in December of the same year as the boom was
> reaching its peak, and falling to 494,800 by June 1975 in the course of the long run-
> down to the present slump.[26]

This increase in part-time women workers is the clearest expression of a general feature
of the position of the majority of women workers. British capitalism's increasing need
for a manoeuvrable section of the labour force, the political and economic limits on
previous sources of such labour, and the uniquely accommodative nature of family
relations outside of direct exchange relations, reinforces the position of women as a
distinct and subordinate group. Part-time work visibly illustrates the way in which the
sexual division of labour is built into the strategies of management to meet their fluctuating labour needs. Part-time work on wages lower than subsistence is *only possible*
because of women's domestic obligations and dependence. In this way, far from a steady
erosion of the sexual division of labour, sections of the production process are organized
on the basis of compromise. The general fluctuations in women's employment as
compared to men's are shown in figure 4.3.

The way in which the sexual division of labour and the fluctuating labour requirements of the economy interlock to keep the majority of unskilled and semi-skilled
women in their subordinate position contrasts sharply with the position of women in
the 'career' sector of the job market. In this sector the specific capacities of each
individual are central to the needs of the employer. Once women have been drawn into
this sector because of shortages, and once the women involved have through their
relatively high income transferred their domestic commitments to private services, bough
on the market, there is no basis other than overt discrimination on which they can be
treated differently. In this sector of the job market, where workers are hired for their
individual merits as distinct from being units of undifferentiated labour power, tendencie
towards meritocracy are strong. There is little to be gained from treating women differently. Prejudice still exists but it is becoming increasingly anomalous. It is at this level of
the job market that the Sex Discrimination Act is likely to have some effect. In the
unskilled/semi-skilled labour market the individual capacities of each worker are

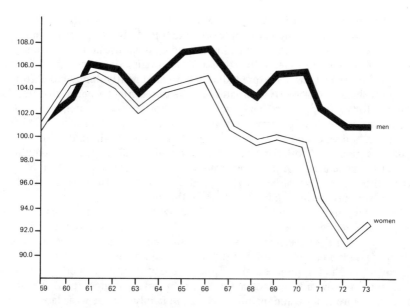

Figure 4.3   Index of Male and Female Employment in Manufacturing Industry, 1959–73

Source: CIS Report, *Women Under Attack* (1976), p. 11.

irrelevant. They are selling a general capacity to work which the employer will then control and use. What is important is the controllability of this capacity to work. If certain groups of workers have particular characteristics which enhance the ability of management to control when and how their work capacity is utilized, these characteristics will be harnessed to the production process. This is what has happened to the present family system and women's dependent position within it. It is the way that this has become integral to employers' labour needs that gives the lie to optimistic generalizations from the increasing presence of women in the higher echelons of British society.

THE HISTORICAL ROOTS OF THE PRESENT DIVISION OF LABOUR

So far we have concentrated on the problem of how the sexual division of labour is reproduced. Our analysis does not imply that these processes *caused* the division of labour. It merely implies that there is no automatic tendency towards its erosion within the institutions of modern capitalism. To explain the basic features of women's position we need to re-examine the transition from feudalism to capitalism. How were relations between the sexes transformed in the course of this transition between two modes of production?

Historians argue correctly that a major consequence of the industrial revolution was the destruction of the family as a unit of production. As one historian describes it: 'Each stage in industrial differentiation and specialization struck also at the family economy, disturbing customary relations between man and wife, parents and children, and differentiating more sharply between 'work' and 'life'.[27] But this was not simply a change whereby all those processes which in pre- and early industrial Britain came under the category of production were, in the course of industrialization, transferred from the family to the factory or office. The pre-industrial, predominantly family-based form of production involved the fusion of what later became two distinct aspects: that is, a fusion of production for some sort of exchange with production for the maintenance of the family. The dairying, care of poultry and pigs, brewing, growing of vegetables and fruit, spinning of flax and wool and other similar work that was done within the family in varying degrees, was done both for exchange and for the family's direct consumption. Similarly, future generations of producers were reared and were taught their trades in the place where those trades would be practised: within the family. They also received medical care from inside the family, usually from the mother.

For the feudal family the consequences of the growth of capitalism were not simply an increasing differentiation between 'work' and 'life'. They can be more accurately described in terms of the severing of this feudal fusion between labour involved in the production of goods and the labour required for the maintenance of human life. But factory production did not permeate the whole sphere of family production, nor did it entirely strip the family of its economic functions. In varying degrees it left the labour involved in the reproduction and maintenance of the family outside wage labour and exchange relations. This aspect of production remained within the private sphere of the family, to be carried out on the basis of the sexual division of labour in which the man — because of a pre-existing sexual division — was the main wage-earner and the woman the housewife. The housewife occasionally became a wage-earner, but this was only when the insufficiency of the man's wages coincided with employers' needs for more labour.

The fact that this sphere of housework and child-rearing was not itself directly organized according to the laws of the market and wage labour does not mean that it was not integrated into, and at various times modified by, the emerging capitalist relations of production. Essential to the wage system is the fact, referred to above, that it is the individual worker, and not the family unit, who is directly involved in the productive process. In general the family was not recognized as in any sense an economic unit. At times this was the case: wages were so low that wives and children frequently had to become individual wage labourers and the family's role in the maintenance of the labour force came near to collapse, However it was soon realized by employers and those concerned with the long-term development of their own enterprises and the economy as a whole, that this virtually complete destruction of the working-class family without alternative institutions (apart from the stopgap measure of the workhouse) undermined the health and work capacity of the present and future workforce. This realization, combined with innovations in machinery that periodically reduced employers' labour needs, led to pressures on women to give priority to their domestic obligations. These pressures included legislation which made it difficult for women to opt for a more independent existence. Between 1802 and 1898 a series of Factory Acts at first protected and then drastically reduced the employment of women. Parallel with this, and resulting from the increasing strength of the organized working class, wages began to be successfully demanded to cover the cost of subsistence of both the worker and his dependent wife and children. The possibility of women becoming dependent home labourers

as given a further material boost after the First World War by the successful campaigns
ɔr family allowances in the 1920s and 30s. But as labour needs remained either static
ː even below the supply of male labourers, there was very little possibility for women
● break out of their position as housewives. Nor was there any impetus for the trad-
ional role and skills of the housewife to be supplanted by labour-saving food and
ɔpliances, familiar to us since the post-war boom created a demand for labour. Similarly
ιere was no pressure on the state to provide nursery or other facilities, until, for the
ιration of the Second World War, women's labour was required on a massive scale.
ɔcause of the relationship between the position of women and the rate of industrial
owth, the productive capacity of a family of the pre-industrial era eventually became
tegrated into the industrial economy. In the course of this integration the subordination
˙ women, which in the feudal family had been characterized by authority relations
ther than the nature of work, took the form of a rigid division of labour.

The above is only a brush-stroke picture of the division of labour as expressed in the
vision between domestic and wage labour. These processes of industrial development
so shaped the division expressed within the labour market. Before the development of
ɔdern production methods women worked in almost every type of trade, industry and
ɡriculture. For example, until the Colliery Act of 1842 women worked in the mines,
ιshing wagonloads of coal along the underground rail track to the bottom of the shaft,
˙ landing, weighing, picking and screening, although not hewing, the coal. Until the
ːcline of family industry in the course of the seventeenth and eighteenth centuries,
ɔmen were working as blacksmiths, metal workers, printers, bakers, millers, brewers,
ιnners and many other crafts, trades and professions in whose modern workshops
ɔmen play little or no role. Through this productive activity they made their indepen-
ιnt contribution to the prosperity of their families. The idea that a man should main-
in his wife through his own work, while she was restricted to production purely for
ɔmestic consumption, was rarely accepted. The business responsibilities that women in
ιdor England took on in the absence or incompetence of their husbands, the skilled
ɔrk that craftswomen performed in a variety of fields, the heavy manual work carried
ιt in agriculture and mining, all demonstrate the historically specific nature of the
esent division between the sexes.[28]

What precisely were the processes which in the course of industrial development laid
e foundations of the present occupational division of labour by both squeezing women
ɔmpletely out of particular trades and by relegating them to unskilled work through
ιich it was impossible to earn sufficient for an independent life? The expansion of the
ɔductive forces and the disruptive effects of this on feudal family relationships had
ffering consequences for the situation of women according to the economic position
˙ the family. In the case of the wealthiest families who, through an intermixing of
ɔlitical position and landed wealth with merchant prosperity and business acumen,
ːre in the vanguard of capitalist expansion, the energetic life of the Elizabethan business
rtner and wife gave way to the leisurely, ornamental existence of the Restoration lady.
ιe growth of surplus wealth meant that owners of large amounts of capital were no
nger themselves required to engage in the productive process. Women were therefore
● longer needed to fulfil the managerial functions that they had previously performed
ι *the basis of their marriage.* They were replaced by men who were hired *on a com-*
ːrcial basis* to manage estates and finances. The possession of a purely decorative wife,

or in less wealthy families a wife solely engaged in feathering the domestic nest, gradually became an important symbol of wealth and success; in fact so much so that not only capitalists bút also higher-paid wage-earners became proud to have a wife whose energies were devoted primarily to strengthening the family as a private haven.

Just as in the case of wealthy families the downfall of the woman was primarily a result of work deriving from a marriage relationship being replaced, in all but an increasingly narrow domestic sphere, by work performed through commercial relationships, so it was in the case of the craftswoman. Whereas in the past marriage had involved her directly in production, with the spread of hired managerial skill her marriage relationship became an obstacle to any involvement. There were three main aspects of this change: first, because a woman's involvement in the craft or trade was generally dependent on the possibility of work in the home, the move towards factory production made it more and more difficult for her to undertake many types of work. The constraining effects of domestic commitments were reinforced by the fact that it was her husband who had learnt the craft through an apprenticeship and therefore had the formal qualifications required by the employer for skilled work. The woman had usually only learnt from experience, and the replacement of rules of custom by formal rules of capitalist production meant that she could not enter the skilled sectors of production. For example, even in the case of baking where in the past women's domestic experience stood them in good stead as skilled workers, it became increasingly rare to find women involved except at the most menial level. A second factor, closely related to the customary way in which women learned their trade through family relationships, was that when craftsmen began to organize themselves in order to protect their interests from encroachment by employers, they made use of the remains of guild organization to restrict their numbers and therefore to force wages up. This involved tightening the rules governing skill qualifications, and lengthening the period of apprenticeships. This further strengthened the process whereby, when trying to maintain some degree of economic independence, women were faced with increasingly limited, unskilled and unlucrative options. The effect of this pressure is further demonstrated by the fact that the few crafts which were initially dominated by women, such as upholstery, millinery and brewing, had particularly weak forms of guild organization. Thus, in general, by the beginning of the nineteenth century a woman in a skilled job was a rare exception. Furthermore, the higher wages that skilled male workers obtained through increased organization gave their wives a means of subsistence through dependence on the husband's wage, which in the past would have been inconceivable. This materially aided their subjective adaptation to, and acceptance of, the job market which could give them neither the monetary nor the psychological satisfaction necessary to make working outside the home a permanent part of their lives. So the elimination of the craftswoman laid foundations for women becoming a flexible, unskilled reserve labour force.

In the case of the poorest families who even before the spread of mass wage labour, being unable to sell the products of their labour directly on the market, were partially dependent on wages, the effects of capitalist development depended on the position of their industry in the British economy. The different industries, of which spinning was a necessary part, illustrate this relationship well. As a result of the Industrial Revolution the linen and the silk industries declined and it was no longer possible for a large number of female spinners, who had earned at least part of their living, to secure a subsistence wage from working in these industries. The women who had previously gained some minimal independence through their spinning joined the growing numbers of paupers dependent on the parish and on their husbands and were obliged to act as a reserve labour force for employers wanting sweated labour or menial domestic servants. However, in the wool industry, the major growth-point of early British capitalism, the situation was very different. Here there was a high demand for labour and although wages were not commensurate with this demand, nevertheless it was possible for women to earn a living wage for themselves and their children from spinning wool.

These factors constitute the beginnings of the sexual division within the occupational structure, the continuity of which has not been persistently challenged until now. These divisions arose, not from some egalitarian Golden Age but from a society in which patriarchy was deeply entrenched. However, the economic relations of which this patriarchy was a part *did* entail the involvement of women in all levels of production, even though it was on the basis of their marital relationship. The new economic relations of capitalism undermined the productive relevance of this relationship and as a result women were squeezed out of business, out of the majority of skilled trades, and out of the professions whose new scientific basis undermined the custom-based medical and teaching practice that were almost exclusively women's role in pre-capitalist Britain. These were the foundations of man's world and woman's secondary place within it. The continuity underlying this is that whereas the growth of capitalism broke the direct connection that women, on the basis of familial relationships, had with all levels of production, it never permanently upset the way in which those same relationships tied women to private domestic labour. The commitments of this labour have persistently constrained women from any thoroughgoing challenge to the dominant position that men achieved in productive work after the disintegration of family industry.

CONTRADICTIONS AND ALTERNATIVES

The central argument of this chapter has been that the unequal position of women in modern Britain is a product of the division, on a sexual basis, between social labour for the market and private labour for immediate consumption within the family. This sex-based separation has its roots in the transition from feudal to capitalist Britain. More specifically the basis for the present form of women's subordination (the argument does not imply that this is the only form, or that sex inequality is unique to capitalist societies) was established with the growth of an economy in which the capacity to work became a commodity, controlled by those with the wealth to buy it. The crucial link between this and the sexual division of labour is that employers have only been concerned about the workers' capacity to work. As long as this is adequate they, and the state also, have no interest in how the commodity is reproduced. This is left to the private labours of women within the family; others only intervene when the quality and supply of labour power require modification. The present analysis has briefly sketched the origins of these structures and the ways in which they transformed the lives of women in all classes. It has also traced the different ways in which this basic sex division has been reinforced by the contemporary institutions which shape people's day-to-day choices. In conclusion, the analysis will now identify the sources of conflict in these

relationships and the growing challenges and alternatives which women are creating out
of such conflicts.

The fundamental source of instability lies in the breakdown of the sex boundaries
between social and domestic labour; that is, the mass entry of married women into the
labour market. (The boundaries were never entirely complete but were sufficient to
appear natural.) The timing of this breakdown has been important in producing its
destabilizing effects. It occurred at a time when a massive expansion was taking place in
higher and further education. As we have seen, women benefited from this expansion.
Not equally it is true, but sufficiently to generate high expectations of equal opportunities when they entered the job market. Another feature of the timing of the mass
influx of married women into paid jobs, was that it coincided with a period of trade
union strength and expansion. The unions were on the offensive to achieve closed shops
and to move into new un-unionized spheres, for example in the offices and in the
services. The result was that not only did women enter the labour force but it was not
long before many of them joined trade unions, though it is only recently, as a result of
women's pressure and self-organization, that the unions have paid special attention to
the needs of women workers.

Against this background we need to explore more deeply why the breakdown of the
boundaries between waged labour and private domestic labour, by the rapid growth of
the numbers of workers who straddle both, should produce conflict. As we have seen, the
two institutions of paid labour and unpaid housework do not automatically clash. In fact
employers and the state have put considerable effort into achieving harmony between
them. The partial breakdown of the separation appears only to have produced a new
accommodation based on the usefulness of married women as a source of cheap flexible
labour.

The root of the conflict lies in the fact that, although employers depend on the
specific obligations and constraints which women face outside of production and which
partially negate their position as wage labourers, they have to buy women's labour on
essentially the same formal contractual basis as men's. They have to turn women into
wage labourers, free to sell their labour power to the highest bidder and with, in principle,
access to all the political, educational and economic rights of wage labourers. The significance of this is seen by contrasting the position of women with that of migrant
workers, the other major source of reserve labour for European capitalism. They face an
entirely different kind of labour market. Capitalism has been able to deny to the migrant
workers, the other major source of reserve labour for European capitalism. They enter
into an entirely different kind of labour contract. Capitalism has been able to deny to the
migrant worker, implicitly or explicitly, all the citizenship and trade union rights which
have been conceded to other wage labourers. It has been able to separate migrant workers
labour power constrained by relations extraneous to his relation with his employer, but
his relationship to his employer is itself only formally one of a wage labourer to a buyer
of labour power. The employer's control is over the labourer himself, not merely over
his labour power. This makes the relationship closer to one of short-term slavery. Thus
the relations involved in the migrant's situation have tended to be unbroken and unfree.
In the case of women, however, there is a greater disjuncture created between their rights
as wage labourers and the constraints they face as housewives. In spite of all the obstacles
from employers and trade unions alike, as workers or potential workers they have begun

to utilize their trade union and political rights, and in the case of many activists in the women's movement, their educational background, to make the elementary demands which are a pre-condition of independence: the demand for a living wage and secure employment. The rising rate of increase in the number of women involved in strike action is an illustration of the over-riding strength of the pressures, expectations and traditions that induce women to make these demands and thus prevent employers from having the best of both worlds.

For women, especially women with children, the right to a living wage and secure employment conflicts with their private domestic obligations. This conflict is taking many different forms. Its resolution will be a long struggle requiring a transformation of paid work as well as domestic work. On the one hand the issue of social provision for housework, particularly childcare, has been put on the agenda of the trade unions, and higher on the agenda of some parts of the Labour party, especially innovating local authorities like Sheffield and the GLC. The TUC now has a charter for women which includes the demand for nursery facilities as a right for all children under five. And major unions such as the TGWU and NUPE have passed similar resolutions at their conferences. Women's councils, women's schools and women's committees are springing up to follow through these paper commitments with programmes of positive action.

On the other hand many of these same groups of women are focusing their attention on the organization of paid work: men's as well as women's. The sexual division of labour can never be overcome simply by the socialization of housework, the social provision of nurseries and cafés. There will always be work to be done in the home and there will always need to be time for individual care of children. Time in fact is at the heart of the issue which women are raising. They ask, and increasingly demand: Why cannot work be so organized to meet the needs of workers as parents, as fathers as well as mothers, and as people desiring a personal life that is more than recovering from work? Unemployment has made the issue of the 35-hour week a high priority in the trade union movement, so the opportunity for radical demands is there, though the industrial strength to back them up is frequently absent.

Whether this strength can be rebuilt around the new demands for shorter hours and more flexible working arrangements which women are raising in the unions will depend a lot on how quick the unions are to respond to the new position of women within the economy. For though, as we have seen, women are in one sense on the margins of the economy — in terms of status and occupational grade — in terms of potential economic power they are at the centre. This can best be seen by adding to our detailed picture of the trends in women's employment a quick sketch of the trends in men's employment. The two most important trends are, first, the decline and in some instances collapse of the main industries dominated by male employment: shipbuilding, heavy engineering, and mining. Secondly, other traditional centres of male employment, such as printing and mechanical engineering, are undergoing technological changes which entirely undermine the exclusive position and therefore power of the skilled craftsman. A strategy for re-building the trade unions in these industries will have to find new sources of strength, this time built on equality and unity rather than exclusivity and subordination.[30]

The trade unions are only one area where women are making their needs and demands felt. In the communities, too, women are becoming increasingly confident in fighting for social solutions to the problems which used to drive them to tranquilizers and other personal solutions. Women have therefore been taking independent action and dragging others behind them. They have occupied council offices and university and polytechnic administration blocks, demanding nursery facilities. In almost every major town women have created centres through which they coordinate their struggles, support each other and reach out to others just beginning to reject their traditional position. The increasing consciousness among women has also generated cultural alternatives in literature — including school books — history, films, music and in personal relationships.

Once women themselves question their domestic role, all the institutions and assumptions which have historically given it credibility begin to be revealed and confronted. One such assumption is that there is a necessary bond between sexuality and procreation, enforced practically in abortion legislation and the organization of contraceptive facilities. The bond is no longer primarily biological; it is based on the moral and social relations of family and marriage. The demand of women to control their own sexuality and fertility involves a direct rejection of the bond. The growing number of women who are making this rejection is indicated by the size of the movement which mobilized a demonstration of 40,000 against attempts to place further restrictions on abortion facilities.

Within every area of social life, from nursery and primary schools to the health service, housing, the unions and political organizations, women are identifying and challenging the way in which everyday activities and institutions are based on their being in a secondary position. This challenge is organized through networks of loosely linked groups and journals. Its strength is diffused but this is partly a function of the way in which the sexual division of labour is sustained — that is, not only by the institutions of the state. The terrain is therefore not suitable for a focused political movement of the conventional form.

The above analysis implies that political transformation is a necessary condition for the elimination of the sexual division of labour.[31] But, for such a transformation to be effective, it must involve resistance to institutions and ideas deeply rooted in areas of private and social life which, until they are challenged, appear unconnected with politics. It is partly for this reason that the existing legislation is having little impact. It only skims the surface. It does not present a threat to the groundwork of gender inequality which it has been the purpose of this chapter to understand.

Notes to Chapter 4

1 Since then there has been an outpouring of analyses of women's position. Useful summaries and general contributions include Michele Barrett, *Women's Oppression Today* (London 1980); Anna Coote and Beatrix Campbell, *Sweet Freedom* (London 1982). A useful reader covering a wide range of issues in the sociology of sex and gender is A. Oakley and J. Mitchell (eds), *The Rights and Wrongs of Women* (Harmondsworth 1978).

2 This is documented in detail in Ann Oakley, *The Sociology of Housework* (London 1974), ch. 1.

3 *Social Trends* (HMSO 1972, 1974 and 1982).

4 J. S. Mill, *The Subjection of Women* (1869, Everyman edn. 1970).

5 Though some parts of the suffrage movement were more radical than others, see J. Liddington and J. Norris, *One Hand Tied Behind Us* (London 1978), on the suffrage movement amongst working-class women in the North of England.

6 See Jean Coussins, *The Equality Report* (London 1976) for a thoroughly documented analysis of the inadequacies revealed in the implementation of this legislation. See also P. Ashdown-Sharp, 'Women's Rights: the missed opportunity' in *The Sunday Times* (20 February 1977). See also S. Roberts with A. Coote and E. Ball, *Positive Action For Women – The Next Step* (NCCL 1981); and A Coote and B. Campbell, *Sweet Freedom*, ch. 4.

7 F. Parkin's, *Class Inequality and Political Order* (London 1971) provides the clearest illustration of this.

8 The analysis of J. Westergaard and H. Resler in *Class in a Capitalist Society* (Penguin edn. 1975) starts from this limitation. It therefore concludes that sex inequality merely 'accentuates class divisions' (ch. 6). There is no hint that sex inequality is a product of social divisions which are distinct from, though related to, class divisions; its basis is referred to merely in terms of 'handicaps' and 'sex discrimination'.

9 This involves a contrasting emphasis to that of Engels in *The Origins of the Family* (London 1940). Engels stresses the process of inheritance through the male line as the basis of women's subordination. He traces this back to the origins of surplus wealth and class divisions. Surplus wealth developed in the sphere of male labour in primitive society. It consequently gave men the power to overthrow the matriarchal and matrilineal family relations which according to Engels characterized

pre-class societies. This overthrow of inheritance according to the female line of descent was thus, in Engels' words, 'the world historical defeat of the female sex'. Our analysis would imply, in terms of a debate with Engels, that the 'world historical defeat of the female sex' came with the separation of the labours of production for immediate need from those of production for exchange (see pp. 235-9). This would tend to entail inheritance through the male line because only the man would usually be directly involved in the processes of investment and accumulation. But patrilineal inheritance would thus only be a product of a more basic structure – a structure which is most apparent among those directly involved in production.

10   M. Young and P. Wilmott, *The Symmetrical Family* (London 1973), p. 183.

11   For a fuller description see L. Mackie and Polly Patullo, *Women at Work* (London 1977).

12   For a description of the sexual division of labour in the medical profession see E. Gamarnikow, 'Sexual Division of Labour: The Case of Nursing' in A. Kuhn and A. Wolpe, *Feminism and Materialism* (London 1978).

13   Office of Manpower Economics, *Report on Equal Pay Act* (1972).

14   See J. Hurstfield, *The Part-Time Trap*, Low Pay Unit (London 1980).

15   This rule, according to calculations in *Women's Report* (March–April 1976), deprives at least 8,000 mothers and 1,000 widows of their benefits and pensions every year. Moreover, there is little sign that the rule will be modified: the Supplementary Benefits Commission has produced a defence of the basic principles behind it in *Living Together as Husband and Wife* (HMSO 1976).

16   William Beveridge, *Report on Social Insurance and Allied Services*, Cmnd 6484 (HMSO 1968), pp. 49, 52-3; for a fuller analysis of the Welfare State's relation to women, see Elizabeth Wilson, *Women and the Welfare State* (London 1977).

17   M. Mead, *Male and Female* (Penguin edn. 1962).

18   R. Hartley, 'A developmental view of female sex-role identification' in J. Biddle and E. J. Thomas (eds), *Role Theory* (Chichester 1966); J. Kagan and H. A. Moss, *Birth to Maturity: a study in psychological development* (Chichester 1967).

19   A very clear and sympathetic account of Freud's theory of femininity and masculinity – from one feminist viewpoint – is given by Juliet Mitchell in *Psychoanalysis and Feminism* (London 1974).

20   See J. Kamm, *Hope Deferred: girls' education in English history* (London 1965).

21   *Schools Council Working Paper*, No. 45 (London 1972).

22   Maria Loftus, 'Learning Sexism and Feminimity' in *Red Rag*, 7 (June 1974).

23   For a fuller description of the patterns of sexist ideology in education see Sue Sharpe, *Just Like A Girl* (Penguin 1976), ch. 4.

24   For a detailed discussion of this see H. Braverman, *Labor and Monopoly Capital* (New York 1974), esp. ch. 15.

25   For a vivid and detailed description of the relations of unfreedom enslaving the migrant worker, see J. Berger and J. Mohr, *A Seventh Man* (Penguin edn. 1975).

26   Counter Information Services, *Women Under Attack* (London 1976).

27   E. P. Thompson, *The Making of the English Working Class* (Penguin edn. 1968).

28   Alice Clark, *The Working Life of Women in the Seventeenth Century* (1919, reprinted London 1968). Most of the information in this section comes from this invaluable book.

29 See J. Berger and J. Mohr, *A Seventh Man*. This situation is also being challenged as migrant workers become organized, catalysed by the political struggles of their fellow workers and peasants at home in Portugal, Spain and Greece.
30 This argument is developed through a detailed study of craft trade unionism in the print industry by Cynthia Cockburn, *Brothers* (London 1983).
31 Anne Philips, *Hidden Hands* (London 1983) lays out very clearly the economic strategy necessary for such a political transformation.

I would like to thank Julie Madden for help in updating the tables in this article and for helpful discussion of the ideas.

5

Elites and Privilege[*]

Philip Stanworth

INTRODUCTION

The term 'elite' retains a distinctively Gallic ring even when printed in English without its accent (a practice that has only recently become usual). The importation of the term was an indirect one, however, since it was the Italian writers Pareto and Mosca who mor than any others were responsible for popularizing it as a concept in social and political analysis. In the works of these two authors, the notion of elite was introduced to suppo a critique of Marxist theories of class and class domination. Such theories tie together economic and political power in a way which Pareto and Mosca found unacceptable, an moreover, they envisage the coming of a form of society in which, through the trans-cendence of classes, the domination of man over man will be overcome. Against these views they developed the thesis that in all societies, apart from perhaps the most simple and small-scale, there exists an irremediable division between those who exercise power – political elites – and those who are subjected to it; while the composition of elites may change, the domination of the mass by a minority of power-holders is as inevitable in a socialist society as it is in a capitalist one.

It is not the purpose of this chapter to examine such all-embracing issues; we refer to them here only briefly in order to trace some main strands in the history of the concept of elite, and thereby to develop a clear framework within which to analyse elites in British society. For while they made use of the notion of elite in order to criticize class theory, the classical elite theorists also retained the terminology of class, using 'political class' as equivalent to 'ruling elite', thereby helping to propagate conceptual confusions which have dogged work in this field for decades.

Following the classical elite theorists, the notion of elite has been used in three con-trasting contexts. First, the concept has been adopted and adapted by numerous author of the 'pluralist' persuasion who have used it to make arguments which diverge sub-stantially from those involved in both classical elite theory and in Marxism. In their writings, elites appear as fragmented groups each of whose power is limited by that of t others. Some of these writers recognize that a ruling class existed in nineteenth-century capitalism, but hold that it has long since become splintered into a series of distinct and often competitive elites. Second, the concept of elite has been taken up by certain authors – most notably C. Wright Mills – who have retained the idea of a unitary, dom inant elite, but have given this quite a different moral thrust from that of classical elite theory, the implications of which were expressly reactionary.[1] Mills, however, explicitly distinguished his 'power elite' from the Marxist 'ruling class' on the same sort of grounds that the classical elite theorists had done, namely that the latter notion assimilates political and economic power.[2] Finally, the term elite has been used by some Marxists themselves to refer to sectional groups within the ruling class.[3]

If all this were not confusing enough, the notion of elites has also been at the centre of a debate of a methodological kind: that concerned with problems arising from the empirical study of power. Writers of all persuasions have been interested in examining elite formations in order to analyse the distribution of power within national or local communities. But there has been no clear consensus as to how this should be accomplished. Many studies depend upon the so-called 'positional' method, in which elites are simply defined in terms of formal positions of authority, e.g. cabinet ministers, directors of large companies, high-ranking civil servants, etc. Others have been strongly critical of this sort of approach, and have insisted that authority must not be defined as power, and that elites should be regarded as clusters of effective power-holders, regardless of whatever formal authority they may hold.[4]

The controversies generated by elite studies have often been obscured by conceptual ambiguities, and in the face of these it is important to insist upon a number of elementary distinctions. In what follows the term 'elite' will be used in a very general sense to refer to those occupying high positions of authority within an organization, without in any way prejudging the issue of how far that authority reflects the actual power they may wield. Elites thus defined may be examined from three angles. First, in respect of processes of recruitment to elite positions: the kinds of social background from which the members of elite groups are drawn, and the factors that characteristically influence the progress of their careers. Second, in respect of the integration of elites: which includes an examination not only of the interconnections that exist between the members of particular elites and between different elite groups, but also an inquiry into the extent of ethical or ideological solidarity within and between elite groups. Finally, it is important to seek as far as possible to analyse in a direct way whatever types of power may rest in the hands of those in elite positions. The latter implies studying the capability of such individuals to take or to influence major decisions in conformity with definite sets of interests. But it is a mistake to suppose that this exhausts the study of power relations. Power is mediated not only through decision-making, but through structures which express asymmetries of life chances, and which form the parameters within which certain issues are 'decisionable',[5] and others are not. This reunites 'elite' and 'class', which in this discussion we shall treat as independent but equally useful concepts: the recruitment, integration and power of elite groups represent important aspects of class structuration, and it is fundamental to connect them with the reproduction of privilege in the class system.[6]

THE DISTRIBUTION OF WEALTH AND PROPERTY

Personal Wealth in General

Trends in the distribution of income between occupations are discussed elsewhere in this book but income is not as relevant to the study of elites as is wealth. To begin with,

wealth is a main source of income for the most affluent sections of the population –
much more so than vice-versa. But more important than this, wealth in the form of
property, in the means of production, is central to any examination of the relationship
between elites and classes.

The analysis of the distribution of wealth in Britain is a complex exercise, not least in
establishing a reliable set of data. Two modes of estimating the distribution of wealth are
ordinarily recognized, one depending upon information derived from estate duties at
death, the other using projections from investment income. The basic sources of data
are the Annual Reports of the Inland Revenue which utilize a system of mortality
multipliers in order to discover the division of wealth among the living from an investigation of the estates of those dying each year. Critics of these estimates have ranged
from those who argue that such figures overstate the degree of concentration by omitting
millions of adults who appear to own nothing,[7] to those who claim that the official
figures seriously understate the wealth of the richest who are able to conceal their real
worth by tax avoidance, settlements, trusts and similar arrangements.[8] Both positions
have been considered (and refuted) by Atkinson and Harrison in a sophisticated critique
of Inland Revenue methodology and statistics.[9] Writing in 1978 Atkinson and Harrison
argued that although official figures underestimated total wealth somewhat (£566 billion
in 1980),[10] the Revenue's estimates of the level of concentration were broadly accurate.
According to the official figures, the top 1 per cent of wealth-holders owned 29.9 per
cent of total wealth, whereas Atkinson and Harrison regarded estimates of between 31.4
and 34.7 per cent to be more accurate, depending on the method used to evaluate assets.[11]
More recent figures from the Inland Revenue (1981–2) give the top 1 per cent of wealth-
holders approximately one-quarter of total marketable wealth, and the top 2 per cent
about one-third (see table 5.1). The figures reveal little change in the officially estimated
distribution of wealth since 1974, and, in the light of the criticisms of Atkinson and
Harrison, probably underestimate the level of concentration. The richest 1 per cent
owned on average nearly £300,000 each while the poorest 50 per cent of the adult
population owned on average just over £1,500.

The data on the changing distribution of wealth over time, like those expressing the
level of concentration in any one year, must be treated with a good deal of caution. On
the face of it they would appear to suggest that, since the 1920s, there has been a marked
diffusion of wealth downwards. According to table 5.2 the share of total wealth held by
the wealthiest 1 per cent has declined substantially from 58 per cent in the period
1924–30 to 30 per cent in 1970 (Atkinson and Harrison's figures). The data published by
the Royal Commission on Wealth[12] show a more pronounced decline in the percentages
of total wealth held by the richest 1 per cent – from 69 to 28 per cent between 1911–13
and 1973, the share of the top 5 per cent decreasing from 87 per cent to 51 per cent over
the same period. However, much of the redistribution is accounted for not by an increase
in the share of wealth held by the bulk of the adult population, but by the improved
position on the part of the top 2 to 10 per cent of wealth-holders. The figures produced
by Atkinson and Harrison reveal that the share of the top 2 to 10 per cent of wealth-
holders moved from 29 per cent in 1924–30 to 39 per cent in 1970. Within these
percentiles, the share of the top 2 to 5 per cent of wealth-holders remained more or less
stable – 22 per cent in 1924–30 and 24 per cent in 1970. The share of the next 6 to 10
per cent of wealth-holders increased from 7 per cent to 15 per cent over the same period.

Table 5.1   Distribution of Wealth in the UK, 1980

Percentages and £s thousand million	1980
Marketable wealth	
Percentage of wealth owned by:	
Most wealthy 1 per cent of population [1]	23
Most wealthy 2 per cent of population	30
Most wealthy 5 per cent of population	43
Most wealthy 10 per cent of population	58
Most wealthy 25 per cent of population	81
Most wealthy 50 per cent of population	94
Total marketable wealth (£s thousand million)	566

[1] Aged 18 and over

Source: *Social Trends* (London 1983), p. 78.

Table 5.2   Trends in the Distribution of Wealth, 1924–70

| | England and Wales | | | Great Britain | | |
	1924–30	1936	1951–6	1960	1965	1970
	Percentages					
Top 1%	58	54	44	34	33	30
5%	80	77	72	60	59	54
10%	87	86	–	72	72	69
20%	93	92	–	84	86	85

Source: Atkinson and Harrison, p. 165.

Figures published by the Royal Commission broadly confirm these changing shares.[13]

The significance of the decline in the proportion of total wealth owned by the very wealthiest is a matter of much discussion. The most obvious and plausible explanation of a substantial amount of this transfer is that it reflects the passing of wealth *inter vivos* to a range of heirs and relatives. Whereas in the past the tradition of primogeniture remained the normal practice for wealthier families, now it is probable that wealth is spread among family members or vested in trusts and settlements which involve a whole range of kin members. Furthermore, estate duty could be minimized by wealth-holders divesting themselves of their possessions well in advance of death – a practice which might further depress the apparent wealth of the rich. Unfortunately, wealth statistics relate to individuals and reveal nothing of the kin-relationships that may exist between these individuals. The sociological significance of the redistribution of wealth indicated in the data would be different if it had occurred between unrelated individuals rather than, as is more probable, within an interconnected web of already prosperous families. In this sense Schumpeter was correct to emphasize that the 'family' is the real unit of class theory.[14] Here the family should be understood to be the economically effective kinship unit amongst the wealthy – to be discovered only through direct empirical investigation – rather than the 'nuclear family'.

The continuing significance of family relationships among the rich is indicated by evidence produced by Harbury and Hitchens on the importance of inheritance as the basis of large fortunes.[15] Their work, based on an examination of 734 top wealth-leavers between 1956 and 1973 (leaving £100,000 or more) revealed that 67 per cent had received an inheritance of £25,000 or more from their fathers. Such figures understate the significance of inheritance for they omit any reference to the transmission of property from one generation to the next, other than that from father to son. There is some debate over the extent to which 'self-made men' have been successful in joining the ranks of the very wealthy. Harbury and MacMahon report that there was 'no very marked change in the relative numbers of self-made men as distinct from those with inherited wealth . . . between the mid-fifties and mid-sixties'.[16] Rubinstein, however, detects an increase in the numbers of self-made millionaires since the end of the Second World War, their wealth often associated with the retail and property sectors of the economy. He suggests that between 14 and 35 per cent of millionaires deceased in the 1960s might be regarded as self-made, depending on how the term is defined. Perkin notes a decline in the 'self-made' man recently after a post-war eruption of nouveaux riches.[17]

The distribution of wealth is directly affected by the changing relative values of different assets, and the changing distribution of these assets among the population. For instance in 1976, 34 per cent of the wealth held by those possessing assets valued at £200,000 or more was accounted for by company shares whereas, in holdings of £10 to £20,000, shares comprised only 2 per cent. Also, a fall in the Stock Market valuation of shares, such as occurred in the early 1970s, has the effect of redistributing wealth, though there is no gain by those with little or no wealth. This phenomenon may be compared with the spread of house-ownership. In the 1980s well over half the dwellings in Britain were owner-occupied compared with less than 10 per cent in 1914. This very important transformation has created a band of wealth-holders whose main asset is their house. Of the wealth held by those with between £10 and £20,000 in 1976, 51 per cent was accounted for by houses. The rise in the value of houses relative to other assets in recent decades, allied to the diffusion of owner-occupation, has had a major impact on the redistribution of wealth. Some observers go so far as to claim that increases by the 'rest' at the expense of top wealth-holders are attributable, in the last two decades at least, to these two factors.[18] In both cases those who do not own shares (the vast majority) and those living in rented accommodation (approximately 40 per cent) gain nothing from a fall in the price of shares or the rise in house prices.

Figures on the distribution of wealth refer to all manner of possessions, but some forms of property are more significant than others with respect to class structure, since they yield substantial 'unearned' income and may also be associated with the control of companies. Capital investment is, in this sense, the key form of private property and its principal forms are deposits in banks and building societies, insurance policies, government bonds and securities, land and company shares. As the foundation of private enterprise capitalism, company shareholdings are of crucial significance and represent one of the most concentrated forms of wealth. Though the percentage of shares held by persons has fallen to 37.5 per cent of those listed in 1975, the top 1 per cent of wealth-holders owned 54 per cent of these shares, and the top 5 per cent no less than 80 per cent.[19] The pattern for the ownership of land (excepting that around houses) is broadly similar and the top 1 per cent of wealth-holders also hold nearly two-thirds of listed

British government securities held in personal ownership.[20]

It is often argued that even if wealth in Britain remains highly concentrated this is not of great significance for other aspects of privilege, since property ownership has declined significantly in importance, both in the means whereby individuals reach elite positions and in relation to the power they are thus able to command. This view is expressed in various convergent threads of social theory that centre on the idea of the obsolescence of private property in advanced, industrialized countries. It is not that property disappears, but it is claimed it becomes progressively less salient to the central features of the social organization of the advanced societies. However, it is the basic contention of this chapter that the unequal concentration of private wealth remains of fundamental importance in the social structure of Britain, with respect to each of the aspects of elite formation: recruitment, integration and power — and that these in turn reflect broader aspects of the class structure that also depend upon the continued significance of private property.

ELITE RECRUITMENT

Studies of the social backgrounds of elites in British society focus traditionally on the proportions of those in elite positions who were educated at public schools and Oxford or Cambridge, as compared to those having other types of educational experience. The method has received a considerable amount of criticism, some of it justified. It has been rightly pointed out that shared educational experience in a particular type of school does not necessarily generate a coherent ethos or culture among elite groups; nor, on the whole, does it follow that because individuals are drawn from a common and distinctive sort of background they will necessarily promote qualities that favour the interests of the social groups to which they belong. Yet despite these qualifications the study of the educational backgrounds of the members of elite groups is still of value. If it does not prove an overall coherence of views and interests, the demonstration of shared educational experience in such distinctive institutions does indicate one important element in the socialization of those who hold elite positions which is certainly relevant to a possible coherence.

Apart from this, available material about the social origins of the members of elite groups is often sketchy. The differentiation of public school education from the state sector of education provides a useful complement to whatever direct information about social origins is available. There is only a tiny minority of non-fee-paying pupils at public schools, and a public school education usually indicates that a person is not of lowly social origins, especially if he or she was educated at one of the more prestigious public schools. Since a high proportion of Oxbridge students have been drawn traditionally from the public schools (especially prior to 1939), it can be presumed that attendance at Oxford or Cambridge is also a general indicator of social background, although as a criterion this is obviously more fallible than attendance at public school. As a general indicator of social background, education is then of some avail, though it should be supplemented by other information.

There is available a range of studies of recruitment to elite positions in the major institutional spheres in Britain: the church, the armed forces, the judiciary, the Civil

Service, Parliament, and business.

The Church

Analysis of the social backgrounds of bishops shows that as recently as 1940 to 1959, 64 per cent were from families located in the higher ranks of industry, the professions, and the church or the aristocracy.[21] The contribution of landed families fell from over a third in 1860 to 2 per cent in 1960, but those bishops with professional or higher administrative backgrounds increased in number substantially. The proportion of bishops whose fathers were clergymen also increased over the same period, indicating that as the church has moved to the margins of secular power its elite has become more specifically ecclesiastical.

In 1960-2 there was a marked contrast between the episcopate and the lower clergy; only just over one-quarter of the latter had been educated at public school, compared with 85 per cent of bishops.[22] More recently, the public school component has declined a little. In 1983, 70 per cent of bishops had been educated at a public school, 73 per cent had attended Oxford or Cambridge, and 60 per cent both a public school and one of the ancient universities.

The Armed Forces

Otley's study demonstrated that in 1959, 39 per cent of army officers of the rank of lieutenant-general or above were the sons of 'land-owners or entrepreneurs', and 44 per cent the sons of higher professionals and managers.[23] In an overlapping study Abrams found that 32 per cent of lieutenant-generals or above in 1960 were either 'upper' or 'upper middle class' in origin, a further 28 per cent being traced to other professional or managerial origins.[24]

The army elite is dominated by those of public school education. In 1970, 86 per cent of officers of the rank of major-general or above had attended public school, a notably higher proportion than in 1939 (64 per cent). The percentage of officers educated at Oxford or Cambridge also rose from a mere 3 per cent in 1939 to 24 per cent in 1970. Only 8 per cent were graduates of other universities in 1970 – most of Scottish universities. The internal career provided by the Royal Military Academy, Sandhurst, has however retained the pre-eminent position.[25] In 1970 about one-third of major-generals or higher had been educated there. Sandhurst seems to be undergoing a definite widening of its recruitment base at the present time, a trend which is too recent to be reflected yet in the highest ranks, but is probably associated with the declining attractiveness or prestige of a military career. As Otley notes, by the end of the century it is likely that the army elite will be recruited from outside the ranks of the upper echelons of the class structure for the first time since the days of Oliver Cromwell. However, it is clear that the most prestigious regiments remain extremely selective in terms of social class when recruiting new officers. Between 1976 and 1978, of 73 new officers entering the Guards or Royal Green Jackets 62 had attended a small group of high status public schools. Not one attended a state school.[26] During the same period 75 per cent of candidates for entry to Sandhurst were rejected; yet 65 per cent of those from the most prestigious public schools were successful, compared with only 22 per cent of all candidates educated at other types of schools. The highest levels of the navy and air force are less solidly recruited from those of public school or Oxbridge background than the corresponding ranks in the army. Nevertheless, in 1971 two-thirds of the air force officers of the rank of air vice-marshal and above had attended public schools — a proportion virtually unchanged since 1939. Public school education is much less prominent in the navy, largely it seems because of the influence of Dartmouth Naval College, through which over half of the top leadership has passed.[27]

The Judiciary

Assessed in terms of social origin and educational background, the judiciary is probably the most exclusive of all elite groups in Britain. Brock's study shows that, whereas 67 per cent of High Court Judges sitting between 1820 and 1875 were of 'upper' or 'upper-middle' class backgrounds, the figure rose to 76.8 per cent for the period 1951-68.[28] Since the relevant information was unavailable for 14 per cent of the total, this leaves only 9 per cent who originated from what were designated as of 'lower-middle class' (8 per cent) and 'working class' (1 per cent) origin. These figures indicate a consistent and exclusive pattern of recruitment. Griffiths hints that a rather more broadly recruited population of barristers since the 1960s may provide a less narrowly drawn group of High Court Judges in the 1990s, but, as yet, Lord Justice Lawton's comment in 1975 that judges were 'drawn from all ranks of society' seems remarkably wide of the mark.[29] There is also evidence of increasing levels of internal recruitment between generations within the judiciary and legal profession as a whole.

Of those on the Bench between 1960 and 1969 well over three-quarters of High Court Judges received their education in public schools. Of the principal judges, 81 per cent received a public school education, a figure that has remained fairly consistent since the 1920s, although it reached a peak of 92 per cent in 1940-49. A striking feature of the data is the number of judiciary who were educated at ȏne of a handful of major public schools; in 1960-69 over 40 per cent of principal judges had been to one of these so-called 'Clarendon Schools'. Notably, nearly 80 per cent of High Court judges in office between 1960 and 1969 had attended Oxford or Cambridge, compared with 63.4 per cent of the 1900-9 cohort. Interestingly, the contribution of non-Oxbridge universities declined considerably during the first seven decades of the century. Certainly over this period the educational experience of High Court judges has become in this sense more uniform. However, there may be some slight hint of change in Young's figures based on an analysis of the educational experience of 31 judges appointed to the High Court between 1970 and 1975.[30] 68 per cent went to public school and 74 per cent attended Oxford or Cambridge.

The Civil Service

Alone among the institutions discussed here, entry to the Civil Service is based almost entirely upon success in public examinations. There used to be two methods of entry. Method 1 was the more traditional, and consisted of a written examination plus an interview. Method 2 was created after the Second World War, and involved a series of interviews and other techniques of evaluation; it has now wholly replaced method 1, following a period when they operated side by side.

Whether or not this is due to the use of examination as a method of selection, the Civil Service elite does emerge (with Parliament) as the most open, or it would be more apt to say, the least closed, of the professions analysed in this chapter. In 1967, 17 per cent of civil servants of the rank of Under Secretary or above were from manual work backgrounds; almost one-third had fathers in either manual or routine non-manual occupations. The proportion of higher civil servants from such relatively humble origins has risen steadily over the past half-century or so. Thus in 1929, 7 per cent of civil servants of equivalent rank to that just mentioned (Assistant Secretary and above) were from manual backgrounds, 12 per cent from manual plus non-manual origins combined.[31] The success of those from lowly backgrounds seems to be due mainly to promotion from the lower levels of the Civil Service, rather than a consequence of the examination system as such. There is some indication, however, that method 1 favoured those from less privileged backgrounds, and that therefore the abandonment of this method of entry will in some part diminish the chances of those from less privileged backgrounds.[32] The increasing penetration of the higher echelons of the Civil Service by those from less well-to-do homes has accompanied a decline in the proportion having a public school education. In 1939, 84 per cent of Under Secretaries or above had attended public schools; the comparable figure for 1970 was just over 60 per cent. The contribution of the grammar schools (which however underwent considerable reorganization after 1944) over this period rose from 6 per cent to 28 per cent. In contrast, the proportion of Permanent Secretaries who had attended a Clarendon school declined from 1 in 3 in 1950 to 1 in 8 in 1980.[33]

The influence of Oxford and Cambridge diminished much less than that of the public schools which indicates that an Oxbridge education has been of considerable importance to those entering the Civil Service elite from the state sector – with the exception of London, other universities barely appear in the picture. In 1970, 2 per cent of Under Secretaries and above had attended provincial universities, 10 per cent London University, and 69 per cent Oxford or Cambridge. However, it is possible this figure may decline for the percentages of Assistant Principals attending either Oxford or Cambridge fell from 85 per cent in 1960 to 57 per cent in 1970.[34] It is from Assistant Principals that the highest ranks of the Civil Service generally emerge. But on past form, the Oxbridge entrants may be expected to be more successful, especially those from Oxford. For instance, in 1977, while Oxbridge provided 30 per cent of all graduates holding the position of Principal or above, at the rank of Deputy Secretary and above, 74 per cent had received an Oxford or Cambridge education. In the Foreign and Commonwealth Office, the Treasury, and the Cabinet Office, the most prestigious of departments, 79, 68, and 54 per cent of those at Principal or above level were graduates of Oxbridge. In the same departments, the proportions of graduates having been educated at Oxford or Cambridge were 86 per cent, 77 per cent and 70 per cent respectively.[35]

Unlike the professions, the Civil Service has a more limited type of elite, but this does not seem to restrict recruitment to those with a privileged social background. The proportion of Permanent Secretaries who went to public school reflects the same trend towards a diminution in exclusive recruitment that appears at the lower level of the Civil Service hierarchy. There also occurred a marked dropping-off in the percentage of Permanent Secretaries coming from the leading public schools, and the proportion with a public

school background declined from 64 per cent in the 1900–19 period to 54 per cent in
the post-war years. However, the role of Oxford and Cambridge remained more important than in lower ranks; the proportion of Permanent Secretaries who attended one or
other of the ancient universities varied between 80 and 90 per cent between 1900 and
1963. By 1980, however, this figure had declined to 70 per cent. Such evidence leads
Kellner and Crowther Hunt to conclude that: 'today's mandarins tend to come from
families of great diligence and little prosperity, rather than great prosperity and little
diligence'. While the second part of this summary may be true, it would be misleading to
suggest that top civil servants are now drawn proportionally from all sections of the
population. As Kellner and Crowther Hunt themselves point out, public schools educate
less than 1 in 15 children but provide 40 per cent of applicants to the administrative
Civil Service, and secure 7 out of 10 of the top positions. They conclude that the recruitment procedures of the Civil Service Selection Board do 'favour a privileged background'.[36]

Parliament

A much greater variety of studies of the political elite has been carried out than any of
the other groups analysed in the preceding sections, and the material available on the
social and educational background of politicians is more complete and detailed than any
referred to so far. There have, of course, been massive changes in the nature of British
politics in the last hundred years, far too complex to detail here, but their basic pattern
in regard to social background is clear enough. There has been a steady decline in the
landed interest compared with the growing significance of MPs with links with the
financial, commercial and industrial sectors. This latter development has been counter-
balanced in part by the emergence of the Labour movement in Parliament springing
from the enfranchisement of the working classes.

The decline in the representation of landowning interests and the growth in the
importance of industrial and commercial elements affected both major parties (Liberals
and Conservatives prior to 1918); yet the process affected the Liberal Party most of all,
which by the turn of the century had been abandoned by most of the landowners. At
this time the Liberals were at the height of their success, but quite suddenly the number
of Liberal MPs dropped to 115 in 1919, and to 40 in 1924 as the Labour Party's parliamentary representation grew. During this period MPs linked to industrial and commercial
business interests moved into the ranks of the Conservative Party. Although the majority
of MPs and Cabinet members were now drawn from industrial, commercial and professional backgrounds, they shared certain social characteristics with those from landed
stock. In particular, attendance at public school and Oxford or Cambridge had become
an increasingly common feature of an MP's experience. The traditional channels of entry
into the higher political circles were thus strengthened and not weakened by this change
in the political elite.

The emergence of the Labour Party, in contrast, did introduce major changes in the
composition of the House of Commons and establish a new mode of access into national
politics through the Trade Union and Co-operative movements, and the Labour Party
itself. In 1906 all 26 Labour MPs were from manual, working-class backgrounds and in
1918 all but one of 57. Initially, this established a marked contrast in Parliament between

the social origins of Tory and Labour politicians, but this has been much less notable in recent Parliaments as the manual working-class element in the Parliamentary Labour Party has declined. Guttsman estimated that by 1970 only 27 per cent of Labour MPs were drawn from the working class compared with 43 per cent in 1945,[37] and in 1972 Johnson found that an increasing proportion of 'safe' Labour seats were going to candidates of middle-class origins.[38] He demonstrated that each succeeding cohort of candidates in the 1960s and early 1970s tended to be more middle class than the last. Johnson concluded that, within a decade or so, working-class participation in the political elite would be extinguished and that a working class 'effectively excluded' from direct political participation would be represented by MPs from the middle class and upwards in the social hierarchy. An analysis of the class structure of Cabinets confirmed this tendency. Between 1924 and 1935 over one-half of Labour Cabinets were working class in origin, while the middle classes contributed just over one-third. Between 1955 and 1970 the proportions were almost completely reversed — nearly two-thirds of Labour Cabinet members were drawn from the middle classes, while a third were of working-class origin.

However, returning to discuss the parties' elites in 1983, Johnson noted that the convergence of the 1960s, between the social profiles of the Tory and Labour leadership, had not continued.[39] The Labour victory of 1945 produced a generation of mainly middle-class, Oxbridge educated future leaders who later took control of the Party in the sixties and seventies. By 1983, however, the transformation of the Party's fortunes has been accompanied by a retrenchment of MPs with working- and lower-middle-class origins within the leadership to produce an elite that echoed that of the early forties.

Within the Conservative Party between 1918 and 1945 the social origins of MPs changed relatively little. There was a discernable move away from the very highest levels of class structure (though a strong upper-class element remained in the Tory ranks), the solid core of Conservative MPs being drawn from the upper ranks of the middle class as the sons of fathers who worked in the established professions: banking, commerce, industry and farming. Guttsman's analysis of the class structure of Cabinets confirms this trend. Between 1916 and 1935 the aristocratic share of Tory Cabinets stood at 36 per cent, whereas this figure fell to 21 per cent between 1955 and 1970. The percentages for 'middle-class' representation during these periods were 62.4 and 79, though in Guttsman's analysis these figures undoubtedly include many who were, on other criteria, non-aristocratic members of the upper class. Johnson argues that between 1974 and 1983 the Tory leadership has been changed by the elimination of the upper-class paternalists and their replacement by a mobile group drawn from the lower echelons of class structure. The bulk of the Cabinet is, however, still based around MPs drawn from the upper middle classes though some of its most influential members come from rather more modest backgrounds.

Analysis of the educational backgrounds of MPs demonstrates a marked difference between the Labour and Conservative Parties, though a less stark contrast at present than in the past.[40] As expected on the basis of the information on social background, a far higher proportion of Conservative MPs has been educated at public school than their Labour counterparts. However, in recent parliaments newly-elected Tory MPs have been drawn increasingly from the state sector (perhaps as beneficiaries of the 1944 Education Act). Between 1918 and 1974 three-quarters or more of Tory MPs had attended public school but this figure declined to 63 per cent in 1983.[41] The proportion of Conservatives who attended Oxford or Cambridge rose from 40 per cent during the inter-war period to 55 per cent in 1966, declining from then on to 44 per cent in 1983, as the numbers of newly-elected, Oxbridge educated, Tory MPs fell (33 per cent in 1983). By 1979 a quarter of Tory MPs had gained degrees at universities other than Oxford or Cambridge. The percentage of Conservatives attending both public school and Oxbridge, which hovered between 45 and 50 per cent between 1945 and the mid-1970s, appears to have declined in recent years. Between 1918 and 1935 76 per cent of Labour MPs had only received an elementary school education, 9 per cent had attended a public school, and 8 per cent attended either Oxford or Cambridge. With the introduction of compulsory secondary education so the proportion of 'elementary only' Labour MPs declined to less than one-tenth in the 1970s. However, the proportion of Labour MPs who attended grammar school rose from 15 per cent during the period between the wars to 52 per cent between 1951 and 1970, later declining to 40 per cent in 1979. Public school representation among Labour MPs moved to a peak of 25 per cent in the late fifties and early sixties and then declined to 8 per cent in 1979.[42] University attendance is far more common in the present era than in the past among Labour MPs. In 1945 15 per cent had been to either Oxford or Cambridge and 20 per cent to other universities; in 1979 the figures were 22 per cent and 40 per cent respectively.

In the present era, then, Tory MPs are far more likely to have attended a public school than Labour MPs though a public school education is not so dominant in Tory ranks as once was the case. Attendance at university is a far more common occurrence among MPs than in the past and it is twice as likely that a Tory MP will have attended Oxbridge than in the case of a Labour parliamentarian. Similarly, although universities other than Oxford or Cambridge are now better represented amongst Tory MPs, Labour MPs are much more likely to have attended a non-Oxbridge university.

The educational experience of Cabinets has differed substantially from that of MPs as a whole. A consistently higher proportion of Labour Cabinets have been educated at public school than the rest of Labour MPs. In 1924, 40 per cent of the Labour Cabinet had attended public school. After some vacillation this figure declined to 32 per cent in 1979. Similarly, Oxford and Cambridge were well-represented in Labour Cabinets at between 20 to 25 per cent between 1924 and 1950. This figure rose to 43 per cent in the 1964 to 1970 Cabinets, then declined to just over a third in 1979 (almost entirely Oxford).

Tory governments have been very narrowly drawn in terms of the educational experience of their members. Between 1951 and 1964, of thirty-three Tory ministers 90 per cent had attended a public school including a third at Eton alone, while 79 per cent had received degrees from Oxford or Cambridge (two-thirds from Oxford). Johnson detects a change since then with the fall of the 'patrician Oxford men'.[43] By 1979 the Etonian share in the Cabinet was down to 23 per cent, and Cambridge then outnumbered Oxford by 2 to 1 amongst the Tory ministers. After the Election in 1983, only one ageing Etonian remained in the Cabinet. In all, public school representation in the Thatcher government reached an all-time low for the Conservatives at 71 per cent, while the state sector contributed just over one-fifth of the Cabinet. The Oxbridge representation remained high at 76 per cent and just over two-thirds of the Cabinet had attended public school and Oxford or Cambridge.

Few MPs enter Parliament in the modern era without first embarking on another career. Again, the Conservative Party presents a more uniform picture than the Labour Party. In 1945, 47 per cent of Tory MPs had worked in the professions, while 37 per cent had been employed in the business sector. By 1974 those with business backgrounds had increased to 46 per cent and the professional element reduced to 35 per cent. During the same period farming remained well-represented at around one-tenth of all Tory MPs. Three occupations, barrister, director and farmer, provided over half of Tory MPs between 1945 and 1974.[44] Though the figures are not truly comparable (since they refer to the occupations held by MPs after, as well as prior to, their election), it is clear that these occupations are still well-represented in 1983. After the 1983 election, 48 per cent of Conservatives were directors, 28 per cent consultants or advisors, 25 per cent barristers or solicitors, and 12 per cent farmers. Mellors' figures show that between 1966 and 1974 the percentage of businessmen among new Tory MPs increased notably from 36 to 63. Directors accounted for approximately one-third of new Conservatives in 1974 and barristers nearly one-quarter. However, in 1983 a new breed of Tories appeared to emerge since only 18 per cent of new Tory MPs were directors, 16 per cent were barristers, and none were farmers. Many are drawn from teaching, journalism, accountancy, and 'consultancy and advising'. The proportion of solicitors (12 per cent) was much higher than among established Tory MPs (6 per cent).[45]

Analysis of the occupational backgrounds of Labour MPs reveals the decline of those who were employed as manual workers and an increasing professional element. The percentage of manual workers in the Labour ranks in Parliament declined from 28 per cent in 1945 to 12 per cent in 1974 while the professional representation increased from a third to over a half during the same period. By the early eighties nearly three-quarters of Labour MPs had professional occupational backgrounds. Employment in education has become far more common among Labour Members of Parliament, rising from 12 per cent in 1945 to 28 per cent in 1974, and then declining to 20 per cent in 1979. Thus, in the present era, Labour MPs are drawn in the main from a diverse selection of professions, especially the newer and/or less prestigious professions, though the Party has a small but declining working-class rump. Tory MPs have more homogeneous social backgrounds rooted in business and the more prestigious and established professions. The latest cohort of Tory MPs suggests that there is also a significant move into the Party of grammar school educated 'self-made' men − products of the extension of educational opportunity and affluence of the fifties and sixties.[46] In both parties service in local politics has become common proving ground.

Industry and Finance

In the course of the Cambridge elites study, material was gathered on the social and educational background of directors of the largest financial and industrial organizations in Britain over the years 1960–70. The companies studied included firms from each of the major sectors of industry − general manufacturing, shipping, oil, brewing, iron and steel, railways (up to 1948) − the largest clearing and merchant banks, and the major insurance companies (the latter after 1946). The financial directors were more consistently drawn from the 'upper class', as defined in the study, than their equivalents in industry. In both cases, there occurred a decline between 1906 and 1970 in the proportion of individuals of upper-class origin, but the trend was more consistent for industrial directors. Most of the change was accounted for by the increase in the percentage of directors, both industrial and financial, drawn from 'upper-middle-class' backgrounds; particularly important here was a rise in the proportion of those whose fathers were in a professional occupation. The data do indicate the movement into Britain's boardroom of 'career' managers, but these seem to be in the main from the modestly affluent section of the middle class. There is little indication of long-range mobility from the manual working class (between two-thirds and four-fifths of the population during this period). In this respect, directors of the largest companies which dominate the economy seem to be far more homogeneous in social occupation than the more diverse ranks of senior management.

A more detailed breakdown of the origins of those ranked as upper class in background shows that there has been a fairly consistent proportion of directors of aristocratic descent during the present century (that is the sons or grandsons of Barons, Viscounts, Earls, Marquesses and Dukes) although there has been a considerable change in the composition of the nobility since the latter part of the nineteenth century when truly industrial peers were first admitted to the House of Lords. Approximately 11 per cent of the industrial directors and 15 per cent of the financial directors in each annual sample prior to 1970 had such a family background. Similarly the proportion of directors who had inherited titles (not necessarily from their fathers or grandfathers) remained at around 12 to 13 per cent for industrial directors and 13 to 17 per cent for financial directors. Only in 1970 was there any evidence of a decline in the proportion of directors with aristocratic origins.

Table 5.3   **Directors with Fathers who were Directors, Proprietors or Partners in 'Large' Businesses, 1946–70**

	1946	1952	1960	1970
Industry	32.0	24.4	25.8	19.7
Finance	38.3	36.3	35.9	23.1

Source: A Giddens and P. Stanworth, Cambridge Elites Project (1971–4).

There is also some evidence of a decline in the proportion of directors whose fathers had themselves sat on the boards of, or were proprietors in, large businesses. Given the poor quality of information available in publicly available sources with regard to the comparative sizes of nineteenth-century industrial and financial enterprises, only data relevant to directors holding seats in the period after the Second World War is presented in table 5.3. From this fragmentary information it appears that the boardrooms that now constitute the apex of the private sector of the economy are more broadly recruited in the sense that their fathers are less likely to have been on the boards of major corporations themselves. However, when Hall and Amado-Fischgrund studied the chief executives of 120 large British companies at the end of the 1960s, they found that 70 per cent of their sample were the sons of business owners, executives and professionals, and less than 10 per cent were from the working class.[47] This broadly confirmed the findings of the Cambridge elites study which, focusing on only the largest companies, found chairmen to have more select social backgrounds than other members of the boardroom.

According to Perkin, 72 per cent of top company chairmen in 1970 were drawn from the upper classes.[48]

It seems reasonable to conclude that boardrooms have been rather more widely recruited in recent years than in the past. However, the broadening of recruitment has been largely restricted to the upper echelons of the class structure. There is little evidence that this elite has been similarly opened to individuals from the working- or lower-middle classes.

Table 5.4   Percentage of Directors Educated at Various Types of School and Oxford or Cambridge Universities (Birth Cohorts)

		1820–39	1840–59	1860–79	1880–99	1900–19	1920–39	Total sample
Unknown	I	43.8	26.5	20.5	14.8	8.9	11.1	16.7
	F	50.0	19.2	18.0	9.0	6.8	5.2	
Local grammar	I	3.1	5.4	3.9	13.3	10.5	13.3	7.1
Proprietary and Elementary	F	7.1	3.3	1.0	8.1	9.8	5.2	
Total	I	31.2	44.7	58.3	62.3	72.6	73.3	62.5
Public School	F	32.1	47.5	75.9	76.3	78.1	79.9	
Total	I	28.1	31.8	35.7	33.4	35.5	35.5	37.9
Clarendon	F	28.6	40.8	46.5	50.7	46.5	46.6	
Privately	I	7.8	11.3	6.0	2.3	0.7	0.0	3.9
	F	3.6	10.0	2.6	1.4	0.7	0.0	
Other	I	6.3	8.8	6.4	4.9	6.6	2.2	5.9
School	F	3.6	10.0	5.2	3.8	3.4	7.8	
Oxford or	I	22.0	28.0	32.9	33.1	48.3	42.2	40.2
Cambridge University	F	24.9	39.2	44.8	47.4	58.0	52.6	
Number of	I	64	204	283	263	304	45	1,163
Directors	F	28	120	194	211	295	116	964

Source: A. Giddens and P. Stanworth, Cambridge Elites Project (1971–4).

Analysis of the educational background of the business elite shows an overall trend towards the increasing significance of public school and Oxbridge education among both industrial and financial directors. Table 5.4 represents the distribution of types of school and university in the educational background of cohorts of directors born within the discrete periods indicated. The proportion of directors attending public schools has risen from about one-third in the first cohort to three-quarters in the most recent one. There is some evidence of the social differentiation of the City and industry in the consistently higher proportions of financial directors attending a Clarendon school in all cohorts but that of 1820 to 1839. The position of Eton is particularly notable, accounting as it does for approximately one-third of City directors in each annual sample taken this century. As in the case of public school education an increasing proportion of each succeeding cohort of directors attended either Oxford or Cambridge. Similarly there has been a tendency towards an education embracing both public school and Oxbridge. For instance in 1906 36.8 per cent of financial directors attended both a public school and Oxford or Cambridge; in 1970 the figure was 51.9 per cent. The chairmen of these boards have an even higher proportion of public school educated men and Oxbridge scholars among their number than do the bulk of the already selectively educated directors.

Therefore, despite the huge expansion of State education since 1870, and the increase in the number of places at 'redbrick' universities, the directors in our sample have been drawn from the narrow confines of the public school system and the universities of Oxford and Cambridge. This contrasts with Leggatt's finding that amongst *managers* employed in companies generally to be found outside the ranks of the very largest, grammar school representation had grown considerably, though at the expense of elementary and secondary schools since the public school educated managers had maintained their share.[49] Certainly grammar school products seem to be providing an increasing share of the top managerial pool from which a proportion of directors are drawn. Whether or not they will be successful in gaining access to the boardroom in anything but small numbers is doubtful.

Summary

The material described and referred to in the preceding sections is deficient in certain respects and does not provide a basis for any sort of precise comparison between the elites in different institutions. Nevertheless, a number of conclusions can be drawn from it and other relevant data with respect to the social origins and education of British elites:

1. Despite a recent broadening in the recruitment of specific elites they remain dominated by persons from privileged social backgrounds. The contribution of the upper classes to most elites has declined but remains significant. Increasingly, British elites are drawn from the upper middle classes, and, to a much lesser extent, the lower middle classes. Though the less prosperous sections of the population are contributing an increasing minority to elites, there has been little working-class penetration of these institutional elites, with the exception of Labour Cabinets and that episode of political history seems to be waning.
2. The public schools and Oxbridge continue to play a pre-eminent role in elite recruitment. The hold of the most prestigious schools is now less secure as minor and direct grant schools have become more important. However, it should be noted that schools which educate between 2 and 5 per cent of British children have usually provided 60 to 80 per cent of those holding elite positions. Conversely, the contribution of the state sector has always remained small. Oxford or Cambridge educations have become more common amongst most elites in the last eighty years or so. Only in the last decade has there been a slight reversal of this trend.

Furthermore, the proportion of individuals who have attended public schools *and* Oxford or Cambridge has remained stable or increased in most elites during this century.

3. It is generally the case, though not universally so, that the higher the level of what is to count as the 'elite' is placed in any of the institutions covered in this chapter, the greater will be the proportion having public school and/or Oxbridge backgrounds.

4. Though long-range mobility is rare, Oxford and Cambridge appear particularly important avenues for the small number of 'lower' class mobile individuals who gain elite positions.

5. British elites have been almost exclusively male though the classes from which they are differentially drawn consist of men and women. The pattern of gender discrimination is far more stark than that relating to class structure in respect to elite recruitment.

THE INTEGRATION OF ELITES

In order to analyse the integration of elites, it is not enough to discuss the ties which may exist between members of different elites today; for any such discussion must be placed against the sweep of social change that has brought about the centralization of the economy and the polity during the course of this century.

The Centralization of Economic Life

The levels of industrial concentration in the country today are very high, higher than in the United States, for example. Industrial concentration increased gradually in Britain from the later decades of the nineteenth century into the 1930s. During and after the Second World War the degree of concentration in the industrial sector of the British economy declined marginally, but since the middle of the 1950s it has climbed steeply. The top eighty companies by asset size in 1957 accounted for 53 per cent of the total net assets of publicly quoted industrial companies; ten years later, this proportion had increased to 62 per cent and the top three hundred companies accounted for some 85 per cent of the total. Much of this growth in the sixties and seventies is accounted for by merger activity as opposed to the internally generated growth of large firms. Indeed Hannah argues that between 1919 and 1969 mergers were the most important cause of increasing concentration. In 1970 the largest 100 firms in manufacturing accounted for 45 per cent of total net output (see table 5.5).[50]

It is more difficult to assess the concentration of financial, as opposed to industrial, assets. On the one hand it is clear there has been a process of institutional centralization reducing, for instance, the number of clearing banks from 16 in 1957 to 9 in 1983, dominated by the 'Big Four'. However, the number of banks (of all types) operating in the City has risen from approximately 100 in 1957 to 348 (many foreign) in 1978. There had also been significant changes in the assets held by banks. In 1957 assets of £8.5 billion were held almost entirely in sterling, whereas in 1978 65 per cent of the assets of £219 billion were held in foreign currencies.[51] These figures re-emphasize the

Table 5.5   Shares of the Largest 100 Firms in Manufacturing, Net Output, 1909-70

	Percentages		Percentages
1909	15	1948	21
1919	17	1953	26
1924	21	1958	33
1930	26	1963	38
1935	23	1968	42
1939	23	1970	45

Source: L. Hannah, *The Rise of the Corporate Economy*, p. 216.

City's international orientation and increasingly its international character (over half the assets of banks in Britain were held by foreign banks at the end of the 1970s.)

However, in recent years, financial institutions have become more significant within Britain as the owners and controllers of large amounts of company shares. In 1957 21 per cent of shares in UK companies were owned by financial institutions; by 1980 the figure had reached over 60 per cent.[52] Personal ownership of shares had dropped to just over one-third, though that ownership was highly concentrated in the top 5 per cent of wealth-holders. The ostensible diffusion of equity in the British economy resulting, in particular, from the activities of the pension funds and insurance companies in mobilizing the small savings of millions, is an illusion. As Minns demonstrates, the 'facts' of ownership conceal the concentrated control and management of these funds in a relatively small number of institutions. For instance he estimates that pension funds own 16.8 per cent of shares but control only 5.6 per cent (see table 5.6). On the other hand, banks and stockbrokers own a mere 1.1 per cent of company shares but effectively control 23.9 per cent, discretion having been passed from formal owners to the financial experts of the City.[53] In 1982 'over half' of British industry was reported to be formally owned by financial institutions and while this does not deliver the intricacies of industrial production into their hands it has enhanced the ability of the City to influence the general constraints under which industry operates.[54]

Analysis of interlocking directorships gives some sort of index, although an inherently crude and limited one, of the degree to which the rising level of economic concentration has been accompanied by the proliferation of connections among large corporations, and between industry and finance. The Cambridge elites study mapped the directorial connections between the top fifty quoted companies, railways (up to 1945), leading banks and insurance companies (after 1945) between 1906 and 1970. The results indicate a steadily increasing range of interconnections between the major corporations. In 1906 less than half of the 85 enterprises in the sample were connected by shared directorships, 34 organizations joined by 41 links making up the major network (6 other companies were linked in 3 separate pairs). The banks (especially the Bank of England) and railways figured prominently in these connections since only 16 of the top industrial corporations entered any of the networks. In 1970, by contrast, 47 of the industrial firms had entered the major network, 29 of them being linked to other industrial companies by at least one shared director. Moreover the banks and insurance companies

Table 5.6   Ownership and Control of Company Shares, 1975

	Percentages	
	Ownership	Control
Persons	37.5	29.9
Charities and other non-profit-making bodies	2.3	0.2
Stockbrokers (and jobbers)	0.4	6.3
Banks	0.7	17.6
Insurance companies	15.9	17.1
Pension funds	16.8	5.6
Unit trusts	4.1 }	11.1
Investment trusts and other financial companies	10.0	
Industrial and commercial companies	3.0	3.0
Public sector	3.6	3.6
Overseas sector	5.6	5.6
Total value of assets £44,560 million.	100	100

Source: R. Minns, 'The concentration of corporate power' in the *New Statesman* (24 October 1980), p. 11.

had sprouted a series of new links with industrial firms as well as with each other to become the most 'connected' elements in the network. In the 1970 sample, 73 out of 85 organizations in the study appeared in a network of 193 linkages (see table 5.7).[55]

Table 5.7   Interlocking Directorships, 1970

	Top 50	Clearing Banks	Merchant Banks	Bank of England	Shipping	Insurance	National-ised Industry
Top 50	(33)	37	24	6	4	27	5
Clearing Banks	37	(0)	5	0	4	16	0
Merchant Banks	24	5	(0)	4	3	13	1
Bank of England	6	0	4	–	0	1	1
Shipping	4	4	3	0	(0)	3	1
Insurance	27	16	13	1	3	(0)	5
Nationalised Industries	5	0	1	1	1	5	(0)
Total links	103	62	50	12	15	65	8
Total links including interlinks	136	62	50	12	15	65	8

Source: Cambridge Elites Study.

In a similar study of 43 large industrial and 27 financial companies, Whitley discovered 56 of the corporations to have at least one link with another company in the sample; in addition 62 were connected if other overlapping directorships in companies not included in the original 67 were taken into account.[56] Further work by Johnson and Apps in 1977 found that of the 200 top industrial companies and 35 largest financial corporations 160 were connected in an extensive network.[57] Likewise, L'isle Williams' very detailed work on the City demonstrates complex patterns of interlocking directorships between financial and industrial enterprises.

The significance of these interlocking directors is a matter of some dispute. Pahl and Winkler are sceptical of their importance while Useem, Scott and others[58] are more inclined to support Wright Mills' observation that:

'Interlocking Directorate' is no mere phrase: it points to a solid feature of the facts of business life, and to a sociological anchor of the community of interest, the unification of outlook and policy, that prevails among the propertied class . . . As a minimum inference, it must be said that such arrangements permit an interchange of views in a convenient and more or less formal way among those who share the interest of the corporate rich . . .[59]

However, the proper evaluation of the significance of interlocking directorships requires much additional information drawn from company histories on capital formation and policy orientation supplemented by, if possible, direct observation of directoral behaviour.

The Centralization of Government

The centralization of political life over the past century is demonstrated in various ways: in the concentration of political functions at both the local and national level; in the 'professionalization' of politics, and in the consolidation of the organization of the major party machines.

At both the local and national level there has been a centralization of political functions. The bureaucratization of the relationship between state and civil society has rationalized political relationships and delivered the formally enfranchised but (in terms of electoral, and local party, participation at least) increasingly indifferent citizen in the safekeeping of larger scale urban and metropolitan authorities and the massified national state. The scope and efficacy of 'local' autonomy in decision making has been much reduced and even in its present consolidated form may be further eroded as a central government seeks to reduce the economic independence of local authorities. The proposals by the Conservative government to impose financial penalties on local authorities that 'overspend', and even to abolish metropolitan authorities (introduced by an earlier Tory administration), may be interpreted as another step towards greater political centralization. As Patrick Jenkin, Environment Secretary, said: 'in this respect, we live in a unitary state'.

It may also be argued that the local importance and influence of MPs has been reduced. While MPs may spend a good deal of time in consulting with constituents and may intervene successfully on occasion on behalf of particular constituents on specific issues (miscarriages of justice, etc.), they have little individual influence over political decisions which affect the mass of their constituents (e.g. the effect of cuts in public spending on inner city areas). Generally they have little more at their disposal than persuasion in attempting to affect economic decisions about plant closure which have direct consequences for the level of employment in their constituency.

Over the course of the present century, politics has become more professional in two senses: being an MP is a more full-time occupation than it was formerly; and both the skills and tasks of politicians have become more specialized. In the past MPs often devoted much of their energy to involvements outside and in this sense politics at the national level was often the amateur pursuit of landed gentlemen and ambitious local entrepreneurs. However, in the present era, although nearly all MPs retain outside commitments of many kinds, politics is the main pursuit of the majority of those who sit in the Commons. The character of the House is now determined by those for whom politics is their principal professional concern. Those who used Parliament principally as a means of promotion in their extra-parliamentary careers are far fewer today. Politics has, in the post-war period, in Mellors' words 'established itself as a profession in its own right'.[60] However, it differs in important respects from other professions in that elections can terminate membership (although in most post-war elections two-thirds of seats have been 'safe') and that in crucial matters, such as voting, action is subject to strict party discipline.

Something of an index of the internal consolidation of the parties from the latter part of the nineteenth century up to the present day is provided by the incidence of 'Whip divisions' on Parliamentary legislation in the Commons. Thus, in 1836, when the Liberals formed the government, the party put its Whips on in less than 50 per cent of the divisions in the House; in 1908, when the Liberals were again in power, this had risen to 96 per cent. A similar rise is manifest for the Tory Party.[61] The proportion is marginally higher today in both Tory and Labour Parties. Whereas a century ago a considerable proportion of legislative proposals in Parliament were drafted and introduced privately, today private members' bills are unusual. Moreover the work of preparing legislative action has become largely bureaucratic and operates through the Civil Service. Within the Parliamentary Party organizations, the Cabinet and Shadow Cabinet have come to assume more and more pre-eminence — although the power of Cabinet Ministers is a matter of some controversy. The attempts to revitalize 'community politics', introduce the compulsory re-selection of MPs, and the proposal for the devolution of parliament may be seen as different responses to this pervasive process of political centralization.

Interconnections between Polity and Economy: the Business Interests of MPs

In the nineteenth century, and at least up to the First World War, the connections between property and political power were naked and direct. In both Tory and Liberal Parties more than a few MPs were wealthy men. The 1895 Parliament contained thirty-one millionaires as well as others nearly as wealthy. Rubinstein remarks: 'Since there were probably at that time 200 living millionaires in Britain, many of whom were members of the House of Lords, it seems likely that any State opening of Parliament during the period saw a greater concentration of Britain's economic wealth in one place at one time than ever in British history, and possibly in the annals of any legislature anywhere.'[62] Those in the Commons included a substantial number of 'regional entrepreneurs': Brunner and Mond represented Cheshire constituencies; Spencer Charrington, Mile End, Stepney; Harland and Wolff, Belfast North and Belfast East respectively. Today there are certainly fewer of the very wealthy who sit in the House of Commons; although since estimates of wealth depend upon the tracing of estates, it is not possible to build up an accurate picture for recent years. Of the post-war MPs for whom Rubinstein was able to gather information, none were millionaires and only two (both members of the Conservative Party) left over £500,000, in spite of the fact that the numbers in the country as a whole owning this much wealth or more have risen since the turn of the century. The advent of the Labour Party has obviously had an effect. Labour MPs are overwhelmingly of modest circumstances, even if they have included a few individuals of moderate wealth: four Labour members of the 1922 Parliament, for example, left estates of £50,000 or more.

It would be a mistake to suppose that the fact that there are fewer wealthy MPs today than there were a hundred years ago means that the erstwhile connections between political and economic elites have become severed, or that such connections are no longer important in the distribution of power in British society. Rather, they have become altered and ramified as a consequence of the twin processes of centralization of the political and economic orders. Of course, even in the nineteenth century the ties between political and economic elites were often indirect, or mediated through other institutions. One should not over-emphasize the significance of the presence of the wealthy in the forum of politics itself. Most played only a minor role themselves in parliamentary affairs, and very few rose to positions of any eminence in the Commons.[63]

Studies show that a complex series of direct ties exist between members of the Commons and industry in recent Parliaments. For instance, in the 1960–66 sessions of the House of Commons MPs held 770 directorships and 324 posts as chairman, vice-chairman or managing director of an industrial or financial organization. The vast majority – in the order of 90 per cent – were held by the Conservatives. Within the ranks of the Tory businessmen, there were elements of what Roth calls 'Political Lysenkoism' – on leaving the House of Commons a person passes on directorships in politically sensitive companies to fellow MPs.[64] Thus, when the chairman of the Wellman Smith Owen Engineering Corporation planned to retire from the House, Quinton Hogg (Lord Hailsham) became a director of the company; Daniel Awdry, Conservative MP for Chippenham became a director of the BET Omnibus Co. when Sir Herbert Butcher, another member of the Board, was defeated. The affinity between the brewing industry and the Conservative Party is well established. Mellors identified 25 Tory MPs who had direct connections with the brewery business.[65] The same author also noted that of 273 'sitting' directors elected between 1945 and 1974, 245 were Tories. Roth's analysis of business connections among MPs in the 1970s suggested that approximately two-thirds of Conservatives were directors or equivalents in some kind of business enterprise. Applying the same criterion to the whole House, Roth estimated that nearly half had business involvements of this kind. Furthermore, of those MPs with no directorships a proportion were barristers who acted for business clients, or held posts in the City. On the basis of this kind of data Johnson has argued that whatever the social and occupational characteristics of MPs, the majority had business connections. The business interest so constituted is almost the same size as a major party and more than twice as numerous as Trade Union sponsored MPs.[66]

The Broader Scope of Interconnections: Personal and Kinship Ties

In any context, the integration of elites depends upon two elements: the existence of
direct ties of association, friendship or kinship, that can potentially be called upon to
mobilize obligations; and the existence of a common culture of belief, habit, and outlook that mediates and facilitates new social contacts. We have noted earlier that a shared
type of social or educational background does not in itself generate shared interests.
But it is difficult not to accept that shared backgrounds provide a basis for ready communication for those exposed to them, and that the pre-eminence of the public schools
and Oxbridge, whose students only constitute a small minority of the total school and
university populations, is the medium of the perpetuation of an 'elite culture'.

Three principal means have been used in the literature on elites to attempt to examine
the forms of direct connection that exists between the members of elite groups; each is
only partially satisfactory. One method is to treat membership of private clubs as a mode
of personal networks and ties. Another is to work out whatever close kin connections
exist between elite members. These, however, only indicate potential types of association and influence that may be developed, rather than showing whether such connections are mobilized in any significant way by those involved. The third method, which is
to study the patterns of interaction among elite members, in particular sets of circumstances in which nominally hidden ties become revealed, turns up more detailed
information than the other two, but one cannot be certain how 'typical' the specific
situation studied is.

Private clubs, centred mainly in London, perpetuate into adult life the atmosphere
and even style of the major public schools and ancient universities. Nowadays they are
alleged to have declined into convenient venues for lunch, but access to the most
prestigious still remains a signal mark of social acceptance among the higher circles. On
the available, rather sketchy, evidence club membership is more diffused and less frequent
among elites than once was the case. In 1906, for instance, 57 per cent of directors
investigated as part of the Cambridge Elites study were members of one or more of eight
extremely select London clubs, compared with only 35 per cent in 1970. However,
another 22 per cent in 1906, and 34 per cent in 1970, were members of other metropolitan clubs, the number of clubs involved being considerably greater in the latter
case. This still creates the potential for a considerable number of interconnections
between large corporations through club membership. In Whitley's study of large financial and industrial enterprises, 28 per cent of the industrial directors and 46 per cent of
financial directors were members of one or more of eight 'prestigious and aristocratically
connected clubs'. This web of cross-cutting club membership created a network of
linkages between 29 of the 40 companies in the study.[67]

There is evidence of a decline in the membership of particular clubs by specific elites;
judges provide a good example. Of those High Court judges in office between 1900 and
1909, no less than 83 per cent were members of the Atheneum. However, of the 1960
to 1969 cohort, only 19 per cent enjoyed its hallowed portals. This, and other, data
suggests a less specifically oriented club membership on the part of elites than in the
past.[68]

Whitley's research also included an analysis of kinship connections between, rather
than within, companies. He found that 15 of the 40 industrial companies studied were

connected through directors mentioned in *Burke's Peerage* and *Burke's Landed Gentry*. This was only a loosely connected network, compared to that existing among financial organizations. In the case of the latter, 26 out of the 27 firms were thus connected forming a highly integrated network of ties. With the two types of organization taken together, 18 of the industrial firms entered the network with the financial companies (see figure 5.1). The studies showed that those industrial firms dominated internally by kinship networks – 'family firms' – stand apart from the networks that link most of the other organizations. It should be noted that this type of research, depending upon the two source books of the aristocracy and landed gentry, is only likely to provide a minimal estimate of the extent of kinship networks.[69] L'isle Williams' examination of the City also reveals a continuing tradition of inter-married kinship systems joining the best families and most prestigious finance houses in a complex and dense web of inter-connections. In this case the rationalization of economic organization has not eroded the significance of family. Nor are such networks fortuitous for L'isle Williams demonstrates that they are an outcome of conscious strategies designed to reconcile family control with the technical requirements of the most advanced forms of corporate operations.[70]

One of the very few pieces of research that attempts to develop an analysis of kinship connections from an examination of a particular set of circumstances involving top 'decision-makers', is Lupton and Wilson's now classic study of the Bank Rate Tribunal.[71] The Tribunal was set up to report in 1956 on allegations that an impending change in the bank rate had been leaked prior to the event. Lupton and Wilson tried to show how evidence given at the proceedings of the Tribunal indicated the importance of a 'culture of expectations' within which the everyday interactions between individuals prominent in finance, politics and public administration are carried out; shared beliefs and confidence in customary procedures gear to a range of informal contacts that cut across formal allegiances and relations of authority. A good example came out during the examination of witnesses. The Attorney General asked Lord Kindersley (a director of the Bank of England) why he, and not Mr Cobbold (the Governor of the Bank of England), had gone to see Lord Bicester about the possible effect of the bank rate rise on the Vickers issue and on relations between the 'City and the Bank of England'. Lord Kindersley replied: 'I consider it perfectly natural that I should be allowed to go and talk to a colleague at the Bank of England . . . I do not think that Lord Bicester would find it in the least surprising that I should come to him and say to him: "Look here, Rufie, is it too late to stop this business or not?", and: "I have discussed this with Jim – the Governor – and I am coming on to see you."'

Lupton and Wilson attempted to document in some detail the kinship connections of leading figures appearing in the Tribunal proceedings, for example Lord Kindersley and Cobbold. By tracing through parents, siblings, spouses and children they were able to build up 'family trees' that often joined up with one another. The categories represented included Cabinet Ministers and other Ministers of the Crown (A); senior Civil Servants (B); directors of the Bank of England (C); directors of the Big Five clearing banks (D); directors of merchant banks or discount houses (E); directors of insurance companies (F).

The Overlapping of Elite Groups

One cannot leave the topic of the integration of elites without considering, despite the

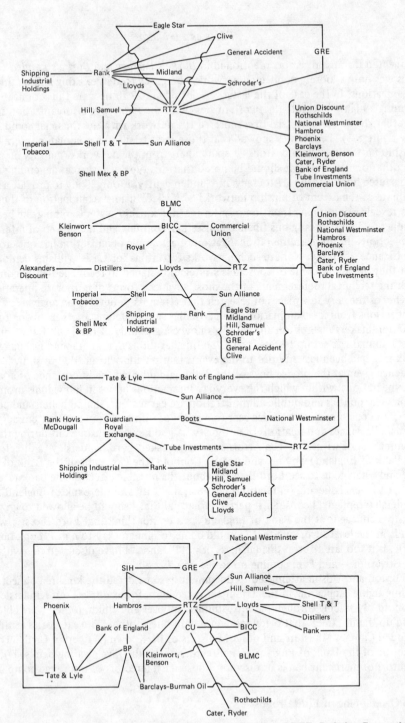

Figure 5.1 Kinship Relations of Hill, Samuel, Lloyds Bank, GRE and RTZ, Omitting Connections between Financial Institutions

Source: R. Whitley, 'The City and Industry' in P. Stanworth and A. Giddens, *Elites and Power in British Society* (Cambridge 1974).

lack of data, how far the interlocking of elite positions extends beyond the spheres of the political and economic elites themselves, and, second, what degree of individual move-ment there is from one elite group to another. At least two methods of examining elite linkage by way of multiple position-holding may be distinguished: first, that based on comparing annual samples which illustrate the extent of elite interlocking of particular years, and therefore when compared give an indication of how the pattern of interlocking has changed over time. The concern in this case is to discover those individuals who hold more than one elite position at a particular time. This method, however, fails to pick up those individuals who may never have held more than one elite position at any particular time, but who have held several such positions at different points in their career. Thus, while the first method might reveal the links current between the boards of large banks and the House of Commons in, for instance, 1906, it would not indicate the number of MPs who had once held seats on major boards, or vice versa. Similarly, it would not show the number of High Court judges for that year who had formerly sat as MPs. This latter type of information can only be revealed by the second method which concen-trates on the careers of individuals holding elite positions and reveals the extent to which elites have been joined through the movement of individuals from one sphere to another over a period of years. Given the lack of any comprehensive study for elite groups as a *whole*, there is no clear indication of how, and to what extent, the patterns of linkage of either type have changed over the years. However, though a comprehensive study is not yet available, there are data which relate to certain distinct elites and illustrate their links with other elites in both the senses mentioned.

Some of the most recent information emanates from work done in the Cambridge elites study. Changes in the pattern of interlocking between the companies and the banks themselves have been indicated above. Data dealing with the links between the boards of major companies and other elites are shown in table 5.8.

This documents a cohort analysis, taking the careers of individual directors in order to compare the extent to which they entered other elites during the course of their working lives (the figures for the last two cohorts are almost certainly under-estimates, since some of the directors included have not yet completed their careers and may still 'accumulate' other elite positions). It is apparent that the proportion (and number) of directors also taking a seat in the House of Commons has declined during the present century, a trend which undoubtedly reflects the increasing full-time, professional, nature of both pursuits. This form of institutional separation is reflected in the figures for par-ticular years. For instance, in 1906 90 of the directors of the major industrial corpor-ations sampled for that year had been, or still were, Members of Parliament. In 1970, the equivalent figure was 16. Among directors of the main banks sampled in 1906, 26 had been, or still were, MPs. In 1970, only 13 bank directors had this kind of connection with politics. However, the diminution in linkages between the House of Commons and the boards of the very largest corporations must be tempered by the information dis-cussed earlier which points to the continued connections of MPs in smaller business enterprises.

It is interesting to note, however, that the cohort analysis reveals that the proportion of both financial and industrial directors who actually served in a government adminis-tration in a ministerial rank rose for those born in each successive decade of the nineteenth century. Only for those directors born in the twentieth century do the figures reveal a fall in the 'ministerial connection', and as pointed out earlier, these latter figures are under-representations. The figures for connections between the economic and other elites may be briefly summarized. A higher proportion of each succeeding generation of directors has served on government advisory councils, commissions, etc. Likewise, service on the boards of universities and nationalized industries has become more common, both among succeeding cohorts of directors, and for annual samples taken over the last seventy years for universities, and since 1945 for nationalized industries. As universities have proliferated, so business has maintained its links with the academic world. Similarly, the public sector of the economy has drawn increasing numbers of board members from among the directors of the larger industrial corporations and banks. The numbers of directors who had achieved positions of Under-Secretary or above (or equivalent) in the higher Civil Service and similar posts in the Foreign Service and Diplomatic Corps, though always very low, have also increased. In 1906, 2 financial directors and 2 industrial directors had served in such a capacity; in 1970, 8 industrial directors and 12 financial directors (18 different men, since 2 had directorships in both the financial and industrial samples) had reached senior appointments in the higher Civil Service (or equivalent) prior to their directorships. The 'pantouflage' so characteristic of the French Civil Service appears to be entering the British scene. Kellner and Crowther-Hunt report that between 1974 and 1977, of 32 Permanent Secretaries leaving the Civil Service, 23 took up new posts (one died); 11 moved quite unambiguously into the private sector of the economy, including Lord Armstrong, former Head of the Civil Service, who moved onto the Boards of both the Midland Bank (Chairman) and Shell Transport and Trading.[72] Including 'quangos' and international organizations, a clear majority of these former Permanent Secretaries took up posts that depended on the patronage of either industry or Whitehall. Between 1974 and 1977 32 Under-Secretaries and above received permission from the government to enter private industry.

The proportion of directors who inherited a peerage and therefore had access to the House of Lords (prior to the introduction of Life Peerages) reveals a rise and later decline. Those directors having titles (from knights upwards) and sitting on boards also declined in number. In 1960 41 per cent of those on the boards of the financial companies included in the Cambridge study had titles of some kind; in 1970 the figure was 24 per cent. Similarly 134 directors in the industrial sample had titles in 1970 (17 per cent) whereas ten years earlier the number had been 143 (18 per cent). Large numbers of directors have, of course, had military experience as a result of two World Wars. However, the proportion of full-time professional soldiers amongst their number is small, and there appear to have been very few former members of the military elite on the boards of Britain's largest corporations.

The data for the links between the Cambridge sample of directors and other elite sectors between 1906 and 1970 are summarized in table 5.8. Table 5.9 illustrates the extent of multiple interlocking between directors who held at least three elite positions.

There appears to be no long-term study of links between the House of Commons and other elite groups. The work of Guttsman, Johnson and others has provided an enormous amount of information on the political elite, but we still lack a comprehensive account of the extent to which the patterns of linkage between political and other elites have changed. Our data on directors illustrates a sharp decline in multiple position-holding between Parliament and the top boardrooms. However, Guttsman's analysis of cross-

Table 5.8   Elite Interlocks: Percentage of Directors of Large Industrial and Financial Institutions with Links to other Elite Sectors (Birth Cohorts)

		1820-39	1840-59	1860-79	1880-99	1900-19[1]	1920-39[1]
House of	I	40.6	34.4	23.7	13.4	5.9	6.7
Commons	F	39.2	22.5	18.6	13.3	5.1	0.9
House of Lords	I	11.0	23.2	21.1	24.3	15.2	8.8
	F	7.2	15.0	22.7	24.1	17.3	6.2
Government advisory	I	4.7	6.4	7.4	8.8	4.7	4.4
councils etc.	F	0.0	2.5	8.2	10.4	5.4	0.9
Higher Civil Service	I	3.1	1.5	2.8	0.8	1.6	0.0
	F	0.0	2.5	3.6	1.9	4.8	1.7
Nationalized	I	–	–	0.7	6.9	12.9	8.9
industries	F	–	–	0.5	6.6	13.2	8.4
Military elite	I	0.0	1.0	0.7	2.7	0.3	0.0
	F	0.0	0.0	0.5	3.3	0.0	0.0
University board of	I	4.7	6.4	7.8	11.0	14.8	4.4
governors	F	10.7	4.2	7.2	13.8	16.3	6.0
Royal Commissions	I	15.1	16.1	27.5	24.8	27.6	4.4
	F	10.7	17.5	26.8	27.5	29.5	6.0

Note:
1 The careers of some of the directors in these cohorts have yet to be completed and the figures for the various linkages may yet rise.

Source: A. Giddens and P. Stanworth, Cambridge Elites Project (1971–4).

membership of elite groups between 1945 and 1955, in which members of the Labour and Conservative administrations figure prominently, demonstrates that the political elite was far from 'isolated' at that time.[73]

One type of linkage particularly subject to comment in the early decades of the twentieth century was that between the Bench and Parliament.

Laski observed that 80 of the 142 High Court Judges who occupied a position on the Bench between 1832 and 1906 had also been MPs.[74] Table 5.10 shows that this 'channel of entry' is much less common than once was the case. The proportion of judges with parliamentary experience in the House of Commons has fallen for each succeeding decade of the present century. The actual numbers, as opposed to percentages, show a rather less dramatic decline, with a rise in the most recent decade (25, 27, 24, 21, 18, 11 and 18 for each respective decade). In the earlier part of the century some of the judges had shown little inclination for a continuous involvement in the processes of law until elevated to the Bench. Some appointments were notoriously political; at the present time appointments are monopolized by practising members of the legal profession. Just as judges are less likely to have parliamentary experience, so too the number holding high

Table 5.9   **Multiple Position by Directors Holding at Least Two Other Elite Positions, 1906–70**

Number of directors		House of Commons	University Governors	Government Administration	House of Lords	Higher Civil Service	Nationalized Industries	Military Elite
(289)	House of Commons		27	89	63	2	4	1
(177)	University governors	27		18	25	6	18	1
(108)	Government administration	89	18		52	4	5	0
(187)	House of Lords	63	25	52		3	11	3
(47)	Higher Civil Service	2	6	4	3		4	0
(94)	Nationalized industries	4	18	5	11	4		2
(15)	Military elite	1	1	0	3	0	2	

Note: Of 289 directors who sat in the House of Commons, 27 were also on University Boards of Governors, 89 served in Governments and so on.

Source: A. Giddens and P. Stanworth, Cambridge Elites Project (1971–4).

Table 5.10   **High Court Judges who have sat as Members of Parliament**

On Bench	Percentages						
	1900–9	1910–19	1920–9	1930–9	1940–9	1950–9	1960–70
All high court judges	44.2	43.6	39.4	30.0	22.6	13.4	9.5
Principal judges	52.9	46.5	44.8	36.7	29.7	18.8	15.4
Number	57	69	61	70	80	82	128

Source: A. Giddens and P. Stanworth, Cambridge Elites Project (1972–4)

office in a government administration (usually Solicitor General, or occasionally Home Secretary) has fallen from 17.6 per cent (10 in number) for 1900–9 to 4 per cent (5 in number) for 1960–70. Of those High Court Judges who did sit as MPs, between one-half and two-thirds sitting in each decade investigated had been Conservatives. These figures present further evidence of a demographic separation of two elites, in this case the House of Commons and the High Courts. However, just as many MPs retain links with business so, too, the legal profession is extremely well-represented in Parliament. In the 1979–83 session 76 barristers and 26 solicitors in current practice were to be found in the Commons, a figure roughly in line with that for the last three decades. A fair proportion represent the legal interests of business corporations (40 per cent in 1972).

Class, Ethos and Elite

In his work on the very rich in Britain Rubinstein casts considerable doubt on the validity of a number of widely held assumptions about British social development.[75] He challenges the idea that during the process of industrialization the richest families were based in industry and manufacturing. Further, Rubinstein also rejects the notion that the nineteenth-century middle class were similarly linked to industrial enterprise. Finally, he does not accept the contention that the new manufacturing towns of the North of England gave birth to an industrial upper and middle class of sufficient size and wealth to constitute the dominant element in Victorian society. Rather, Rubinstein produces an impressive array of evidence to give weight to the idea that the very wealthy made their fortunes primarily in commerce and finance, and that while the lower levels of class structure were transformed by industrial work, the dominant element among the newly rich was involved in commerce and financial enterprises. Consequently, London retained, and increased, its position as the principal location of wealth making. At the heart of this process lay, not metropolitan industry, but the financial and commercial institutions of the City. Provincial industry, concentrated in the smaller towns surrounding Manchester, Liverpool and Leeds, failed to produce wealth and fortune on anything like the same scale. Landed wealth provided the largest fortunes right to the end of the nineteenth century though urban holdings in burgeoning cities often supplemented the traditional estates.[76]

Rubinstein goes on to suggest the sociological significance of these findings. Respectable society dominated by landed wealth was far more open to the newly rich based in commerce and finance than those associated with manufacturing. City and estate were linked by their Anglicanism, their public school and Oxbridge educations, and Tory politics. Industry, in contrast, was often non-conformist, frequently provincial, and inclined towards the Liberals. Gentility was compatible with the financial and mercantile pursuits but not with manufacturing. There were significant social obstacles to the penetration of the higher circles by new industrial wealth which did not affect the *nouveaux riches* of the City. As the century came to an end there was a degree of integration between the formerly distinct forms of wealth. Industrial wealth lost some of its Northern and/or provincial character and was incorporated into the social milieu dominated by landed, banking and mercantile wealth.

An important aspect of this process of amalgamation was the public school education.[77] The public school system expanded enormously in the nineteenth century in response to the growth of newly enriched classes. A truly national system of education for the sons of those belonging to the upper echelons of class was created. Characteristically, and significantly, these schools were much concerned to inculcate a particular set of values and attitudes. The production of 'Christian Gentleman' required long hours of classical rote learning in order to attain the traditional sign of gentility. A distinctive form of speech became almost universal amongst the upper middle and upper classes which even today remains a remarkably accurate, though not infallible guide to educational background. The cult of sport of the gentleman amateur, the stiff upper lip, and regular chapel moulded 'muscular Christianity' as bourgeois conceptions of competition were mellowed and 'civilized'. These schools, guided by reforming headmasters, were intended to produce men fit to run an empire, to administer the state, to be responsible *for* but not *to* the masses they governed by the divine ordinance of being British gentlemen. There was little or no place for science, or for 'moderns', or anything that smacked of the blood and guts of industrial production. The once proud captains of industry were replaced by generations of 'synthetic gentlemen'. This social emasculation of the industrial bourgeoisie has long been the subject of comment, and recently Weiner has revived the charge that it was this 'cultural highjacking' of industry which stood at the core of Britain's industrial decline.[78] While the weight given to such factors is a matter of some debate, the limited impact of industry on Britain's upper classes was remarkable (though in view of Rubinstein's findings it has become more comprehensible). Thus, the values of Britain's first capitalist class, a class of agrarian capitalists, withstood the emergence of industrial *nouveaux riches*, who in numbers and wealth were inferior to the more gentlemanly bankers, merchants and landowners of the British upper class.

It was from this peculiar class amalgam, particularly as embodied in public school reform and the slow transformation of major institutions such as the Civil Service, that the distinctive ethos associated with the upper echelons of British class culture emerged. The institutional variations of this outlook, in the officer corps, among higher civil servants, political leaders, leading business executives and judges, have a common stress. Firm leadership softened by a proper sense of service (paternalism), loyalty, conformity and initiative conditioned by self-restraint were highly valued. In all spheres technical expertise was regarded as inferior to the general all-round skills of the amateur – the embodiment of which was the administrator, politician or soldier who, with a mind disciplined by classical scholarship, could turn his hand to any task that might befall him. Such men expected the exercise of power to be governed by internalized norms rather than explicit rules – by a gentlemanly consensus. This mirrored their consensual view of society, politics and the economy, and produced between the holders of power, divided though they might be on certain issues, a mutual comprehension, a sense of homogeneity and integration. These values have been and continue to be important in the recruitment and career socialization of those who enter British elites, whatever their background. For instance the analysis, by Salaman and Thompson, of the selection and testing methods used on potential officer cadets leaves little doubt that class cultural factors feature prominently in the process of selection.[79] Arguing in a similar vein, Garnier notes that although more candidates from ordinary middle-class homes are entering Sandhurst, the principal ideological components of military life, deriving from quite a different style of life, remain secure.[80] Cultural uniformity is ensured by the strong class structure of the wider society, effective selection procedures which reject the ideologically incompatible, and the effectiveness of the army's own socialization procedures. In the Civil Service the 'cult of the generalist' owes its longevity in part to similar processes and has proved resistant to attempted reform.[81] This and other evidence emphasizes the importance of examining career socialization when analysing elites – especially when social and educational backgrounds are becoming a little more diverse.

ELITES AND THE DISTRIBUTION OF POWER

The study of social power poses notorious conceptual and methodological difficulties. Power, in a certain sense, only comes to light when used, although it nonetheless refers to a 'capacity'; it is not a constant, and can be 'expanded' by the development of new resources at the disposition of individual or collective actors. It is important to distinguish two aspects of power that are immediately relevant to the analysis of the relationship between class structure and institutional power or authority. The first is what Giddens has referred to as the institutional mediation of power, meaning by this the structure of power as represented by asymmetries in the reproduction of life chances across the generations. This refers above all to the general form of economy and state within which elite groups operate. The second, the 'mediation of control', refers to the capability of members of elite groups to take or influence policy decisions.[82]

Power in Industry: the Impact of Managerialism

The thesis of managerialism has a curious history in the literature dealing with corporate power. In the third volume of *Capital*, Marx discussed the rise of the joint-stock company and the concomitant 'obsolescence of the capitalist'. The fragmentation of shareholding in public companies, according to Marx, means that the control of the affairs of the firm passes out of the hands of the owners of property into the hands of managerial executives. For Marx, this signals incipient socialism within capitalism: the joint-stock company, although necessarily still operating within a framework of capitalist production, shows that the functioning of modern industry has no need of the capitalist. In Marx's writings, the internal transformation of capitalism is due to be complemented by the accession to power of a socialist labour movement that will complete politically the socio-economic changes that have already in substantial part transformed the system from within.[83]

In more recent writings on the topic, the presumed transfer of power to the managers is presented from a different aspect — not a socialist revolution as anticipated, but on the contrary as undercutting the possibility of such an occurrence. The modern debate over managerialism dates from the publication in 1932 of *The Modern Corporation and Private Property*, and James Burnham's account of the 'managerial revolution'.[84] Most of those who have contributed to the controversy from the non-Marxist side have (unlike Burnham himself) held that the coming to prominence of the propertyless managers produces a dispersion or fragmentation of economic power. Later Marxists who have entered the debate have mostly done so with the object of showing that the proportion of large companies that are dominated by their managers rather than their shareholders is much lower than that claimed by 'managerialist' authors.

The following points are relevant in assessing the issues involved in the protracted controversy over the internal distribution of corporate power, insofar as it relates to Britain:

1 Even among very large corporations, family companies are far from having completely disappeared: not all the mega-corporations are public joint-stock enterprises.

2 In public companies in which stock ownership is widely dispersed, ownership of relatively small blocks of shares can be sufficient to allow those who own them to intervene effectively in the running of the corporation. Moreover, forms of corporate control exist whereby such minority interests can yield a ramified set of powers extending through various companies: as where a minority shareholding controls a parent company that in turn holds interests which effectively dominate other subsidiary firms.

3 There is a difference between 'power' and 'administration'. It is certainly the case that among the large corporations the old-style entrepreneurial company is rare, and that

day-to-day administration of the firm is in the hands of directors and executives. But it still may be the case that propertied interests can intervene when they feel it necessary to do so, and thus that they ultimately control the policies followed within the company.

4 Not all stock carries voting rights, and there may be concentrated ownership of voting shares where non-voting stock is dispersed among a large number of un- enfranchized shareholders.

5 There is a growing amount of institutional stock ownership in large companies in Britain, especially insurance companies. The intertwining of firms through insti- tutional ownership is very difficult to trace out, but may represent one of the most significant mechanisms in the modern economy whereby ownership of private property is tied directly to economic power.

The nature and forms of economic control obviously are likely to vary by type of company and perhaps by industrial sector. But some general conclusions seem warranted as outcomes of the debate on managerialism. The original claims of those who, following Berle and Means, have held that the ownership of private property is now only of marginal significance to corporate power within large companies, can really no longer be sustained. It seems undeniable that the picture is more complex than such authors tend to suggest: and indeed that managerial positions can be used to accumulate property that can then yield an extended range of power. Certainly the advent of the large corporations and the fragmentation of shareholding does not express a movement beyond the capitalist structure of the enterprise itself, as is frequently suggested. If, in many large companies, directors are not themselves major shareholders in those companies, never- theless most own shares in some form which ensures that their interests are not too discrepant from those of property owners in the means of production as a whole. And the companies whose fortunes they direct necessarily operate within a framework of profit- making and the sustaining levels of investment.[85]

The voluminous literature dealing with managerial themes depends for the most part upon reference from statistical material. Nyman and Silberstone combine this kind of approach with information derived from the intensive case-studies of twenty large British companies and further work on the top 250 firms.[86] They identify proprietory control of a company by reference to three criteria: the percentage of votes held by a known individual, institution or cohesive group; the percentage of votes owned by the board of directors and their families; and the identities of the Chairman and Managing Director, their relationship to the firm's founder and his family. Nyman and Silberston regard that 5 per cent or more of voting shares delivers potential control of a company to the owner of such a stake. Their emphasis on the roles of Chairman and Managing Director is justified, they contend, since it is they who normally exercise discretion in the appoint- ment and dismissal of senior management. The investigation of the 250 largest UK companies yielded a minimal 56 per cent which could be so defined as owner-controlled. Of these 126 firms, 77 were controlled by the shareholdings of either their Boards of Directors or family chairmen or managing directors (see table 5.11). Compared with Sargant Florence's study completed in 1951 there had been an increase in owner- controlled companies — a finding quite contrary to managerialist contention of the secular rise to pre-eminence of professional propertyless managers.[87] Further, there

Table 5.11   Owner-controlled and Management-controlled Large Companies

Rank in Times 1000 by turnover	Number of companies owner-controlled	Number of companies management-controlled	Total	% owner-controlled
1 – 50	23	19	42	54.7
51 – 100	24	19	43	55.8
101 – 150	22	15	37	59.4
151 – 200	19	20	39	48.7
201 – 250	24	13	37	64.9
251 –	14	12	26	53.8
Total	126	98	224*	56.25

* Some companies were excluded on the ground they were foreign-owned, were subsidiaries of other companies, or failed to meet certain criteria in relation to asset size or sales.

Source: S. Nyman and A. Silberston, 'The ownership and control of industry', *Oxford Economic Papers*, Vol. 30 (1978).

appeared to be no greater incidence of management control among the top hundred or so companies that dominate the private sector of the industrial economy. In a related piece of work which explored the stages of control through which large corporations have passed, Francis also noted the continued significance of owner (and often family) control.[88] However, he also points to the growing ownership stake of financial institutions. A detailed examination of seventeen firms employing criteria of control similar to those employed by Nyman and Silberston revealed that six could now be classified as controlled by financial institutions. In L'isle Williams' work on the City the continuance of family control is shown to be quite compatible with the most advanced forms of corporate operation. Within the major Accepting Houses the significance of kinship is not an anachronism but part of a conscious strategy of organizational transformation which has given the private shareholder control over capital far in excess of that which is formally their own. Minns' work, mentioned earlier in the chapter, also demonstrates that the extension of institutional ownership has done little to ameliorate the capitalist orientation of investment managers. These studies throw considerable doubt on managerialist assumptions about the ownership status of large-scale industry and the behavioural consequences purported to follow from 'management' control.

There are few studies of the actual operations of power inside companies, but one such is reported by Pahl and Winkler.[89] These authors concentrate on relations between the board-room and other managerial staff rather than on those between shareholding interests as such. They are particularly concerned to point to the insufficiencies of previous research, arguing that it has typically identified the holding of office with effective power and contacts between the members of elite groups (e.g. interlocking directorships) as signifying mutual influence. In analysing decision-making at board level, they distinguish two types of boards of directors – 'pro-forma boards' and 'functioning boards'. The first has only a nominal existence, in accordance with legal requirements; it plays no part in the actual running of the company and may perhaps not even meet at all.

Pro-forma boards are characteristic of business organizations dominated by a single individual or a tiny minority of oligarchs – who may be members of the same family in a family firm, a block of shareholders, or a small group of managerial executives. A functioning board is one which does not participate as a collective entity in the government of the affairs of the corporation. But Pahl and Winkler emphasize that functioning boards usually possess only limited power. 'Any group which purports to be an instrument of decision-making in any institution, yet only meets once a month or less, as most boards do, is inevitably cast in the role of gatekeeper, weighing proposals for future action, letting some go through, rejecting others. Unless it organizes and exerts itself in a way we never observe, the initiative passes over to individuals or to a permanent secretariat/management.' Most of the matters that come before the board are 'pre-packaged' by managers and executive directors in such a way as to manipulate the information available about the proposals; thus, what the board tends to do is merely to ratify decisions that are actually taken from below.

Pahl and Winkler argue that their research carries direct implications for the managerialism debate. Most contributors to the controversy, they claim, have treated property rights as equivalent to control, without differentiating between such rights. They suggest a distinction between 'allocative' and 'operational' control. The first refers to the power to distribute economic resources, the second to what we have earlier called the 'administration' of such resources. Allocative control may derive from ownership of capital, but need not do so. It is particularly important, they point out, to notice that not only managers but also propertied interest may take advantage of the diffusion of shareholding within large public companies. Thus, asset-strippers deliberately buy up scattered holdings in such a way as to enforce take-overs; and institutional investors, whose allocative control is now very considerable indeed, come to dominate companies in which their actual stock-holdings are relatively small.

Scott locates the core of upper class (or business or property class) within the directorate of the largest British companies and banks.[90] He argues that the executive focus of the propertied class is to be found amongst those who participate in the strategic control of those companies that constitute the monopoly sector of the British economy (the top 1,000 – but predominantly the top 250 companies). Scott is at present engaged in the analysis of the capital histories of the major companies, particularly with the patterns of capital allocation and control in order to identify those who are responsible for the major features of corporate policies. Such work will highlight the managerial reorganization of the propertied class around the network of large-scale impersonal corporations. Family property vested in a whole range of enterprise by means of a diversity of shareholdings in British and foreign companies links the personal world of kinship with the impersonal and bureaucratic management of giant enterprises. While family remains an important dimension of upper-class structuration, political and economic primacy within the propertied class now lies with those who control the commanding heights of the corporate world.

Relevant here is Useem and McCormack's work on business leadership in Britain.[91] Using a wide variety of materials derived in part from interviews with a cross-section of those who occupy senior positions in the UK's largest and most prestigious industrial corporations and banks, they argue that they have located a core of businessmen whose orientation is towards the welfare of the business class as a whole rather than any particular sectional interest. This contrasts with the businessmen interviewed by Fidler who in general occupied a lower position in the business hierarchy (usually managing smaller companies than those in Useem's sample) and consistently put the interests of their own company first.[92] Useem and McCormack contend that the business leaders they have located perform an important function in the pursuit of business interests, broadly conceived, attempting to conciliate between corporations when overt and unsavoury clashes occur. These men are realistic in recognizing the permanence of such conflict but also see the possibility of a degree of co-ordination and cohesion. In so doing they promote what the authors term a 'class wide rationality'. Such business leaders constitute the politically dominant sector of business, having frequent contact with government and the Civil Service — characteristically their formal positions of authority are located on the boards of the largest corporations and banks, and their careers usually involve an active role in the CBI or similar employers' organizations.

Based though it is around formal bureaucratic positions within the largest corporation, the organization of this grouping is essentially informal and vague. However, Useem and McCormack argue that it is the most authoritative voice of business despite its loose and elusive identity. It is to this inner circle of business that the government turns when seeking the ear and advice of the corporate sector.

Power in Politics: Parliament, Cabinet and Civil Service

Bagehot's celebrated portrayal of government in *The English Constitution* has for many years provided a focus for analyses of the distribution of power within Parliament. Bagehot diagnosed as the 'efficient secret' of British politics the significance of the Cabinet as fusing legislature and executive. The role of the Cabinet and the power wielded by its members, as contrasted with that of MPs in general on the one hand, the Prime Minister and the Civil Service on the other, have remained subjects of chronic dispute. The growing pre-eminence of the Cabinet after the closing decades of the nineteenth century was clearly in substantial degree the outcome of the internal consolidation of the parties within Parliament, and the strengthening of party discipline. The Cabinet has become not a committee in and of the legislature as a whole, as Bagehot represented it, but the apex of the party's organization — 'a committee of the party chosen by the Prime Minister from Parliament'.[93] A Cabinet secretariat, responsible to the Prime Minister, was only created for the first time duirng the First World War.

No one now doubts that the power of the ordinary MP to influence government policy, whether their own party is in or out of power, is limited indeed. But there is considerable disagreement as to how far the power of Cabinet Ministers themselves has been eroded by the twin-influences of Prime Ministerial and Civil Service power. It is difficult to deny that the dominance of the Prime Minister within the Cabinet, although of course always subject to variabilities of personality, has grown over the past seventy years. Lord Morley's much quoted characterization of the position of the Prime Minister in the Cabinet — 'primus inter pares' — today appears less than adequate. The formal authority and certainly the effective power of the Prime Minister has expanded with the centralization of party politics. The range of the Prime Minister's patronage within Parliament includes not only the twenty or so Cabinet Ministers themselves, but also about sixty junior ministerial posts. The number of ministerial appointments has grown steadily over the decades of this century. In the Conservative administration of 1900, 42 of the 402 Tory MPs held ministerial positions. In 1983 the Government team numbered 85.

So long as the Prime Minister retains the general support of the Parliamentary party, these rights of patronage enable even a moderately forceful leader to wield a great deal of power over the formulation of general policy. Surveying the role of the Cabinet, the most plausible conclusion, at least in the post-World War Two period, is that policy is dominated by what Crossman called 'Prime-Ministerial government'. Crossman quoted Lord Home: 'Every Cabinet Minister is in a sense the Prime Minister's agent – his assistant. There is no question about that . . . If the Cabinet discusses anything it is the Prime Minister who decides what the collective view of the Cabinet is. A Minister's job is to save the Prime Minister all the work he can. But no Minister could make a really important move without consulting the Prime Minister . . .'[94] The Prime Minister not only is able to control the organization of the Cabinet through his or her rights of patronage, he or she is also able to determine the agendas in Cabinet meetings. The 'Information control' that Pahl and Winkler speak of in regard to board meetings in business organization is applied from two directions so far as Cabinet Ministers are concerned – from 'above' through the control of the Prime Minister, and from 'below' through the channelling of information on the part of Civil Service advisers.

Until well into the nineteenth century, the higher posts in the Civil Service were patronage appointments, staffed by relatives or friends of Ministers and other MPs whose political support was deemed necessary to the government. The fall of the government was likely to mean that some leading Civil Servants lost their appointments; also promotion within the Civil Service was in some degree tied to the success or otherwise of the political parties. As a consequence, the Civil Service was dependent upon Parliament and in terms of the formation of policy decisions, undoubtedly very largely subordinate to it in terms of power. The modern Civil Service, as a professional organization, dates effectively from the reforms instituted by Robert Lowe in 1870, which replaced patronage by competitive examinations administered by the Civil Service Commission, and formally separated off the members of the 'administrative class' from those at lower levels. As the Civil Service has become more professional, it has increased enormously in size, while the Cabinet has remained virtually the same size. In 1980 there were 2,000 Assistant Secretaries and above, including 150 Deputy Secretaries, and 50 Permanent Secretaries alone. The stability and permanence of the Higher Civil Service today contrasts with the transitional status of Cabinet Ministers, who are reshuffled fairly frequently and may lose their Cabinet membership even when their party is in power. This proved an important element in the Civil Service's successful defence of its own interests when faced with the proposed reforms contained in the Fulton Report – in particular to undermine the 'cult of the generalist' and to unify the class structure of the Service.

A former Conservative Cabinet Minister aptly expressed the contrast between the 'temporary' politician and the permanent office:

> One of the very first lessons my Permanent Secretary thought fit to teach me was 'whatever you may think of me or any other Civil Servant here, you cannot sack us'. I had no desire whatever to sack any of the Ministry of Agriculture Civil Servants, all of whom I had learned to admire. But I was amazed to find that in fact a Minister had no individual control over his staff, from the newest joined junior clerk or typist right up to the top.[95]

The limited range of knowledge most Ministers possess of technical aspects of matters with which they must deal and the shortness of time in which they are in charge of particular departments, drastically confines any initiatives they might be able to take in modifying pre-existing viewpoints or policy orientations in Whitehall. The possibility of Ministers becoming anything remotely approaching 'tycoons' in the sphere of business is negated by these elements; unlike business leaders, a Minister has no authority to either promote, transfer or dismiss the staff with whom he works. The range of 'information controls' used to present issues in specific ways seems to be potentially much greater than is possible in most industrial settings. Moreover, a Minister simply cannot devote most of his time to the administration of the affairs of the Department which he leads, as an executive director in business enterprises can do, since he must spend a considerable time in the House of Commons replying to questions, and dealing with his general duties as an MP. It is contact between Civil Servants, rather than between Cabinet Ministers as such, that preserves co-operation between different Departments in Whitehall — such contact often being mediated through the Treasury which, as the Department most responsible for economic questions, has become central to the co-ordination of the Civil Service as a whole.

So far as the distribution of power in the higher circles of the British polity is concerned, then, it would seem most plausible to conclude that power is normally concentrated in the hands of the Prime Minister, often acting in conjunction with an 'inner circle' of trusted advisers, usually drawn from the Cabinet but not operating significantly within the sphere of official Cabinet meetings, and associated with small numbers of Civil Service officials. This is not to suggest, of course, that these constitute an integrated circle with an internally consistent outlook; the power of Whitehall may be used to blunt ministerial initiatives that emanate from the Prime Minister. But the Cabinet functions more as what Headey has termed an 'inter-departmental battleground' rather than as 'a forum for collective deliberation on policy'.[96] As Crick has remarked: 'The evidence is great that the Cabinet no longer makes policy and that, in any case, little reliance is to be put on the old concept that the Cabinet represented a kind of coalition of the diverse forces from a great party and was, therefore, in itself an effective check on the powers of the executive.'[97]

The State, Economy and the City

During the present century, especially since the Second World War, there has been an enormous expansion and proliferation in the activities of the state. In no area of national life has this been more important than in the economic sphere. The crude data give some indication of this process although they fail to specify important developments in the structural relationships between state and economy. In 1914, for instance, public expenditure represented a mere 14 per cent of GNP, a figure which passed 50 per cent in the mid-1970s. At that time the output of nationalized industries accounted for just over one-tenth of GNP and the public sector employed more than 1 in 3 of the labour force. State purchases from the private sector amounted to 12 per cent of total output in 1970 and current and capital expenditure by central and local government on goods and services rose by 24 per cent in real terms between 1971 and 1981, by when they accounted for 21 per cent of GNP.

The first two decades after the Second World War were characterized by the emergence and consolidation of a Welfare State reflecting particular features of the organization of capital labour and government in Britain.[98] At the heart of this Keynsian compromise lay the attempt to reconcile the demand from a well-organized and politically influential Labour movement for raising real wages, improving welfare benefits, and full employment, with the requirements of capital for a sustained process of accumulation. Prominent features of this effort to ameliorate the contradictions between capital and labour in a growing economy were large scale increases in public spending, taxation and public sector employment. In theory at least, the growing significance of public spending gave the government the potential to influence aggregate demand by varying current and capital expenditure through adjusting taxation and money supply. In this manner the deleterious consequences of the business cycle, rising unemployment and prices, and fall in production were to be offset through government manipulation of the general economic climate. The resulting fractured economic tempo gave rise to the uniquely British experience of the 'Stop–Go' economy.

The economic policy preferences of successive governments carried the mark of City influence. The close relationship between the Bank of England and the Treasury facilitated the ability of the City to protect and maintain those conditions on which its international commercial operations depended, and one such, prior to the emergence of the euro-dollar market (and other 'stateless' currency), was a strong governmental commitment to the continued international role of sterling and defence of its value. The Bank of England was (and is) able to marshal a formidable array of financial expertise in exerting control over monetary policy. It is in effect the City's representative in Whitehall. This influence, in part, explains why the financial sector has never been required by government to play a more direct role in financing a long-term programme of industrial expansion. Neither has industry in general asked for funds from the City, since short-term and expensive credit (among other factors) has encouraged industrial companies to supply most of their own investment. In this respect Britain contrasts with Federal Germany and France in the preference for fiscal manipulation of broad economic variables over a more centrally-directed process of planned industrial development in seeking economic growth. However, the policy choices of British governments should not be viewed solely as expressions of the influence of the City for they also evidence the failure of industry to develop an organizational basis from which to present government with viable political alternatives.

By the 1960s it had become clear that, despite a period of growth unprecedented in British experience, the national economy had performed relatively poorly compared with its major international competitors. This was especially the case in comparison with those nations in which co-ordinated and consistent plans of industrial expansion had been implemented to stimulate the growth of a free-market economy on the basis of a controlled flow of investment. Rather timid attempts were made to promulgate a policy of planning and the beginnings were made to create an institutional basis for the rationalization and re-organization of the industrial sector. In 1961 a Conservative government introduced the National Economic Development Council, a tripartite body including representatives of capital, labour and government, through which government could consult and seek advice in the formulation of economic policy. This movement towards a 'corporatist' strategy of governmental action was further exemplified by the formation of the Industrial Reorganization Corporation by the Wilson government in 1966. Though its task was only vaguely demarcated, the IRC acted on the assumption that the units of production in British industry were, in many cases, too small to compete effectively on the international market. As the government's merchant bank, the IRC encouraged mergers and rationalization in what were regarded as critical sectors of industrial production. This experiment was a notable mix of government, business and Civil Service and initially received some support from business. However, as it developed a capacity for independent action, so too its brittle popularity waned. In 1972 it was declared 'out of control' and abolished by the Heath government before the latter's brief embrace with the 'corporatist' mentality.

None of these attempts to amalgamate the organs of representation and intervention in order to legitimate government-led industrial reorganization made much impact on the bureaucratic hegemony of the Treasury and the Bank of England. The planners remained truly marginal men, institutionally isolated from the real centres of policy formation, and unable to shake the primacy of fiscal considerations in matters of economic policy. The sanctity of the balance of payments and the international role of sterling indicated the continued unwillingness or inclination of British governments to impose conditions on the City which might directly benefit industry and involve the state in a more interventionist role in the revitalization of industry.

In the 1970s the British state began to encounter a major fiscal crisis even though its revenues were bolstered by oil revenues from the North Sea. A failing economy, growing unemployment and the expanding financial, welfare, defence, etc., obligations of the state introduced another phase of British political economy. Once again, fiscal policy was utilized to produce a 'solution' to the economic afflictions of the day. An attempt has been made to combine control of the money supply with public spending cuts. This has exacerbated unemployment, 'disciplined' the labour force, and weakened Trade Unions, thus lessening the need to continue the historic compromise that marked relations between labour and capital in the era of the 'post-war settlement'. Furthermore, it has become increasingly difficult for nationally-based institutions such as Trade Unions to counter the political demands of the business sector, since in many major British companies overseas operations are becoming a more significant aspect of their corporate activity, and the City has always enjoyed a degree of autonomy from the state of the national economy. The re-emphasis by government on the centrality of the market (privatization), the strong commitment to the free flow of capital, and the changing priorities of government spending reflect both the low ebb of the labour movement and the primacy of the internationally-oriented sector of the businesss world — 'multinationals' and the City.

The investigation of the City has much to contribute to an understanding of the 'structuration' of the British upper classes. As Rubinstein has demonstrated, the City has been, and remains, the most important centre of wealth creation for the rich in Britain. Not only is the City the principal source of wealth for the upper classes, it is also the main institutional location for the servicing of their wealth. Merchant banks, for instance, now derive much of their influence from their strategic importance in organizing, administering and advising on, the movement of capital in the private, and in some cases public, sectors of the economy.

The growth of the euro-currency market, the expansion of contractual savings, the merger boom of the sixties and seventies, expensive and restricted credit policies, all enhanced the influence of the City. Of the top 1,000 companies, 600 utilize the services of the Accepting Houses (17 in number) with regard to their capital structure, the raising of credit and the rationalization of their operations. As L'isle Williams observes, City institutions are one of the main agencies through which capitalist rationality is translated into corporate action.[99] However, this is not to argue that finance 'runs' industry. Rather in their dual role of advisers and investors merchant banks exert and diffuse pressure for increased profitability and capital growth, and thereby constrain the policy choices available to industrial corporations. For instance, Minns argues that the phenomenal increase in institutional shareholding, especially by pension funds, has created a situation in which decisions that have long-term implications for productive industry are taken on the basis of short-term financial considerations emanating from the City. One consequence is the tendency of pension funds to invest in very large, established, corporations rather than smaller companies that are a higher initial risk but might have greater potential importance in the development of a new industrial structure for Britain's ailing economy. Pension fund management also directs investment increasingly toward the financial sector itself. In relation to the domestic economy the provision of long-term loans for houses contrasts with the predominance of short-term credit in the productive sector, a notable contrast with Japan.[100]

The growth of the institutional ownership of shares, the relative prosperity of the City at a time when much of British industry is in decline, and the dramatic increase in overseas investment has renewed the debate about the relationship between industrial and financial corporations. A number of brief points are worth mentioning. As Minns has convincingly argued, versions of the finance-capital argument that depend on the purported fusion of financial and industrial capital do not stand up to close examination. Rather, British capitalist development has been characterized by a division of interests between the worlds of finance and industry, reflected not only in distinct modes of operation and organization, but also in diverse styles of life of their denizen. The City has generally enjoyed a superior access and mutuality with the government when compared with industry. In part, this is related to Britain's central role in the growth of a world economy, the importance of Empire, and the social compatibility of metropolitan finance and Whitehall. In consequence of these and other factors, the maintenance of those conditions associated with the optimal operation of the City institutions have been long-established as the *sine qua non* of responsible government. In contrast, concern with the optimization of industrial production has had lower priority (except in war-time) especially when it seemed that such considerations might clash with the interests of finance.

In correcting what he shows to be misconceived notions of the City's role in the British economy, Ingham emphasizes the commercial, as opposed to financial, operations of City firms.[101] The commercial interests and operations of the City preclude the direct control of industrial production, as implied in many models of finance capitalism, and also provide the essential element in the symbiotic relation of government and the square mile. Thus Ingham stresses:

> ... many of the City's 'banking' activities are fundamentally *commercial* practices insofar as discounting or short-term lending pre-empt any *financial control* of the borrower by the intermediaries.[102]

The commercial transactions in money, shares, commodities and services create a market structure directed toward a rapid turnover of saleable assets. Throughout most of its history City institutions have been neither interested in, nor organizationally equipped for, the direct control of industry. Yet, the international role of the City has required the maintenance of an over-valued sterling and the free flow of capital, commodities and commercial services with deleterious consequences for the health of industry. As one of the principal centres of international banking and commerce, the City has a great stake in retaining untrammelled access to the world economy, even if this imposes further burdens on British industry.

CLASS AND ELITES

Debate on the usefulness of the term 'elite' was a central element in a well-known exchange between Poulantzas and Miliband.[103] In *The State in Capitalist Society*, Miliband attempted to rebut the idea that the property-owning ruling class of nineteenth-century capitalism had become displaced by an amorphous set of elites. It has never been true, Miliband argues, that in modern capitalism the capitalist class has actually 'governed', and he quotes Kautsky to the effect that 'the capitalist class rules but does not govern' since 'it contents itself with ruling the government'. In this way modern industrial capitalism differs from earlier types of society where the dominant class actually ruled directly. Thus while businessmen have often themselves participated, and still do participate quite extensively, in the immediate exercise of governmental power, political and economic elites have largely separate personnel. But the social composition of these and other major elite groups, judged in terms of similarity of background, experience and values, shows that elites in the advanced societies today still compose a unitary dominant class. 'In an epoch when so much is made of democracy, equality, social mobility, classlessness and the rest,' Miliband says, 'it has remained a basic fact of life in advanced capitalist countries that the vast majority of men and women in these countries have been governed, represented, administered, judged, and commanded in war by people drawn from other, economically and socially superior and relatively distant classes.'[104]

For Miliband, therefore, the concept of elite is not incompatible with that of a 'ruling' or 'dominant' class, but can in fact be used to underpin the latter, by showing that elites have a similar class background and display a general unity in outlook or beliefs. Poulantzas on the other hand argues that a satisfactory analysis of problems of class domination, in relation to the state, can only be undertaken if the elite concept is criticized and abandoned. In Poulantzas' words, social classes and the state are 'objective structures' which cannot be reduced to inter-relations between individuals or even groups. Miliband, for example, criticizes managerialist theories by indicating that managerial executives, even where nominally 'property-less', are still profit-seeking in their actions. But, says Poulantzas, neither the existence of capitalism, nor of a dominant capitalist class, are predicated upon the actions or motivations of individuals; they concern instead structural properties of the social system. In the same way, similarities in the social composition of elite groups, divisions and conflicts between elites, and the degree of participation of industrialists in the operations of government, do not establish the existence of a dominant class: that class is an expression of the overall structure of society as a totality. The state in fact may serve the interests of the capitalist class most effectively when the 'ruling class' is not the 'politically governing class', since the ambitions of particular groups, for example, of industrialists, may be inimical to the interests of the survival of the system as a whole.

Miliband's reply to this critique is to suggest that the concept of elite can be detached from the perspective of those who have made the most play with it (the original elite theorists and political pluralists), and turned back against them. Moreover, he adds, Poulantzas still talks about elites, albeit within a different terminology, referring to 'fractions of the dominant class'. It is important, when examining the claims of managerialists, to analyse the behaviour and motives of managers precisely to show in what ways these are constrained by the broader imperatives of the society of which they are a part. Poulantzas dismisses the composition of elites, and what their members do, as of no account; but if we do not study them, we will have no way of analysing the dynamic character of class relationships. We have to avoid a 'structural super-determinism'.[105]

This debate raises general questions of social theory that cannot be tackled here: such as how ideas like 'structure' and 'structural effects' might be most appropriately understood. So far as the use of the term 'elite' in relation to that of 'class' is concerned, it seems perfectly possible to accept Miliband's points without denying the significance of the substance of those made by Poulantzas. Classes are correctly regarded as properties of the social totality, insofar as they express definite forms of alignment between economy and polity: 'private property' here is of fundamental importance both for supplying a legitimating framework of contract and exchange, and for providing the material medium of investment, price and profit in the economic system. But the particular form of the groups and group relations that become consolidated round class divisions, i.e. the nature of class structure, is influenced by a variety of factors, including ones specific to the particular development of a given society. These have to be studied directly, at any level of the class system. The dimensions of elite group formation analysed in this chapter thus represent basic aspects of the structure of the dominant class, but are not by any means exhaustive, since a more comprehensive account of class domination in British society would have to relate them to a broader institutional setting.

Notes to Chapter 5

*   This chapter is a revised version of that written with Anthony Giddens for the first edition of this book.

1   For an examination of the changing use of the term 'elite' see P. Bachrach, *The Theory of Democratic Elitism* (London 1969)

2   C. Wright Mills, *The Power Elite* (London 1956), p. 277.

3   R. Miliband, *The State in Capitalist Society* (London 1969).

4   These issues are discussed at length in A. Giddens, 'Elites in the British class structure', *Sociological Review* (1972); and the same author's, *The Class Structure of the Advanced Societies* (London 1973).

5   Giddens (1973), ch. 9.

6   The concept of structuration is elaborated in Giddens (1973), ch. 6.

7   See G. Polanyi and J. B. Wood, *How Much Inequality?* (London 1974).

8   See M. Meacher, 'Wealth' in N. Bosanquet and P. Townsend (eds), *Labour and Inequality* (London 1980).

9   A. Atkinson and A. J. Harrison, *The Distribution of Personal Wealth in Great Britain* (Cambridge 1983).

10   *Social Trends* (London 1983), p. 78.

11   Atkinson and Harrison, *op. cit.*, p. 123.

12   *Inland Revenues Statistics* (London 1982), p. 68.

13   *Royal Commission on the Distribution of Wealth*, Report No. 1, Cmnd. 6172 (London 1976).

14   J. Schumpeter, *Imperialism and Social Classes* (New York 1960), p. 113.

15   C. D. Harbury and D. Hitchens, *Inheritance and Wealth Inequality in Britain* (London 1979).

16   C. D. Harbury and P. C. MacMahon, 'Inter-generational wealth transmission and the characteristics of top wealth-leavers in Britain' in P. Stanworth and A. Giddens (eds), *Elites and Power in British Society* (Cambridge 1974); C. D. Harbury, 'Inheritance in the distribution of personal wealth', *Economic Journal* (December 1962).

17   W. D. Rubinstein, 'Modern Britain' in W. D. Rubinstein (ed.), *Wealth and The Wealthy in the Modern World* (London 1980), p. 87; and H. Perkin, 'The Recruitment of Elites in British Society since 1800', *Journal of Social History* (Winter 1978).

18   Alan Day, *The Observer* (22 September 1974).

19   *An A to Z of Income and Wealth* (London 1980), p. 26.

20 D. Massey and A. Catalano, *Capital and Land* (London 1978), p. 11.
21 D. M. J. Morgan, 'The Social and educational background of diocesan bishops of the Church of England, 1860–1960', MA thesis (University of Hull 1961).
22 K. Thompson, 'Church of England bishops as an elite' in P. Stanworth and A. Giddens (eds), *Elites and Power in British Society* (London 1974).
23 C. B. Otley, 'The Social Origin of British Army Officers', *Sociological Review* (1970).
24 P. Abrams, 'Democracy, technology and the retired British army elite' in S. P. Huntingdon (ed.), *Changing Patterns of Military Politics* (New York 1962).
25 D. Boyd, *Elites and their Education* (Windsor 1973).
26 K. MacDonald, 'The persistence of an elite: the case of British Army Officer cadets', *Sociological Review* (August 1980).
27 Boyd, *op. cit.*, pp. 82-3.
28 J. Brock, 'The social class origins of the judiciary of the superior courts (1820–1968)', MPhil thesis (University of London 1972).
29 J. A. G. Griffiths, *The Politics of the Judiciary* (Glasgow 1979), p. 29. Lawton's comment is contained in the Riddell Lecture published in the *Law Society Gazette* (18 June 1975).
30 H. Young in *The Sunday Times* (5 October 1975).
31 R. K. Kelsall, 'Recruitment to the Higher Civil Service: how has the pattern changed?' in Stanworth and Giddens, *op. cit.*, p. 172.
32 *Ibid.*, p. 177.
33 Figures up to 1970 from Boyd *op. cit.* for 1980 from *Who's Who* (London 1980).
34 P. Kellner and Lord Crowther-Hunt, *The Civil Servants* (London 1980), p. 193.
35 *Ibid.*, p. 192.
36 *Ibid.*, p. 124.
37 W. L. Guttsman, 'The British Political elite and the class structure' in Stanworth and Giddens, *op. cit.*
38 R. W. Johnson, 'The British Political Elite 1955–72', *European Journal of Sociology* (Summer 1973).
39 R. W. Johnson, 'Cambridge in command', *New Society* (3 March 1983).
40 In addition to the contributions of Guttsman and Johnson, data from C. Mellors, *The British MP*, has also been utilized in this section.
41 'Tory MPs: the new breed', *Labour Research* (August 1983).
42 This figure of 8 per cent is probably an underestimate since it is taken from the *Times House of Commons* (1979) which, as Mellors argues, tends to understate the contribution of public schools, see C. Mellors, *op. cit.*, p. 11.
43 Johnson (1983), *op. cit.*, p. 347.
44 Mellors, *op. cit.*, ch. 5.
45 'Tory MPs: the new breed', *Labour Research* (August 1983), p. 208.
46 *Ibid*, p. 208.
47 D. Hall and C. Amado-Fischgrund, 'Chief executives in Britain', *European Business*, 20 (1969).
48 Perkin, *op. cit.*, p. 231.
49 T. Leggatt, 'Managers in Industry: their background and education', *Sociological Review*, Vol. 26 (1978).

50 L. Hannah, *The Rise of the Corporate Economy* (London 1976), p. 216.
51 R. Minns, *Take over the City* (London 1982), p. 31; and *Pension Funds and British Capitalism* (London 1980).
52 R. Minns, 'The concentration of corporate power', *New Statesman* (24 October 1980), p. 11.
53 *Ibid.*, p. 11.
54 *New Statesman* (16 April 1982), p. 3.
55 P. Stanworth and A. Giddens, 'The Modern Corporate Economy: Interlocking Directorship in Britain, 1906–70', *Sociological Review*, 23 (1975).
56 R. Whitley, 'The City and Industry: the directors of large companies, their characteristics and connections' in Stanworth and Giddens (1974), *op. cit.*
57 P. S. Johnson and R. Apps, 'Interlocking directorates among the UK's largest companies', *Antitrust Bulletin*, Vol. 24 (1979); M. L'isle Williams, 'Continuities in the English Financial Elite', paper given to BSA/PSA conference (January 1981).
58 R. Pahl and J. Winkler, 'The economic elite: theory and practice' in Stanworth and Giddens (1974), *op. cit.*; M. Useem, 'Classwide rationality in the politics of Managers and Directors in the US and Great Britain', *Administrative Science Quarterly*, Vol. 27 (1982); J. Scott, *The Upper Classes* (London 1982), p. 141.
59 C. W. Mills, *op. cit.*, pp. 122-3.
60 C. Mellors, *op. cit.*, p. 124.
61 S. H. Beer, *British Politics in the Collectivist Age* (New York 1967).
62 W. D. Rubinstein, 'Men of Property: occupations, inheritance and power' in Stanworth and Giddens (1974), *op. cit.* See also his *Men of Property: the wealthy in modern Britain* (London 1980).
63 Rubinstein in Stanworth and Giddens (1974), *op. cit.*, pp. 168-9.
64 A. Roth and J. Kerbey, *The Business Backgrounds of MPs* (Parliamentary Profiles) (London 1972), p. 12.
65 C. Mellors, *op. cit.*, p. 71.
66 R. W. Johnson (1973), *op. cit.*
67 R. Whitley in Stanworth and Giddens (1974), *op. cit.*
68 Data from the Cambridge Elite Study.
69 R. Whitley in Stanworth and Giddens (1974), *op. cit.*
70 M. L'isle Williams, 'The social and economic significance of the British merchant banks', paper presented to EGOS conference (York 1981).
71 T. Lupton and C. S. Wilson, 'The social background and connections of "top decision makers"', *Manchester School*, 27 (1959).
72 Kellner and Crowther-Hunt, *op. cit.*, pp. 194-6.
73 Guttsman (1963), *op. cit.*, p. 361.
74 H. J. Laski, *Studies in Law and Politics* (London 1932), p. 168.
75 In addition to Rubinstein's work cited earlier the following should be consulted: 'Wealth, elites and class structure in modern Britain', *Past and Present*, No. 76 (1972); 'The Victorian middle classes: wealth, occupation and geography', *Economic History Review*, Vol. 30 (1977).
76 See P. Lindert, 'Who owned Victorian England?', Working paper No. 12, Agricultural History Centre, University of California, Davis.
77 On public schools, see J. R. de S. Honey, *Tom Brown's Universe* (London 1977);

T. Bamford, *The Rise of the Public Schools* (London 1967); R. Wilkinson, *The Prefects* (London 1964); E. C. Mack, *The Public Schools and British Opinion*, 2 Vols (New York 1975).

78 M. J. Wiener, *English Culture and the Decline of the Industrial Spirit 1850–1980* (Cambridge 1981).

79 G. Salaman and K. Thompson, 'Class culture and the persistence of an elite: the case of army officer selection', *Sociological Review*, Vol. 26 (1978).

80 M. Garnier, 'Changing recruitment patterns and organizational ideology: the case of a British Military Academy', *Administrative Science Quarterly*, Vol. 17 (1972).

81 Kellner and Crowther-Hunt, pt. 1; R. Putnam, 'The Political Attitudes of Senior Civil Servants in Western Europe', *British Journal of Political Science*, Vol. 3 (1973).

82 Giddens (1973), *op. cit.*, pp. 275–94.

83 K. Marx, *Capital*, Vol. 3 (New York 1967), pp. 436-41.

84 A. A. Berle and G. C. Means, *The Modern Corporation and Private Property* (Chicago 1932); J. Burnham, *The Managerial Revolution* (New York 1941).

85 For the 'decomposition of capital' argument see R. Dahrendorf, *Class and Class Conflict in Industrial Society* (London 1959). For a contrary view see P. Burch, *The Managerial Revolution* (Lexington 1972).

86 S. Nyman and A. Silberston, 'The ownership and control of Industry', *Oxford Economic Papers*, Vol. 30 (1978).

87 P. S. Florence, *The Logic of British and American Industry* (London 1953).

88 A. Francis, 'Families, firms, and finance capital', *Sociology*, Vol. 14 (1980).

89 Pahl and Winkler in Stanworth and Giddens (1974), *op. cit.*

90 Scott (1982), *op. cit.*, ch. 6; see also his *Corporations, Classes and Capitalism* (London 1979).

91 M. Useem and A. M. McCormack, 'The Dominant Segment of the British Business Elite', *Sociology*, Vol. 15 (1981).

92 J. Fidler, *The British Business Elite* (London 1981).

93 B. Crick, *The Reform of Parliament* (London 1981), p. 34.

94 R. H. S. Crossman, 'Introduction' to W. Bagehot, *The English Constitution* (London 1964).

95 R. H. Dorman-Smith, *The Times* (25 June 1954).

96 B. W. Headey, *British Cabinet Ministers: the roles of politicians in executive office* (London 1974).

97 Crick, *op. cit.*, pp. 37-8.

98 See B. Jessop, 'The transformation of the state in post-war Britain' in R. Scase (ed.), *The State in Western Europe* (London 1980).

99 L'isle Williams, 'Social and economic . . .', *op. cit.*

100 Minns (1982), *op. cit.*

101 G. Ingham, 'Divisions within the dominant class and British "exceptionalism"' in A. Giddens and G. Mackenzie (eds), *Social Class and the Division of Labour* (Cambridge 1983).

102 *Ibid.*, p. 217.

103 R. Miliband (1969), *op. cit.*; N. Poulantzas, 'The problem of the capitalist state' in R. Blackburn (ed.), *Ideology in Social Science*; R. Miliband, 'The Capitalist State: a reply', *New Left Review*, No. 59; R. Miliband, 'Poulantzas and the capitalist

State', *New Left Review*, No. 82.
104   R. Miliband (1969), *op. cit.*, p. 62.
105   N. Poulantzas, *Political Power and Social Class* (London 1973).

6
Deviance and the Law

Steve Redhead

INTRODUCTION

In the relatively short time since the publication of the first edition of this book, 'law and order' themes have become ever more widely promulgated in law enforcement, parliamentary and mass media discourses. Forms of deviance, and even more specifically forms of criminality, that is the breach of criminal law rather than wider social and moral rules, have become the focus of an intense public interest in UK society. This is an interest, moreover, which is no longer attributable — indeed if it ever was — merely to moral panics or hysterical over-the-top social reaction by politicians, policemen or others in positions of social and moral authority. Deviance is much more likely to be acknowledged by social scientists today as a *real* social problem. To take one example at random, few sociologists of deviance in the 1980s would regard glue sniffing as a positively liberating activity as they undoubtedly would have viewed the use of drugs like marihuana a decade or more earlier. Real social problems, however, are inevitably part of a process which is negotiable in its outcomes and highly dependent on the discretionary practices of the agents of rule-enforcement. This, on the other hand, does not mean that deviancy studies have slipped back into the dark ages: not everyone, even in the bleak political and economic climate of the present decade, has gone back to arguing that deviants are either biologically or psychologically abnormal or else simply morally wicked.

Theories of crime and deviance, rather like the judicial, penal and welfare measures designed to eradicate the various rule-breaking behaviours, can accurately be described as being in a state of chaos. Traditional criminological explanations, namely Classicism and Positivism, have set up a traditional dichotomy: *either* deviants have the capacity of free will and make rational choices to behave in an irrational (that is, law or rule-breaking) fashion *or* they are determined or propelled into such action, through no fault of their own, by internal or external factors. Labelling or new deviancy theories, emanating from symbolic interactionist or phenomenological roots, undermined much of the thinking from traditional criminology, but in turn dug up as many problems as solutions. 'New' or radical criminologies which have followed on from the sociology of deviance have tended to rule out *any* biological or psychological factors in the search for a social theory of deviance, a practice which is tantamount to throwing out the baby with the proverbial bath water. However, historical studies of criminal law in the eighteenth and nineteenth centuries, and of popular culture in the twentieth century, have helped to redress the balance by focusing on the connections between legal rules and the formation of particular ideologies – the 'rule of law', 'equality before the law', and popular notions of 'law and order' and justice, for instance.

But what exactly is the status of the concept of 'deviance' as a social problem in contemporary society? What sense can we make of the seemingly endless calls for 'law and order' and the (re-)establishment of the 'rule of law' in a nation which is said by leading Chief Constables, such as ex-Metropolitan Police Commissioners, Sir David McNee and Sir Robert Mark, and James Anderton, Chief Constable of Greater Manchester Police, to be crime-ridden as never before? In this chapter I want to suggest some answers to these questions by reference to observations about crime and deviance today and the varied legal responses to such phenomena. A number of themes relating to deviance and the law will be discussed in order to come to some general conclusions about certain aspects of the operation of the criminal justice system. In particular, the chapter will focus on: deviance and youth; law and social class; and law and the state. We shall first look at the connection between youth, deviance and the law and the images of deviance which have been engendered in and through the practices of legal regulation of juvenile law-breaking, especially since the 1950s. Two such 'images' will be specifically considered: black youth and football hooligans.

IMAGES OF A LAW AND ORDER SOCIETY

How many times have we heard the claim that UK society is breaking down, and that the evidence for such a contention is in the deviant behaviour of its youth? Northern Ireland has been the single most significant geographical terrain for the emergence of such a notion: since the early 1970s television news screens have been filled almost nightly with images of stone and petrol bomb-throwing youth. But ever since the 1950s (and indeed well before) youthful deviance and particularly working-class delinquency have been held out as if they were a spectre hanging over Western civilization equivalent to the threat of Russian invasion. In this section I want to examine some of the developments in the response to specific forms of youth deviance in post-war Britain and to draw out a few lines of inquiry which can be linked to the role of law in modern society. There is no space here to discuss specific legal interventions in the field of juvenile justice – for instance, the Children and Young Persons Act of 1969 or the Criminal Justice Act of 1982 – nor to cover all the myriad pieces of research into forms of juvenile law-breaking and deviancy.[1] What can be done, however, is to present some selected snapshots of youth deviance and their connections with the law. First, let us consider black youth and the law.

Young, Labelled and Black

The civil disorders on the British mainland in 1981 helped to firmly establish in the public mind a connection between black youth and crime – particularly looting, generalized street violence, assaults on the police, damage to property, and so on. However mistaken this impression, the 'law and order' campaigns of the previous decade, emphasizing the threat to British society posed by the young, black 'mugger',[2] paved the way for mass media portrayals of 'alien hordes' rioting on the mainland's formerly peaceful streets.[3]

Less violent but equally misleading images of deviant black[4] youth subcultures — for instance, rastafarians[5] — have increasingly come to signify the threat of social instability and change for respectable society, and police training and strategy is organized accordingly.[6] Furthermore, the connection between black youth and certain forms of criminality has been explicit in official criminal statistics. (I have, incidentally, deliberately eschewed the use of tables of criminal statistics in this chapter because nowhere is it more clear that such apparently 'hard' social facts do not speak for themselves and tend to mislead as much as inform us.)[7] Such statistics become widely publicized precisely because of the alleged connections. For instance, the Metropolitan Police released statistics in March 1982 which were widely interpreted[8] in the mass media as proving that London's street crime problem was due overwhelmingly to young, black 'muggers'. However, as has been argued in interpreting studies by the Home Office itself, 'it would be a mistake to see mugging as necessarily being a type of crime committed mainly by blacks'.[9] There are further difficulties with such statistics, of course, such as the fact that 'mugging' itself is not a legal category (no crime of 'mugging' exists in English law), but what is really at stake here is the significance of the developments in the relations between black youth and law enforcement agencies over recent decades. The notorious 'sus' law,[10] or the suspected persons offence under section 4 of the Vagrancy Act of 1824, though now officially repealed and to some extent rehabilitated in the Criminal Attempts Act of 1981, lives on in folklore of the inner-city black communities, especially the young.[11] By the early 1980s it is clear that the important issue is not just how many young blacks commit forms of street crime[12] but the process of blanket labelling of all young black people as 'muggers' or 'criminally inclined rastafarians' or whatever.[13] As Simon Frith pointed out, during the riots:

> The most savage episodes (Brixton, Toxteth, Moss Side) involved the police and blacks. West Indian youth face the most systematic discrimination in their search for work, places to go, and the effect of such discrimination is to put them up against the police continually. Black youth, living on the street, have to subsist on street skills (small-scale hustling, pilfering, dealing). The dividing line the police like to draw between villains and decent citizens is impossible to define, and so all young blacks are treated as muggers and thieves (as Chief Constables blandly admit).[14]

It is this criminalization of black youth culture *as a whole* which is the most obvious outcome of recent trends in the policing of inner-city areas. Racial discrimination in law[15] and policing[16] — as in other spheres such as employment, housing, and so on — has been visible and well-documented since the 1950s and in part led to the passing of successively ineffectual pieces of legislation, namely the Race Relations Acts of 1965, 1968 and 1976, designed to combat it. But by the 1980s a clear, distinct figure has emerged in the discourses of 'law and order' — he is young, black, male, probably unemployed, and living in specific parts of Britain's inner cities. It is, moreover, a figure which has come to symbolize, better than any other, the much heralded 'crisis' facing the courts, police and prisons in UK society. In Stan Cohen's well-chosen phrase, for many in Britain today black youths are 'symbols of trouble'.[17]

Trouble on the Terraces

Black youth, in a sense, are only the latest in a series of post-war 'folk devils'.[18] From the teddy boys in the 1950s through mods, rockers, hippies and skinheads in the 1960s to punks and rastas in the 1970s, youth subcultures have been identified as 'symbols of trouble'. Initially, too, such subcultures were class based. Only the hippies and their 1950s predecessors, the beats, were *clearly* middle class in origin. Other youth subcultures have all emanated — albeit partially and hesitantly — from a wider working-class youth culture. But, as Stan Cohen has recognized, most youth are not 'in' subcultures and even if they are it is the worthlessness of jobs, emptiness of education and lack of optimism for the future which mark their existence rather than rebellion, however ritualized.[19] Fatalism, not hope, is more often the order of the day. Soccer hooligans are probably the best example of such a youth group, emerging on the scene as a 'social problem' in the 1967–8 League season when skinheads and football violence first converged.[20] Not that the history of crowd 'misbehaviour' began in the 1960s. As several social historians have shown,[21] the 1880s and 1890s were at least as unruly as the 1970s and 1980s as far as professional football was concerned. But the modern subcultural violence surrounding professional soccer games and grounds, to the extent that it is distinctive in its form with 'organized' terrace cultures, the defending and taking of 'ends' and so on,[22] is significant for the response it has evoked from the increasingly aggressive 'law and order' society.

Numerous official[23] and unofficial reports have delved into the apparent causes of the phenomenon. Newspapers,[24] radio and television have repeatedly, over the last fourteen or fifteen years, focused on the soccer hooligan 'problem' as a major reason for the decline in football match attendances, and criminologists continue to seek 'objective facts' regarding the ways in which courts and police process 'football hooligans'[25] through the criminal justice system. All kinds of theories — sociological, psychological, economic, biological, even zoological[26] — have been advanced to account for the various deviant behaviours grouped under the label 'football hooliganism', some with considerably more credibility than others.[27] However, what is important about the explosion of interest in the folk devil 'football hooligan' is the consequences for the organization of law enforcement which have ensued. This is not just simply due to the oft-quoted example of the deviancy-amplification spiral, where social reaction transforms primary deviance into secondary deviance, tertiary deviance, and so on.[28] It is part of a wider process which is redefining the football spectator,[29] and subsequently the social meaning of the game itself. In this process there is a growing tendency, especially since the late 1960s, to perceive the deviant behaviour of spectators (and interestingly enough players, too) as a problem for the football industry and government to solve. An apparently innocuous piece of licensing legislation, the Safety of Sports Grounds Act of 1975, ostensibly confined to safety criteria, was to contribute to an already continuing set of practices which were transforming the football 'audience', from participatory crowd to passive spectators, from predominantly skilled and male working-class 'fans' to more middle-class 'consumers'. The reason for safety legislation playing such a role is that its practical implementation over a number of years has specifically aided the already operational surveillance by police forces, frequently involving Special Patrol Group or equivalent 'elite' police squads and also closed circuit television and other methods of crowd control, targeted at the terrace supporter. Note that it is the terrace supporter *en bloc* rather than a labelled 'hooligan' element in that area of the football ground that has become the object of the all-seeing police operations. Difficulties with the scope – it has proved difficult to ensure strict surveillance outside the grounds, for instance – and content of the legislation have been experienced, but the Safety of Sports Grounds Act has played its part in helping to monitor one particular section of the football crowd. By delimiting the terrace area (in some cases massively reducing the standing capacity for fans) and requiring the erection of new barriers and fences the Act has contributed to a whole network of techniques and strategies designed to 'cage' and 'pen' the terrace supporter. The process in which this legislation has participated is seen by many pundits as a necessary repackaging of the football product, remarketing it as Jimmy Hill – TV sage and former Chairman of the Players' Union (now the PFA) and Coventry City FC – has recently put it, for the 'non-hooligan' consumer. Hill's own efforts to put this into practice at Highfield Road, Coventry were rudely rebuffed when the all-seater stadium, the first of its kind in the Football League, was vandalized by visiting Leeds United supporters early in the 1981–2 season.

It is well known, to those who care to look or remember, in Britain, Europe and elsewhere that seating soccer spectators does not curb 'football hooliganism'. But the importance of the identification and isolation of a whole section of a football crowd as a problem is not so much its effectiveness as a solution to vandalism, drunkenness and crowd 'riots', rather for what it tells us about changes in law enforcement, police strategies and civil liberties. To observe the common practice (by the 1980s) of arbitrary ejection of football spectators who *look* as if they are likely to cause 'trouble' – based as always on stereotypical images of what hooligans wear, do, say, etc. – is to witness the erosion of civil liberties which are supposedly part and parcel of the coveted 'rule of law'. So, too, is the enforced imprisonment of 'away' supporters in one terrace section of the ground for anything up to three-quarters of an hour at the end of the game, not to mention their tightly-monitored progress to and from the stadium. As one senior policeman observed to me on a research 'tour' of North-West soccer grounds, 'You won't see much *law* here!'

Here the 'football hooligan', like another figure we have identified, 'black youth', is something more than a mere scapegoat. As Garry Whannel has acutely observed:

> The structuring process of public discussion has constructed two figures around which the debate is formed: the FOOTBALL HOOLIGAN and the FAMILY AUDIENCE. The hooligan took its place within an increasingly formalized mode of explanation; the label HOOLIGAN came to reference a whole section of the terrace sub-culture.
>
> The FAMILY AUDIENCE only makes full sense if it is understood to refer to the affluent middle class consumer. The presence in development plans of squash courts, hairdressing salons, executive boxes and expensive restaurants indicates that football clubs are increasingly looking to the top end of their market for economic salvation.
>
> What is significant here for the concept of deviance labelling is that the folk devil FOOTBALL HOOLIGAN does not simply become part of a law-enforcement induced amplification as a figure in a more general discourse, the real basis of which remains unspoken.[30]

What I have tried to indicate in this section of the chapter, by selection of two prominent figures in 'law and order' discourse — black youth and football hooligans — is that to identify someone as deviant or criminal and to subsequently process them through the criminal justice system (from arrest and detention through court trial to punishment) is never just an isolated act of law enforcement. It does not take place in a social or political vacuum. Of course, this is not to imply that 'images thus engendered are wholly fictitious: mods and rockers, teddy boys, skinheads, violent criminals, hippies, drug addicts are after all not just inkblots on to which fantasies are projected.'[31] But images of deviance, such as black youth or football hooligans (or, to spell out the ultimate 'law and order' nightmare, black football hooligans!), inevitably come to signify lawlessness, the breakdown of an older traditional form of 'discipline', and the need for a strengthening of the forces of 'law and order'. They are images, moreover, which are key elements in the mobilizing of opinion and policy. As Stuart Hall has put it:

> We are now in the middle of a deep and decisive movement towards a more disciplinary, authoritarian kind of society. This shift has been in progress since the 1960s . . . This drift into a 'law and order' society is no temporary affair . . . Governments in trouble, it might be said, always have a strong temptation to reach for discipline and regulation in times of social crisis. These are not times when human freedoms and civil liberties flourish. But the new aspect to this ancient habit is the capacity of those in power to use the augmented means of communication now available to them, in order to SHAPE public opinion, constructing a definition of 'the crisis' which has, as its inevitable corresponding echo, a popular demand for 'more law and order'.[32]

As we have noted already there are a number of outstanding features of the images of a 'law and order' society. They are explicitly linked with the overall themes with which this book is concerned — work, urbanism and inequality, or more appropriately, given the context of the UK in the 1980s, unemployment, the inner city and social class. The selected images we have presented here are highly specific: they are representations of a particular form of working-class culture at a 'moment' in British history where the long-term decline of the economy impinges on a working-class youth in an acute though often contradictory manner, involving mass youth unemployment and a radically changing youth labour market. This brings us to more traditional sociological concerns, especially the questions of social structure or social class, and the changing nature of state activity. Both of these issues, in so far as they relate to law and deviance, will now be considered. Firstly, law and social class.

LAW AND SOCIAL CLASS

Inequality Before the Law

Just as the sociology of deviance has attempted to account for, amongst other things, the way in which division of labour, environment and social background are linked to deviance and crime, its related discipline, the sociology of law (or 'socio-legal studies', 'law and society' or 'law in society' to give it its rather ambiguous pseudonyms) has tried to come to terms with the role of law, in both its civil *and* criminal aspects. The way in which social structure and law interact is a classical problem for the sociology of law. The founding fathers' — Marx, Durkheim, Weber — wrestled with various conceptual frameworks which would adequately account for law's relationship to class or group 'interests', and their unresolved endeavours have inevitably left their impact on modern sociology of law, which in its infancy in the 1960s and early 1970s turned on a rather crude polarity between consensus and conflict theories.[33] Consensus theory, roughly equivalent to Parsonian functionalism, saw law as a representation of general social interests opposed only by deviants at the margins of society. Conflict theory, on the other hand, at the opposite end of the theoretical spectrum claimed that law was, more or less, the imposition of the interests of a ruling elite on an unwilling majority; that is, the rest of society.[34] Dissatisfaction mounted with both of these 'extremes' as more and more empirical studies of law failed to conform to either pole. Law, it seemed, was not simply a reflection of the wishes of the majority of the population, nor merely an 'iron fist' with which a ruling minority represses its subjects. Subsequently, more sophisticated explanations[35] — both pluralist and Marxist — have come to dominate the stage in accounting for law's relationship to social structure. In this section I want to consider the ways in which the notion of 'equality before the law' might be questioned by the relations between law and social class. There are three spheres in which this may occur: the emergence of law, the enforcement of law and the provision of legal services.

The Emergence of Law

The sociology of law and sociology of deviance have produced numerous law-creation or 'emergence' studies, mainly of the process by which criminal (rather than civil)[36] laws have been made by Parliament or judges. It has been argued[37] that conflict theory has dominated this field of study with a number of negative consequences emerging as a result. One such consequence is the conspiratorial[38] impression which has pervaded much of this work. Ruling elites, or ruling classes (in the more Marxist inclined studies), appear to create criminal law in some way or other, either through parliamentary or extra-parliamentary pressure or via the law-making of the judiciary. There is interminable debate in sociology of law and jurisprudence about whether judges simply declare law[39] (made by Parliament) or create it, either by complex rules of interpretation of previous statutes and cases or outright invention of new rules.[40] If the creativity argument is upheld — as it most frequently is by case-studies — the social background of the judiciary comes into play. Because the judiciary comes from a remarkably narrow social elite, the argument runs, when judges create law they will do so in accordance with such social background,[41] with unfortunate consequences for certain 'deviant' groups[42] in society who are the 'natural' targets for their prejudices. Certainly the judiciary is overwhelmingly and increasingly[43] drawn from those with a public school and Oxbridge background; it is also well known for its male exclusivity (very few women become judges), its racial origins and its age. But this does not *necessarily* mean that judges are biased in their law-making (or law enforcement) in terms of social class, gender, race or age: any more than a similar preponderance of white upper-middle class male MPs write their own biases onto the statute book when passing legislation through Parliament.

The major problem with such contentions about law creation, whether parliamentary or judicial, is its reliance on a sociological reductionism. This assumes that legal and political actions and institutions are to be explained by the social class composition of their agents. For instance, judges interpret and make criminal laws; they are overwhelmingly homogeneous in their social, political and educational background; therefore, they cannot help but make judgements (especially in politically sensitive cases) which fit in with such factors. Social class thus determines the creation of legal rules. In this (slightly) caricatured picture of explanations of law-making which come under the rubric of conflict theory, the major difficulty is that social class 'interests' are taken as given, then assumed to be reflected in political and legal institutions. There is no acknowledgement of the role of law in constructing such interests in the first place or the limits on judicial creativity set by other legal rules and procedures, political structures, 'public opinion', mass media investigaton and other factors. Moreover, the more sophisticated accounts of law-making in both pluralist and Marxist paradigms have difficulty in avoiding these same pitfalls of reductionism. Precisely how class or group 'interests' are formed, and the role of law in their formation is a complex question which has not been answered satisfactorily in studies of law creation so far.

The Enforcement of Law

It is in the everyday enforcement of law that deviancy studies have detected an even more obvious flaw in the mythology surrounding the notion of 'equality before the law'. The stereotyping practices[44] of the agencies of law enforcement have long been identified as discriminatory on the grounds of social class, race, gender and age. As we saw in the first section of this chapter the images of 'law and order' society are built up from identikit pictures of law-breaking, gained to some extent from police–citizen interaction in everyday contexts: the pub, the street and other 'public' places. Those who conform to such identikit images are likely to be more vulnerable than those who do not, whether or not they have committed 'rule-breaking' activity. This, as labelling theorists from Howard Becker to Stan Cohen and beyond have displayed in their accounts of deviancy, can lead to inefficiency in law enforcement in two distinct ways. There can be cases of 'mistaken identity',[45] that is, innocent victims can be identified and processed through the criminal justice system as guilty. Or, on the other side of the coin, there can be law-breakers who are never caught. Of course all sorts of other factors besides stereotyping contribute to such inefficiencies: witness the human error and technological incompetence of the police in the Yorkshire Ripper case, for example.

Further, social class has been linked more specifically to the enforcement of the criminal law in the historical studies of 'white-collar crime'. Breaches of pollution, food and drugs, factory and consumer legislation have classically been inspected – by special regulatory bodies such as the Factory Inspectorate and Trading Standards Officers – rather than prosecuted by the police. They are, nevertheless, breaches of the criminal law and frequently, as in the case of chemical factory explosions or asbestos manufacture for instance, have even more serious consequences for property and personal welfare than most everyday theft, burglary and assaults. The enforcement policy of such bodies towards these crimes is frequently dictated by a deep-rooted desire in the history of the organizations concerned to promote conciliation and harmony between the agency and the management or owners, rather than discord and legal conflict in the courts. Secondly, the relatively lenient attitude taken by the magistracy and the judiciary towards these crimes, both in determination of guilt and sentence, has led such inspectorates to prosecute only in rare and legally watertight cases. Research[46] which I carried out in the early

1970s into the enforcement of harassment and illegal eviction provisions of the Rent Acts in one North West city revealed that Local Authority Officers responsible for such breaches of the criminal law were conditioned by these factors. The result of their (in)action was often to allow thoroughly unscrupulous and blatantly criminal landlords to evade the provisions of the Rent Acts, many of whom are perpetrating similar illegalities today. Perhaps the best-known studies of this 'class' distinction in law enforcement are the researches of W. G. Carson into the history of the Factory Acts. Carson in a number of papers has charted the stages in which 'offences against the Factory Acts moved towards the position where, today, they are accepted as customary, are only rarely subjected to criminal prosecution, and, indeed, are often not regarded as really constituting crimes at all'.[47] He has further shown how:

> ... one important segment of the new bourgeoisie in nineteenth century Britain, early textile manufacturers, managed to reserve a vital area of illegality for its own use within the context of securing an adequate and cheap supply of labour to man the prototypical factories of emergent industrialization ... (and) despite a succession of criminal laws purporting to restrict the hours of labour to be performed by children and young persons in cotton and other textile mills, their early nineteenth century employers successfully retained a 'right', if not to totally uncontrolled violation in this respect, at least to substantial immunity from the penal and other adverse implications of their criminal conduct.[48]

We have now looked at two areas where inequalities before the law, and specifically class inequalities, have been seen to occur. Now let us consider a third: the provision of legal services.

One Law for the Poor

Inequality before the law has been obvious in the access of various sections of the population to the legal system and particularly the services of the legal profession. The Royal Commission on Legal Services[49] was created by the 1974–9 Labour government in response to various public criticisms of the legal profession, not least that its clienteles were overwhelmingly middle class and that large portions of the rest of the population required legal services but for a number of reasons were unable to obtain them. The Royal Commission's report has been widely criticized, particularly for appearing to be 'designed' to improve the public image of lawyers rather than to lay the foundations for any future strategy.[50] It had been well established prior to the setting up of the Royal Commission that the use of legal services was narrowly restricted. For example a report[51] in the early 1970s, prepared for the Law Society of Scotland, found that users of legal services in Scotland 'tend to come from "better off" sections of the community' – in other words, 'the higher the social class the greater the extent of contact with a solicitor'. Numerous other studies into what has come to be known as 'unmet legal need' have confirmed such a picture. Zander, Abel-Smith and Brooke,[52] for instance, in a study of Islington, Southwark and Tower Hamlets in the late 1960s found that there was substantial unmet legal need 'particularly among those with low incomes and of low social class'.[53]

Despite the existence of a system of Legal Aid covering legal advice and also assistanc with preparation of cases and representation at court or tribunal hearings, the impression that there is one legal system for 'the poor' and one for 'the rich' undoubtedly lives on. This is particularly evident in the lack of legal representation before administrative tribunals (where in most instances there is no Legal Aid available) and at Magistrates Court cases. Despite the operation of Duty Solicitor schemes[54] in a number of towns and cities in England and Wales since 1972, many defendants are still not legally represented, and those that are (as in Crown Court cases) face heavy pressure from their legal representatives to plead guilty irrespective of innocence in return for an offer of a reduced charge or sentence; in other words to indulge in the dubious practice of plea-bargaining.[55]

In general, various socio-legal studies have established that the poorest sections of the community have the most unequal access to the law. But inequality before the law is not simply a matter of equating legal services with middle-class usage. Various legal aid systems, for example, have been noted for their creation of means and other criteria which exclude middle-income earners who are thus unable to afford to go to law. As I have suggested in this section the relationship between law and social class in UK society today is by no means a strightforward one to establish. What makes it even more difficult to summarize precisely is the changing class relations in post-war society and in particular the role of the state in this period.

LAW AND THE STATE

The 'Rule of Law' in the 1980s

Just as with the relationship between law and social class, the theorization of law and the state has languished in the wake of nineteenth-century sociological debates, particularly Marxist-inspired ones. The 'resurrection' of twentieth-century Marxist legal theorists such as Karl Renner and E. B. Pashukanis in the 1970s contributed to rigorous analysis of the relationship between capitalism and the rule of law, but was unable to escape the fundamental tenet of Marx and Engels' work which was that the demise of capitalism also meant the withering away of law.[56] In the earlier 'new criminology'[57] a similar romanticism about crime had persisted. However, the harsh realities of world recession, mass unemployment and the erosion of civil liberties turned the attention of law and deviancy studies to the potential of law for the protection of the poorest communities, especially in the inner cities and the transformation of society itself.[58] These about-turns in the sociology of deviance and sociology of law have, of course, been accompanied by growing public debates about forms of accountability of the judiciary, police and prisons and can be traced back to earlier theoretical arguments about the accuracy of social historian, E. P. Thompson's claim that:

> . . . if the actuality of the law's operation in class-divided societies has, again and again, fallen short of its own rhetoric of equity, yet the notion of the rule of law is itself an unqualified good . . . If we suppose that law is no more than a mystifying and pompous way in which class power is registered and executed, then we need not waste our labour in studying its history and forms. One Act would be much the same as another . . .[59]

In order to suggest the nature of the battleground which the notion of the 'rule of law' has become I want in this final section to analyse briefly one element — the recent debates over criminal procedure.

The Criminal Procedure Debates, 1972–82

I have concentrated in this chapter on English law (applying in England and Wales and to some extent in Northern Ireland), and it is in England where debates about criminal procedure have been at their fiercest over the latest decade, although that by no means minimizes the significance of developments in Northern Ireland (such as the so-called 'Diplock courts' where judges sit without a jury to try 'terrorist' offences) and Scotland where legislation such as the Criminal Justice (Scotland) Act of 1980 has been seen as the portent for future changes in criminal law in England and Wales. The criminal procedure debates of the last decade had their origin in the Criminal Law Revision Committee's Eleventh Report,[60] published in 1972 after a long period of deliberation. The Committee's report reflected the pressure (particularly from the police) to restrict suspects' rights, such as the 'right to silence', but proposals were initially beaten back. Next, the then Metropolitan Police Commissioner Robert Mark gave a Dimbleby Lecture[61] on television in November 1973 which further supported the restriction of citizens' rights on the grounds that too many criminals were avoiding conviction. Much debate ensued on this specific issue. Were too many criminals avoiding conviction, were they 'professional' criminals, etc?[62] But the most significant event of the decade as far as changes in criminal procedure were concerned was the celebrated Confait case[63] involving the wrongful convictions of three youths for the murder of Maxwell Confait, a homosexual prostitute and transvestite, in highly dubious circumstances. A report[64] on the case by a High Court judge, Sir Henry Fisher, provoked the creation in 1977 of a Royal Commission on Criminal Procedure to look into various aspects of suspects' rights. Many of the recommendations of its subsequent highly controversial report[65] — especially those increasing police powers — found their way into the Police and Criminal Evidence Bills of 1982 (which lapsed when the 1983 General Election was called) and of 1983.

The importance of such debates, which will continue apace in the coming years, lies in their capacity to signify the meaning of the term the 'rule of law' in UK society in the 1980s. For E. P. Thompson the rule of law, even in the eighteenth century when the law was clearly made and enforced by the gentry, still meant real limits on upper-class rule, real 'inhibitions upon the actions of rulers'.[66] The 'law and order' society of the 1980s with its parliamentary democracy is clearly a very different creature, but it still requires its legal inhibitions. The capacity of the guardians of the 'rule of law' (pressure groups, judges, politicians and others) to maintain its inhibitory power will be reflected in the criminal procedure debates of the *next* ten years.

CONCLUSION

The three themes which have structured this chapter — 'law and order', 'equality before the law' and the 'rule of law' — are familiar to anyone concerned with the relationship between law and deviance. But they are not unambiguous terms; indeed they only mean anything at all intelligible in the contexts I have placed them. The capacity of a 'law and order' society to maintain 'equality before the law' is most uncertain. It is the contradictory reconciliation of such themes in Britain today which make deviance such a highly negotiable phrase. I began by looking at two highly familiar images of deviance — black youth and football hooligans. The recent appearance of a more blatantly political image, that of women peace campaigners (at Greenham Common, for instance), with all the difficulties which that poses for mass media and judicial discourses (women as mothers, women as 'non-violent', women as 'non-political', and so on), reinforces this negotiability of deviance. The radical non-interventionism of labelling theorists (that is, the injunction to *stop* labelling) may be less and less fashionable as deviancy studies face up to the very real social problems on their doorstep in Britain in the 1980s, but the variable legal responses to deviance which I have dealt with in this chapter should remind us that social class, age, race and gender are vital determinants of the practice of law.

Notes to Chapter 6

1 For an excellent review of the field, see Howard Parker and Henri Giller, 'More and less the same: British Delinquency Research Since the Sixties' in *British Journal of Criminology*, Vol. 21, No. 3 (1981), pp. 230-45.

2 See Stuart Hall *et al*, *Policing The Crisis: Mugging, the State and Law and Order* (London 1978).

3 For an effective demolition of the myths surrounding the notion of a peaceful British 'past', see Geoffrey Pearson, *Hooligan: A History of Respectable Fears* (London 1983); and Martin Kettle and Lucy Hodges, *Uprising! The Police, The People and the Riots in Britain's Cities* (London 1982), especially the introduction.

4 'Black' has come to signify *all* coloured races especially in 'law and order' discourses.

5 See, for example, Dick Hebdige, *Subculture: The Meaning of Style* (London 1979), Ch. 3.

6 See Louis Blom-Cooper and Richard Drabble, 'Police Perception of Crime: Brixton and the Operational Response' in *British Journal of Criminology*, Vol. 22, No. 2 (1982), pp. 184-7.

7 See Paul Corrigan's comment on this point in the first edition of this book, Philip Abrams (ed.), *Work, Urbanism and Inequality: UK Society Today* (London 1978), p. 251.

8 For a useful discussion of why criminal statistics themselves are a problem for the sociology of deviance, see Paul Wiles, 'Criminal Statistics and Sociological Explanations of Crime' in W. G. Carson and Paul Wiles (eds), *The Sociology of Delinquency in Britain*, Vol. 1, The British Tradition (London 1971).

9 Malcolm Ramsay, 'Muggings: Fears and Facts' in *New Society* (25 March 1982), p. 467.

10 See Clare Demuth, *'Sus': A Report on the Vagrancy Act, 1824* (Runnymede Trust 1978).

11 For an enlightening account of one black community's relationship with the police, see Derek Bishton and Brian Homer (eds), *Talking Blues* (Birmingham 1978).

12 For an ethnographic account see Ken Pryce, *Endless Pressure: A Study of West Indian Life-Styles in Bristol* (Harmondsworth 1979), esp. Ch. 5.

13 Paul Gilroy, 'Police and Thieves' in Centre for Contemporary Cultural Studies, *The Empire Strikes Back: Race and Racism in 70's Britain* (London 1982).

pp. 143-82.

14 Simon Frith, 'Youth in the Eighties: A Dispossessed Generation' in *Marxism Today* (November 1981), p. 12.

15 See, for example, Rudy Narayan, *Black Community on Trial* (London 1976).

16 See Phil Scraton, 'Policing and Institutionalized Racism on Merseyside' in David Cowell, Trevor Jones and Jock Young (eds), *Policing the Riots* (London 1982), pp. 21-38; and Lord Scarman's Report, *The Brixton Disorders*, Cmnd 8427 (HMSO 1981).

17 See Stan Cohen, *Folk Devils and Moral Panics* (Oxford 1980), introduction to the new edition, page i.

18 *Ibid*.

19 See Stuart Hall and Tony Jefferson (eds), *Resistance Through Rituals* (London 1976).

20 See John Clarke, *Football Hooliganism and the Skinheads* (Centre for Contemporary Cultural Studies, University of Birmingham 1973).

21 See, for instance, Wray Vamplew, 'Ungentlemanly Conduct: The Control of Soccer Crowd Behaviour in England, 1888-1914' in T. C. Smout (ed.), *The Search for Wealth and Stability: Essays in Economic and Social History Presented to M. W. Flinn* (London 1979); and John Hutchinson, *The Football Industry: The Early Years of the Professional Game* (Glasgow 1982), esp. pp. 56-7.

22 See David Robins and Phil Cohen, *Knuckle Sandwich: Growing Up in the Working-Class City* (Harmondsworth 1977), esp. pp. 133-53.

23 See, for instance, *Report of the Working Party on Crowd Behaviour at Football Matches* (the Lang Report) (HMSO 1969).

24 See Garry Whannel, 'Football, Crowd Behaviour and the Press' in *Media, Culture and Society*, Vol. 1, No. 2 (1979), pp. 327-42.

25 Eugene Trivizas, 'Offences and Offenders in Football Crowd Disorders' in *British Journal of Criminology*, Vol. 20, No. 3 (1980), pp. 276-88; and Eugene Trivizas, 'Sentencing the "Football Hooligan"' in *British Journal of Criminology*, Vol. 21, No. 4 (1981), pp. 342-9.

26 See Desmond Morris, *The Soccer Tribe* (London 1981).

27 For example, Morris, *ibid.*, is notable for its factual inaccuracies and theoretical absurdity.

28 See Ian Taylor, 'Soccer Consciousness and Soccer Hooliganism' in Stan Cohen (ed.), *Images of Deviance* (Harmondsworth 1971), pp. 134-64. For some elements of self-criticism of this labelling approach, see Ian Taylor, 'On the Sports Violence Question: Soccer Hooliganism Revisited' in Jennifer Hargreaves (ed.), *Sport, Culture and Ideology* (London 1982), pp. 152-96.

29 See Whannel, *op. cit.*; and Steve Redhead, 'Some Aspects of Legal Regulation in the Post-War Football Industry' in Alan Tomlinson (ed.), *Explorations in Football Culture* (Brighton 1983).

30 Whannel, *op. cit.*, p. 342.

31 Stan Cohen and Jock Young, *The Manufacture of News: Deviance, Social Problems and the Mass Media* (London 1981), p. 164.

32 Stuart Hall, *Drifting into a Law and Order Society* (Cobden Trust 1980), p. 3.

33 See, for instance, William Chambliss and Robert Seidman, *Law, Order and Power*

(first edition, Reading, Ma. 1971).

34   See R. Lefcourt (ed.), *Law Against the People* (New York 1971).

35   See Bob Roshier and Harvey Teff, *Law and Society in England* (London 1980),
      Ch. 2.

36   As S. D. Stein, 'The Sociology of Law' in *British Journal of Criminology*, Vol. 20,
      No. 2 (1980), p. 104, points out, this is a major problem since most of the Acts
      'passed in most Western industrial societies fall under the heading of what is gene-
      rally referred to as civil law'.

37   *Ibid.*; see also W. G. Carson, 'The Sociology of Crime and the Emergence of
      Criminal Laws' in Paul Rock and Mary McIntosh (eds), *Deviance and Social Control*
      (London 1974), pp. 67-90. '

38   See, for instance, Stein's discussion, *op. cit.*, p. 106.

39   Known as the 'declaratory theory' for obvious reasons.

40   The former Master of the Rolls, Lord Denning, is the most notorious modern
      example of such a judicial law-maker.

41   See John Griffith, *The Politics of the Judiciary* (first edition, London 1977),
      esp. pp. 187-216.

42   For instance, students and trade union members, *ibid.*, pp. 150-71.

43   See Malcolm Dean, 'Narrower Choice for Legal Elite' in *The Guardian* (17 August
      1982).

44   For a summary of research into police stereotyping, see Roshier and Teff, *op. cit.*,
      pp. 79-95.

45   There are numerous well-documented cases; see, for example, Peter Hain, *Mistaken
      Identity: The Wrong Face of the Law* (London 1976).

46   See my unpublished LL.M. thesis, 'Case Presentation and Litigant Choice in
      Proceedings Before Administrative Tribunals' (University of Manchester 1974).

47   W. G. Carson, 'The Conventionalization of Early Factory Crime' in *International
      Journal of the Sociology of Law*, Vol. 7, No. 1 (1979), p. 38.

48   *Ibid.*, pp. 37-8.

49   (Benson Report) Cmnd 7648 (HMSO 1979).

50   Roshier and Teff, *op. cit.*, p. 199.

51   Colin Campbell and R. J. Wilson, *Public Attitudes to the Legal Professional in
      Scotland*, Summary of the Research Report presented to the Law Society of
      Scotland.

52   Michael Zander, Brian Abel-Smith and Rosalind Brooke, *Legal Problems and the
      Citizen: A Study in Three London Boroughs* (London 1973).

53   *Ibid.*, p. 226; for a very useful review of the 'unmet legal need' debate, see Ian
      Duncanson, 'Legal Need in England and Wales in the Sixties and Seventies: A
      Retrospect' in *University of New South Wales Law Journal*, Vol. 4 (1981), pp.
      113-27.

54   For a study of one such scheme, see Michael King, *The Effects of a Duty Solicitor
      Scheme: An assessment of the impact upon a magistrates court* (Cobden Trust
      1976).

55   See John Baldwin and Michael McConville, *Negotiated Justice: Pressures on
      Defendants to Plead Guilty* (Oxford 1977).

56   See my essay, 'Marxist theory, the Rule of Law and Socialism' in Piers Beirne and

Richard Quinney (eds), *Marxism and Law* (New York 1982), pp. 328–42.

57 Ian Taylor, Paul Walton and Jock Young, *The New Criminology: For a Social Theory of Deviance* (London 1973).

58 See Ian Taylor, *Law and Order: Arguments for Socialism* (London 1981), Jock Young and John Lea, *What is to be done about Law and Order?* (London 1984).

59 E. P. Thompson, *Whigs and Hunters: The Origin of the Black Act* (London 1977), p. 267.

60 Criminal Law Revision Committee, *Eleventh Report Evidence (General)* Cmnd 4991 (HMSO 1972).

61 Robert Mark, *Minority Verdict* (BBC 1973).

62 For a review of the evidence by one of the debate's participants, see Michael Zander, 'What is the Evidence on Law and Order?' in *New Society* (13 December 1979), pp. 591-4.

63 See Christopher Price and Jonathan Caplan, *The Confait Confessions* (London 1977).

64 *The Confait Case. Report by the Hon. Sir Henry Fisher*, HC90 (HMSO 1977).

65 *Royal Commission on Criminal Procedure: Report* Cmnd 8092 (HMSO 1981).

66 Thompson, *op. cit.*, p. 264.

7 ·
Social Welfare

Paul Corrigan

INTRODUCTION

Over the decade between the two editions of this book the study of UK society has changed considerably. These changes have been wrought by developments in two main and interrelated areas: first, in the nature of the concerns of the society itself; and secondly the way in which sociology has studied that society. These developments move continually over history. Yet at any one moment history can fool us into believing that a particular moment, its particular concerns, fears and worries are natural and inevitably there for all time. It is necessary always to remind ourselves that society and history are full of movement, movement from the past to the present and from the present to the future.

Much of this is clear when we compare sociology textbooks over a ten-year period — issues appear and disappear as matters of importance. In the field of interest of this chapter the change has been dramatic.

Most of the authors of this book have grown up within a period of UK society which has taken the institutions called the 'Welfare State' entirely as an inevitable part of the stability of British society. The institutions of health, social security, housing and personal social services have simply been there; perhaps not achieving as much as they might, but substantially existing around us, as permanent as the rest of our social wallpaper.

Alongside this has gone the belief that if a severe social problem was identified by a large enough section of society then something would be done about it. Thus, as we shall see later in this chapter, when the early 1960s saw the 'rediscovery of poverty' in Britain it became inevitable that governments, at a local and a national level, would do something about this rediscovered problem for millions of people.

Both these permanent fixtures, the welfare institutions themselves and the will to solve social problems, are now distinctly shaky and indeed appear to be becoming historical rather than contemporary facts.

This change may be obvious to most readers and represents one of the movements I mentioned in the opening paragraph. Less obvious has been the transformation in the way in which sociology and social science have studied the Welfare State and deprivation. The changes in methods of inquiry have come about primarily because of wider social changes, as the welfare institutions themselves become politically and socially impermanent. Rather than study institutions from inside their own rationale, once that rationale is in question socially, it is much more likely that sociologists will utilize a range of theoretical perspectives to question those institutions. Thus, as we shall see, it may well be common sense to assume that the social security system aims at the alleviation of poverty. If this assumption is fairly universal, as it was in the 1950s and 1960s, then it is likely that social scientists will ask questions within this assumption. For example, they would analyse the difficulty of ensuring that everyone received all their benefits, would look at ways in which supplementary benefits could be made more inviting, or the system made fairer.

Once, however, the whole institution's viability was questioned then a much wider range of sociological questions emerged. Similarly, the belief that, once a social problem was identified, political actions would follow to remedy that problem had a severe impact upon the way social scientists studied problems such as deprivation. For if through detailed study we could 'prove' that a large-scale problem existed, then political action might well be taken to improve the situation. Our role was confined to 'discovering' and detailing the extent and nature of the problem at hand.

This chapter explores both the development of the post-war welfare services *and* the different sociological ways of characterizing the social meaning of this aspect of society. Achieving both such aims at once contains a logical problem; the only way we can discuss the last forty years of UK welfare society is by using some form of theoretical framework as there can be no pure, atheoretical understanding. Social scientists should overcome this intellectual problem, not by pretending to discuss the social world from an abstract, theory-free, perspective; rather they should explain their own position and place it within the other theoretical viewpoints. We shall be trying to separate out these theories later.

I take my own theory for an analysis of welfare state activities from the point of view which sees those institutions as resulting from *class* struggle.[1] As we shall see, this regards growth, decline and change as the result of powerful forces arguing and fighting over each aspect of society. It looks at the specific movement within each period, analysing the way in which different classes understood and fought for their perspectives within that period. The theory *expects* change and conflict, rather than understanding welfare as a set of immutable functions.

WAYS OF SEEING WELFARE

Nineteenth Century through to the War: Keeping People off the Welfare

Table 7.1 provides the national baseline for expenditure on welfare services. Whilst, in the late 1970s and early 1980s, there began a detailed discussion about *how* this growing amount of money should be spent, most of the debate up until this moment was about the quantity of the gross national product to be spent on welfare. The rise in expenditure is variously explained, but no one denies the scale of this social change. Indeed, in political terms (even if this is not the case for this chapter), the size and scale of welfare expenditure is usually expanded by the addition of education. Thus, usually when public expenditure on social and welfare services is referred to, education is included as a major section. Whilst Robert Burgess' chapter covers this area in detail there are inevitably occasions we will discuss it here.

Social scientists all agree that our present welfare services can be traced back to the ways in which the state intervened in the nineteenth century.[2] Here the state intervened in creating the conditions for both the creation and the maintenance of industrial capitalism in the UK. The New Poor Law of 1834 was the first major national network of social policy and covered the area of social security. It created two of the most powerful realities within the working-class experience of welfare; the means test and the workhouse. The means test remains simple. Before anyone could claim any form of income from social security they had to demonstrate that they had no independent means. Such a 'test of means' ensured that if someone received any benefit they had to be genuinely destitute. If they had any private resources these would have to be expended first. The test was seen to be essential in order to prevent people who were receiving benefit from being better off than those in work.

Table 7.1   Social Expenditure in the UK, 1910–51

	1910	1921	1937	1951	1961	1971	1975
			Percentage of GNP at factor cost				
All social services (of which)	4.2	10.1	10.9	16.1	17.6	23.8	28.8
Social Security		4.7	5.2	5.3	6.7	8.9	9.5
Education		2.2	2.6	3.2	4.2	6.5	7.6
Total state expenditure	12.7	29.4	25.7	44.9	42.1	50.3	57.9

Source: *The Government's Expenditure Plans 1982-3 to 1984-5.*

Ensuring that, for whatever reason, the receipt of welfare benefit did not give those out of work a superior way of life to those in employment became one of the major tasks for one theme of social security policy. In the nineteenth century this task was not easy, for the wage labourer and his family were living in the most appalling squalor. Whilst the chance of survival for children was limited, the prospects of any steady secure life-style was also feeble. Consequently, it took all of Victorian ingenuity to establish an institution which would ensure that the experience of welfare was worse than the already difficult life of the wage labourer. This was the workhouse. The New Poor Law planned that every person who applied for social security would have to enter the workhouse to receive it. There should be no benefit given outside of the walls of the workhouse. Within this setting life and labour would be deliberately harsh; the family would be split up, repetitious and arduous work would be expected. Its aim was that no one would enter such an institution voluntarily but only under the compulsion of the hardest need.

Therefore both the means test and the workhouse test were deliberately aimed at keeping people out of the welfare sector of society. This would reduce expenditure and, more importantly, keep people as dependent as possible on what they could garner from the labour market. The birth of welfare services was not based upon UK society wanting to look after the weakest members of society in their adversity. Rather its major components were intended to put people off from claiming benefit; to link obtaining benefit with some form of pain. Whilst such a link was not universally achieved, the nineteenth and early twentieth centuries saw the painful workhouse, putting people off from the welfare, as the major powerful motif in UK society. Its success in making life horrible set the seal in the development of all the institutions that followed.

1940s: Reconstructing Welfare

The Poor Law officially finished in 1948. Much had changed since the early nineteenth century, but the 1930s still saw savage treatment of unemployed people by the welfare agencies of the period.[3] Crucially, working people simply could not construct the power to create any institution which challenged the power of the market mechanism. In the 1930s, as in the 1830s, the social security system was aimed specifically at making life out of work as horrible as possible. This experience was there not only for the unemployed, but for the majority of the elderly and the sick. Any interruption of earning led to great hardship; a hardship which could only be alleviated by finding wage labour or by using the 'savings' that had accrued in previous wage labour. Thus virtually all of the needs of a working-class family were expected to be met through their endeavours at work. This meant that the health, happiness and home were entirely dependent upon the way in which the market mechanism distributed wages and salaries. Any divergence from this was on the margins and should not be depended upon to provide mass relief from the vagaries of the market.

World War II represented a detailed and serious departure from this. Whilst it is often pointed out that the post-war Labour government and the welfare services that were constructed were far from socialism,[4] it needs re-asserting in the light of the last decade that they did represent a serious check to the power of the market in certain distinctive areas.

The power base for this change was to be found in the war itself. There is no space to explore fully the changes wrought in the experiences of all classes during World War II,[5] but in the fight *against* fascism it became essential to discover something concrete to fight *for*. This became equality and democracy; two principles which had not been transferred into real experiences for working-class people before the war. The army, the blitz, sacrifice and rationing had to be more equally experienced than previous hardships since the active consent of working people was crucial. Total war needed total commitment on all fronts and few people would enthusiastically fight for the insecurity of the 1930s. So real changes had to be made, real changes promised and real mechanisms for change constructed.

The wartime state had to take this seriously, both for the duration and in planning the future. It had to intervene in every aspect of life, including the previously sacrosanct market mechanism. State planning became necessary at every level. Those who had been heroes of free enterprise in the late 1930s by buying cheap and selling dear, became vicious black marketeers. Those who had been dismissed as absurd visionaries when they had argued for a planned economy became senior civil servants putting planning into practice. The normal market was outlawed; the impossible became normal.

In the midst of these changes a Liberal peer, Lord Beveridge, was given the task of planning for post-war social security. His plan was one of the most ambitious of any state document this century. We should not forget that it was only partially implemented, but still its vision was seen as a major part of the war effort. This vision was, as I shall outline later, the classic one of social democracy. Beveridge's plan incorporated a national health service and a fiscal policy that would ensure full employment. He believed that it was possible to defeat the five main evils of pre-war society: want, disease, idleness, ignorance and squalor. This was not a light matter − it involved a planned contract between individual and the state with the aim of abolishing most of the problems of deprivation for ever. The cause of these deprivations was inadequate wages for the working family to provide for itself, alone, during any interruption of earnings. Whilst the family would pay for some of this through an insurance stamp, the rest of the stamp would be paid by employer and the state.

Beveridge anticipated an insurance scheme which would pay out pensions, not on a test of means, but as of right. These pensions would be based upon a level of benefit ensuring the fact that they would become real liveable minimums. Thus, means-tested benefits would disappear except for a very small number of people who would need a 'safety' net.

So Beveridge and the post-war welfare institutions aimed, not just at easing the work effects of the market mechanism, but at breaking the seemingly inevitable link between the amount of benefit received and the wages received whilst in employment. Benefits would be adequate and would not be linked to wage levels. In this way the market was being attacked twice.

Alongside Beveridge's social security plan, the creation of the National Health Service and the increase in the number of council houses to be built both saw the state massively intervening in areas that had previously been totally dominated by the market. As we shall see, the results of these changes were much less complete than outlined here. However, for millions of working people a real and detailed change was provided by the post-war welfare services: a change which was due to their practical and political struggle; a change strongly aimed at destroying the worst excesses of the market relation of capitalism; a change which used large central state institutions as the main source of change.

It is this which marks the major motif of post-war state welfare institutions. They were massive centralized institutions which through the power invested in them by Act of Parliament were prepared to struggle with major social problems. Through this power their services would equalize some of the real existing deprivations and provide some real security. They were centralized institutions precisely because it was felt inevitable to involve the power of the central state in combating the worst excesses of market forces, both in the labour market and in the distribution of goods and services. As we shall see, whilst it was certainly true that centralized state power was necessary, the very size and bureaucratic nature of these institutions caused problems later on.

The 1960s and Early 1970s

UK Society in the 1950s was characterized by a growing mass affluence. Welfare was felt to play a significant role by ensuring that a large group did not get left behind. The Welfare State in alliance with a rising rate in real wages was felt to have succeeded in diminishing, if not eradicating, the vast majority of social problems in society. Indeed the major debate in welfare was whether the Welfare State had gone too far[6] and the 'middle classes' were being taxed out of existence. Macmillan's election in 1959 seemed to set the seal on a period of achievement and complacency for welfare.

However, the 1960s saw 'the rediscovery of poverty', a condition which, once socially 'refound', could not be forgotten completely. Social scientists played a significant role in this rediscovery. Abel-Smith and Townsend in both academic and popular forums pointed out that in the 1940s and 50s, far from abolishing poverty, the numbers of people on the official poverty line had increased.[7] Similarly, the numbers of people who experienced the inquiring detail of the means test had risen enormously. At the same time the nature of homelessness was revealed by the play *Cathy come home* and the viciousness of Rachman experiences, which were not simply around the lack of a roof but also underlined the continued experience of the market.

Thus the two major aims of the post-war welfare institution, the attack upon the absolute numbers of those in deprivation and a change in the way in which welfare services were delivered, were seen to have failed. It is important though to unpick the actual process of the rediscovery of poverty. It was not simply a matter of publishing results of surveys and the citizenry being horrified and clamouring for change. Over a few years this information became a part of the political process. Most importantly, 1964 saw a general election which was preceded by one of the longest campaigns ever. The issues of poverty, deprivation and failure were continual themes and had some impact on the result, at least on the loss of votes for the Conservative Party. Thus this 'rediscovery' was a political process involving a change of government and the Labour Party in a particularly crusading form.

The political and social reaction to the rediscovery of welfare in the 1960s tells us a great deal about theories of welfare in the UK. The society had, almost universally, believed that increasing affluence plus welfare had destroyed deprivation; once that central myth had itself been destroyed it became necessary for the society to explain the continuation of poverty. Three social explanations could have found credibility.

First, it could have been said that poverty and inequality still existed precisely *because* of the Welfare State and not despite of it. This argument sees the increase in welfare expenditure and welfare provision as undermining the real way in which working-class people have to 'fend for themselves'. It also undermines the power of the market mechanism to provide fully for people. Some fifteen years later this solution came to be identified with the sobriquet 'Thatcherism'. It is significant that in the mid-1960s this represented a minority view within the Conservative Party and did not gain either popular or powerful support at that time.

Alternatively, the re-emergence of poverty could be explained from the Left by the theory that poverty and inequality are intrinsic and inevitable aspects of capitalist social relations. They are not accidental by-products but will always exist as a part of our capitalist society. Any policy to abolish them is, within this argument, doomed as it fails to confront their real cause. All social policy then is at best doomed to complete failure and at worst makes the situation much worse by deflecting the poor from their real task — the abolition of the society itself. This explanation also represented a minority view of social policy and deprivation in the 1960s and whilst it may have become, by the 1980s, more convincing to a large number of intellectuals, it remains a minority view within contemporary society.

The third view, that characterized by a re-worked form of social democracy, reflected and won the hearts and minds of majority opinions. This tinkers with some of the basic tenets of social democratic theory whilst leaving the basic corpus the same. The poor were still there because, whilst the Welfare State and higher real wage rates had affected large numbers of people, the services had been both under-financed and not quite outward-going enough to reach everyone. Consequently, a substantial residue of people had been 'left behind' by the affluence; left behind because they did not understand the opportunities in the system and because there had been inadequate funding in their area

Basically, the promise of Beveridge was to be maintained but re-worked in the 1960s. The 1964 Labour government of Harold Wilson, re-elected in 1966, won both elections on a programme not only of welfare but also of modernization. The 1960s saw a string o detailed Royal Commissions looking closely at a wide range of institutions. Nearly all of them recommended some form of expansion (Seebohm on social services; Skeffington on planning; Robbins and Plowden on education) and nearly all of them fel that the services under discussion should become more responsive.[8] It seemed to be agreed that, whilst it was still necessary for deprivation to be dealt with through the agency of powerful central government institutions, it was also true that these bureaucracies had become closed to ordinary people. This closure was to be remedied by involving 'the community' and by providing much more information about services.

Sociologically speaking, the belief that there was a consensus in society about the nature and solution to social problems was maintained. When problems are posed in tern of communication, a belief that information simply has not got through, then society assumes that the simple provision of that information will not only be understood but acted upon by all concerned. It believes that everyone, say on both sides of the service under discussion, will agree about the aims of that service. Just a little more knowledge all round will mean that those in power will better understand what it feels like to be powerless; and those without power will better understand the system and how to use i

One important example from this period is the social security system. The two systen set up in 1948 had continued as separate entities with different benefit levels and different ways of distributing benefit. The National Assistance Board provided benefits that could only be received if the claimant had, when applying, undergone a test of their existing means. Thus people had to apply and be prepared to provide information on their income. The Ministry of Pensions and National Insurance provided pensions to people who had paid a certain number of National Insurance stamps. If the stamps had been paid then the benefit was provided as a right when the recipient was sick, unemployed or retired. Obviously the two schemes had very different ethoses; the offices hac different atmospheres and the recipients felt very differently.

The level of benefit provided by national assistance was for many claimants higher than that which might be received by national insurance. However, given that the forme had to be *applied for* there were millions of people who did not receive it. The consensu answer to this problem is to assume that the persons not claiming were missing out on benefit through ignorance; the problem was called 'non take-up' of benefit. It was as if t whole thrust of the National Assistance Board was to give out money; a fact of which the non-recipient was simply unaware.

Consequently, campaigns of information were run which did indeed bring many people into National Assistant Board offices. Similarly, the Labour government change the name of the NAB to the Supplementary Benefits Commission (SBC) in an attempt to cut the image of the institution off from the Poor Law of the past and give the impression that its benefits would in fact *supplement* other forms of benefit.

However, this assumes a single-minded approach on behalf of the NAB/SBC which is at odds with, not only the way in which it works, but also its whole aim. For it is undoubtedly the case that the Poor Law of 1834, the National Assistance Board of 1948 and the Supplementary Benefits Commission of 1966 have, as a major part of their remit, the importance of checking that only those who deserve it actually receive benefit. This inevitably creates social relationships in the benefit offices which are at best difficult for clients and at worst humiliating. At best, then, there is a contradiction within supplementary benefits between that aspect which wants to encourage the 'take-up' of benefit and that which minutely checks every claimant.

In trying to encourage the take-up of benefits the information stresses the rights of the individual; however, once the individual applies he or she experiences a very thorough and threatening interrogation. The information tries to overcome the stigma linked to application, but the experience of claiming adds to that stigma. As a consequence, the simple provision of knowledge about benefits does not ensure that all people who should get them do. The consensus model of institutions simply did not work in institutions which had other sets of goals than simply providing a service to meet a need.

The example of the social security systems can be replicated for changes in health and social services.[9] Whilst more resources were expended, and some attempts to open up the relationship between client and service were noted, the services failed to eradicate social deprivation.

The 1970s and the Basis of Thatcherism

The promise of welfare made in the 1940s and re-made in the 1960s was never, and probably never could be, fully kept. Reading the Royal Commissions of the 1960s is a curious experience in the 1980s since they represent a highly confident set of policies and commitments. They would work; social problems *could* be solved. It is partially on the failure of these extravagant promises that the Thatcherite policy alternative is founded. Politically and economically, the social democratic social policies had been backed, perhaps not as strongly as wished by some, but they had been tried and re-tried. In challenging this normal approach Thatcher called into question the whole basis of post-war British social policy.

Conservative government since 1979 has been attempting to roll back the 'frontiers of the state'. Across the widest range of policy areas it has been trying to challenge the state itself as the organizer and provider of welfare. It would be wrong to overemphasize their success in this area (see table 7.2), but this should not decry from the reality that this represents the dominant political welfare philosophy of the early 1980s. The philosophy is outlined in a later section; here we need to outline the ways in which welfare institutions have been changed.

One of the dominant experiences of welfare that Thatcherism has criticized is the lack of choice posed by Welfare State institutions for welfare clients. Choice itself is exemplified in consumer choice. The social security office, the hospital and the social work team are all shown to be different from the corner shop where the consumer can *choose* between different consumer brands. This contrast represents one of the continual themes of the policy: to introduce choice into the system, it is necessary to introduce the market mechanism since it is that which creates consumer choice. The

Table 7.2　　Shares of Public Expenditure in the UK, 1976-7 to 1983-4 (percentages)

	planned					
	1976-7	1978-9	1979-80	1980-1	1982-3	1983-4
Defence	11.3	11.4	12.0	12.0	12.2	12.8
Law and Order	3.1	3.1	3.3	3.4	3.6	3.7
Education	12.7	12.3	12.1	12.2	11.1	10.4
Health and Personal Social Services	10.9	11.3	11.5	12.2	11.8	11.9
Housing	7.0	5.6	6.1	5.0	3.0	2.2
Social Security	21.2	24.9	25.1	25.1	27.8	27.6

Source: *The Government's Expenditure Plans, 1982-3 to 1984-5.*

market has to be introduced through private enterprise providing a series of alternatives, just like the choice between brands of tea.

The social democratic Welfare State had itself always allowed a significant strand of the market to be maintained within welfare in this country. The state education sector had evolved alongside a public school system which operated within the market mechanism. The 1945 and 1964 Labour governments had not abolished this part of the education system. Indeed its dominance as a form of education was still strong. Similarly, within the field of housing, owner-occupation had grown to over half of the housing sector; many more people were buying their own houses, once more taking part in a market process for the distribution of the good of housing. The state social security system had allowed and encouraged the growth of independent private pension schemes, allowing vast numbers of pensioners to opt out of state welfare. Finally, the National Health Service had grown up alongside a private healthcare system, allowing the market into the distribution of medicine.

Therefore, Thatcher's underlining of the market mechanism as a way of distributing services associated with welfare did not in fact come entirely out of the blue. Instead she was arguing for a growth in influence of an already existing mechanism; what is more, a mechanism which has considerable weight within every other section of society. Markets and welfare were not total strangers.

The cutting edge of Thatcherist policy is to encourage the market itself to undermine state welfare. If millions of people choose to use private health then it is not necessary to cut the NHS — as a mass service it would inevitably diminish. Similarly, with the rise in owner-occupation for council house sales, it increases the private sector totally at the cost of state control. Even the most powerful Thatcherite does not envisage the complete abolition of state welfare services. A residuum is to be maintained for those sections of society who cannot afford the private market. This would provide a minimal form of service, meeting the barest needs and in no sense competing with the market mechanism in the rest of the market. Consequently, it is an inevitable part of this philosophy and policy that state institutions should not have as good facilities as private ones, otherwise why should people choose them at all?

On some occasions, and most dramatically with unemployed people, those in receipt of state benefits should in some very distinct way be made worse off than those in work, not just financially, but in other ways. Otherwise, the thinking goes, why should the people in work bother to go? This represents the most obvious and important continuation of the Poor Law of 1834 with its principle of less eligibility.

However, the process of social change does not simply follow the pattern of changes in government ideologies. As table 7.2 shows, in the first few years of Thatcherism the state has not been successfully 'rolled back' in expenditure terms. In the field of housing expenditure much has been achieved and more planned. But this represents the only area where capital spending, mainly on building, can be easily cut back. In other areas institutions have maintained their importance, even more obviously in the field of unemployment benefit, given the rise in unemployment.

Consequently, the Welfare State in 1984 represents a wide variety of frequently contrasting policies. The social democratic institutions built up in the post-war period and the 1960s still hold enormous sway over the actual distribution of welfare to millions of people. However, that takes place against the background of an ideology in government committed to a thorough challenge of both these ideas and institutions. Extremely powerful social forces are at play in this defence and attack, ensuring that welfare services and public expenditure will remain one of the central political issues of the 1980s.

WAYS OF UNDERSTANDING

Analysing society needs more than history and contemporary empirical material. One of the most powerful lessons that sociology has taught the study of welfare is that we must make our theoretical perspectives explicit. Equally, the theories need to be developed as *theories* in order to understand more fully how we approach the issue. Whilst this is a general issue within sociological studies[10] it has proved of specific major importance in the study of welfare in the UK.

Indeed there is a strong case to be made that the origins of British sociology are to be found in the empirical study of poverty and deprivation.[11] It is certainly the case that the first university social science departments were founded on the basis of teaching voluntary social workers.[12] However, the bulk of this early study, and indeed most welfare study until the 1960s, was carried out without an explicitly theoretical framework. To be sure, as we shall see, a theory was used, but it was a theory which had been developed inside the welfare institutions themselves, and therefore inevitably failed to ask important questions of those institutions. British social science is unique in developing a specific 'discipline' for this purpose called 'social administration'.[13] Indeed whole degrees and courses have been taught within that framework — specifically aimed at the study of welfare institutions in the UK. It is this perspective which has dominated the study and indeed the actual construction of welfare and it is in debate with this that the other theories have developed. Consequently, we will start with this model.

Social Democratic Theory and Welfare

The label of social democracy has a substantially longer history than the creation of the party with that title. It describes a political theory of society; a theory which places welfare institutions at its core. There is, as in the three theoretical categories I outline, a wide variety of views within this perspective. They all, however, believe that the major social problems of our society are soluble.

Such a statement may seem to be a truism and indeed for most of the post-war period this was the case. As we saw in the Beveridge Report (in the 1940s) and Seebohm and Plowden (in the 1960s), there is a heady and determined optimism contained in this approach. Want *can* be abolished, inequality massively reduced, children educated to their utmost capacity, etc., etc., through an active, restless determined set of interventions aimed at real detailed success. Social democracy evolved in this optimistic form in order to pave itself firmly against *laissez-faire* approaches to social problems. Obviously the belief in solutions to problems must be based upon an understanding of where these problems come from. If they are seen as 'innate' in human nature then obviously they are not soluble. If they are seen as inextricably linked up with every aspect of our society then equally, without the total transformation of that society, they are not soluble. However, social democracy sees them as residual problems which are by-products of other elements of society. For example, the market mechanism in the distribution of money through wages and salaries fails to provide for any low wage earners with large families. The form of poverty is seen as a by-product and can be remedied by a combination of interventions around family allowances.

Social policy, therefore, is aimed at the alleviation of problems which are vital to the people concerned, but which are soluble because they are by-products of the essential social relations of society.

However, this active intervention to solve these problems needs a vehicle to carry it forward, a way of solving the problems. The major vehicle used by social democracy is the state. Over and over again it is state intervention which is argued for, planned and implemented. Indeed the very title 'Welfare State' underlines the importance of the state, not only as provider of the funds but as organizer of the services. In some ways we should not be surprised since the size of the social problems are enormous, but as we shall see it is not necessary for the state to be so heavily involved throughout the whole process of welfare provision.

Equally, as we saw in the 1960s, the form of state chosen by social democracy has been of prime importance. Essentially large units with central control have been used, partly to ensure that the problems can be substantially dealt with, but also because control can be maintained by those people who run the state. Social democracy posed public intervention and state control as the necessary powerful tools to provide welfare.

Policy change within this model has primarily been viewed as assisting the institutions to get it right, to improve their solutions. At the same time, it is the work of social scientists to improve the state's knowledge of the existence of social problems. Therefore once a remedy to a researched problem has been thought out, the state can step in and use it. The assumption is that, by and large, there is general agreement within society about such issues. If a consensus doesn't actually exist then one can be mobilized through well-presented argument and pressure group politics.

The role of the intellectual, usually the social scientist, in this process is central. They research the problems, work through the solutions and organize the consensus and then, in many cases, actually run the organizations involved. Social democracy puts the 'expert' and the professional in a dominant position in the whole process — a position where their rationality can be most used. The argument is then used in conjunction with pressure groups to mobilize consensus around a particular change in the form of welfare.

Throughout, social democracy poses basically different methods of distributing resources from that of the market. The most powerful exposition of this difference is in the work of Richard Titmuss, in particular his book *The Gift Relationship*, which poses the question of market mechanism versus giving, in looking at the distribution of blood.[14] He points out how the 'giving' of blood is not only morally better, but is also less likely to lead to the distribution of infected blood.

As I have outlined in the historical section, despite intellectual critique from the Left and massive government attack from Thatcherism, social democracy remains the dominant trend in welfare ideology.

Market Mechanism as Distributor of Welfare

This theory has dominated the politics of welfare in the 1980s. Its hallmark is essentially contained within the relationship between state and individual responsibility, especially in terms of the freedom of the individual to choose.

The market is viewed as the 'natural' system for distributing goods and services; any interference in that mechanism interferes with the best possible system. The market works for individuals in that they have control over how they save or spend the money that they earn. Public expenditure on state welfare takes away this choice in two ways. First, it leaves less money for the individual or family to make choices about, less because state welfare takes taxes to pay for social services. Consequently, cuts in public expenditure are not only anti-state expenditure but should, through lower taxes, allow the individual to exercise greater choice. Secondly the sum total of these millions of rational choices through the market mechanism assures that the best and cheapest forms of welfare services are maintained and extended. Inefficient or unpopular services disappear because they do not appeal to sufficient people through their choices.

Obviously the state has no place in this mechanism except to ensure that competition remains as healthy as possible. At extremes this theory would allow all those who were economically unable to make any choices to suffer without; indeed the provision of any safety net which can be landed on without pain acts as a disincentive to remaining economically independent. Therefore the philosophy sees economic independence as of enormous moral importance since it is only through that state that people can exercise their full potential. Any state welfare measures which interfere with this undermine the very humanity which they claim to protect.

Much of the popular appeal is based upon the everyday nature of the market which people experience in buying tea, cigarettes and cars. Here we are used to the mechanism: we simply do not see, in the market place, those people who cannot afford to enter. They are quite simply absent. This then is the major problem for this approach. Those people who do not have the economic capacity to choose, those people who do not experience the social and economic world as a set of opportunities for ever opening up to them, are simply outside of the model. If there are only a few of them their absence passes quietly. If there are many they may make their voices heard in a variety of other, more political, ways.

Marxist Theories: Determination or Class Struggle

Other chapters of this book have also discussed the importance of Marxist theories in the study of society. Two specific issues need clarifying here. First, seen as political theories on which powerful policies might have been based, Marxism has been of much less importance than either social democracy or the theory of market forces. Market forces represent one of the most powerful themes within a capitalist society and therefore they provide a base for all sorts of policy activity within existing social relations. Similarly, social democracy as an optimistic theory of social improvement has provided the powerful base for much post-war social policy. By contrast, Marxist thought in this area has been of critical intellectual importance, but has not secured sufficiently powerful political or mass support to influence the creation of policy. Consequently, it represents much more an analysis, rather than describing detailed policy; a feat that it could only attain in a society in which it had greater power, that is a socialist society.

Secondly, there are two very distinct and opposing interpretations of Marxist theory within the Welfare State, which utilize different bases within Marxist thought. It is wrong to think of Marxist thought as continuing a simple unity. There are continuing intellectual and political disagreements within it. On the one hand, stress is put upon the way in which the capitalist class not only dominates economic life, but also dominates all state relations including the Welfare State; on the other, the Welfare State is seen as representing direct contradictions between existing classes, leaving some aspects of it as progressive and some reactionary.

The power of the first form of Marxism is in its direct contrast to social democratic analysis of welfare. Since that form of analysis represents such a central part of understanding welfare, it was inevitable that it should receive the sharpest criticisms. Most importantly the institution chosen by social democracy to carry out the analysis, that of the state, comes under the most rigorous re-thinking. The state is seen as an organization which represents the interests of the ruling class of any society. Thus, in a feudal society the state represents aristocracies; the interests of the serfs are taken into account only when they happen to coincide with those of the aristocracy. When there is any form of clash in these interests the state takes the side of the ruling class.

Similarly, within a capitalist society it is the capitalist class which uses the state for its own interest. As a consequence all of the actions of the state in the field of welfare, however beneficial they may seem to working people, can only be understood in terms of the interests of capitalism. For example, the National Health Service provides services for working people in order to maintain both their ability to work and their ability to reproduce workers in the family. Similarly, social security exists, both to provide some finance for poor people to spend on consumer goods, thereby bolstering the market, but also to ensure that workers are cared for whilst unemployed or sick to enable them to recommence employment. Consequently, within this argument it is entirely wrong for social reformers to look to the state as the institution which will improve their condition since this would only happen if that improvement was in the interests of the rich and powerful.

There is also a direct challenge to the belief that social problems can find any overall solution within our society. Beveridge's promise of the end of want, disease, ignorance, idleness and squalor is seen at best as misguided and, at worst, as an attempt to deliberately hoodwink working people. All of these deprivations are seen as intrinsic aspects of a capitalist society and cannot be adequately dealt with as long as that society exists. Like social democracy, the market mechanism is seen as a major cause of these social problems; unlike social democracy though, their solution cannot be achieved without the powerful delimitation and eventual destruction of the market mechanism. What social democrats may see as the 'worst effects' of the market are seen as an inevitable element of capitalist social relations.

Therefore, the only really thorough social policy can be one which overturns capitalism as a whole. Such a philosophy, far from being pessimistic, shifts the possibility and importance of social policy for progress out of this epoch and into the future: socialism. It does, however, mean that the major thrust of any practical political activity must be aimed at revolutionary change.

In contrast, the alternative Marxist perspective underlines the importance of working-class action within a capitalist society. It puts stress upon the working class as the *agency* of social progress and change; the people who will actually carry it out. As a consequence it sees real possibilities for specific achievement *within* a capitalist society. However, it would agree that these can only really fully come about when capitalism has been overthrown. Until that time social progress through welfare policy has two major rationales. It can marginally improve some aspects of the lives of working-class and oppressed people, they can be given some security from the vagaries of the market. It also builds up the confidence of working-class people as historical actors. If it is possible for the working class to successfully represent its interests in one area, then it is also possible to carry this out in a much wider and more powerful way in the future.

This is not simply a prescriptive part of the theory, it can also be used to analyse the history of policy. For rather than seeing the state as inevitably acting in the interests of the ruling class, this approach sees the state as reflecting the balance of class forces in the society as a whole. It rejects any notion that the state is neutral, but sees that it can be struggled over and, at specific times and in specific forms, can reflect the interests of working-class people. However, it cannot do this totally until they are in charge throughout the rest of the society, in every institution.

Thus it says that if we want to understand anything about a particular social policy, we have to look at the balance of political, ideological, social and economic class forces that exist at that particular time. For example, in the period after World War II working-class people had, through the elections, represented their interests through the Labour Party. Ideologically, following the war, there was considerable stress upon the ideas of equality, democracy and progress. This gave some considerably powerful elements to welfare policy of the time. However, socially working-class people were not put in charge of the institution of welfare; they did not influence the organizational framework. Economically, too, working people were still very far from influence let alone control.

Thus, the state policy on welfare reflected the different strengths and weaknesses of the classes involved. If you were to analyse those factors in the 1980s, it might explain some of the major changes in policy.

CONCLUSION

The organization of this chapter may seem odd since it represents two very distinct formats: on the one hand a very schematic history of state welfare in UK; on the other a thematic approach to the three main models of welfare. I believe it is only through a historical understanding of theoretical models that it is possible to approach welfare. Given the increasing intellectual and political importance of the area of social study in the 1980s, the development of those theoretical models within the sphere of political practice itself will be of major importance in social change.

Notes to Chapter 7

1 See P. Corrigan, 'The Welfare State on an Arena of Class Struggle', *Marxism Today* (March 1977).
2 See R. Pinker, *Social Theory and Social Policy* (London 1971); and N. Ginsburg, *Class, Capital and Social Policy* (London 1979).
3 For an account, see G. Orwell, *The Road to Wigan Pier* (London 1937).
4 For example, R. Miliband, *Parliamentary Socialism* (London 1973); and D. Coates, *The Labour Party and the Struggle for Socialism* (Cambridge 1975).
5 See A. Calder, *The People's War* (London 1969).
6 I. Macleod and E. Powell, *The Social Services' Needs and Means*, Conservative Political Centre (1952).
7 B. Abel-Smith and P. Townsend, *The Poor and The Poorest* (London 1965).
8 Seebohm, *Committee on Local Authority and Personal Social Services* (HMSO 1968); Skeffington, *People and Planning* (HMSO 1969); Robbins, *Committee on Higher Education* (HMSO 1963); and Plowden, *Children and their Primary Schools* (HMSO 1966).
9 See L. Doyal, *The Political Economy of Health* (London 1979); and S. Bolger in S. Bolger, P. Corrigan, J. Docking and N. Frost (eds), *Towards Socialist Welfare Work* (London 1981).
10 See J. Rex, *Key Problems in Sociological Theory* (London 1961).
11 P. Abrams, *The Origins of British Sociology* (Chicago 1968); and R. Pinker, *op. cit.*
12 See C. Jones, *Social Work, the State and the Working Class* (London 1982).
13 R. M. Titmuss, *Essays on the Welfare State* (London 1963).
14 R. M. Titmuss, *The Gift Relationship* (London 1970).

Select Bibliography

The Bibliography is organised in six sections: **1. General Sources and Works of Reference** concerned with the aspects of contemporary UK society treated in this volume; **2. Cities and Urban Problems** – the principal sources used for chapter 1 of this volume together with other recommended works on urbanism and urban change in the UK since 1945; **3. Education** – the principal sources used for chapter 2 of this volume together with a selection of other works on education and socialisation; **4. The Division of Labour** – the principal sources and recommended works on work, occupations and the political economy of gender relationships which are the subjects of chapters 3 and 4; **5. Inequality** – the main sources used for chapter 5 together with selected recommended works on elites, deprivation and class structure in the UK; **6. Deviance, Law and the Welfare State** – the principal sources used for chapters 6 and 7 and a selection of other works on these topics. The bibliography is in no way comprehensive and many of the works listed in one section are of course also of relevance for other topics.

1. GENERAL SOURCES AND WORKS OF REFERENCE

CENTRAL OFFICE OF INFORMATION, *Britain – an Official Handbook*, HMSO, London, annual.
CENTRAL STATISTICAL OFFICE, *Annual Abstract of Statistics*, HMSO, London.
CENTRAL STATISTICAL OFFICE, *Facts in Focus*, HMSO, London, 1975.
CENTRAL STATISTICAL OFFICE, *Social Trends*, HMSO, London, annually since 1970.
DEPARTMENT OF EDUCATION AND SCIENCE, *Education Statistics for the United Kingdom*, HMSO, London, annually since 1967.
DEPARTMENT OF EMPLOYMENT, *Employment Gazette*, HMSO, London, monthly.
DEPARTMENT OF EMPLOYMENT, *Family Expenditure Survey*, HMSO, London, annual.
DEPARTMENT OF THE ENVIRONMENT, *Census Indicators of Urban Deprivation*, HMSO, London, 1975.
DEPARTMENT OF THE ENVIRONMENT, *Trends in Population, Housing and Occupancy Rates 1861–1961*, HMSO, London, 1971.
DEPARTMENT OF HEALTH AND SOCIAL SECURITY, *Health and Personal Social Services Statistics for England and Wales*, HMSO, London, 1972.
HALSEY, A. H. (ed.), *Trends in British Society since 1900*, Macmillan, London, 1972.
HALSEY, A. H., *Change in British Society*, Oxford University Press, Oxford 1978.
HAMMOND, E., *An Analysis of Regional Economic and Social Statistics*, University of

Durham, Rowntree Research Unit, Durham, 1968.
MARSH, D. C., *The Changing Social Structure of England and Wales 1871–1961*, Routledge and Kegan Paul, London, 1965.
MAUNDER, W. F. (ed.), *Reviews of United Kingdom Statistical Sources*, Vols. 1-5, Heinemann, London, 1973–6; Vols. 6-15, Pergamon, Oxford, 1978–81.
MITCHELL, B. and DEANE, P., *Abstract of British Historical Statistics*, Cambridge University Press, Cambridge, 1962.
NOBLE, T., *Structure and Change in Modern Britain*, Batsford, London, 1981.
SILLITOE, A., *Britain in Figures*, Penguin Books, London, 1971.

2. CITIES AND URBAN PROBLEMS

AMBROSE, P. and COLENUTT, B., *The Property Machine*, Penguin Books, London, 1975.
ASHWORTH, W., *The Genesis of Modern British Town Planning*, Routledge and Kegan Paul, London, 1954.
BALL, M., *Housing Policy and Economic Power. The Political Economy of Owner Occupation*, Methuen, London, 1983.
BELL, C. and NEWBY, H., *Community Studies*, Allen and Unwin, London, 1971.
The Brixton Disorders 10–12 April, 1981, Report of an Inquiry by the Rt. Hon. The Lord Scarman, HMSO, London, 1981.
BROADY, M., *Planning for People*, Bedford Square Press, London, 1968.
CAMERON, G. (ed.), *The Future of the British Conurbations*, Longman, London, 1980.
CASHMORE, E. and TROYNO, B. (eds), *Black Youth in Crisis*, Allen and Unwin, London, 1982.
CASTELLS, M., *The Urban Question*, Edward Arnold, London, 1976.
CASTELLS, M., 'Y-a-t-il une sociologie urbaine', *Sociologie du Travail*, No. 1, 1968.
CENTRE FOR URBAN STUDIES, *London: Aspects of Change*, MacGibbon and Kee, London, 1964.
CHISHOLM, M. and MANNERS, A., *Spatial Policy Problems of the British Economy*, Cambridge University Press, Cambridge, 1971.
CLAWSON, M. and HALL, P., *Planning and Urban Growth, an Anglo-American Comparison*, Johns Hopkins University Press, Baltimore, USA, 1973.
COUNTER INFORMATION SERVICES, *The Recurrent Crisis of London*, London, 1973.
CULLINGWORTH, J. B., *Housing Needs and Planning Policy*, Routledge and Kegan Paul, London, 1960.
CULLINGWORTH, J. B., *Owner Occupation in Scotland and in England and Wales*, NHRBC, London, 1969.
DAMER, S., 'Wine Alley: the Sociology of a Dreadful Enclosure', *Sociological Review*, vol. 22, No. 2, 1974.
DAVIES, P. and NEWTON, K., 'The Social Patterns of Immigrant Areas', *Race*, vol. XIV, No. 1, 1972.
DEAR, M. and SCOTT, A. (eds), *Urbanization and Urban Planning in Capitalist Society*, Methuen, London, 1981.
DENNIS, N., *People and Planning*, Faber and Faber, London, 1970.
DENNIS, N., HENRIQUES, F. and SLAUGHTER, C., *Coal is our Life*, Eyre and Spottiswoode, London, 1956.
DEPARTMENT OF THE ENVIRONMENT, *Census Indicators of Urban Deprivation*, Working Note No. 6, 1975.
DEPARTMENT OF THE ENVIRONMENT, *Housing and Construction Statistics 1972–*

1982, HMSO, London, 1983.

DEPARTMENT OF THE ENVIRONMENT, *Policy for the Inner Cities*, Cmnd. 6845, HMSO, London, 1977.

DEPARTMENT OF THE ENVIRONMENT, *Study of the Inner Areas of Conurbations*, HMSO, London, 1975.

DONNISON, D. and EVERSLEY, D. (eds), *London: Urban Patterns, Problems and Policies*, Heinemann, London, 1973.

DONNISON, D. and SOTO, P., *The Good City. A Study of Urban Development and Policy*, Heinemann, London, 1980.

DURANT, R., *Watling: A Survey of Social Life on a New Housing Estate*, P. S. King and Son, London, 1959.

ELLIOTT, B. and McCRONE, D., 'Landlords in Edinburgh: some preliminary findings', *Sociological Review*, vol. 23, 1975.

ELLIOTT, B. and McCRONE, D., 'Urban development in Edinburgh: a contribution to the political economy of place', *Scottish Journal of Sociology*, vol. 4, 1980.

ENGLISH, J. and NORMAN, P., 'One Hundred Years of Slum Clearance in England and Wales', *Discussion Papers in Social Research*, No. 1, University of Glasgow, Glasgow, 1974.

EVANS, A. and EVERSLEY, D. (eds), *The Inner City, Employment and Industry*, Heinemann, London, 1980.

EVERSLEY, D., 'Landlords' Slow Goodbye', *New Society*, 15 January 1975.

EVERSLEY, D., *The Planner in Society. The Changing Role of a Profession*, Faber, London, 1973.

FERRIS, J., *Participation in Urban Planning*, Bell, London, 1972.

FORD, J., 'The Role of Building Society Managers in the Urban Stratification System', *Urban Studies*, vol. 12, No. 3, 1975.

FOTHERGILL, S. and GUDGIN, G., *Unequal Growth, Urban and Regional Employment Change in the UK*, Heinemann, London, 1982.

GLASS, R., 'The Evaluation of Planning: Some Sociological Considerations', *International Social Science Journal*, vol. XI, No. 3, 1959.

GOODMAN, R., *After the Planners*, Penguin Books, London, 1972.

GREVE, J. and PAGE, D., *Homelessness in London*, Scottish Academic Press, Edinburgh, 1971.

HADDON, R., 'The Location of West Indians in the London Housing Market', *New Atlantis*, vol. 2, No. 1, 1970.

HALL, P., *The Inner City in Context*, Heinemann, London, 1981.

HALL, P., GRACEY, H., DREWITT, R. and THOMAS, R., *The Containment of Urban England*, Allen and Unwin, London, 1973.

HAMNETT, C., 'Social Change and Social Segregation in Inner London 1961–71', *Urban Studies*, vol. 13, No. 3, 1976.

HAMNETT, C. and WILLIAMS, M., 'Social Change in London: a study of gentrification', *The London Journal*, vol. 6, 1980.

HARRISON, P., *Inside the Inner City*, Penguin, Harmondsworth, Middlesex, 1983.

HARVEY, D., *Social Justice and the City*, Edward Arnold, London, 1973.

HOME OFFICE, *Racial Attacks*, HMSO, London, 1981.

JACKSON, A., *Semi-Detached London*, Allen & Unwin, London, 1973.

JEFFREY, P., *Migrants and Refugees. Muslim and Christian Pakistani Families in Bristol*, Cambridge University Press, Cambridge, 1976.

JOHNSTON, R. J., *Urban Residential Patterns*, Bell, London, 1971.

JONES, C. (ed.), *Urban Deprivation and the Inner City*, Croom Helm, London, 1979.

KEMENY, J., 'Home Ownership and Privatization', *International Journal of Urban and Regional Studies*, vol. 4, 1980.

KINGSTON POLYTECHNIC, *The Buxton Report*, London, 1976.

KNOX, P. and CULLEN, J., 'Planners as Urban Managers: an exploration of the attitudes and self-image of senior British planners', *Environment and Planning*, vol. 13, 1981.

KUPER, L., *Living in Towns*, Cresset Press, London, 1953.

LAMBERT, C. and WEIR, D., *Cities in Modern Britain*, Fontana, London, 1975.

LAWLESS, P., *Urban Deprivation and Government Initiative*, Faber, London, 1979.

LAWLESS, P., *Britain's Inner Cities*, Harper and Row, London, 1981.

LIPSKEY, M. et al., *Theoretical Perspectives on Urban Politics*, Prentice Hall, Englewood Cliffs, New Jersey, 1976.

MELLOR, J. R., *Urban Sociology in an Urbanized Society*, Routledge and Kegan Paul, London, 1977.

MITCHELL, C. D., LUPTON, T., HODGES, M., and SMITH, C., *Neighbourhood and Community*, Liverpool University Press, Liverpool, 1954.

MOGEY, J. M., *Family and Neighbourhood: Two Studies in Oxford*, Oxford University Press, Oxford, 1956.

MOSER, C. and SCOTT, W., *British Towns: A Statistical Study of their Economic and Social Differences*, Oliver and Boyd, Edinburgh, 1961.

MUCHNICK, D., 'Urban Renewal in Liverpool', *Occasional Papers on Social Administration*, No. 33, Bell, London, 1970.

MUMFORD, L., *The City in History*, Secker and Warburg, London, 1961.

NOWIKOWSKI, S. and WARD, R., 'Middle Class and British? An analysis of South Asians in Suburbia', *New Community*, vol. 7, 1978.

ORLANS, H., *Stevenage: A Sociological Portrait of a New Town*, Routledge and Kegan Paul, London, 1952.

PAHL, R., *Readings in Urban Sociology*, Pergamon Press, Oxford, 1968.

PAHL, R., *Whose City?*, Longman, London, 1970.

PAHL, R., *Urbs in Rure: the Metropolitan Fringe*, London School of Economics, Geographical Papers, No. 2, 1965.

PAHL, R., *Urban Sociology: Critical Essays*, Tavistock Publications, London, 1976.

PEACH, C., *West Indian Migration to Britain*, Oxford University Press, Oxford, 1968.

PEACH, C. (ed.), *Ethnic Segregation in Cities*, Croom Helm, London, 1981.

POLICY STUDIES INSTITUTE, *Police and People in London*, PSI, London, 1983.

PRATT, G., 'Class analysis and urban domestic property: a critical examination', *International Journal of Urban and Regional Research*, Vol. 6, 1982.

Report of the Committee on Housing in Greater London, HMSO, Cmnd. 2605, 1965.

REX, J. and MOORE, R., *Race, Community and Conflict: a study of Sparkbrook*, Oxford University Press, Oxford, 1967.

RICHARDSON, H., VIPOND, J. and FURBEY, R., *Housing and Urban Spatial Structure, A Case Study*, Saxon House, Farnborough, 1975.

ROBINSON, F. and ABRAMS, P., *What we Know about Neighbours*, University of Durham, Rowntree Research Unit, Durham, 1977.

ROBINSON, V., 'Asians and Council Housing', *Urban Studies*, vol. 17, 1980.

ROBINSON, B. T., *Urban Analysis*, Cambridge University Press, Cambridge, 1969.

SAUNDERS, P., *Urban Politics*, Hutchinson, London, 1979.

SHELTER, *Council House Sales: who pays?*, Shelter (The Scottish Campaign for the Homeless), Edinburgh, 1979.

STACEY, M., 'The Myth of Community Studies', *British Journal of Sociology*, vol. 20, 1969.

TEBBUTT, M., *Making Ends Meet: Pawnbroking and Working Class Credit*, Leicester University Press, Leicester, 1983.
WEBER, M., *The City*, trans. D. Martindale and G. Neuwirth, Free Press, New York.
WILLIAMS, M., 'The New Raj: the gentrifiers and the natives', *New Society*, 14 January 1982.
WILMOTT, P., *The Evolution of a Community*, Routledge and Kegan Paul, London, 1963.
WILLMOTT, P. and YOUNG, M., *The Symmetrical Family*, Routledge and Kegan Paul, London, 1973.
WIRTH, L., 'Urbanism as a Way of Life', *American Journal of Sociology*, vol. 44, 1938.
YOUNG, M. and WILLMOTT, P., *Family and Kinship in East London*, Routledge and Kegan Paul, London, 1957.

3. EDUCATION

ACKER, S., 'No Woman's Land: British Sociology of Education 1960–1979', *Sociological Review*, vol. 29, No. 1, 1981.
ARCHER, M. S., *The Social Origins of Educational Systems*, Sage, London, 1979.
BALL, S. J., *Beachside Comprehensive: A Case Study of Secondary Schooling*, Cambridge University Press, Cambridge, 1981.
BALL, S. J. (ed.), *Comprehensive Schooling: A Reader*, Falmer Press, Lewes, 1984.
BAMFORD, T., *The Rise of the Public Schools*, Nelson, London, 1967.
BANKS, O., 'The Sociology of Education, 1952–1982', *British Journal of Educational Studies*, vol. 30, No. 1, 1982.
BANKS, O., *The Sociology of Education*, Batsford, London, 1976.
BARKER LUNN, J., *Streaming in the Primary School*, National Foundation for Educational Research, Slough, 1970.
BARNES, J., *Educational Priority: Curriculum Innovation in London's Educational Priority Areas*, vol. 3, HMSO, London, 1975.
BARTON, L. and WALKER, S. (eds), *Race, Class and Education*, Croom Helm, London, 1983.
BENN, C. and SIMON, B., *Half Way There*, Penguin, Harmondsworth, Mddx., 1972.
BERNSTEIN, B., *Class Codes and Control*, vol. 1-3, Routledge and Kegan Paul, London, 1971–75.
BLACKBURN, R. M., STEWART, A. and PRANDY, K., 'Part-time Education and the "Alternative Route"', *Sociology*, vol. 14, No. 4, 1980.
BURGESS, R. G., *Experiencing Comprehensive Education: A Study of Bishop McGregor School*, Methuen, London, 1983.
BYRNE, D. S., WILLIAMSON, W. and FLETCHER, B., *The Poverty of Education*, Martin Robertson, London, 1975.
BYRNE, E., *Women and Education*, Tavistock, London, 1978.
BYRNE, E. M., 'Inequality in Education – Discriminal Resource-allocation in Schools', *Educational Review*, vol. 27, No. 3, 1975.
COHEN, L., THOMAS, J. and MANION, L. (eds), *Educational Research and Development in Britain 1970–1980*, National Foundation for Educational Research, Windsor, 1982.
CORMACK, R. J. and OSBORNE, R. D. (eds), *Religion, Education and Employment: Aspects of Equal Opportunity in Northern Ireland*, Appletree Press, Belfast, 1983.
CRAFT, M. and CRAFT, A., 'The Participation of Ethnic Minority Pupils in Further and

Higher Education', *Educational Review*, vol. 25, No. 1, 1983.

CRAFT, M., RAYNOR, J. and COHEN, L. (eds), *Linking Home and School*, Harper and Row, London, 3rd edition, 1980.

DALE, R., ESLAND, G. and MACDONALD, M. (eds), *Schooling and Capitalism: A Sociological Reader*, Routledge and Kegan Paul, London, 1976.

DARBY, J., 'Divisiveness in Education', *The Northern Teacher*, Winter, 1973.

DARBY, J., 'Educational Provision in Northern Ireland', *The Northern Teacher*, vol. 12, No. 4, 1977.

DAVIE, R., BUTLER, M. and GOLDSTEIN, H., *From Birth to Seven*, Longman, London, 1972.

DEEM, R. (ed.), *Schooling for Women's Work*, Routledge and Kegan Paul, London, 1980.

DEEM, R., *Women and Schooling*, Routledge and Kegan Paul, London, 1978.

DELAMONT, S., 'All too familiar? A Decade of Classroom Research', *Educational Analysis*, vol. 3, No. 1, 1981.

DELAMONT, S., *Interaction in the Classroom*, Methuen, London, 1976.

DELAMONT, S., *Sex Roles and the School*, Methuen, London, 1980.

DEPARTMENT OF EDUCATION AND SCIENCE, *Aspects of Secondary Education in England: A Survey by HM Inspectors of Schools*, HMSO, London, 1979.

DEPARTMENT OF EDUCATION AND SCIENCE, *Children and their Primary Schools* (Plowden Report), HMSO, London, 1967.

DEPARTMENT OF EDUCATION AND SCIENCE, *Education: A Framework for Expansion*, Cmnd. 5174, HMSO, London, 1972.

DEPARTMENT OF EDUCATION AND SCIENCE, *The Organisation of Secondary Education*, HMSO, London, 1965.

DEPARTMENT OF EDUCATION AND SCIENCE, *Primary Education in England: A Survey by HM Inspectors of Schools*, HMSO, London, 1978.

DOUGLAS, J. W. B., *The Home and the School*, MacGibbon and Kee, London, 1964.

DOUGLAS, J. W. B., ROSS, J. M. and SIMPSON, H. R., *All Our Future*, Peter Davies, London, 1968.

DRIVER, G., *Beyond Underachievement*, Commission for Racial Equality, London, 1980.

EGGLESTON, J. (ed.), *Contemporary Research in the Sociology of Education*, Methuen, London, 1974.

EDWARDS, E. G. and ROBERTS, I. J., 'British Higher Education: Long Term Trends in Student Enrolment', *Higher Education Review*, vol. 12, 1980.

GALTON, M. and MOON, B. (eds), *Changing Schools . . . Changing Curriculum*, Harper and Row, London, 1983.

GLEESON, D. (ed.), *Youth Training and the Search for Work*, Routledge and Kegan Paul, London, 1983.

GOODSON, I. F., *School Subjects and Curriculum Change*, Croom Helm, London, 1982.

GOODSON, I. F. and BALL, S. J. (eds), *Defining the Curriculum*, Falmer Press, Lewes, 1984.

HALSALL, E., *The Comprehensive School*, Pergamon, Oxford, 1973.

HALSEY, A. H., *Educational Priority: EPA Problems and Policies*, vol. 1, HMSO, London, 1972.

HALSEY, A. H., FLOUD, J. and ANDERSON, C. A. (eds), *Education, Economy and Society*, Free Press, New York, 1961.

HALSEY, A. H., HEATH, A. F. and RIDGE, J. M., *Origins and Destinations: Family, Class and Education in Modern Britain*, Oxford University Press, Oxford, 1980.

HAMMERSLEY, M. and WOODS, P. (eds), *The Process of Schooling*, Routledge and Kegan Paul with Open University Press, London, 1976.

HARGREAVES, A. and TICKLE, L. (eds), *Middle Schools: Origins, Ideology and Practice*, Harper and Row, London, 1980.

HARGREAVES, D. H., *The Challenge for the Comprehensive School*, Routledge and Kegan Paul, London, 1982.

HARGREAVES, D. H., *Social Relations in a Secondary School*, Routledge and Kegan Paul, London, 1967.

HARLAND, M. (ed.), *Education for the Inner City*, Heinemann, London, 1980.

Higher Education (Robbins Report), HMSO, London, 1963.

HONEY, J. R. de S., *Tom Brown's Universe*, Millington, London, 1978.

JACKSON, B., *Streaming: An Educational System in Miniature*, Routledge and Kegan Paul, London, 1964.

KAGAN, J. and MOSS, A. H., *Birth to Maturity: a Study in Psychological Development*, Wiley, New York, 1967.

KAMM, J., *Hope Deferred: Girls' Education in English History*, Methuen, London, 1965.

KARABEL, J. and HALSEY, A. H. (eds), *Power and Ideology in Education*, Oxford University Press, Oxford, 1977.

KELLY, A. (ed.), *The Missing Half: Girls and Science Education*, Manchester University Press, Manchester, 1981.

KELSALL, R. K., POOLE, A. and KUHN, A., *Graduates: the Sociology of an Elite*, Methuen, London, 1972.

KING, R., *All Things Bright and Beautiful? A Sociological Study of Infants' Classrooms*, Wiley, Chichester, 1978.

LACEY, C., *Hightown Grammar: The School as a Social System*, Manchester University Press, Manchester, 1970.

LAWTON, D., *The Politics of the School Curriculum*, Routledge and Kegan Paul, London, 1980.

LITTLE, A., 'Education and Race Relations in the United Kingdom' in J. Megarry, S. Nisbet and E. Hoyle (eds), *World Yearbook of Education*, Kogan Page, London, 1981.

LITTLE, A., 'Performance of Children from Ethnic Minority Backgrounds in Primary Schools', *Oxford Review of Education*, vol. 1, No. 2, 1975.

LITTLE, A. and WESTERGAARD, J. H., 'The Trends of Class Differentials in Educational Opportunity in England and Wales', *British Journal of Sociology*, vol. 15, 1964.

LODGE, P. and BLACKSTONE, T., *Educational Policy and Educational Inequality*, Martin Robertson, London, 1982.

MACK, E. C., *The Public Schools and British Opinion*, Greenwood Press, New York, 1973.

MAIN, B. and RAFFE, D., 'The "Transition from School to Work" in 1980/81: A Dynamic Account', *British Educational Research Journal*, vol. 9, No. 1, 1983.

MORTIMORE, J. and BLACKSTONE, T., *Disadvantage and Education*, Heinemann, London, 1982.

MURPHY, J., *Church, State and Schools in Britain 1800–1970*, Routledge and Kegan Paul, London, 1971.

NASH, R., *Schooling in Rural Societies*, Methuen, London, 1980.

RAFFE, D., 'The "Alternative Route" Reconsidered: Part-time Further Education and Social Mobility in England and Wales', *Sociology*, vol. 13, No. 1, 1979.

RAMPTON, A., *West Indian Children in Our Schools: Interim Report of the Education of Children from Ethnic Minority Groups*, HMSO, London, 1981.

REES, T. and ATKINSON, P., *Youth Unemployment and State Intervention*, Routledge and Kegan Paul, London, 1982.

ROBERTS, H., 'After Sixteen: What Choice?' in R. Burgess (ed.), *Exploring Society*, British Sociological Association, London, 1982.

ROBINSON, P., *Perspectives on the Sociology of Education*, Routledge and Kegan Paul, London, 1981.

RODERICK, G. and STEPHENS, M. (eds), *The British Malaise: Industrial Performance, Education and Training in Britain Today*, Falmer Press, Lewes, 1982.

ROY, W., *Teaching Under Attack*, Croom Helm, London, 1983.

RUBINSTEIN, D. and SIMON, B., *The Evolution of the Comprehensive School*, Routledge and Kegan Paul, London, 1971.

RYRIE, A. C., 'Social Class, Examination Success and School Differences', *Scottish Education Review*, vol. 13, No. 1, 1982.

SALTER, B. and TAPPER, T., *Education, Politics and the State*, Grant McIntyre, London, 1981.

SHARPE, S., *Just Like a Girl*, Penguin, Harmondsworth, Middx., 1976.

SHINMAN, S., *A Chance for Every Child? Access and Response to Pre-School Provision*, Tavistock, London, 1981.

SILVER, H. (ed.), *Equal Opportunity in Education*, Methuen, London, 1973.

SIMON, B. and TAYLOR, W. (eds), *Education in the Eighties: The Central Issues*, Batsford, London, 1981.

SPENDER, D., *Invisible Women: the Schooling Scandal*, Norton, London, 1982.

SZRETER, R., 'Opportunities for Women as University Teachers in England since the Robbins Report of 1963', *Studies in Higher Education*, vol. 8, No. 2, 1983.

TAYLOR, G. and AYERS, N., *Born and Bred Unequal*, Longmans, London, 1969.

UNIVERSITIES CENTRAL COUNCIL FOR ADMISSIONS, *Statistical Supplements to Reports*, UCCA, Cheltenham, annual.

VENESS, T., *School Leavers*, Methuen, London, 1962.

WALFORD, G. (ed.), *Sociological Perspectives on the Public Schools*, Falmer Press, Lewes, 1984.

WALKER, S. and BARTON, L. (eds), *Gender, Class and Education*, Falmer Press, Lewes, 1983.

WHITE, R. and BROCKINGTON, D., *Tales out of School*, Routledge and Kegan Paul, London, 1983.

WILKINSON, R., *The Prefects*, Oxford University Press, London, 1964.

WILLIS, P., *Learning to Labour*, Gower, Farnborough, Hants, 1977.

WOODHEAD, M., *Intervening in Disadvantage: A Challenge for Nursery Education*, National Foundation for Educational Research, Slough, 1976.

WOODS, P., *The Divided School*, Routledge and Kegan Paul, London, 1979.

WOODS, P. (ed.), *Pupil Strategies*, Croom Helm, London, 1980.

WOODS, P., *Sociology of the School: An Interactionist Viewpoint*, Routledge and Kegan Paul, London, 1983.

WOODS, P. (ed.), *Teacher Strategies*, Croom Helm, London, 1980.

WOODS, P. and HAMMERSLEY, M. (eds), *School Experience*, Croom Helm, London, 1977.

YOUNG, M. F. D. (ed.), *Knowledge and Control: New Directions for the Sociology of Education*, Collier-Macmillan, London, 1971.

4. THE DIVISION OF LABOUR

ABRAMOWITZ, M. and ELIASBERG, V. F., *The Growth of Public Employment in Great Britain*, Princeton University Press, Princeton, New Jersey, 1957.

AMSDEN, A. H. (ed.), *The Economics of Women and Work*, Penguin, Harmondsworth, Mddx., 1980.

BAIN, G. S., *The Growth of White Collar Unionism*, Oxford University Press, Oxford, 1970.

BAIN, G. S. (ed.), *Industrial Relations in Britain*, Blackwell, Oxford, 1983.

BAIN, G. S. and PRICE, R., 'Who is a White Collar Employee?', *British Journal of Industrial Relations*, vol. 10, No. 3, 1972.

BALDAMUS, W., *Efficiency and Effort*, Tavistock Publications, London, 1961.

BANKS, J., *Trade Unionism*, Collier-Macmillan, London, 1974.

BARKER, D. L. and ALLEN, S. (eds), *Sexual Divisions and Society: Process and Change*, Tavistock Publications, London, 1976.

BARKER, D. L. and ALLEN, S. (eds), *Dependence and Exploitation in Work and Marriage*, Longman, London, 1976.

BARRETT, M., *Women's Oppression Today*, Verso, London, 1980.

BECHHOFER, F. and ELLIOTT, B., 'An Approach to the Study of Small Shopkeepers and Class Structure', *Archives Européenes de Sociologie*, vol. 9, 1968.

BECHHOFER, F. et al., 'The Petit Bourgeois in Industrial Society', *Archives Européenes de Sociologie*, vol. 17, 1976.

BECHHOFER, F. and ELLIOTT, B. (eds), *The Petite Bourgeoisie*, Macmillan, London, 1981.

BELL, C. and NEWBY, H., 'Capitalist Farmers in the British Class Structure', *Sociologia Ruralis*, vols. 1 and 2, 1974.

BENDIX, R., *Work and Authority in Industry*, Wiley, New York, 1956.

BERGER, J. and MOHR, J., *A Seventh Man*, Penguin, Harmondsworth, Middx., 1975.

BEYNON, H., *Working for Ford*, Penguin Books, London, 1973.

BEYNON, H. and BLACKBURN, R. M., *Perceptions of Work – Variations within a Factory*, Cambridge University Press, Cambridge, 1972.

BLACKBURN, R. M., *Union Character and Social Class*, Batsford, London, 1967.

BLACKBURN, R. M. and MANN, M., *The Working Class in the Labour Market*, Macmillan, London, 1979.

BRANNEN, P. (ed.), *Entering the World of Work: Some Sociological Perspectives*, HMSO, London, 1975.

BRAVERMAN, H., *Labor and Monopoly Capital*, Monthly Review Press, New York, 1974.

BROWN, R. K., CURRAN, M. M. and COUSINS, J. M., *Changing Attitudes to Employment?*, Research Paper No. 40, Department of Employment, London, 1983.

BULMER, M. (ed.), *Working Class Images of Society*, Routledge and Kegan Paul, London, 1975.

CARTER, M., *Into Work*, Penguin Books, London, 1966.

CENTRAL OFFICE OF INFORMATION, *Occupations and Conditions of Work*, HMSO, London, 1976.

CHILD, J. (ed.), *Man and Organization*, Allen and Unwin, London, 1973.

COCKBURN, C., *Brothers. Male Dominance and Technological Change*, Pluto Press, London, 1983.

COOTE, A., and CAMPBELL, B., *Sweet Freedom*, Picador, London, 1982.

COUNTER INFORMATION SERVICES, *Women Under Attack*, London, 1976.

COUSINS, J. M., *Values and Value in the Labour Market*, Working Papers in Sociology No. 9, University of Durham, Durham, 1976.

COUSSINS, J., *The Equality Report*, National Council for Civil Liberties, London, 1976.

DEPARTMENT OF EMPLOYMENT, *British Labour Statistics: Historical Abstract 1886–1968*, HMSO, London, 1971.

DEPARTMENT OF EMPLOYMENT, *British Labour Statistics Yearbook*, HMSO, London, 1969–76.

DEPARTMENT OF EMPLOYMENT, *Classification of Occupations and Directory of Occupational Titles*, HMSO, London, 1972.

DEPARTMENT OF EMPLOYMENT, *New Earnings Survey*, HMSO, London.

DURKHEIM, E., *The Division of Labour in Society*, Free Press, New York, 1933.

ELDRIDGE, J. E. T., *Sociology and Industrial Life*, Nelson, London, 1971.

ENGELS, F., *The Origins of the Family*, Lawrence and Wishart, London, 1940.

ESLAND, G., SALAMAN, G. and SPEAKMAN, M. (eds), *People and Work*, Holmes McDougall, London, 1975.

ESLAND, G. and SALAMAN, G. (eds), *The Politics of Work and Occupations*, Open University Press, Milton Keynes, 1980.

FORESTER, T. (ed.), *The Microelectronics Revolution*, Blackwell, Oxford, 1980.

FOX, A., *Beyond Contract: Work, Power and Trust Relations*, Faber and Faber, London, 1974.

FRASER, R. (ed.), *Work: Twenty Personal Accounts*, Penguin Books, London, 1968.

GARDINER, J., 'The Political Economy of Female Labour in Capitalist Society', *New Left Review*, No. 89, 1975.

GARNSEY, E., 'Women's Work and Theories of Class Stratification', *Sociology*, vol. 12, No. 2, 1978.

GERSHUNY, J., *After Industrial Society? The Emerging Self-Service Economy*, Macmillan, London, 1978.

GERSHUNY, J., *Social Innovation and the Division of Labour*, Oxford University Press, Oxford, 1983.

GERSHUNY, J. I. and PAHL, R. E., 'Britain in the Decade of the Three Economies', *New Society*, 3 January 1980.

GIDDENS, A. and MACKENZIE, G. (eds), *Social Class and the Division of Labour*, Cambridge University Press, Cambridge, 1982.

GOLDTHORPE, J. H. et al., *The Affluent Worker – Industrial Attitudes and Behaviour*, Cambridge University Press, Cambridge, 1968.

HAKIM, C., *Occupational Segregation*, Research Paper No. 9, Department of Employment, London, 1979.

HAKIM, C. and HAWES, W. R., 'The Labour Force' in *Labour and Income*, Statistical Sources, D.291, Open University Press, Milton Keynes, 1982.

HEDGES, N. and BEYNON, H., *Born to Work*, Pluto Press, London, 1982.

HEMINGWAY, J., *Conflict and Democracy*, Oxford University Press, Oxford, 1976.

HUNT, A., *A Survey of Women's Employment*, HMSO, London, 1968.

HUNT, A., *Women and Work: A Statistical Survey*, HMSO, London, 1974.

HYMAN, R. and BROUGH, I., *Social Values and Industrial Relations*, Blackwell, Oxford, 1975.

JAHODA, M., *Employment and Unemployment – A Social-Psychological Analysis*, Cambridge University Press, Cambridge, 1982.

JAQUES, E., *Equitable Payment*, Penguin Books, London, 1967.

JOHNSON, T. J., *Professions and Power*, Macmillan, London, 1972.

KINNERSLEY, P., *The Hazards of Work*, Pluto Press, London, 1973.

KUHN, A. and WOLPE, A. M., *Feminism and Materialism*, Routledge and Kegan Paul, London, 1978.

LANE, T., *The Union Makes Us Strong*, Arrow, London, 1974.

LITTLER, C. R. and SALAMAN, G., *Class at Work*, Batsford, London, 1984.

LOCKWOOD, D., *The Blackcoated Worker*, Allen and Unwin, London, 1958.

MACKIE, L. and PATULLO, P., *Women at Work*, Tavistock, London, 1977.

MANN, M., *Workers on the Move*, Cambridge University Press, Cambridge, 1973.

MILLERSON, G., *The Qualifying Associations*, Routledge and Kegan Paul, London, 1964.

MUMFORD, E. and BANKS, O., *The Computer and the Clerk*, Routledge and Kegan Paul, London 1967.

NICHOLS, T., *Ownership, Control and Ideology*, Allen and Unwin, London, 1969.

NICHOLS, T. (ed.), *Capital and Labour*, Fontana, Glasgow, 1980.

NICHOLS, T., 'Social Class: official sociological and Marxist' in J. IRVINE et al. (eds), *Demystifying Social Statistics*, Pluto Press, London, 1979.

NICHOLS, T. and BEYNON, H., *Living with Capitalism: Class Relations and the Modern Factory*, Routledge and Kegan Paul, London, 1977.

OAKLEY, A., *The Sociology of Housework*, Martin Robertson, London, 1974.

OAKLEY, A. and MITCHELL, J., *The Rights and Wrongs of Women*, Penguin, Harmondsworth, Middlesex, 1978.

PALMER, G., *British Industrial Relations*, Allen and Unwin, London, 1983.

PARKER, S. R., *Leisure and Work*, Allen and Unwin, London, 1983.

PARKER, S. R., BROWN, R. K., CHILD, J. and SMITH, M. A., *The Sociology of Industry*, Allen and Unwin, London, 1972 (4th edition 1981).

POLLARD, S., *The Genesis of Modern Management*, Edward Arnold, London, 1965.

POND, C. and WINYARD, S., *The Case for a National Minimum Wage*, Low Pay Unit pamphlet No. 23, London, 1983.

PRANDY, K., *Professional Employees*, Faber and Faber, London, 1965.

PRANDY, K., STEWART, A. and BLACKBURN, R. M., *White-Collar Work*, Macmillan, London, 1982.

PRICE, R. and BAIN, G. S., 'Union Growth in Britain: retrospect and prospect', *British Journal of Industrial Relations*, vol. 21, No. 1, 1983.

ROUTH, G. G. C., *Occupation and Pay in Great Britain, 1906–1979*, Macmillan, London, 1980.

SADLER, P., 'Sociological Aspects of Skill', *British Journal of Industrial Relations*, vol. 8, No. 1, 1970.

SALAMAN, G., *Community and Occupation*, Cambridge University Press, Cambridge, 1974.

SCASE, R. and GOFFEE, R., *The Entrepreneurial Middle Class*, Croom Helm, London, 1982.

SECCOMBE, W., 'The Housewife and her Labour under Capitalism', *New Left Review*, No. 83, 1974.

SHOWLER, B. and SINFIELD, A. (eds), *The Workless State*, Martin Robertson, Oxford, 1981.

SINFIELD, A., *What Unemployment Means*, Martin Robertson, Oxford, 1981.

STEWART, A., PRANDY, K. and BLACKBURN, R. M., *Social Stratification and Occupations*, Macmillan, London, 1980.

THOMPSON, E. P., 'Time, Work Discipline and Industrial Capitalism', *Past and Present*, No. 38, 1967.

THOMPSON, P., *The Nature of Work*, Macmillan, London, 1983.
WARR, P. and WALL, T., *Work and Well-being*, Penguin Books, London, 1974.
WEDDERBURN, D. and CROMPTON, R., *Workers' Attitudes and Technology*,
  Cambridge University Press, Cambridge, 1972.
WEIR, M., *Job Satisfaction*, Fontana, Glasgow, 1976.
WILLIAMS, W. M., *Occupational Choice*, Allen and Unwin, London, 1974.
WILSON, E., *Women and the Welfare State*, Tavistock, London, 1977.

5. INEQUALITY

ABEL-SMITH, B. and TOWNSEND, P., *The Poor and the Poorest*, Occasional Papers in
  Social Administration, No. 17, Bell, London, 1965.
ABRAMS, P., 'Democracy, Technology and the Retired British Army Elite', in S. P.
  Huntington (ed.), *Changing Patterns of Military Politics*, Free Press, New York, 1962.
ATKINSON, A. B., *The Economics of Inequality*, Oxford University Press, Oxford,
  1975.
ATKINSON, A. B., *Poverty in Britain and the Reform of Social Security*, Cambridge
  University Press, Cambridge, 1969.
ATKINSON, A. B., *Unequal Shares: Wealth in Britain*, Penguin Books, London, 1974.
ATKINSON, A. B. (ed.), *Wealth, Income and Inequality*, Penguin Books, London, 1973.
ATKINSON, A. B. and HARRISON, A. J., *The Distribution of Personal Wealth in
  Britain*, Cambridge University Press, Cambridge, 1983.
BACHRACH, P., *The Theory of Democratic Elitism*, University of London Press,
  London, 1969.
BOSANQUET, N. and TOWNSEND, P. (eds), *Labour and Equality*, Heinemann, London,
  1980.
BOYD, D., *Elites and their Education*, National Foundation for Educational Research,
  Windsor, 1973.
BROWN, M. (ed.), *The Structure of Disadvantage*, Heinemann, London, 1983.
CHILD POVERTY ACTION GROUP, *Poverty: The Facts,* London, 1975.
COATES, K. and SILBURN, R., *Poverty: The Forgotten Englishmen*, Penguin Books,
  London, 1970.
DAHRENDORF, R., *Class and Class Conflict in an Industrial Society*, Routledge and Kegan
  Paul, London, 1959.
FIDLER, J., *The British Business Elite*, Routledge and Kegan Paul, London, 1981.
FIELD, W., *Are Low Wages Inevitable?*, Spokesman Books, Nottingham, 1976.
FRANCIS, A., 'Families, Firms and Finance Capital', *Sociology*, vol. 14, 1980.
GARNIER, M., 'Changing Recruitment Patterns and Organisational Ideology: the case
  of a British Military Academy', *Administrative Science Quarterly*, vol. 17, 1972.
GIDDENS, A., 'Elites in the British Class Structure', *Sociological Review*, 1972.
GIDDENS, A., *The Class Structure of Advanced Societies*, Hutchinson, London, 1973.
GIDDENS, A. and HELD, D. (eds), *Classes, Power and Conflict*, Macmillan, London,
  1982.
GLASS, D. (ed.), *Social Mobility in Britain*, Routledge and Kegan Paul, London, 1954.
GOLDTHORPE, J. H., *Social Mobility and Class Structure in Modern Britain*, Oxford
  University Press, Oxford, 1980.
GRIFFITHS, J. A. G., *The Politics of the Judiciary*, Fontana, Glasgow, 1979.
GUTTSMAN, W. L., *The British Political Elite*, MacGibbon and Kee, London, 1963.
HANNAH, L., *The Rise of the Corporate Economy*, Methuen, London, 1976.

HARBURY, C. D. and HITCHENS, D., *Inheritance and Wealth Inequality in Britain*, Allen and Unwin, London, 1979.

HARRIS, J. S. and GARCIA, T. U., 'The Permanent Secretaries: Britain's Top Administrators', *Public Administration Review*, March 1966.

HEATH, A., *Social Mobility*, Fontana, Glasgow, 1981.

HOPE, K. (ed.), *The Analysis of Social Mobility*, Oxford University Press, Oxford, 1972.

JOHNSON, R. W., 'The British Political Elite 1965–1972', *Archives Européenes de Sociologie*, 1973.

KELLNER, P. and Lord CROWTHER-HUNT, *The Civil Servants*, Raven Books, London, 1980.

KELSALL, R. K., *Higher Civil Servants in Britain*, Routledge and Kegan Paul, London, 1955.

LEGGATT, T., 'Managers in Industry: their background and education', *Sociological Review*, vol. 26, 1978.

LUPTON, T. and WILSON, S. C., 'The Social Background and Connections of "Top Decision Makers"', *Manchester School*, 27, 1959.

LYDALL, H. F. and TIPPING, D. G., 'The Distribution of Personal Wealth in Britain', *Bulletin of the Oxford Institute of Economics and Statistics*, vol. 23, 1961.

MASSEY, D. and CATALANO, A., *Capital and Land*, Arnold, London, 1978.

MILIBAND, R., *Parliamentary Socialism*, Allen and Unwin, London, 1961.

MILIBAND, R., *The State in Capitalist Society*, Weidenfeld and Nicolson, London, 1969.

MILLS, C. W., *The Power Elite*, Oxford University Press, New York, 1956.

NYMAN, S. and SILBERSTON, A., 'The Ownership and Control of Industry', *Oxford Economic Papers*, vol. 30, 1978.

OPEN UNIVERSITY, *Patterns of Inequality*, Milton Keynes, 1976.

OTLEY, C., 'The Educational Background of British Army Officers', *Sociology*, vol. 7, No. 2, 1973.

OTLEY, C., 'The Social Origin of British Army Officers', *Sociological Review*, vol. 18, 1970.

PAHL, R. E. and WINKLER, J., *The Corporate State*, Centre for Studies of Social Policy, London, 1976.

PARKIN, F., *Class Inequality and Political Order*, MacGibbon and Kee, London, 1971.

PARKIN, F. (ed.), *The Social Analysis of Class Structure*, Tavistock Publications, London, 1974.

PERKIN, H., 'The Recruitment of Elites in British Society since 1800', *Journal of Social History*, Winter, 1978.

POLANYI, G. and WOOD, J. B., *How Much Inequality?*, Heinemann, London, 1974.

PRESTON, B., 'Statistics of Inequality', *Sociological Review*, vol. 22, No. 1, 1974.

REID, I., *Social Class Differences in Britain*, Open Books, London, 1974.

ROSE, R., 'The Making of a Cabinet Minister', *British Journal of Political Science*, vol. 1., No. 1, 1971.

ROWNTREE, S. B., *Poverty: A Study of Town Life*, Nelson, London, 1910.

ROYAL COMMISSION ON THE DISTRIBUTION OF INCOME AND WEALTH, Reports No. 1-8, HMSO, London, 1975–9.

RUBINSTEIN, W. D., 'Wealth, Elites and the Class Structure of Modern Britain', *Past and Present*, No. 76, 1977.

RUBINSTEIN, W. D., *Men of Property: the wealthy in modern Britain*, Croom Helm, London, 1980.

RUBINSTEIN, W. D. (ed.), *Wealth and the Wealthy in the Modern World*, Croom Helm,

London, 1980.

RUNCIMAN, W. G., *Relative Deprivation and Social Justice*, Routledge and Kegan Paul, London, 1966.

RUTTER, M. and MADGE, N., *Cycles of Disadvantage*, Heinemann, London, 1976.

SALAMAN, G. and THOMPSON, K., 'Class Culture and the Persistence of an Elite: the case of army officer selection', *Sociological Review*, vol. 26, 1978.

SCASE, R. (ed.), *The State in Western Europe*, Croom Helm, London, 1980.

SCOTT, J., *Corporations, Classes and Capitalism*, Hutchinson, London, 1979.

SCOTT, J., *The Upper Classes*, Macmillan, London, 1982.

SPIEGELBERG, R., *The City: Power Without Accountability*, Blond and Briggs, London, 1973.

STANWORTH, P. and GIDDENS, A. (eds), *Elites and Power in British Society*, Cambridge University Press, Cambridge, 1974.

STANWORTH, P. and GIDDENS, A., 'The Modern Corporate Economy: interlocking directorships in Britain, 1906–70', *Sociological Review*, vol. 23, 1975.

TOWNSEND, P., *Poverty in the United Kingdom*, Penguin, Harmondsworth, Mddx., 1979.

URRY, J. and WAKEFORD, J., *Power in Britain*, Heinemann, London, 1973.

USEEM, M. and McCORMACK, A., 'The Dominant Segment of the British Business Elite', *Sociology*, vol. 15, 1981.

WEDDERBURN, D. (ed.), *Poverty, Inequality and Class Structure*, Cambridge University Press, Cambridge, 1974.

WESTERGAARD, J and RESLER, H., *Class in a Capitalist Society*, Heinemann, London, 1975 (Penguin edition 1975).

WIENER, M. J., *English Culture and the Decline of the Industrial Spirit, 1850–1980*, Cambridge University Press, Cambridge, 1981.

6. DEVIANCE, LAW AND THE WELFARE STATE

ABEL-SMITH, B. and TOWNSEND, P., *The Poor and the Poorest*, Bell, London, 1965.

ABRAMS, P., *The Origins of British Sociology*, Chicago University Press, Chicago, 1968.

BALDWIN, J. and McCONVILLE, M., *Negotiated Justice: Pressures on Defendants to Plead Guilty*, Martin Robertson, Oxford, 1977.

BEIRNE, P. and QUINNEY, R. (eds), *Marxism and the Law*, Wiley, New York, 1982.

BEVERIDGE, W., *Report on Social Insurance and Allied Services*, HMSO, London, 1968.

BISHTON, D. and HOMER, B. (eds), *Talking Blues*, Affor, London, 1978.

BLOM-COOPER, L. and DRABBLE, R., 'Police Perception of Crime: Brixton and the Operational Response', *British Journal of Criminology*, vol. 22, No. 2, 1982.

BOLGER, S., CORRIGAN, P., DOCKING, J. and FROST, N., *Towards Socialist Welfare Work*, Macmillan, London, 1981.

BROWN, M. and MADGE, N., *Despite the Welfare State*, Heinemann, London, 1982.

BUTTERWORTH, E. and HOLMAN, R. (eds), *Social Welfare in Modern Britain*, Fontana, Glasgow, 1975.

CALDER, A., *The People's War*, Calder, London, 1969.

CARSON, W. G. and WILES, P. (eds), *The Sociology of Delinquency in Britain*, Martin Robertson, Oxford, 1971.

CENTRE FOR CONTEMPORARY CULTURAL STUDIES, *The Empire Strikes Back: Race and Racism in 70's Britain*, Hutchinson, London, 1982.

CHAMBLISS, W. and SEIDMAN, R., *Law, Order and Power*, Addison-Wesley, Reading,

Ma., 1971.

CLARKE, J., *Football Hooliganism and the Skinheads*, Centre for Contemporary Cultural Studies, Birmingham, 1973.

COATES, D., *The Labour Party and the Struggle for Socialism*, Cambridge University Press, Cambridge, 1975.

COHEN, S., *Folk Devils and Moral Panics*, Martin Robertson, Oxford, 2nd edition, 1980.

COHEN, S. (ed.), *Images of Deviance*, Penguin, Harmondsworth, Mddx., 1971.

COHEN, S. and YOUNG, J., *The Manufacture of News: Deviance, Social Problems and the Mass Media*, Constable/Sage, London, 1981.

THE CONFAIT CASE, Report of the Hon. Sir Henry Fisher, HC90, HMSO, London, 1977.

COWELL, D., JONES, T. and YOUNG, J. (eds), *Policing the Riots*, Junction Books, London, 1982.

DEMUTH, C., *'Sus': A Report on the Vagrancy Act 1824*, Runnymede Trust, London, 1978.

DONNISON, D., 'Supplementary Benefits: Dilemmas and Priorities', *Journal of Social Policy*, vol. 5, part 4, 1976.

DOYAL, L., *The Political Economy of Health*, Pluto Press, London, 1979.

GINSBURG, N., *Class, Capital and Social Policy*, Macmillan, London, 1979.

HAIN, P., *Mistaken Identity: The Wrong Face of the Law*, Quartet, London, 1976.

HALL, S. and JEFFERSON, J. (eds), *Resistance Through Rituals*, Hutchinson, London, 1976.

HALL, S. et al., *Policing the Crisis: Mugging, the State and Law and Order*, Macmillan, London, 1978.

HEBDIGE, D., *Subculture: the Meaning of Style*, Methuen, London, 1979.

JONES, C., *Social Work, the State and the Working Class*, Macmillan, London, 1982.

KETTLE, M. and HODGES, L., *Uprising! The Police, the People and the Riots in Britain's Cities*, Pan, London, 1982.

KINCAID, J., *Poverty and Equality in Britain*, Penguin Books, London, 1973.

LAND, H., *Large Families in London*, Occasional Papers in Social Administration, No. 20, Bell, London, 1969.

LEFCOURT, R. (ed.), *Law Against the People*, Random House, New York, 1971.

MACLEOD, I. and POWELL, E., *The Social Services: Needs and Means*, Conservative Political Centre, London, 1952.

MARSHALL, T. H., *Social Policy*, Hutchinson, London, 1975.

MARSHALL, T. H., *The Right to Welfare and other essays*, Heinemann, London, 1981.

NARAYAN, R., *Black Community on Trial*, Blackbird Books, London, 1976.

ORWELL, G., *The Road to Wigan Pier*, Gollancz, London, 1937.

PARKER, H. and GILLER, H., 'More and Less the Same: British Delinquency Research since the Sixties', *British Journal of Criminology*, vol. 21, No. 3, 1981.

PEARSON, G., *Hooligan: A History of Respectable Fears*, Macmillan, London, 1983.

PEOPLE AND PLANNING, (Skeffington Report), HMSO, London, 1969.

PINKER, R., *Social Theory and Social Policy*, Heinemann, London, 1971.

PRICE, C. and CAPLAN, J., *The Confait Confessions*, Marion Boyars, London, 1977.

PRYCE, K., *Endless Pressure: A Study of West Indian Life-Styles in Bristol*, Penguin, Harmondsworth, Mddx., 1979.

REDHEAD, S., 'Some Aspects of Legal Regulation in the Post-War Football Industry' in A. Tomlinson (ed.), *Explorations in Football Culture*, Brighton Polytechnic, Brighton, 1983.

REPORT OF THE WORKING PARTY ON CROWD BEHAVIOUR AT FOOTBALL

MATCHES, (The Lang Report), HMSO, London, 1969.

REPORT OF THE COMMITTEE ON LOCAL AUTHORITY AND PERSONAL SOCIAL SERVICES, (Seebohm), HMSO, London, 1968.

REPORT OF THE COMMITTEE ON ONE PARENT FAMILIES (Finer Report), HMSO, London, 1974.

ROBINS, D. and COHEN, P., *Knuckle Sandwich: Growing up in the Working-Class City*, Penguin, Harmondsworth, Mddx., 1977.

ROCK, P. and McINTOSH, M. (eds), *Deviance and Social Control*, Tavistock, London, 1980.

ROSHIER, R. J. and TEFF, H., *Law and Society in England*, Tavistock, London, 1980.

ROYAL COMMISSION ON CRIMINAL PROCEDURE, Report, Cmnd. 8092, HMSO, London, 1981.

SCARMAN, Lord, *The Brixton Disorders*, Report, Cmnd. 8427, HMSO, London, 1981.

STEIN, S. D., 'The Sociology of Law', *British Journal of Criminology*, vol. 20, No. 2, 1980.

TAYLOR, I., *Law and Order: Arguments for Socialism*, Macmillan, London, 1981.

TAYLOR, I., 'On the Sports Violence Question: Soccer Hooliganism Revisited' in J. Hargreaves (ed.), *Sport, Culture and Ideology*, Routledge and Kegan Paul, London, 1982.

TAYLOR, I., WALTON, P. and YOUNG, J., *The New Criminology: For a Social Theory of Deviance*, Routledge and Kegan Paul, London, 1973.

TITMUSS, R. M., *Essays on the Welfare State*, Allen and Unwin, London, 1963.

TITMUSS, R. M., *The Gift Relationship*, Allen and Unwin, London, 1970.

TRIVIZAS, E., 'Offences and Offenders in Football Crowd Disorders', *British Journal of Criminology*, vol. 20, No. 3, 1980.

TRIVIZAS, E., 'Sentencing the "Football Hooligan"', *British Journal of Criminology*, vol. 21, No. 4, 1981.

WHANNEL, G., 'Football Crowd Behaviour and the Press', *Media, Culture and Society*, vol. 1, No. 2, 1979.

ZANDER, M., ABEL-SMITH, B. and BROOK, R., *Legal Problems and the Citizen: A Study in Three London Boroughs*, Heinemann, London, 1973.

Index